The Voices of Sus
Their Translation in Thrillers

APPROACHES TO TRANSLATION STUDIES
Founded by James S. Holmes

Edited by   Henri Bloemen
                   Cees Koster
                   Ton Naaijkens

Volume 39

The Voices of Suspense and Their Translation in Thrillers

Dutch/Jewish accent — Muller.
Look at Brumme bk. z read.

Edited by
Susanne M. Cadera and Anita Pavić Pintarić

Amsterdam - New York, NY 2014

P.196
Pontive Modality (subjunctive)
Deontic - duty/Obligation
boulomaic - Ponibility/necenity
evaluative exprenion
verba sentiendi - what character
feels - she noticed
        it annoyed her that

P.197
Reflector-character — 3rd person,
narrator with accen to character's
thoughts.
Mn. oliver - Direct speech + free
indirect thought
        interior monologue — Organised
+ rational
        stream of consciousness -
        often disjunted thoughts. Rules
of grammar do not apply.
        Free indirect discourse 3rd person
narrative embodying the thoughts/
emotions of the main character.

Cover image: www.dreamstime.com

Cover design: Studio Pollmann

The paper on which this book is printed meets the requirements of "ISO 9706:1994, Information and documentation - Paper for documents - Requirements for permanence".

ISBN: 978-90-420-3822-6
E-Book ISBN: 978-94-012-1069-0

Table of contents

Dialogue esp. important in crime fiction.

read *polar bk but a lot on terms descriptive of narrative* *Genette?*

read *Creative rewriting* *Very relevant*

read *How he used an actual criminal!*

read *good for terms, & scholarship on dialect* *translation & ...* *Pryalos German*

"mon ami" etc in Poirot. What happens when FF translated repatriated?

No *different langs. in 'international' films. Note referencing of films.*

semiotic devices: E.g. nodding, laughing
images, music, gestures, mimic ✱
Non-verbal

P. 185. French use of dash for conversation makes it look more like a script.

P. 190 Important comments re footnotes in crime fiction.

* Agatha Christie using French in
her novels P. 131
- Vocab. relatively basic
- Semantically speaking, it is 'empty'
It has a semiotic purpose rather
than a semantic one, i.e. signalling
foreignness

Abbreviations used in this volume

P. 116 Elision to reproduce oral quality
e.g. v'là for voilà

ST   Source Text

TT   Target Text

TT1   If there is more than one version discussed, numbers indicate each distinct version or versions in different languages

SL   Source Language   Code switching - betw.
langs
TL   Target Language

Gen. vocab
illocutionary force
There's a snake under you -
Illocutionary force of a warning
Polysemy. word/phrase that has many
meanings.
* Semiotics - signs as they
communicate things - spoken &
unspoken.
- Common signs understood globally
e.g. traffic signs, emojis.
- intertextuality, puns, metaphors,
cultural commonalities.
inflected langs - gendered endings, def. articles
Frozen metaphor
He's a snake
P. 253 TA expectations.
P. 136 Venuti - invisible translator.
P. 185. Purpose of dialogue (other)

<u>Transliteration</u> - letters in one
script transcribed into another

Pocc ИЯ - transliteration Rossiya,
means Russian.

<u>Diatopic</u> register - dialect P.114
(geographical)
<u>Diastratic</u> register - <u>Sociolect</u>   "

a Discursive resource, e.g. response
    P.69   curiosity.
62 } <u>metalinguistic</u> - register
23 } <u>Paralinguistic</u> - gestures

Homodiegetic - Narrator is/protagonist
or character in the novel.
Heterodiegetic - Narrator who does <u>not</u>
take part in the plot.
p64 in media res - in the midst of the
plot.

  analepsis - flashback } P.64.
  prolepsis - flashforward

Pragmatics - how <u>context</u> contributes to
              meaning.
P.66 Ellipsis points ...

P.141 Diachronic - how lang. develops thro'
time.

Discourse markers - words/phrases
which organise discourse into sections
e.g. well/I mean

Introduction: Creation of suspense through dialogue and its translation

Susanne M. Cadera and Anita Pavić Pintarić

1. Background and aims of the approach

The interest in the creation of suspense through dialogue in literature and film and its recreation in translation arises from research into the translation of fictive dialogue. Such an approach has been followed in two projects funded by the Spanish Ministry of Science and Innovation since 2007, and whose results have been published in several volumes.[1] Whereas the first project (*Feigned Orality: Description and Translation*, OFDYT, 2007-2009) focused on the description and translation of the recreation of orality in contemporary narrative fiction and theatre, the second one (*Translating Fictional Dialogue. Literary Texts and Multimodal Texts*, TRADIF, 2010-2013)[2] seeks to consider how fictive orality is represented in different genres and in different media; written and audiovisual fiction.

A general and global overview of results has been published by Rodopi in 2012 (Brumme and Espunya (eds) *The Translation of Fictive Dialogue*). In this volume, the most important concern was to discuss the theoretical background considered during the development of the two projects and its application to different types of original and translated texts within narrative, theatrical and film fiction. All studies focus on the spoken language dimension, its recreation in fiction and its translation.

The present volume focuses on a single but very broad and popular genre where suspense is used as one of the most important means or techniques to create uncertainty, anxiety and excitement: different modes of crime fiction in both, fiction and film including sub-genres like psychological and crime thriller, detective story or novel, mystery, hardboiled or *noir* fiction. Because of the variety of text and film types there has not been consensus about the denomination of a genre that could be valid for all. Hence our interest here does not lie in a definition of genre, rather we will follow Scaggs (2005: 1-2) who uses the general term *crime fiction* "to classify an otherwise unclassifiable genre" because of its endless sub-genres. The focus on crime fiction is due to the

homogeneity – uniformity.
heterogeneity – diversity

initial observation that the use of dialogue is one of its most prevailing characteristics. Dialogue in crime fiction literature and film has different purposes: it confers more realism on the scenes represented, it confers more clearness and simpleness on the receptor, it represents different social strata of the characters, or it indicates specific language uses of the different professions (police, lawyer, doctor etc.):

> El lenguaje cumple la función referencial. Los discursos se supeditan a la claridad, sencillez y rapidez de la lectura. Se trata de textos especialmente dialógicos que reproducen el plurilingüismo social: el discurso del hombre de la calle, del policía, de la prostituta, del camarero, etc. (de Castro and Montejo 1990: 61)
> The language acts as a reference. The discourse is submitted to the clarity, the simpleness and the speed of reading. The texts are most dialogical and reproduce the plurilingual social context: the language of the man of the street, of policemen, of prostitutes, of the barman etc. [*our translation*]

All these functions of dialogue can be frequent in other literature and film genres, but in crime fiction and film, dialogue is an essential device that is structured by the author / script writer, in order to create the plot that has to guide the reader or spectator to the resolution of the crime. But dialogue is also a vehicle to show the psychology of the characters, their fears, their intentions, their lies, or their sincerity. In addition, the constant use of dialogue creates the sensation of immediacy, as if the plot were happening at the same time as reading about it (Galán Herrera 1988: 63). In this way, the information about the crime in the dialogues, or through the organisation of dialogue, is given in small units, creating both a sensation of suspense, and the animation to anticipate possible resolutions by the reader.

As the study of fictive dialogue and its translation is the guideline of the two projects, crime fiction acquires particular interest in the second one because of its popularity and high translation index.[3]

The special interest in dialogue comes from the host of roles it plays in literature and film. In literature, fictive dialogue evokes[4] orality, everyday speech and confers authenticity and lends credibility to the plot. One of its main functions is to depict the characters and to contribute to the development of their personality, distinguishing them from others taking part in the action of the story.

As a narrative strategy, dialogue is an important resource that enables the writer to shape the characters and the plot. The creation of fictive dialogue takes place basically on two levels. Firstly, on the linguistic level, fictive dialogue is represented through different speech types or linguistic variations. These can take the form of dialect, slang, informal speech, as well as other characteristics of orality, such as simple phrasing, filler words, particles, repetitions, and redundancy. Non-verbal communication can also be used to create the notion of fictive dialogue. Secondly, on the narrative level, fictive dialogue is represented in the form of specific narrative techniques and graphic presentations within the text through oral markers such as punctuation marks, paragraph marks, spacing etc. (Cadera 2012a: 37-38). In films, one of the most important functions of dialogue is character portrayal (Zabalbeascoa 2012: 64), but besides the verbal utterances, the semiotic components increase the creation of special effects and the manipulation of the spectator's perception.

> In films, the director and the screenwriter enter into dialogue with the spectators by carefully arranging all of the non-verbal items, including camera angles and movements, the choice of cast, manipulation of the weather conditions to provide greater impact of the words; and vice versa, a character's lines are carefully constructed to lend greater impact to the visual and sound effects. (Zabalbeascoa 2012: 67-68)

Several studies have been published on the topic of crime fiction and film in general, and particularly on the topic of suspense creation.[5] In contrast, in translation studies there has not been a visible interest in the topic. The aim of this volume is therefore to strive for a clearer vision of how suspense is created and translated into other languages. The different chapters compiled in this volume focus uniquely on this topic, but they study different aspects of it in order to offer a wider perspective.

2. Methodology

From the very beginning of our work we place special interest on the prior analysis and description of the devices used in the source text, combined with the study of traditions, conventions, literary norms and the evolution of innovative creations of fiction and films. The aim is to identify the specific resources that authors of literary or audiovisual fiction use to represent real spoken language. This feigned or fictive orality[6] has been studied by researchers from different disciplines like Linguistics, Literature Studies and Discourse Analysis.[7] Whereas to date, the main subject of our research has been the representation of orality in literature and film and its recreation in translations, the studies of the present volume lead us to consider a somewhat different point of view. The interest in how suspense is created through dialogue leads us to consider not only the recreation or evocation of real orality but also aspects related to fictional constructions without any direct comparison in reality; for example the use of foreign words or multilingualism in the dialogues, or special artificial effects like music, weather changes or illumination in film.

The methodological approach of the studies presented in this volume offers a prior inner-linguistic and inner-narrative analysis of the source text or texts in order to establish the elements that are responsible for the creation of suspense. Special focus is given to how dialogue, dialogue structure or any elements of speech have an influence on suspense building. In addition, most of the chapters consider research into crime fiction or film, the historical context and the literary or film tradition.

The second step of the analysis consists of a comparison of the respective translations in one or more languages in order to find out how translators transfer those specific devices observed in the source text, what kind of translation strategies the translator uses to evoke the same sensation of suspense in the target text; or, otherwise, what kind of translation strategies are not able to create the same sensation,

Furthermore, this detailed analysis of both source and target text allows us to learn more about translation shifts or translation deficits, as well as about aspects presenting special translation challenges. As a theoretical framework, most of the contributions of this book share the concepts of descriptive translation studies set out by Gideon Toury (1995).

3. General characteristics of suspense building

In general terms, suspense in crime fiction can be defined as a feeling of uncertainty, anxiety and excitement that is created within the story. The spectator / listener / reader feels uncertain about the outcome of a character's intention in a certain situation, in this case, in a fictional one.

As mentioned above, the fictional elements that create suspense are partially different to the elements analysed by the researchers in preceding volumes that essentially aimed at "identifying the specific resources authors and translators have used [...] in order to analyse to what extent they differ from the traits of real spoken discourse, both in original works and in their translation" (Brumme and Espunya 2012: 15). The chapters in this volume will show that suspense comes through different literary or filmic devices or constructions and that the mimesis or evocation of real spoken discourse is only a part of it.

Thus, with the term *voice* used in the title of this volume, we try to designate all those resources used in the written and audiovisual media used to create suspense. Narrative *Voice*, as proposed by Genette (1972), has been discussed by different researchers. Its use referring to different concepts has led to some confusion and the adequacy of the term applied to written text has been discussed.[8] Genette applied the term to denote a concept that corresponds to the question "who speaks in the text" and that is related to the questions, "when and from where does he / she speak" including in the concept *voice* the three narrative aspects of person, time and level, but separating it from aspects of perspective (Aczel 1998: 468). It has been shown that Genette's categories of voice ("who speaks") and perspective or point of view ("who sees") are really inseparable (Coste 1989), and both are responsible for evoking "a consistent real-world schema from the textual surface structure" (Fludernik 2001: 635). Chatman (1978) and Tacca (1973) interpret *voice* from the other, the reader side, defining the reading process as "audible", where the reader "hears" the voices from the narrator, the characters, the addressees involved, and from the story itself (Tacca 1973: 15). Aczel (1998) also argues along these lines, insisting on the audibility of narrative texts and the importance of the question "how a particular voice speaks". He points to the need for restoring "the realm of "how" –tone, idiom, diction, speech-style– to a central position among the configuration of essential first questions of narrative voice" (Aczel 1998: 469).

In relation to suspense in literary and audiovisual fiction, we will formulate the questions from all these points of view, yet the findings of the authors in this volume show that the voices of suspense are present on both linguistic and narrative levels. If we take into account the question "how does a particular voice, narrator or character speak?", we will find different linguistic devices to arouse suspense in the reader / spectator. If we formulate the questions "who speaks?" and "who sees?", the narrative aspects will be the reason for suspense. In the studies of the present volume, "hearing" the voices of suspense is analysed on the following levels:

1. Speech or dialogues of the characters
Evil or maleficent protagonists can be marked by a special manner of speaking. The use of variational aspects of language (standard and non-standard varieties, colloquial or formal language use, slang, dialect, etc.) can create a social distance between the characters. In addition, the reader can be able to identify the characters or the narrator through language use.

In some of the contributions of Part I and II of this volume, "exotic" language use, or multilingualism, have been shown to be a particular device of the genre to create the sensation of the strange, foreign, or 'ununderstandable' *i.e. deepers the mystery.*

2. Character portrayal
In fiction or film where the focus is on the protagonist, suspense can be produced by the character's mental or physical reactions towards the other characters (Iwata 2005). Character portrayal can be presented through epic or narrative discourse describing the character from the outside or through direct or indirect speech through the mode of speech of the character itself. In the case of audiovisual fiction, character portrayal is achieved through the speech of the characters and through semiotic devices like images, music, gestures or mimic.

3. Point of view
In crime fiction and film the character's voice is part of the process of creating suspense. The dimensions of narrator categories and modes of speech as well as the thought representations are a fundamental stylistic component. The point of view helps the reader or spectator to identify with the characters. Suspense is produced when the reader feels the trouble of the character (Iwata 2005: 177). If

13

the point of view is focused on the evil or nefarious character, the creation of anxiety is even more intense.

4. Plot or narrative structure
The reader or spectator is guided by plot or script in order to feel suspense, tension or surprise. According to Iwata (2005: 168) the sensation of suspense usually depends on clearly bifurcating plot lines or on the delay in showing the resolution. Emmott and Alexander (2010: 340-346) explain how reader manipulation is responsible for suspense creating. Also, other devices like long parts of detailed narrative, or dialogue description, or repetitions, can create suspense by prolonging the tension and the outcome of the crime. (Emmott and Alexander 2010: 332)

5. Semiotic aspects
Non-verbal aspects of communication appear in written and audiovisual fiction. In written fiction there are restricted to the narrative discourse that accompanies the interventions of the characters or through the speech of other characters as receptors. In audiovisual fiction, semiotic elements like music, sounds etc. are a very important factor in the creation of suspense.

All these linguistic and narrative aspects show how complex the voices used to create suspense sensation in crime fiction or film are. This complexity has to be taken into account when translating it into another language.

As a general result of this volume, it has been proved that the interventions of the translator can affect or change the quality of the suspense experience of the reader, in both directions, decreasing or increasing the suspense sensation.

Referring to linguistic devices, the use of language varieties and multilingual language elements presents a special challenge for translators. Studies on this topic have shown that it is impossible to draw a correspondence between varieties of different languages which are closely linked to geographical and social settings (Brumme and Espunya 2012: 21). In crime fiction and film, where the speech of the characters is one of the most important resources in suspense building, the translator has to compensate in some way for this impossibility. In the present volume, the authors show how some translators create their own system from target languages in order to produce the colloquial tone and the rhetorical style of the narrator. The very characteristic foreign elements in crime fiction are treated in very different manners, from neutralization or omission of the foreign element in the translations, to the use of foreignised features in the translation of greetings and commonplace sayings, giving the characters an exotic flair, although in the original they are not foreigners.

Other linguistic elements such as the use of interrogative sentences in some source novels, signalling that characters discover clues themselves, have not always been taken into account by the translators of the examples presented in this volume. This is the case when the narrator intervenes in the translation more than in the original; the target readers face a higher degree of explicitation, and the suspense decreases. In some text examples, explicitation can be found in the footnotes, which can disturb the suspense in a novel and turn the readers' attention in another direction. Suspense can also be neutralized by prologues or glossaries which are sometimes used by the translator to help the readers understand the overused slang or other substandard features of the characters.

Concerning the translation of narrative elements, it has been shown that in translations of suspenseful texts, narrative strategies employed by the author of the original text have sometimes been modified. In more recent studies the importance of considering the narrative techniques and structures of the target text while translating it into another language has been emphasized.[9] The manner of translation of narrative aspects in literary works can even have an impact on how the work is received in the target culture. Hewson (2006), for example, explains how the first French translation of Franz Kafkas *Die Verwandlung* (*The Metamorphosis*) has been misunderstood because of the change from free indirect style of the original into a first person narrator. The free indirect style in the original creates a special ambiguity between reality and irreality, whereas the French translation was interpreted as something that really happened to the main character, and therefore caused the reaction of rejection and revulsion among the French readers. In the case of crime fiction, this kind of change in the point of view increases the suspense sensation, whereas the inverse case decreases it.

Finally, some source novels show a higher degree of expressivity, of displaying emotions. The translation of nonverbal behaviour expressing characters' emotions presents another challenge for the translator because of the cultural implications. Semiotic elements can influence the feeling of suspense and the creation of suspense achieved in the original.

The complexity of and difficulty in transferring the voices of suspense seems to lead us to the conclusion that it is impossible to take into account all devices in the same way as they are used in the source text. Nevertheless, the aim of this volume is to detect both translator decisions that change or eliminate the suspense of the original, and translation strategies that are able to create similar or the same sensations.

As a topic that has not been studied yet, this volume aspires to be considered as a first step and inspiration to further studies on the translation of suspense in literary and filmic crime fiction.

4. The content of this volume

The chapters in this volume are a selection[10] of the papers originally presented at the International Conference *The Voices of Suspense and their Translation in Thrillers*, held at the Universidad Pontificia Comillas in Madrid (Spain) on October 18th and 19th, 2012.[11] Our goal was to bring together researchers specialising in crime fiction and film, and in translation of the genre and its subgenres, to study fictional dialogue as a means of creating suspense and its translation in crime fiction (novels and films). The book comprises three parts and 16 chapters.

In Part I, *Creating suspense in literature and film*, the authors present definitions of suspense in different types of crime fiction in order to define the topic of the book. All chapters exemplify their definitions with detailed analyses of novels and films.

Dirk Delabastita focuses on two bestsellers from the late Victorian period: Bram Stoker's Gothic novel *Dracula* (1897) and George du Maurier's psychological thriller *Trilby* (1895). These two novels are discussed through exploration of the nature of suspense, which is viewed as a narrative and cognitive phenomenon whose understanding requires close attention to textual devices as well as to response from the audience / readership. **Sanja Škifić** and **Rajko Petković** deal with the stylistic and linguistic creation of suspense in Quentin Tarantino's *Pulp Fiction* and *Reservoir Dogs*. The most prominent linguistic device identified in both films refers to repetition. Analysed in relation to suspense creation, repetition is viewed as a device that creates the effect of suspense primarily by prolonging or slowing down the dialogue. **Soledad Díaz Alarcón** studies dialogue in the French detective novel *Melchior*, by Alain Demouzon, as the device used to build up, qualify, diversify and interrelate the characters, and to create realistic effects. **Leah Leone** investigates the Spanish translation of Faulkner's *The Wild Palms*. The translator employed lexical additions, the transfer of dialogue from one character to another, and the displacement of free-indirect discourse into direct speech to increase the tone of suspense, thereby transforming *Las palmeras salvajes* from psychological narration into a thriller.

Part II, *Translation of language variation and foreign language use*, contains studies of translating slang, multilingualism and greetings, devices that have been shown to be very common in crime fiction and film.

Daniel Linder analyses the overcompansated slang in the Spanish translation of Chester Himes's *For the Love of Imabelle*. In this novel, slang creates realism, an apparent immersion of readers into the imagined criminal underworld. **José Luis Aja Sánchez** investigates translation proceedings of Gadda's *Quer pasticciaccio brutto di via Merulana* (1946-1947), the story of a sordid murder related from police inspector Ciccio Ingravallo's point of view,

[handwritten annotations: "idiolect – individual's distinctive language." above; "dialect Sociolect" mid-page]

and marked by the use of the diatopic and diastratic registers. **Jean Anderson** explores how authors attempt to create a sense of the foreign in thrillers with exotic settings or characters with empty exclamations in the foreign language. The study is based on the French translations of the American author Cara Black's *Aimée Leduc* series, where the French flavour of the Parisian setting and the Frenchness of the (half-American) protagonist are underlined. **Giuseppe De Bonis** explores the semiotic implications of multilingualism in the construction of suspense in Alfred Hitchcock's films. The presence of different languages on screen has three functions in the films directed by the universally acknowledged "master of thrill": realism, conflict and confusion.

In Part III, *Transferring narrative structure, plot and semiotic elements in translation*, the authors analyse how translators transfer suspense built through the use of special narrative structures, by the development of the plot in novels or by semiotic elements in films.

Jenny Brumme analyses detective novels by the Austrian writer Wolf Haas, paying attention to the stylistic features which evoke a spoken context in the original and their translation in the target texts (English, Spanish and French). **Guilhem Naro** and **Maria Wirf Naro** explore reducing the distance between characters, narrator and reader in Steinfest's *Nervöse Fische* and its translation into French. The narrator feigned a certain degree of spontaneity through digressions and comparisons, which appear in the translation, but without the graphic representations (different fonts, dashes, footnotes, italics) from the original that have been used to reduce the distance between narrator and reader. **Anna Espunya** studies translation shifts on the microtextual level, e.g. from one category of narrator to another, or from one mode of speech and thought to another, drawn from Agatha Christie's works featuring Ariadne Oliver. These instances can affect the global articulation of points of view that build suspense. **Karen Seago** analyses how ambiguity, ambivalence, and misdirection are achieved, focusing on dialogue instances between the detective and his / her side-kick. **Laila A. Helmi** sets out to examine how suspense is constructed through the narrative voice(s) and dialogue of the characters in the original text, and its subsequent reconstruction in the Arabic translation, based on a corpus of illocutionary forces in Dan Brown's work. **Bárbara Martínez Vilinsky** analyses features and functions of dialogue in five crime novels written originally in Castilian Spanish and five novels translated from American English into Spanish, all published in the 90s, focusing on the following aspects: vocabulary employed in the characters' speech, the type of structure chosen to convey information, the degree of detail and informational load included in the narrators' dialogue tags. **Anita Pavić Pintarić** and **Sybille Schellheimer** investigate the translation of emotions expressed in nonverbal features of dialogues in Remin's novel *Schnee in Venedig* and its Croatian and Spanish translations. **Camino Gutiérrez Lanza** analyses the contribution of fictive orality to the creation of suspense and its translation from English into Spanish in the film *Repulsion* (Polanski 1965), which was censored in Spain during the 1960s and 1970s.

---

[1] See for example: Brumme (2008), Brumme and Resinger (2008), Andújar and Brumme (2010), Cunillera and Resinger (2011), Brumme (2012), Brumme and Espunya (2012), Fischer and Wirf (2012).

[2] The complete references of the projects are: *Oralidad fingida: Descripción y Traducción*, OFDYT, 2007-2009 (HUM2007-62745) and *La traducción del diálogo ficcional. Textos literarios y multimodales*, TRADIF, 2010-2013 (FFI2010-16783).

[3] Besides the genre of crime fiction, it has also been studied the literature and films for children and young people because of the high incidence of dialogue. See Fischer and Wirf Naro (2012).

[4] The concept of evocation applied on translation studies has been described by Freunek (2007); see also Brumme (2012), Brumme and Espunya (2012), Cadera (2012b).

[5] See for example: Bönnemark (1997), Derry (1988), Iwata (2008), Scaggs (2005), Vorderer / Wulff / Friedrichsen (1996).

[6] There are several terms in use to name the phenomenon of representation of orality in literature. Feigned orality (from German *fingierte Mündlichkeit*) has been introduced by Goetsch (1985). There is also used the terms "fictional" or "fictive" orality, see Brumme and Espunya (2012: 12-15).

[7] See Brumme and Espunya 2012: 7-31.

[8] See Chatman (1978), Lanser (1981), Coste (1989) and further Patron (2011), Aczel (1998), Fludernik (2001).

[9] See, for example Alsina (2008), Cadera (2011), Kohlmayer (2004), Zuschlag (2002).

[10] The papers of this volume have been all peer reviewed by an international scientific committee.

[11] The Conference and the present volume are part of the research project *The Translation of Fictional Dialogue. Literary Texts and Multimodal Texts* (TRADIF is its Spanish acronym), reference number FFI2010-16782 (subprogramme FILO, 2010-2013), financed by the Spanish Ministry of Science and Innovation.

Bibliography

Aczel, Richard. 1998. 'Hearing Voices in Narrative Texts' in *New Literary History* 29.3: 467-500.

Alsina, Victòria. 2008. 'El tratamiento del discurso indirecto libre en las traducciones españolas y catalana de *Mansfield Park* de Jane Austen' in Brumme, Jenny and Hildegard Resinger (eds). 2008. *La oralidad fingida: obras literarias. Descripción y traducción.* In collaboration with Amaia Zaballa. Madrid and Frankfurt am Main: Iberoamericana / Vervuert. 15-32.

Andújar, Gemma and Brumme, Jenny (eds). 2010. *Construir, deconstruir y reconostruir. Mímesis y Traducción de la oralidad y la afectividad.* (TRANSÜD. Arbeiten zur Theorie und Praxis des Übersetzens und Dolmetschens). Berlin: Frank & Timme.

Bönnemark, Margit. 1997. *The Mimetic Mystery. A linguistic study of the genre of British and American detective fiction including a comparison with suspense fiction.* PhD Thesis. University of Stockholm.

Brumme, Jenny (ed.). 2008. *La oralidad fingida: descripción y traducción. Teatro, cómic y medios audiovisuales.* In collaboration with Hildegard Resinger and Amaia Zaballa. Madrid and Frankfurt am Main: Iberoamericana / Vervuert.

———. 2012. *Traducir la voz ficticia.* Berlin and Boston: De Gruyter.

Brumme, Jenny and Hildegard Resinger (eds). 2008. *La oralidad fingida: obras literarias. Descripción y traducción.* In collaboration with Amaia Zaballa. Madrid and Frankfurt am Main: Iberoamericana / Vervuert.

Brumme, Jenny and Anna Espunya (eds). 2012. *The Translation of Fictive Dialogue.* (Approaches to translation studies, 35). Amsterdam and New York: Rodopi.

Cadera, Susanne M. 2011. 'Aspectos de oralidad fingida en la narrativa de Mario Vargas Llosa y sus traducciones al alemán' in Cunillera, Montserrat and Resinger, Hildegard (eds). 2011. *Implicación emocional y oralidad en la traducción literaria.* Berlin: Frank & Timme. 153-174.

———. 2012a. 'Translating fictive dialogue in novels' in Brumme, Jenny and Espunya, Anna (eds). *The Translation of Fictive Dialogue.* (Approaches to translation studies, 35). Amsterdam and New York: Rodopi. 35-51.

———. 2012b. 'Reflexiones sobre la traducción de la oralidad fingida en la narrativa' in Romana García, Maria Luisa, Saénz Rotko, José Manuel and Úcar Ventura, Pilar (eds) *Traducción e interpretación. Estudios, perspectivas y enseñanzas.* Madrid: Servicio de Publicaciones de la Universidad Pontificia Comillas.

Chatman, Seymour. 1978. *Story and Discourse: Narrative Structure in Fiction and Film.* Ithaca: Cornell University Press.

Coste, Didier. 1989. *Narrative as Communication.* Minnesota: University of Minnesota Press.

Cunillera, Montserrat and Hildegard Resinger (eds). 2011. *Implicación emocional y oralidad en la traducción literaria.* (TRANSÜD. Arbeiten zur Theorie und Praxis des Übersetzens und Dolmetschens). Berlin: Frank & Timme.

De Castro García, María Isabel and Lucía Montejo Gurruchaga. 1990. *Tendencias y Procedimientos de la novela española actual.* Madrid: UNED.

Derry, Charles. 1988. *The Suspense Thriller. Films in the Shadow of Alfred Hitchcock.* Jefferson, North Carolina: McFarland & Company, Inc.

Emmott, Catherine and Marc Alexander. 2010. 'Detective fiction, plot construction and reader manipulation' in McIntyre, Dan and Beatrix Busse (eds). 2010. *Language and Style.* Houndmills: Palgrave Macmillan. 328-346.

Freunek, Sigrid. 2007. *Literarische Mündlichkeit und Übersetzung. Am Beispiel deutscher und russischer Erzähltexte.* (TRANSÜD. Arbeiten zur Theorie und Praxis des Übersetzens und Dolmetschens). Berlin: Frank & Timme.

Fischer, Martin B. and María Wirf Naro (eds). 2012. *Translating Fictional Dialogue for Children and Young People.* (TRANSÜD. Arbeiten zur Theorie und Praxis des Übersetzens und Dolmetschens). Berlin: Frank & Timme.

Fludernik, Monika. 2001. 'New Wine in Old Bottles? Voice, Focalization, and New Writing' in *New Literary History* 32: 619-638.

Galán Herrera, Juan José. 2008. 'El Canon de la novela negra y policíaca' in *Tejuelo* 1: 58-74.

Genette, Gérard. 1972. *Figure III*. Paris, Le Seuil.

Goetsch, Paul. 1985. 'Fingierte Mündlichkeit in der Erzählkunst entwickelter Schriftkulturen' in *Poetica* 17: 202-218.

Hewson, Lance. 2006. 'Translation Strategies, or Sorting Out Fiction from Fiction'. Conference held in the Departament of Translation and Interpreting, Universidad Pontificia Comillas de Madrid. 11th of May 2006.

Iwata, Yumiko. 2008. *Creating Suspense and Surprise in Short Literary Fiction: A Stylistic and Narratological Approach*. PhD Thesis. University of Birmingham. On line at: http://etheses.bham.ac.uk. (Consulted: 15 April 2013)

Kohlmayer, Rainer. 2004. 'Literarisches Übersetzen: Die Stimme im Text' in *Actas del Congreso Internacional de Germanistas*. Germany- Italy. 8th – 12th of October 2003. Bonn: DAAD: 465-486.

Lanser, Susan Sniader. 1981. *The Narrative Act: Point of View in Prose Fiction*. Princeton: Princeton University Press.

Patron, Sylvie. 2011. 'Homonymy, Polysemy and Synonymy: Reflections on the Notion of Voice' in Krogh Hansen, Per, Stefan Iversen, Henrik Skov Nielsen and Rolf Reitan (eds). 2011. *Strange Voices in Narrative Fiction*. Berlin and Boston: De Gryter. 13-36.

Scaggs, John. 2005. *Crime Fiction*. London and New York: Routledge.

Tacca, Óscar. 1973. *Las voces de la novela*. Madrid: Gredos.

Toury, Gideon. 1995. *Descriptive Translation Studies – and Beyond*. Amsterdam: John Benjamins.

Vorderer, Peter, Hans J. Wulff and Mike Friedrichsen (eds). 1996. *Suspense: conceptualizations, theoretical analyses, and empirical explorations*. Mahwah, NJ: Lawrence Erlbaum Associates.

Zabalbeascoa, Patrick. 2012. 'Translating dialogues in audiovisual fiction' in Brumme, Jenny and Espunya, Anna (eds). *The Translation of Fictive Dialogue*. (Approaches to translation studies, 35). Amsterdam and New York: Rodopi. 63-78.

Zuschlag, Katrin. 2002: *Narrativik und literarisches Übersetzen. Erzähltechnische Merkmale als Invariante der Übersetzung*. Tübingen: Gunter Narr.

Part I

Creating suspense in literature and film

Chapter 1: Thrilled by *Trilby*? Dreading *Dracula*?
Late-Victorian thrillers and the curse of the foreign tongue

Dirk Delabastita

Abstract
This paper looks at two bestsellers from the 1890s: George du Maurier's *Trilby* and Bram Stoker's *Dracula*. An operational definition of suspense in narrative fiction is provided which attempts to combine an understanding of its cognitive and emotional effects with a repertoire of narrative techniques available to achieve these effects. The model emphasizes the variability of the reader's prior knowledge (in our case, linguistic knowledge) as a factor that turns suspense into a fairly unstable notion. The discussion of the two novels shows that multilingualism and translation are not just things that happen 'after' a suspenseful text and in response to it. Translation and multilingualism may already come into the picture within (source) texts and their fictional universe, potentially serving as a suspense-generating technique. The language gap and attendant problems of comprehension and translation are sometimes highlighted sometimes swept under the representational carpet, depending on the suspense-related needs of the moment. Rhetorical effect always prevails over logical consistency.

Keywords: *Dracula, Trilby*, multilingualism, suspense, translation

1. Introduction

In this paper we shall be looking at two sensational bestsellers from the late Victorian period.[1] Firstly, Bram Stoker's *Dracula* (1897), a Gothic thriller which owes its success in part to the author's consummate narrative skill and suspense management and, secondly, George du Maurier's *Trilby* (1894), which can be described as a psychological thriller; its initial success just as stunning as that of Stoker's masterpiece but far less enduring. These two books will be referred to for their own sake but also to explore several issues of a more general interest. Among the points I want to argue, there are two that stand out.

First, feelings of suspense feed on quite complex interpretive mechanisms, involving many parameters. Careful contextualisation is therefore required and, crucially, this contextualisation has to include the reader or viewer. This means that we cannot avoid acknowledging the heterogeneity of groups of readers and viewers, and thus the variability of their reactions to texts, and consequently the instability of suspense.

Second, multilingualism and translation are not just things that happen 'after' a suspenseful text and in response to it, as translation and multilingualism may already come into the picture within (source) texts and their fictional universe, potentially serving as a suspense-generating technique.[2] With the help of our two novels, we shall not only discuss suspense as a challenge for the translator, but also as something that can find its very origin in language difference and its representations.[3]

2. The two novels

Dracula hardly requires an introduction. Written by Dublin-born Bram Stoker, the book came out in 1897 and instantly established itself as a modern classic. *Nosferatu*, released in 1922, launched the career of the book on the silver screen and in the popular media more widely. Skilfully combining vampire lore with the literary traditions of gothic fiction and the epistolary novel, and tapping into several topical debates and discourses, Stoker definitely created one of the most powerful myths of the modern age.

The one-time popularity of *Trilby* is attested by the presence in English of several lexical items stemming from the book:

trilby = a man's soft hat with a narrow brim and the top part pushed in from front to back

svengali = a person who has the power to control another person's mind, make them do bad things, etc.

in the altogether = (OLD-FASHIONED, INFORMAL) without any clothes on.[4]

Its author was George du Maurier, a close friend of Henry James. The genesis of *Trilby* and the story of its wildfire success are described from James's semi-fictionalized perspective in David Lodge's 2004 novel *Author, Author*.

Most of the story of *Trilby* is set in the 1850s. Two aspiring English painters, William Bagot and Talbot Wynne (nicknamed 'Little Billee' and 'Taffy' respectively), and their Scottish friend Sandy McAllister ('the Laird') form a little band of artistic brothers in the bohemian artistic milieu of Paris. All three fall in love with Trilby O'Ferrall, the novel's heroine. Of half Irish and half Scottish origin, Trilby grew up in Paris and was orphaned as a young girl, having to look after her baby brother Jeannot. She works as an artist's model, occasionally posing "in the altogether" but, after meeting Little Billee, she is filled with shame about this and becomes a laundress. Moral scruples about her past make Trilby feel unworthy of Little Billee's offer of marriage, but the latter's pleadings are so passionate and insistent that she finally gives in. As soon as Billee's mother gets wind of this, however, she comes over from England to talk Trilby out of the engagement again. Miserable and confused, Trilby disappears from Paris, while Billee is heartbroken and decides to go back to England.

Another key character in the book is the master pianist Svengali, who, with his musical friend Gecko, spends a lot of time at the artists' studio. Svengali is a half-Polish, half-German Jew. Amply drawing on anti-Semitic stereotypes, Du Maurier depicts him in the most unfavourable manner as a filthy, greedy, exploitative and manipulative person.

An ellipsis (p. 142) shows Little Billee five years later in England, where he has become a celebrated painter. After Trilby's vanishing act and Billee's return to England, Taffy and the Laird, too, had left Paris and they spent several years travelling around. Now the three friends meet again in London. They hear about a famous singer known as "la Svengali". It turns out that this international star is none other than Trilby. In a state of hopeless distress after the death of her little brother, Trilby had fallen under the hypnotic spell of Svengali, who became her therapist, music teacher, mentor and manager (and probably her lover also). But when Svengali dies in the middle of a concert, Trilby is instantly reduced to her unglamorous, down-to-earth and absolutely tone-deaf self: such was the diva's total dependence on Svengali's hypnotic power. Trilby is hissed off the stage and suffers a fatal nervous shock. She manages one more splendid vocal performance on her deathbed, when she sees Svengali staring straight at her from a photograph, and then passes away. The very day of her burial, Little Billee also sinks into a long and painful decline, leading to his premature death.

Another ellipsis (p. 284) jolts us twenty years into the future. Taffy is married with Blanche, the sister of Little Billee. They are visiting Paris for a second honeymoon. Taffy and Blanche go to a musical show in Paris where they spot Gecko among the musicians. They meet afterwards and Gecko gives Taffy his version of the story of the relationship between Svengali and Trilby: "*There were two Trilbys*. There was the Trilby you knew, who could not sing one single note in tune. She was an angel of paradise" (p. 298), but Svengali could at the flick of a switch turn her into "an unconscious Trilby of marble, who could produce wonderful sounds –just the sounds he wanted, and nothing else– and think his thoughts and wish his wishes– and love him at his bidding with a strange, unreal, factitious love" (p. 299).

There are some striking resemblances with the plot of *Dracula* to the point of suggesting direct forms of influence.[5] Thus, in both *Trilby* and *Dracula*, we meet a trio of good and caring men (Billee, Taffy and the Laird vs. Dr Seward, Arthur Holmwood and Quincey Morris), who are in love with an attractive and basically innocent and virtuous, but less than morally perfect young woman (Trilby vs. Lucy Westenra).[6] Two of the men in the respective trios must learn to repress their amorous feelings, since the third friend of the group (Billee vs. Holmwood) enters into an engagement with the young woman, which will, however, never materialize in marriage. In either case, the young woman falls under the total psychological and physical control of a gothic villain of East-European Jewish origin: Svengali and Count Dracula respectively.[7] Prefiguring the Count, Svengali is described as having "big yellow teeth baring themselves in a mongrel canine snarl" (p. 92).[8] Whether this was intended by Du Maurier in any way or not, *Svengali* is a half-English half-French anagram of *evil sang*, meaning 'evil blood'. The anagram's racial overtones, its allusion to blood and its interlingualism make it particularly apt.

Furthermore, in both books, the themes of mesmerism, repressed sexuality and the split personality play a crucial part, showing that Freudian psychoanalysis was only just around the corner in the 1890s. Last but not least, both novels are highly language-conscious: they lead the main characters out of their native cultural habitat into strange linguistic territory; they present a range of idiolects, dialects and sociolects; they stage linguistic barriers, confront the reader with heterolingual material, and use all such linguistic and interlinguistic devices for the sake of suspense. These are the very aspects that we wish to concentrate on here.

3. The hermeneutics of suspense

Let us briefly recall the basic features of suspense. Suspense is one of the possible cognitive and emotional effects of a narrative, dramatic or filmic text (whatever its exact genre); other possible effects include surprise, mystery, sadness, humour, and so on. Suspense occurs in the reading or viewing *process* and has a strong *emotional component*. In other words, it has an intrinsic temporal and emotional nature. The following model, static as it is, can nonetheless help us understand how suspense operates. The model summarises the field within which the narrative processes of telling and understanding act themselves out:

Table 1. Model of the narrative processes

	the world of the text	general world knowledge (subjective, intersubjective, objective)
WORLD	characters events space time	facts frames scripts
TEXT	medium language time characterization focalization narration	individual texts genres discourses
	the text	intertextuality other texts and discourses
	WITHIN	**BEYOND**

The *world of the text* corresponds with the fictional world (or with what the Russian formalists would have called the *fabula*). The *text*, as understood here, is the ensemble of discursive materials and techniques used in (re)presenting the fictional world (*suzjet*). Both in producing and in interpreting texts, we constantly make use of prior knowledge about the world (*general world knowledge*); we also have permanent recourse to knowledge about ways of speaking about the world (*intertextuality*, understood very broadly as knowledge of existing texts, genres and discursive practices and conventions).[9]

The table with its four interacting subfields contains nothing new, but it is helpful to keep in the back of our minds the interpretive parameters it brings together as we now proceed to present a simple model of suspense. Suspense is usually described as the state of anticipation, curiosity, uncertainty and anxiety regarding the outcome of the story or a particular episode in the story. Upon closer inspection, the effect of suspense depends on the interplay of the following factors:

Table 2. Factors involved in suspense

(Psychology) COGNITIVE AND EMOTIONAL COMPONENTS OF SUSPENSE	*(Literary studies)* SUSPENSE PARAMETERS AS DEFINED IN TERMS OF THE NARRATIVE SQUARE
Reader or spectator involvement: 1. **Positive** attitude **towards protagonists** (involving sympathy and empathy, and implying concern over their well-being) 2. **Negative** attitude towards **antagonists**	A conflict situation in the fictional world with characters who are opposed according to a value scheme (partly text-internal, partly text-external)[10] Textual techniques promoting imaginative immersion (e.g. homodiegetic narration, FDD/DD/FID, internal focalisation)
Uncertainty about what will happen next?	Intertextual knowledge[11]
Specific expectations[12] about what may plausibly happen 1. in the immediate future, 2. in what is for the protagonist a critical, often threatening situation, 3. enabling either a favourable or a negative outcome, 4. with variable degrees of probability (possibly shifting as we approach the critical point of no return)[13]	Hypotheses about likely outcomes are based on text-external knowledge, both real-world knowledge and intertextually based knowledge, as well as on anticipations provided by the text itself, e.g. by means of flashforwards (objective ⇔ subjective) and mise-en-abîme (more ⇔ less obvious)
leading to **curiosity** combined with **strong emotions:** 1. fear (negative outcome) and hope (positive outcome) 2. frustration caused by one's powerlessness as a mere witness of the action 3. frustration caused by the perceived slowness with which one's curiosity is satisfied and emotional relief is provided	emotions possibly heightened by the use of: 1. pathos (e.g. strongly expressive language) 2. dramatic irony (e.g. use of selective viewpoints and unreliable narration) 3. retardation techniques (ellipsis, stretch, descriptive pause, cross-cutting, digression)

As a rhetorical device or effect in fiction, suspense is often discussed together with, but distinguished from mystery and surprise.[14]

Surprise is in certain ways the opposite effect of suspense: to be fully effective in fiction surprise also requires positive attitudes towards the protagonist, but, unlike suspense, it does not involve the creation of expectations which the text is then slow to fulfil or frustrate. The reverse is true, as something happens suddenly and confusingly that one could *not* possibly have expected on the basis of real-world knowledge, intertextually based knowledge or earlier hints within the text. It was either simply impossible to predict the surprising turn of events at all, or we were misled into making a totally wrong prediction.

Mystery concerns the past, not the immediate future in the story's sequence of events. The key question is not so much 'what happens next?' as 'what has happened?' But here too, there are close links with suspense, since the unravelling of a mystery from the past takes place in the present, with the detective and the reader / viewer looking forward to seeing whether their hypotheses will be confirmed or proven wrong, as the investigative process unfolds. In many narratives, crucial future outcomes depend on the successful solution of the past mystery: e.g. the happiness or the career of the detective, the avoidance of further crimes, if the villain is still unidentified and at large, or the sheer victory of morality and justice over evil. In this way the mystery-solving induces a great deal of suspense and past-oriented uncertainties and future-oriented uncertainties become very hard to disentangle.[15]

Clearly, while it makes sense to distinguish suspense, mystery and surprise from an analytical viewpoint, we need to recognize that these effects usually occur together in effective plot management with the common purpose of keeping the reader's or the spectator's attention riveted on the narrative. In distinct but closely related ways all three thrive on temporality and causality, on the interplay of cognition and emotion, and on audience participation.

4. *Dracula*: linguistic othering and narrative axiologies

How does the linguistic management in *Dracula* correlate with its plot and suspense management? *Dracula* has in the past few decades attracted an enormous amount of literary criticism, which has progressively raised the novel's status from that of a professionally written "popular shocker" to that of a multi-layered "proto-modernist text shot through with instability" (Bollen and Ingelbien 2009: 404).[16] Critics have duly noted the linguistic variety and the polyphony of the novel, which combines the conventions of the diary novel and the epistolary novel. At a very basic level of analysis, this linguistic and stylistic variety mirrors the diverse social, regional and national backgrounds of the novel's characters, as well as the range of genres that the different narrators employ (personal letter, business letter, diary, telegram, newspaper article, medical report...), with each genre calling for its proper style or register. If we make abstraction of genre- and situation-bound variation, the following generalisations may be made about how linguistic usage links up with the axiology of good and evil which is so central to the induction of suspense in the book.

With the major exception of Van Helsing (to whom we shall turn in a moment), the 'good' characters all speak or write a form of standard English, which confirms their position as educated members of the British middle class, or at least, in the cases of Quincey Morris (who is a Texan, using a more slangy American English) and Arthur Holmwood (who inherits his father's title before the book is halfway completed), their adherence to the values and aspirations of the British middle class. Clearly, some linguistic variety is tolerated[17] but, on the whole, there is a neat correspondence between linguistic standards of correctness and respect for moral norms.

Not without a certain Dickensian flair, the novel also introduces several uneducated English dialect speakers, who at some point serve the interests of the good characters by providing important information. Thus, in the early Whitby episode we meet old Mr Swales, a retired sailor speaking broad and, occasionally incomprehensible, Yorkshire English; later we hear Cockney English from the London zookeeper, Thomas Bilder, and his wife as well as from rude workmen involved in the transportation of Dracula's boxes; finally there is Mr Donelson, the captain of the ship that takes Dracula back to Transylvania, who speaks Scottish English. In line with romantic valuations of the original purity of dialect, these characters show a natural sense of truth, decency and good humour (especially Mr Swales). But in line with Victorian fears about degeneration and social chaos, the dialect speakers' blatant and linguistically conveyed lack of cultural sophistication may just as well signal the potential danger of slippage into vulgarity, greed, heavy drinking and possibly worse vices. The apparent lack of education in dialect speakers surely reveals their true native qualities as Britons (the man from Doolittle Wharf is a "good fellow all the same", p. 294), but in a modern metropolitan context it also causes some unease. We can always trust true Britons, so the novel tells us, but not without voicing anxieties about whether we can always trust the working classes.

Most continental locals that we meet in Dracula's homeland or *en route* to it speak German (of which Jonathan Harker has a smattering, while the polyglot Van Helsing is said to speak it fluently)[18] but also more impenetrable languages such as Romany, Slovak or Serbian. These locals are either unhelpful in the just fight against Dracula, or they are actually on the wrong side of the conflict as helpers of the Count. Linguistic otherness earmarks these people as either irrelevant to the pursuits of the good characters (in the best case), or as enemies (in the worst).

According to the same logic, one would expect Count Dracula to speak no English, or very bad English, as a linguistic badge of his foreignness and depraved nature. But here an interesting paradox emerges. Dracula turns out to speak more or less perfect English. He has learnt it from books and only feels somewhat uncertain about intonation (a feature which Bram Stoker does not try to represent in print). In point of fact, it is not the Count who thoroughly butchers the English language but his fiercest opponent, the Dutch professor Van Helsing! As Nina Auerbach has observed, "van Helsing is 'good' and has flawed English, Dracula is 'evil' and his English is 'almost flawless'" (Pollner 2002: 214). Conformity to moral norms is here at odds with conformity to linguistic norms. The paradox is easy to resolve though. Dracula has honed his linguistic skills as a speaker of English as a strategy of camouflage and infiltration. Linguistic assimilation enables him to get behind the frontline and blend in. This makes him doubly dangerous.

Turning to Van Helsing, there can never be any doubt about his loyalty to the good cause. He received part of his academic education in London.[19] While not being English he hails from another western, modern and mainly protestant European nation, just the other side of the North Sea. It has been pointed out that 'Helsing' is an anagram of 'English', which can be taken to flag up a profound unity of essence and purpose.[20] A deep personal bond of trust and friendship exists with Dr Seward, which has been sealed by an act of vampirism turned inside out (anticipating the later life-giving blood transfusions for Lucy), namely when Seward saved Van Helsing's life by quickly sucking poison from an infected wound at the risk of his own life. This is how the professor phrases it:

(1)
Were fortune other, then it were bad for those who have trusted, for I come to my friend when he call me to aid those he holds dear. Tell your friend that when that time you suck from my wound so swiftly the poison of the gangrene from that knife that our other friend, too nervous, let slip, you did more for him when he wants my aids and you call for them than all his great fortune could do. (Stoker 2011: 106-107)

This is nothing short of a linguistic massacre. Van Helsing's mangled English is thus not a symbol of his moral otherness but rather a contrasting foil to highlight his commonality of spirit and purpose with the good Anglo-Saxon characters. If the dark forces of evil coming from the East are so strong that they can even cloak themselves in idiomatic English, the force of English virtue is so strong that it can even shine its light through a Dutchman's broken English; in either case, 'even' is the operative word.

As always, context is everything. And so is effect. One effect is that Van Helsing's foreigner's English adds a touch of linguistic authenticity and local colour to his characterisation. Having said this, I can affirm as a native speaker of Dutch that Van Helsing's countless language errors are barely representative of typical Dutch / English linguistic interference.[21] In the only two cases where Stoker just perhaps may have intended to give Van Helsing a phrase in his native Dutch, it actually comes out in German and in faulty German too: e.g. "Gott in [*sic*] Himmel!" (p. 120).

Another effect of Van Helsing's broken English is that it introduces a degree of comic relief into what is otherwise a very grim story. Van Helsing's mistakes can be quite amusing, as in the following pathetic effort by the Professor to throw in an idiomatic phrase:

(2)
'Oh that we had known it before!' he said, 'for then we might have reached him in time to save poor Lucy. However, "the milk that is spilt cries not out afterwards," as you say'. (Stoker 2011: 219)

Or take the following example, where Van Helsing (himself quoted by Seward) uses loose forms of indirect speech and narrative report to convey how the dockworkers summarise the conversations between the captain of the Tsarina Catherine and the Count:

(3)
They say much of blood and bloom and of others which I comprehend not,[22] though I guess what they mean; but nevertheless they tell us all things which we want to know. [...] Whereupon the captain tell him that he had better be quick –with blood– for that his ship will leave the place –of blood– before the turn of the tide –with blood. [...] Final the captain, more red than ever, and in more tongues, tell him that he doesn't want no Frenchmen –with bloom upon them and also with blood– in his ship –with blood on her also. (Stoker 2011: 294-295)

Stoker is laying it on thick here: it looks as if he could not get enough of Van Helsing's unintended punning on 'blood' and 'bloody'.

Last but not least, we should be aware of the rather spectacular variations in the degrees of grammaticality of Van Helsing's English. There are many passages where Van Helsing's English is highly unidiomatic and error-ridden, as in the examples above. But then, there are also passages where his English is confident and nearly error-free, occasionally displaying a lexical bandwidth and a rhetorical élan one would readily ascribe to a native speaker. Such sudden improvements in Van Helsing's proficiency in English occur not only in passages where the professor can fall back on the linguistic routines of the medical register in which he feels more at ease (as suggested by Pollner 2002: 214), but in very different contexts too, for instance in moments of great suspense or pathos, where Stoker must have decided that overdoing the linguistic gaffes of Van Helsing would be a distraction lessening the emotional impact of his speeches. In the following example, mistakes are clearly down to a minimum in order to avoid spoiling the solemnity and pathos of the occasion:

(4)
It may be that you may have to bear that mark till God Himself see fit, as He most surely shall, on the Judgment Day to redress all wrongs of the earth and of His children that He has placed thereon. And oh, Madam Mina, my dear, my dear, may we who love you be there to see, when that red scar, the sign of God's knowledge of what has been, shall pass away and leave your forehead as pure as the heart we know. (Stoker 2011: 276)

On other occasions, Stoker neutralizes the linguistic blundering almost completely to avoid it getting in the way of nail-biting suspense.[23] This is nowhere so clear as in Van Helsing's final memorandum just before Mina takes over for the last five pages, where the professor gives a well-paced and nearly word-perfect account of the build-up to the final climax of the fight against evil:

(5)
5 November, afternoon. – I am at least sane. Thank God for that mercy at all events, though the proving it has been dreadful. When I left Madam Mina sleeping within the Holy circle, I took my way to the castle. The blacksmith hammer which I took in the carriage from Veresti was useful; though the doors were all open I broke them off the rusty hinges, lest some ill-intent or ill-chance should close them, so that being entered I might not get out. Jonathan's bitter experience served me here [...] (Stoker 2011: 342)

A final remark on Van Helsing's English. Even though Van Helsing's discursive presence is extremely strong in the novel as a whole, he hardly ever appears as the 'author' of the documents that make up the textual body of the novel. His many speeches, short or long, are mostly quoted by the narrators who have supposedly authored those documents. The question that arises here is why these narrators (Mina and Dr Seward especially) go out of their way to reproduce Van Helsing's grammatical and lexical blunders, as if these would in any way contribute to the referential accuracy of the report. Both in real life and in fiction, quoters very often do their quotees the linguistic courtesy of tacitly editing their mistakes out, along with hesitations, repetitions and all the other minor verbal accidents that characterize improvised oral speech. Not so here, though. The same question may be asked about the fairly faithful representation of the Yorkshire, Cockney and Glaswegian dialects. Why do Mina (p. 62ff), the correspondent for the *Pall Mall Gazette* (p. 128ff) and Jonathan Harker (p. 212, p. 243ff, p. 323ff) all go to such lengths to represent sometimes extensive speeches in dialect? And how does Mina even manage to transcribe stretches of dialect speech, which she admits she does not actually understand?[24] Clearly, momentary effect (stylistic variation, local colour, creating gaps of understanding, suspense) is more important than overall logic and consistency.

5. *Dracula*: language and knowledge gaps

The same principle –effect prevails over logic and consistency– applies also to how foreign languages are represented in *Dracula*. Jonathan's and Dracula's respective foreign travels essentially follow the same pattern, which we know from countless other travel narratives:

Table 3. Jonathan's and Dracula's trips

	HOME⇨	⇨STRANGE LAND⇨	⇨HOME
1. Jonathan's business trip	**England**	**Transylvania**	**England**
2. Dracula's conquest of England	Transylvania	England	Transylvania
	away trip preparation and control	**return** danger and hurried improvisation	

Ironically, Jonathan's business trip [1] serves to pave the administrative way for the execution of Dracula's evil scheme [2]. We have already referred to how much energy Dracula has invested in preparing himself linguistically for his conquest of Britain. During his enforced stay in the Count's castle, Jonathan offers the latter opportunities to further improve his knowledge of the phonetics and plausibly also the pragmatics of English through conversation. As the aims of Jonathan's trip are less ambitious, we can forgive his linguistic homework for being somewhat more casual. Jonathan has a useful "smattering of German" (p. 5) –we do not know whether he has acquired it or brushed it up for the purpose of this trip– and he has also remembered to bring a "polyglot dictionary" in his travel bag (p. 9), but this is as far as his linguistic preparations go.

Not surprisingly, there are a number of occasions where he runs into the limitations of his foreign-language skills. Here are two examples:

(6)
    Just before I was leaving, the old lady came up to my room and said in a very hysterical way: 'Must you go? Oh! young Herr, must you go?' She was in such an excited state that she seemed to have lost her grip of what German she knew, and mixed it all up with some other language which I did not know at all. I was just able to follow her by asking many questions. (Stoker 2011: 8)

(7)
A band of Szgany have come to the castle, and are encamped in the courtyard. These Szgany are gipsies […] They are fearless and without religion, save superstition, and they talk only their own varieties of the Romany tongue.
I shall write some letters home, and shall try to get them to have them posted. I have already spoken to them through my window to begin an acquaintanceship. They took their hats off and

made obeisance and many signs, which, however, I could not understand any more than I could their spoken language ... (Stoker 2011: 41-42)

Almost at the end of the story Mina finds herself in a comparable situation, when she witnesses the English heroes challenging the gipsies who are transporting Dracula to the safety of his castle:

(8)
The leader, with a quick movement of his rein, threw his horse out in front, and pointing first to the sun – now close down on the hill tops – and then to the castle, said something which I did not understand. For answer, all four men of our party threw themselves from their horses and dashed towards the cart. (Stoker 2011: 348)

Partially understood snatches of text, paralinguistic features, context and a great deal of inferencing may enable the character to tentatively reconstruct the gist of what the foreigners are saying, or perhaps not even that. Situations of linguistic isolation like these clearly add to the suspense. Communicative alienation creates uncertainty and lack of control in what is turning out to be a menacing or even outright hostile environment; it places the good character (and with him / her, the emphatic reader) in a frustrating position of relative powerlessness.

In the examples just looked at, Bram Stoker puts up the language barrier in a visible manner. It is meant to be prominent as an obstacle and potential threat for the good characters and thus becomes a source of suspense for the reader. Interestingly, there are many other situations where Stoker does exactly the opposite in order to achieve the same end. The means are different; the function remains the same. There are indeed several scenes in which, far from showcasing and exploiting the language gap, Bram Stoker simply conjures it away, using the novelist's magic wand to let characters communicate with each other while nothing in the fictional world would suggest they have a language in common. Stoker is here using what Meir Sternberg (1981: 224) has called the homogenizing convention. Here is a small-scale example. Jonathan realises he is a prisoner in Dracula's castle:

(9)
I sat down and simply cried. [...] As I sat I heard a sound in the courtyard without – the agonized cry of a woman. I rushed to the window, and throwing it up, peered out between the bars. There, indeed, was a woman with disheveled hair, holding her hands over her heart as one distressed with running. She was leaning against a corner of the gateway. When she saw my face at the window she threw herself forward, and shouted in a voice laden with menace: –
'Monster, give me my child!' (Stoker 2011: 45)

The local peasant woman mistakes Jonathan for the vampire who has abducted her child. The language that she uses is (deliberately!) not identified, as it can hardly be a language that Jonathan knows. So how could Jonathan understand her utterance and report it? Bram Stoker did not want to forego this poignant moment of great pathos and suspense; thanks to his discrete recourse to the homogenizing convention he can get away with it.[25]

Some of the biggest scenes in *Dracula* depend on this ploy. For instance, take the highly erotic episode where Jonathan seems about to lose his purity to the three woman vampires who are approaching him in Dracula's castle:

(10)
I felt in my heart a wicked, burning desire that they would kiss me with those red lips. It is not good to note this down; lest some day it should meet Mina's eyes and cause her pain; but it is the truth. They whispered together, and then they all three laughed [...]. The fair girl shook her head coquettishly, and the other two urged her on. One said: –
'Go on! You are first, and we shall follow; yours is the right to begin.' The other added: –
'He is young and strong; there are kisses for us all.' I lay quiet, looking out under my eyelashes in an agony of delightful anticipation. (Stoker 2011: 39)

All the ingredients of suspense are present here, and the dialogue between the three lady vampires –with its titillating announcement of what is to follow– plays its part in the process. The suspense is so effective that the reader in his / her impatience is unlikely to notice that Stoker is getting away with a most bizarre representational shortcut. Either the lady vampires are conversing in English (or possibly German?), or Jonathan has miraculously acquired a knowledge of Romanian, Romany, Hungarian, Slovak, Serbian, Wallachian, or whichever local language is used in the Dracula household. Neither option looks plausible in terms of the book's fictional set-up.

The scene continues and, an instant before the first fatal kiss, Dracula arrives to stop the ladies and reprimand them. The conversation goes on in the same representational mode, in supposedly universal English without a visible trace of any form of linguistic mediation.[26] This would stretch the reader's credulity, if (again) it had not been for the overwhelming emotional effect of the scene with its mix of suspense, surprise and violent emotion:

(11)
But at that instant another sensation swept through me as quick as lightning. I was conscious of the presence of the Count, and of his being as if lapped in a storm of fury. [...] In a voice which, though low and almost a whisper, seemed to cut through the air and then ring round the room, he exclaimed: –
'How dare you touch him, any of you? How dare you cast eyes on him when I had forbidden it? Back, I tell you all! This man belongs to me! Beware how you meddle with him, or you'll have to deal with me.' The fair girl, with laugh [sic] of ribald coquetry, turned to answer him: –
'You yourself never loved; you never love!' (Stoker 2011: 39-40)

The tacit, extradiegetic and logically impossible kind of 'translation' that is going on here behind the fictional scene is a mimetic sleight of hand that serves the rhetorical purposes of suspense and plot management.

6. Race, accent and morality

The gothic villain in *Trilby* is a strikingly different character from Count Dracula in a number of ways. Rather than being a "Hebrew capitalist" (p. 172), sophisticated and gifted with the financial, linguistic and other means to infiltrate the host country and acquire a strong position there, Svengali is the stereotype of the vile, poor and smelly Jew that you could spot from a long distance. He is "very shabby and dirty" (p. 11), has a "very thin and mean and harsh" voice (p. 11), "bold, black, beady Jew's eyes" (p. 44) like those of a rat or a black crow, and a typical "Hebrew nose"[27] (p. 240). Half vampire and half Wandering Jew, Svengali was "walking up and down the earth seeking whom he might cheat, betray, exploit, borrow money from, make brutal fun of, bully if he dared, cringe to if he must –man, woman, child, or dog" (p. 42). This "Oriental Israelite Hebrew Jew" (p. 244) is "about as bad as they make 'em". On p. 137 in the first American edition of the book, we find an illustration –made by Du Maurier himself– of Svengali as a spider, weaving webs of entrapment. As Trilby says on p. 52, "he reminds me of a big hungry spider, and makes me feel like a fly!"

Crucially, language and accent become an intrinsic part of this outrageously anti-Semitic portrait:

(12)
And here let me say that these vicious imaginations of Svengali's, which look so tame in English print, sounded much more ghastly in French, pronounced with a Hebrew-German accent, and uttered in his hoarse, rasping, nasal, throaty rook's caw, his big yellow teeth baring themselves in a mongrel canine snarl, his heavy upper eyelids drooping over his insolent black eyes. (Du Maurier 1998: 92)

Svengali's linguistic, articulatory and physical imperfections are inextricably linked with each other –and with his moral depravity– to produce an image of subhuman racial inferiority that is strengthened by the narrator's persistent recourse to animal imagery.

The first words Svengali speaks give an idea of what he sounds like in French:

(13)
'Ponchour, mes enfants,' said Svengali. 'Che vous amène mon ami Checko, qui choue du fiolon gomme un anche!' (Du Maurier 1998: 11)

When his words are reported in English, the foreign accent is toned down in the transposition: the narrator says he will "translate him into English, without attempting to translate his accent, which is a mere matter of judiciously transposing p's and b's, and t's and d's, and f's and v's, and g's and k's, and turning the soft French j into sch, and a pretty language into an ugly one" (p.

23). But telltale symptoms of interference remain, sometimes accompanied by metalingual notes, as shibboleths of Svengali's irreducible otherness:

(14)
[Svengali] found Little Billee sitting in a zinc hip-bath, busy with soap and sponge; and was so tickled and interested by the sight that he quite forgot for the moment what he had come for.
'Himmel! Why the devil are you doing that?' he asked, in his German-Hebrew-French.
'Doing *what*?' asked Little Billee, in his French of Stratford-atte-Bowe.
'Sitting in water and playing with a cake of soap and a sponge!'
'Why, to try and get myself *clean*, I suppose!'
'Ach! And how the devil did you get yourself *dirty*, then?'
To this Little Billee found no immediate answer, and went on with his ablutions after the hissing, splashing, energetic fashion of Englishmen; and Svengali laughed loud and long at the spectacle of a little Englishman trying to get himself clean – *tâchant de se nettoyer!*
When such cleanliness had been attained as was possible under the circumstances, Svengali begged for the loan of two hundred francs, and Little Billee gave him a five-franc piece.
Content with this, *faute de mieux*, the German asked him when he would be trying to get himself clean again, as he would much like to come and see him do it.
'Demang mattang, à votre sairveece!' said Little Billee, with a courteous bow.
'*What!! Monday too!!* Gott in Himmel! you try to get yourself clean *every day*?' (Du Maurier 1998: 47)

This passage calls for a number of further comments. Clearly, *Trilby* mobilizes linguistic and cultural difference for humorous purposes as well. True, part of the humour is quite sinister, exploiting as it does the opposition of ethnic stereotypes along the East-West axis. Both physically and morally, the Englishman is clean whereas the Jew is filthy; the former is full of positive energy, contrasting with the latter's cynical opportunism. Another part of the comedy in this exchange appears more innocent: here, and elsewhere, the efforts by Little Billee (and by the Laird) to speak French are quite pathetic in a most amusing way, producing some good-humoured mirth. Occasionally, but much more rarely, French characters try to speak English, with equally hilarious results:

(15)
'Av you seen my fahzere's ole shoes?'
'I av not seen your fahzere's ole shoes.'
Then, after a pause:
'Av you seen my fahzere's ole 'at?'
'I av not seen your fahzere's old 'at!' (Du Maurier 1998: 55)

Verbal clowning and effects of *couleur locale* aside, the juxtaposition and mingling of French and English in *Trilby* also has symbolic meanings. It helps to set up a second spatially-based moral axis in the novel: the North-South axis, represented by Britain and Paris respectively, with the former standing for decency and morality, and the latter for excesses of passion leading to sexual immorality. Thus, on the horizontal axis, Trilby is the Western victim of a Jewish monster from the "mysterious East", the "poisonous East – birthplace and home of an ill wind that blows nobody good" (p. 282). Moving along the vertical axis, we see her being born as the daughter of British parents but growing up in frivolous Paris and slipping into sexual sin herself, to be saved again from human weakness by Little Billee and his British friends. Being a "sinner that repenteth" (p. 182) abandoning French promiscuity to regain clean English virtue, it is altogether appropriate for Trilby to be a French-English bilingual.

Suspense depends on conflict and on moral schemata. The linguistic management of *Trilby* makes a direct contribution to the build-up of its suspense effects. But there is another, perhaps more unexpected, manner in which language and suspense interact in Du Maurier's novel.

7. Suspense, foreign languages and the reader

Du Maurier was born in Paris of a French father and an English mother. Before settling in England at the age of 26, he spent most of his time in France and Belgium, where he trained to become a painter. These basic biographical elements suffice to account for the writer's bilingualism. Feeling equally at ease in French and English, Du Maurier seems to have taken for granted a fair degree of English / French bilingualism in his readers too, as the novel contains a large amount of French. Or does he? In all fairness, the novel gives very contradictory indications about this. My personal feeling is that he just did not have a clear linguistic roadmap.[28]

There are many cases where Du Maurier goes out of his way to make sure that French words, sentences or passages are duly translated or glossed, be it through a character or through the narrator, and sometimes even by a paratextual explanation. Sometimes the illustrations that the novelist provides in the US editions of the book –not in the original UK edition though– offer a visual, intersemiotic kind of translation to help the monolingual English reader out.

But then, in other instances there is a great deal of French that remains untranslated, unglossed and unillustrated, leaving readers to their own linguistic resources. In this way, several of the jokes in the novel become inaccessible to English monolinguals. Also, several passages that play a key part in the suspense management of the book are largely lost on them. Such loss could be said to start on p. 1, where the book's motto, which creates the expectation of a tragic love story, is given in untranslated French:

(16)
Hélas! Je sais un chant d'amours
Triste et gai tour à tour! (Du Maurier 1998: 1)

Each of the book's eight main 'parts' of the novel is prefaced by a poem, which offers, in most cases, a foreshadowing of what is to follow. Six out of those eight mottos are in untranslated French. The chapters are interspersed by several literary quotations in French which, in some cases, also provide hints about future developments or even a mise-en-abîme of the story (e.g. p. 200-202). Again, these indications are lost on the reader who has no French. Here is a brief example. On p. 52, after having inspected Trilby's vocal organs, Svengali quotes the following (unidentified) lines:

(17)
Votre cœur est un luth suspendu!
Aussitôt qu'on le touche, il résonne...[29]

This is a somewhat ominous foreshadowing of what will follow, as Svengali is here implicitly announcing his wish or his plan to manipulate the heart of Trilby and to 'instrumentalize' her in the various possible senses of the term: he will reduce her to a passive tool for his own purposes and turn her into a musical instrument. One needs good French to grasp this. As it happens, the lines are strongly intertextual as well as heterolingual: they form the motto of E.A. Poe's 'The Fall of the House of Usher',[30] adding an eerie gothic resonance, and further widening the gap between those who work out the motto and those who cannot.

It is not just these suspense-building foreshadowing that may be obscured from monolingual English readers, but also several of the moments where the suspense actually builds to a pitch and comes unbearably close to its resolution. Here is one of them. It is actually one of the climactic moments in the book where –with Svengali dead in his box (but nobody knows that at this stage)– Trilby's voice is completely paralysed:

(18)
The band struck up the opening bars of 'Ben Bolt', with which she was announced to make her début.
She still stared – but she didn't sing – and they played the little symphony three times.
One could hear Monsieur J—— in a hoarse, anxious whisper saying,
'Mais chantez donc, madame – pour l'amour de Dieu, commencez donc – commencez!'
She turned round with an extraordinary expression of face, and said,
'Chanter? pourquoi donc voulez-vous que je chante, moi? chanter quoi, alors?'
'Mais 'Ben Bolt', parbleu – chantez!'
'Ah – 'Ben Bolt!' oui – je connais ça!'
Then the band began again.
And she tried, but failed to begin herself. She turned round and said,
'Comment diable voulez-vous que je chante avec tout ce train qu'ils font, ces diables de musiciens!'
'Mais, mon Dieu, madame – qu'est-ce que vous avez donc?' cried Monsieur J——.
'J'ai que j'aime mieux chanter sans toute cette satanée musique, parbleu! J'aime mieux chanter toute seule!'
'Sans musique, alors – mais chantez – chantez!'

> The band was stopped – the house was in a state of indescribable wonder and suspense. (Du Maurier 1998: 248)

The narrator speaks of "indescribable wonder and suspense" but I would add that, to the reader of the novel, the "wonder and the suspense" in this passage must decidedly come in very variable proportions, depending on that reader's personal familiarity with the story, and on his or her proficiency in French.

True, most untranslated French passages are less important and less thrilling than the one we have just quoted. But that does not really change anything from the viewpoint of the English-only reader, who, after all, has no way of assessing the importance of what remains incomprehensible to him or to her! Potentially, *all* French passages, no matter how irrelevant to plot and suspense, present themselves as big gaps in the processing of the text.

In his *Author, Author* David Lodge has Henry James musing about the use of French in *Trilby*:

> He had to admire Du Maurier's boldness in leaving much of the French dialogue untranslated. He would wager that very few of the masses who had read the story, especially in America, would have been sufficiently competent in the language to construe these passages, yet none as far as he was aware had complained. Perhaps they felt flattered by being assumed to understand the French. Perhaps they were amused by the effort to guess what it meant. Or perhaps its impenetrability strengthened the illusion of being transported to an exotic and unfamiliar time and place. There was, after all, little risk of losing the thread of the story on this account, because the story was so very simple. (Lodge 2004: 222)

James is supposedly thinking these words in January 1895, just months after the publication of *Trilby*. No complaints about the untranslated French had come to Henry James's attention but little could he know that, before the end of the year, the *Trilby* merchandising machine, now revved up to full power, would turn out two publications to contradict him:

> Hawley, John G. 1895. *An Appendix to Trilby. Translations and Notes.* Detroit, Mich.: The Richmond & Backus Co.

> Schönberg, James. 1895. *The Comparative Trilby Glossary French-English.* New York: J. Hovendon & Co.

Harper's Magazine, in which *Trilby* was first serialised, had a wide international readership. At one point Du Maurier even addresses his "Parisian readers" (p. 207), who would have had less of a struggle with the French passages. But Lodge (a literary theoretician as well a novelist), who is here ventriloquizing for Henry James (himself a narratologist *avant la lettre*), was of course right to emphasize the exclusionary effect of the French in *Trilby*, which is partly (but only partly) neutralized by the informational redundancy contained in the novel, as he was also right to highlight the heterogeneity of the novel's readership, divided as it is by foreign-language skills, nationality and social class. This heterogeneity accounts for very different reading experiences, and therefore for the variability of suspense as a crucial part of those reading experiences.

8. Concluding note: afterlives

I have tried to explore the nexus between suspense and language gaps within our two novels. We have not even started to contemplate the further complexities and fascinations that arise in the numerous intralingual, interlingual and intersemiotic translations of both novels. Can the ever-present tendency of over-translating be shown to have an impact on suspense, and could such effects be tested empirically? What voices and what accents are given to Count Dracula in audiobook versions, film versions, stage adaptations and radio plays based on the novel? What happens with the broken English of Van Helsing in terms of correctness, on the one hand, and articulation, on the other? Is it edited in any way in printed translations? What about the ironies of translating Van Helsing's English into Dutch? What is the effect of translating *Trilby* into French, where Du Maurier's French passages may merge invisibly with the English, so that the lines of linguistic difference and moral normality are redrawn? Or into a target culture where French is a very little known language? How do the illustrations influence the flows of information that guide the reader's cognitive and emotional responses? Or what happens with Svengali's linguistic otherness in a century that saw the Holocaust?[31]

Let me conclude by referring to one document that shows that the last question is definitely a relevant one. In 1897, one Alfred Welch jumped on the *Trilby* bandwagon with a polemical reply to Du Maurier's novel. It is called *Extracts from the Diary of Moritz Svengali* and it gives Svengali's side of the story. As a kind of rewrite of *Trilby*, it challenges the demonization of Svengali as the evil Jew from the East, which Du Maurier had needed to get the suspense under steam. The work's motto summarises Welch's critique of anti-Semitism:

> Be just to all mankind, my friend;
> They seek the same as you;
> Their different manners but depend
> On chance and point of view.

Welch humanises Svengali by giving him a first name (Moritz), by giving him the full use of his voice in a document all his own (a diary) –this is, incidentally, a privilege radically denied to Count Dracula, in Stoker's novel of the same year– and, last but not least, by letting him express himself in grammatical, fluent and elegant English. Moritz Svengali supposedly wrote his diary in his native "Polish Hebrew dialect". However, using the fictional ploy of the pseudo-translation, Welch says he thought it best "to abandon all attempts to preserve the peculiarities of the author's style of the form of expression of his native tongue" (Welch 1897: v). Svengali was linguistically and morally alienated in *Trilby* for the sake of a thrill; the curse of the foreign tongue had to be undone to draw Svengali back into the fold of humanity.

---

[1] For both *Trilby* (ed. Elaine Showalter, 1998) and *Dracula* (ed. Roger Luckhurst, 2011) I shall be referring to the Oxford World's Classics edition, with page references given parenthetically.

[2] For what such labels are worth, this paper could thus be situated within what some like to call the 'fictional turn' in Translation Studies.

[3] In discussing these issues, it will become clear that dialogue must always be related to other parts and dimensions of the text (this holds for performative genres such as drama and film, no less than for narrative fiction). If suspense is part of the more general management of text/reader interaction, dialogue is part of the general discursive management of the text and cannot be understood as an isolated phenomenon.

[4] All definitions taken from the online edition of the *Oxford Advanced Learner's Dictionary*. Sitting "for the altogether" was Trilby's own literal translation of sitting "pour l'ensemble", i.e. for the whole body: 'I pose to him for the altogether.' 'The altogether?' asked Little Billee. 'Yes – *l'ensemble*, you know – head, hands, and feet – everything – especially feet' (p. 15).

[5] It is worth remembering that the two books came out within three years from each other and that Stoker and Du Maurier knew each other very well. The 'official' Bram Stoker homepage (www.bramstokerestate.com/) lists Du Maurier as belonging to Stoker's circle of close friends and refers to Du Maurier's cartoon of "Bram Stoker and His Family" for *Punch* (11 September 1886).

[6] See Lucy's remark on the desirability of polygamy, undoubtedly intended as a mild joke in a letter to her best friend Mina, but nonetheless indicating a certain superficiality and sensuality, and a less than full commitment to the conventional ethos of marriage: "Why can't they let a girl marry three men, or as many as want her, and save all this trouble? But this is heresy, and I must not say it" (p. 58) (see also Cranny-Davis 1988: 67-68).

[7] It is true that Bram Stoker never explicitly identifies the Count as a Jew, but there is a very strong case for the view that Dracula would have evoked the image of the alien, parasitical Jew (e.g. Robinson 2009 and Stoker 2011: xxvii-xxviii).

[8] There are more such passages. On p. 246, Svengali has "his teeth bared in a spasmodic grin of hate" in a most vampire-like manner (Du Maurier has a more than common interest in describing the teeth of his characters). The strange symptoms of Trilby and Lucy require the second opinion of an expert doctor called in from the outside (Sir Oliver Calthorpe and Professor Van Helsing respectively). The triangular relationship between Dracula, Mina Harker and Jonathan might profitably be compared with that between Svengali, Trilby and Little Billee. The phrase "Gott im Himmel" (*Trilby*, p. 283) and its grammatically dubious variant "Gott in Himmel" (p. 47), find an echo in Van Helsing's "Gott in Himmel" (*Dracula*, p. 120). Or compare the descriptive phraseology in passages such as the following: "They had not failed to note how rapidly she had aged [...]. Her hands were almost transparent in their waxen whiteness; delicate little frosty wrinkles had gathered round her eyes; there were gray streaks in her hair; all strength and straightness and elasticity seemed to have gone out of her" (*Trilby*, p. 261); "Last night he was a frank happy young man, with strong, youthful face, full of energy and with dark brown hair. To-day he is a drawn haggard old man, whose white hair matches well with the hollow burning eyes and grief-written lines of his face. His energy is still intact" (*Dracula*, p. 280). A more detailed study of Bram Stoker's use of *Trilby* would definitely be worthwhile.

[9] Both distinctions have been challenged and must remain open to critical discussion: e.g. it is very doubtful whether a fictional world is thinkable without some form of textual representation, or whether there is knowledge about the world that exists independently from some form of discursivity.

That is why the scheme visualizes the four fields as being interdependent and having porous borderlines, rather than as discrete categories.

[10] Several authors contributing to the volume *Suspense* (Vorderer, Wulff and Friedrichsen 1996) emphasize the moral basis of the distinction between "good" and "bad" characters.

[11] Can suspense still operate when one re-reads a text, views a film for the second time, watches a film adaptation of one's favourite novel, etc.? The original text with which one is familiar already serves intertextually as a background to later readings, versions or viewings, reducing uncertainty and thus potentially compromising the effect of suspense, since one knows in advance how the story or the sequence will end. Several authors contributing to the volume *Suspense* (Vorderer, Wulff and Friedrichsen 1996) have looked into this problem.

[12] These expectations have to be sufficiently concrete and distinct. Some authors even require that they should be binary and logically opposed.

[13] Most authors assume that the greater likelihood of negative outcomes enhances suspense. Zillmann (1996: 207) refers to empirical research that has demonstrated a correlation between the experience of suspense and degrees of subjective certainty that the negative outcome will materialise: "the intensity of suspense increased with ascending levels of certainty [...] up to a maximum just prior to total certainty". Total certainty will put an end to the suspense as such and produce a different feeling (e.g. sadness and disappointment, or euphoria and relief, as the case turns out).

[14] See several discussions of this issue in *Suspense* (Vorderer, Wulff and Friedrichsen 1996).

[15] It is significant that Rimmon-Kenan (1983: 125-127) speaks of "future-oriented suspense" and "past-oriented suspense" for what most other writers call "suspense" and "mystery" respectively.

[16] Most contemporary criticism aims to present new views on how the novel is informed by various late-Victorian discursive contexts with respect to themes such as Darwinism, progress and degeneration, race, Jews, immigration, the New Woman, female sexuality, the Irish question, democracy, technology, and so on.

[17] Christine Ferguson (2004: 241) goes one further, arguing that the variability, flexibility and even irregularity of language are "a hallmark of the living" whereas linguistic regularity and silence are "a characteristic of vampirism". She concludes that "Dracula's spectacularly anticlimactic physical death is no more than a footnote to the real triumph that has happened elsewhere, that of nonstandard and multimediated English against the deadly tongue of the vampire" (p. 245). The article has excellent points but its overstated conclusion is characteristic of the competitive pressure in literary studies to present strongly worded innovative readings.

[18] David B. Dickens (1998) actually argues that Van Helsing would have been an expatriate German professor teaching in Amsterdam.

[19] See p. 107 in the novel. This makes you wonder about Van Helsing's poor proficiency in English.

[20] According to Bollen and Ingelbien (2009: 412n), the anagram was first noted by John Paul Tiquelme in his 2002 edition of the novel.

[21] David B. Dickens who tries to make the case for "the German matrix of Stoker's *Dracula*" cites a number of recurrent errors in Van Helsing's speech to show that they result from German (not Dutch) linguistic interference (1998: 35-36). However, the author, who is apparently not familiar with Dutch grammar, overlooks the fact that the very same errors could equally be interpreted as resulting from Dutch interference. More basically, he seems to be overstating the level of interlinguistic realism that Stoker wanted to (and would have been able to!) inject into the text. Not knowing Dutch, Stoker may have used his basic knowledge of German to simulate Dutch interference, safe in the knowledge that most of his readers would be familiar with neither foreign language. Moreover, an overwhelming majority of errors are of the intralingual rather than interlingual type.

[22] One suspects that the dockworkers have ample recourse to the unmentionable F-word.

[23] It is not to be denied that sometimes the modulations of the correctness of Van Helsing's English appear simply random and unmotivated by any ulterior narrative or rhetorical purpose. Such sheer inconsistencies can even occur within a single phrase: "We have learnt something – much! Notwithstanding his brave words, *he fears* us; *he fear* time, *he fear* want! For if not, why he hurry

so?" (p. 285; emphasis mine). On p. 280, Van Helsing's English is quite correct, possibly because Dr Seward, through whose recollection it is being reported here ("What he has been saying was, under the circumstances, of absorbing interest. As well as I can remember, here it is […]"), has consciously or unconsciously edited it. But on the next page, we are again treated to a sequence of grammatical howlers. I do not think that the reader can be supposed to attribute such inconsistencies to either the erratic working of Seward's memory or the incoherence of his reporting technique.

[24] See Mina's comment on p. 64: "I nodded, for I thought it better to assent, though I did not quite understand his dialect. I knew it had something to do with the church. He went on: 'And you consate that all these steans be aboon folk that be happed here, snod an' snog?' I assented again". Most modern editions see fit to provide "translations" of the passages in question!

[25] A similar technique is the use of indirect discourse or narrative report as a quotation technique without specifying in which language the quoted words were originally uttered. Here is an example of this:

> Early this morning, one crew took us for a Government boat, and treated us accordingly. We saw in this a way of smoothing matters, so […] we got a Roumanian flag, which we now fly conspicuously. With every boat which we have overhauled since then this trick has succeeded; we have had every deference shown to us, and not once any objection to whatever we chose to ask or do. Some of the Slovaks tell us that a big boat passed them, going at more than usual speed as she had a double crew on board. (p. 332)

The metalingual vagueness involved in the reporting technique somehow manages to keep the reader from asking the awkward question which language Jonathan Harker and Lord Godalming would have used posing as Romanian officials!

[26] Compare this with the extract from the Log of the Demeter (the ship that brought Dracula to Whitby) (p. 79-82): originally drafted by the Russian captain in his mother tongue, it is given in English. But an account of the text's origin is duly provided by the local correspondent of *The Dailygraph* who is quoting/inserting it in his article on the freak storm in Whitby: "Of course my statement must be taken *cum grano*, since I am writing from the dictation of a clerk of the Russian consul, who kindly translated for me, time being short" (p. 78).

[27] Svengali's nose is quite central to his identity and sense of self. When Little Billee punches him in a friendly boxing match and gives him a nosebleed, this "frightened him out of his sardonic wits" (p. 119). Towards the end of the novel, the "violent tweaking of his nose" by Taffy fatally shakes and demoralises him (p. 245).

[28] Du Maurier has a way of using heterolingualism in a random and rather purposeless manner. Consider an example like this:

> Mouths went watering all day long in joyful anticipation. They water somewhat sadly now at the mere remembrance of these delicious things – the mere immediate sight or scent of which in these degenerate latter days would no longer avail to promote any such delectable secretion. *Hélas! ahimè! ach weh! ay de mi! eheu! οἴμοι!* – in point of fact, *alas!*
> That is the very exclamation I wanted. (p. 109)

[29] Your heart is a suspended/poised lute! Whenever one touches it, it resounds/resonates… (*my translation*).

[30] Oddly enough, the Oxford edition (1998, p. 312) has missed this and speaks of an "unidentified source".

[31] See Dror Abend-David's (2003) excellent study of German, Hebrew and Yiddish translations of Shakespeare's *The Merchant of Venice*.

Bibliography

Primary Sources

Du Maurier, George. 1998 [1894]. *Trilby* (ed. Elaine Showalter, notes by Dennis Denisoff). Oxford: Oxford UP.

Lodge, David. 2004. *Author, Author*. London: Secker & Warburg.

Potter, Paul. 2012 [1895]. 'Trilby' in Davis, Tracy C. (ed.) *The Broadview Anthology of Nineteenth-Century British Performance*. Peterborough, Ontario: Broadview Press. 577-642.

Stoker, Bram. 2008 [1897]. *The New Annotated Dracula* (ed. Leslie S. Kinger, introduction by Neil Gaiman). New York and London: Norton.

————. 2011 [1897]. *Dracula* (ed. Roger Luckhurst). Oxford: Oxford UP.

Welch, Alfred. 1897. *Extracts from the Diary of Moritz Svengali. Translated and edited by Alfred Welch*. New York: Henry Holt and Company.

Secondary Sources

Abend-David, Dror. 2003. *"Scorned my Nation". A comparison of translations of* The Merchant of Venice *into German, Hebrew and Yiddish*. Frankfurt am Main and New York: Peter Lang.

Bollen, Katrien, and Raphaël Ingelbien. 2009. 'An intertext that Counts? *Dracula, The Woman in White*, and Victorian Imaginations of the Foreign Other' in *English Studies* 90(4): 403-420.

Bram Stoker. *Official Website for The Bram Stoker Estate*. On line at: http://www.bramstokerestate.com/Home-of-Bram-Stoker-Estate-Gothic-Dracula-Official-website-Bram-Stoker-Estate.html (consulted 03.12.2012).

Cranny-Davis, Anne. 1988. 'Sexual politics and political repression in Bram Stoker's *Dracula*' in Bloom, Clive et al. (eds) *Nineteenth century suspense: from Poe to Conan Doyle*. Basingstoke: Macmillan. 64-79.

Dickens, David B. 1995. 'The German matrix of Stoker's *Dracula*' in Miller, Elizabeth (ed.) *Dracula. The Shade and the Shadow*. Westcliff-on-Sea: Desert Island Books. 1-40.

Ferguson, Christine. 2004. 'Nonstandard language and the cultural stakes of Stoker's *Dracula*' in *ELH* 71(1): 229-249.

Pick, Daniel. 2000. *Svengali's Web. The Alien Enchanter in Modern Culture*. New Haven and London: Yale University Press.

Pollner, Clausdirk. 2002. 'Draculanguage: varieties of English in Bram Stoker's novel' in Todenhagen, Christian and Wolfgang Thiele (eds) *Investigations into Narrative Structures*. Frankfurt am Main and New York: Peter Lang. 209-218.

Rimmon-Kenan, Shlomith. 1983. *Narrative fiction. Contemporary poetics*. London: Methuen.

Robinson, Sara Libby. 2009. 'Blood Will Tell: anti-semitism and vampires in British popular culture, 1875-1914' in *GOLEM: Journal of Religion and Monsters* 3(1): 16-27.

Rosenberg, Edgar. 1960. *From Shylock to Svengali: Jewish stereotypes in English fiction*. Stanford: Stanford UP.

Sternberg, Meir. 1981. 'Polylingualism and reality as mimesis' in *Poetics Today* 2(4): 221-239.

Vorderer, Peter, Hans J. Wulff and Mike Friedrichsen (eds). 1996. *Suspense: conceptualizations, theoretical analyses, and empirical explorations*. Mahwah, NJ: Lawrence Erlbaum Associates.

Zillmann, Dolf. 1996. 'The psychology of suspense in dramatic exposition' in Vorderer et al. (1996): 199-231.

Chapter 2: Stylistic and linguistic creation of suspense in Quentin Tarantino's *Pulp Fiction* and *Reservoir Dogs*

Sanja Škifić and Rajko Petković

Abstract

The paper seeks to address the most prominent stylistic and linguistic devices used to create suspense in Quentin Tarantino's *Pulp Fiction* and *Reservoir Dogs*. The wider conceptual framework for Tarantino's oeuvre is an analysis of the most prominent stylistic strategies identified in his films, particularly the typically postmodern rearranging of ideas and a multilayered narrative idiosyncrasy. Probably the most stylistically oriented contemporary American director, Tarantino is also an adept screenwriter. His scripts are usually fractured into intricate narrative patterns deploying many non-chronological sequences, but their most distinguished characteristic is an inventive dialogue, imbued with pop-cultural references and racist colloquialisms. From a linguistic point of view, the analysis of dialogues in the two films reveals several linguistic devices used with the effect of building up suspense. The most prominent one refers to repetition of parts of characters' utterances. Another device is analyzed via objective clauses and direct objects containing obscene expressions, which are identified as a particular type of image-provoking language and as elements of suspense creation. The paper also addresses additional linguistic devices used to create suspense. They refer to the content of dialogues which at times appears uncorrelated with different contexts of the two plots and/or individual characters.

Keywords: Quentin Tarantino, suspense, inventive dialogue, repetition, image-provoking language

1. Introduction

The paper deals with some of the most interesting features found in *Reservoir Dogs* and *Pulp Fiction*, two of Quentin Tarantino's early films. The focus of interest are three distinct elements which feature prominently in his oeuvre. On the stylistic level, Tarantino has been recognized as one of the most influential modern directors, due to his embracing the notion of postmodern rearranging of ideas and narrative idiosyncrasy. The second topic deals with the treatment of violence in his films. Often accused of being shallow and nihilistic, Tarantino's films prove to be quite the opposite –modern morality plays with the realistic treatment of violence. The third level is linguistic analysis, which focuses on several prominent aspects of the dialogues. The analysis of the verbal interaction between characters allows for the identification of specific linguistic devices which have the effect of building suspense. Repetition appears as the most frequent and easily identifiable linguistic device that helps build suspense, as its usage prolongs the dialogue. Secondly, objective clauses and direct objects containing obscene and vulgar expressions are also identified as linguistic devices used to build suspense, as such expressions have a role in provoking and sustaining intense emotional states. Besides these two most prominent structural devices, there are also other means of building suspense which can be traced via the analysis of dialogues. These refer to the content of dialogues which at times appears uncorrelated with different contexts of the two plots and / or individual characters.

2. Stylistic idiosyncrasies

Although he has made only three feature films in the nineties, Quentin Tarantino is probably the most influential director of the decade. His first film *Reservoir Dogs* was deeply influenced by the legacy of *film noir*, paying homage to established genre classics like *The Killing, The Asphalt Jungle* and *Kansas City Confidential*. Rearranging the novelistic construction of *The Killing*, and borrowing the plot elements from the latter films, Tarantino has managed to create an idiosyncratic mixture of *film noir* and contemporary crime thriller. The palimpsestic nature of Tarantino's style is evident in the analysis of some of his other influences. Apart from borrowing elements from the classics of the *film noir* period, Tarantino has also used elements from the crime thriller *The Taking of Pelham One Two Three* (one of the mainstays of the seventies culture), the Hong Kong classic *City on Fire*, and the Nouvelle Vague films by Jean-Luc Godard, equally filled by pop-cultural references. The influence of French filmmakers is not restricted only to Godard, as the opus of Jean-Pierre Melville has played an equally defining role in shaping the stylistic elements of Tarantino's films, especially *Pulp Fiction*.[1]

Although Tarantino was predominantly influenced by popular cinema, his bold inventiveness can be compared with the masterpieces of art cinema. A seemingly unusual comparison can be made with the films of Andrei Tarkovsky, especially to *Ivan's Childhood*, his first feature film. There are many elements connecting the style of *Ivan's Childhood* with Tarantino's films. Tarkovsky, like Tarantino, disorientates the viewer from the very beginning. *Ivan's Childhood* begins with a dream and has a circular structure. The events in the present are constantly interspersed with flashbacks, showing two parallel structures. Likewise, the events from *Reservoir Dogs*, which take place in the warehouse in the present, are constantly intertwined with flashbacks. Tarkovsky often juxtaposes antagonistic elements (reality and fantasy, fire and water in the same scene) in order to create a multilayered view of reality. The infamous torture scene in *Reservoir Dogs* equally juxtaposes the leisurely rhythm of the catchy pop song with the act of utmost cruelty. According to Skakov, "Tarkovsky's films provide an image of a conventional linear progression of events which gradually, and without any forewarning, evolves into a spatio-temporal maze with characteristic twists and turns" (2012: 41). The same intertwining of linear structure and flashbacks represents the dominant narrative feature of *Reservoir Dogs*.

Although *Reservoir Dogs* has a very unusual narrative structure[2], the narrative organization is even more elaborate in *Pulp Fiction*. The episodic film has a circular structure consisting of seven fragmented and interspersed narrative sequences made up of three separate, but interrelated storylines. The unifying sequence is "The Gold Watch", which, if the events were ordered chronologically, would open and end the film. In his taxonomy of alternative plots in modern films, Charles Ramírez Berg has divided them in twelve categories, and the second part of the title of his paper –'Classifying the "Tarantino Effect"'– provides yet another evidence of the influence of Tarantino's narrative structures on contemporary cinema. Berg quotes Tarantino at the beginning of the paper, arguing for the justification of this type of narrative organization:

> Now the thing is, for both novels and films, 75% of the stories you're going to tell will work better on a dramatically engaging basis to be told from a linear way. But there is that 25% out there that can be more resonant by telling it this [non-linear] way. And I think in the case of both *Reservoir Dogs* and *Pulp Fiction*, it gains a lot more resonance being told in this kinda, like, wild way. (Berg 2006: 5)

In Berg's taxonomy, *Pulp Fiction* is an example of the polyphonic or ensemble plot, where multiple protagonists share a single location, while its distinguishing feature is the unity of time and space. Both *Pulp Fiction* and *Reservoir Dogs* are also representative of the jumbled plot, where the scrambled sequence of events is motivated artistically, by the filmmaker's choice. It is interesting to notice that the causal construction of the films is left intact, but the events are ordered non-chronologically, leaving the viewer to reconstruct the plot by rearranging the jumbled elements of the *syuzhet*. Although not entirely original, this type of narrative structure still presents a major challenge to the dominant type of filmmaking.

3. Violence, nihilism and conversion

American cinema has been imbued with depictions of violent behavior from its very beginning. The landmarks of silent American cinema –*The Great Train Robbery, The Birth of a Nation, Intolerance*– to name but a few, showcased spectacular scenes of violence, including even the decapitation scenes in *Intolerance*. The classic gangster films of the early thirties have revealed an equal fascination with violence and are certainly one of the important reasons for implementing the Production Code, regulating the acceptability of the films' content. Depicting techniques of committing murder or evoking sympathy for criminals was explicitly forbidden. In 1968, the code was replaced by the rating system, although the implementation of the code had already been efficiently bypassed many times, most frequently by films of the *film noir* canon. The late sixties and the seventies have ushered in a new period of depicting violence with the rise of directors such as Sam Peckinpah, Martin Scorsese, Wes Craven, Walter Hill or Stanley Kubrick.[3] Graphic violence has become one of the foundations of American cinema from that period.

The effort to convey the real-life brutality of criminals is probably the reason why there is so much violence in his films, although Tarantino manages to downplay the effect by juxtaposing it with humorous parts. He manages to play with the expectations of the audience by suddenly changing the rhythm of the scene. Tarantino admits: "The thing that I am really proud of in the torture scene in *Dogs* with Mr Blonde, Michael Madsen, is the fact that it's truly funny, up until the point that he cuts the cop's ear off" (Hopper 1994: 17).

Tarantino's films have often been accused of glorifying violence and presenting shallow characters that impersonate the nihilism of the postmodern period. However, a detailed analysis of his first two films presents a different picture. Even the most infamous segment of *Reservoir Dogs*, the torture scene, avoids showing the act of cutting the ear off and instead implies it off-screen. Comparing the different degrees of violence portrayal in films, Devin McKinney has divided them into two broad categories; "strong" and "weak". While films such as *Bad Lieutenant* or *Henry: Portrait of a Serial Killer*, are classified as portraying strong violence, *Basic Instinct* or *Reservoir Dogs* belong to the latter category. In McKinney's opinion, weak violence induces a strong contradiction: "it reduces bloodshed to its barest components, then inflates them with hot, stylized air" (1993: 19). The ubiquitous presence of violence in modern films has a sort of camp aesthetics, where violence is used only as a device with virtually no impact on the audience. Violence shown in Tarantino's films makes the audience disinterested; a viewer does not empathize with any of the characters because they are shown in a cartoon-like, hyperstylized manner.

By comparison, violence depicted in *The Red Circle*, one of the defining works of Jean-Pierre Melville, has a completely different impact on the viewer. Although the characters in Melville's film are equally stylized, the violence committed by them is visceral and deeply felt by the audience. It is interesting to note that the depiction of relations between the criminals in the two films is quite similar. As in the films of Howard Hawks or Sam Peckinpah, the accent is on the sense of honor and belonging to a specific type of community. This is the link shared by Vogel and Corey in *The Red Circle*, and Mr White and Mr Orange in *Reservoir Dogs*. The real centerpiece of *Reservoir Dogs* is not the torture scene, but the interplay between Mr White and Mr Orange. As Kent L. Brintnall has noticed, the bruised, brutalized body of Mr Orange, played by Tim Roth, is the foundational element of the film (2004: 68). While the story goes in all directions, juxtaposing the present with the past, and the flashbacks with the stories of different characters, Orange's bruised body lies almost motionless in the warehouse. Like in the relation between Vogel and Corey, the two characters in *Reservoir Dogs* develop an unusual emotional, almost homoerotic bond. While the film "portrays a hermetically sealed, claustrophobic world of gun-loving, trash-talking, violence-prone men and the carnage they leave in their wake" (Brintnall 2004: 70), their relationship is portrayed as something superior to the harsh world around them. Although hardened criminals, both Vogel and Mr White are ready to take the risk and finally lose their lives in order to protect their code of honor.

Although Tarantino's films have been attacked as nihilistic postmodernist collages, we can find elements that testify to the opposite of these allegations. The centerpiece of *Reservoir Dogs*, the bond between Mr Orange and Mr White, has strong religious undertones. The posture of their bodies at the end of the film is strongly reminiscent of the Pietà[4], and the overall atmosphere of the film has even inspired Brintnall to include Tarantino not among the neo-corruptors of the cinematic morality, but among *neo-theologians* (2004: 75), together with the usual suspects, Martin Scorsese and Francis Ford Coppola.

The religious overtones of *Reservoir Dogs* are even more emphasized in *Pulp Fiction*, turning both films into contemporary morality plays. While the centerpiece of *Reservoir Dogs* is the emotional bond between Mr White and Mr Orange, the most important story element of *Pulp Fiction*, apart from its fragmented *syuzhet* organization, is the notion of divine intervention and the conversion of the hitman Jules. The rhetorical power of divine intervention is unquestionable, because it is placed both at the beginning and at the end of the film. After witnessing the miracle, when a storm of bullets missed him, Jules experiences conversion and decides not to kill the robbers in the restaurant at the end of the film. Although the dialogue is quasi-biblical, in fact it changes very little because Jules acts according to the framework of that text.[5] Tarantino had probably not intended his film to be a Christian allegory, but the fact that the act of conversion "can occur through interaction with the past and images from popular culture rather than through engagement with a spiritual / religious community or a sacred tradition" (Bidwell 2001: 337), certainly captures the *zeitgeist* of the media-saturated society. The arrangement of sequences in *Pulp Fiction* finally leads to a redemptive denouement, and this is what Tarantino intended. The violence in his films is justified because it is not stylized per se, but is an effective means of conveying the sentiment of the author, which is far from nihilistic. As Tarantino has stated in an interview:

> For all the wildness that happens in my movies, I think that they usually lead to a moral conclusion. For example, I find what passes between Mr White and Mr Orange at the end of

Reservoir Dogs very moving and profound in its morality and its human interaction. (Peary 1998: 60)

Apart from being the master of mise-en-scène and probably the most stylistically oriented contemporary American director, Tarantino is also an adept screenwriter. His scripts are usually fractured into intricate narrative patterns deploying many non-chronological sequences, but their most distinguished characteristic is an inventive dialogue, imbued with pop-cultural references and racist colloquialisms.

4. Linguistic creation of suspense in Quentin Tarantino's *Pulp Fiction* and *Reservoir Dogs*

Suspense might be perceived as a vague concept as it is frequently defined as "the withholding of resolution" (Bell 2011: 191), related to a greater extent to "the expectation that a certain specific action might take place" rather than to the more concrete "question of *what* will happen next" (Derry 1988: 31). Creation and maintenance of suspense may be identified in situations in which spectators are given the opportunity "to anticipate plot developments (especially of the threatening variety) before the protagonists themselves" (Derry 1988: 7). However, in processes of the elaboration of the notion of suspense, focus is frequently placed on the very concrete "bipolar tension" that builds up in the spectator, who "not only tries to decide who should win, but also prepares himself to act in the directions of his conflicting wishes and to respond to two opposite situations that are the possible outcomes of the struggle on the screen" (Loker 2005: 28). Moreover, different structural devices –both linguistic and non-linguistic– which are employed to create suspense in films confirm that the process of its creation is not vague at all. Rather, it is a thoroughly planned process, and the different linguistic and non-linguistic devices used reveal that suspense does not occur by chance. Analyses of the ways in which suspense can be built and sustained in films can include practically any genre, but they usually include thrillers because they are particularly saturated with both linguistically and non-linguistically created suspense.

Linguistic structural devices for creating suspense in different types of narratives have been widely discussed, especially in fiction writing. The same might be applied to research on how dialogues are built in films. The most frequently analyzed linguistic structural devices used to create suspense include different grammar techniques and image-provoking language (Noble 1994: 19). The most prominent linguistic technique that represents the focus of the analysis of the creation of suspense in the two films is repetition. Another extremely important technique includes the usage of obscene and vulgar expressions in objective clauses and as direct objects. These will be referred to as elements of image-provoking language rather than elements of "descriptive language" (Webster 2002: 54), as the latter might be used more appropriately in the analyses of narratives other than those presented in films.

4.1. Creation of suspense via repetition

Repetition is one of the most prominent devices used for creating suspense in different types of narratives. It is used with the effect of prolonging or slowing down the dialogue, which creates additional suspense (Johnstone 1996: 48).

The following are examples from *Pulp Fiction* [*our emphasis*]:

(1)
–Also, you know what **they call a Quarter Pounder with Cheese** in Paris?
–**They** don't **call** it **a Quarter Pounder with Cheese**?
–No, they got the metric system there, they wouldn't know what the fuck **a Quarter Pounder** is.
–What'd **they call it**?
–**They call it** the **Royale with Cheese**.
–**Royale with Cheese**. What'd **they call a Big Mac**?
–**Big Mac**'s a **Big Mac**, but **they call it Le Big Mac**.
–**Le Big Mac**. What do **they call** a Whopper?

(2)
–What does Marsellus Wallace **look like**?
–**What**?
–**What** country you from?!
–**What**?
– "**What**" ain't no country I ever heard of! **Do they speak English** in "**What**"?
–**What**?
–**English**, motherfucker! **Do you speak** it?
–Yes.
–Then you know what I'm sayin?
–Yes.
–Describe what Marsellus Wallace looks like!
–**What**?
–Say "**What**" again! Say "**What**" again! I **dare ya**, I double **dare ya** motherfucker, say "**What**" one more goddamn time!
–Well he's... he's... black
–Go on!
–...and he's... he's... bald
–**Does he look like a bitch**?!
–What?
–**Does-he-look-like-a-bitch**?!

(3)
–**In the fifth**, your **ass goes down**. Say it!
–**In the fifth**, my **ass goes down**.

(4)
–**If they find us, they'll kill us, won't they? But they won't find us, will they?**

(5)
–**It's not your fault. You left it at the apartment. You left it at the apartment, it's not your fault.**

(6)
–**What now?**
–**What now?** Let me tell you **what now**...
–I meant, **what now between me and you?**
–Oh, that **what now?** I'll tell ya **what now between me and you.**

(7)
–When you came pulling in here, **did you notice a sign in the front of my house that said "Dead nigger storage"?**
–Jimmie, you know I ain't...
–**Did you notice a sign in the front of my house that said "Dead nigger storage"?!**

What follows are excerpts of dialogues from *Reservoir Dogs* in which repetition is used as a suspense-building device [*our emphasis*]:

(8)
–It **hurts.** It **hurts** her. It shouldn't **hurt.**

(9)
–**Are you a doctor? Are you a doctor?** Answer me please, **are you a doctor?**

(10)
–Joe's gonna get you a doctor, the doctor's gonna fix you up, and **you're gonna be okay.**
–Now **say it: you're gonna be okay. Say it: you're gonna be okay!** Say the goddamn words: **you're gonna be okay!**

(11)
–**I won't tell 'em anything. Look in my eyes, look in my eyes. I won't tell them anything.**

(12)
–We think **we got a rat in the house.**
–I guarantee **we got a rat in the house.**

(13)
–**Are you gonna bark all day, little doggie, or are you gonna bite?**
–What was that? I'm sorry, I didn't catch it. Would you repeat it?
–**Are you gonna bark all day, little doggie, or are you gonna bite?**

4.2. Creation of suspense via objective clauses and direct objects containing obscene expressions

Obscene expressions act as features of image-provoking language which has already been identified as suspense-laden. Such linguistic items represent the backbone of many contemporary films' scripts, especially in comparison to older productions. They represent "uninhibited vernacular speech that includes four letter words that were formerly anathema" (Friedmann 2010: 192) in modern films. Although there is always a chance of such expressions creating the opposite effect if used excessively, in most cases they produce the desired effect of exciting people and eliciting emotion ranging from anger to laughter, and are usually correlated with lack of ambiguity (Rogers 1978: 58, 71). The dialogues between characters in Tarantino's films are extremely rich in such expressions. They possess a superficial appearance of lack of ambiguity. If there was nothing more to them, they would be completely devoid of the suspense character. Namely, the superficial appearance of lack of ambiguity actually creates suspense because the obscene expressions are used in meaningless verbal exchanges about anything other than what the spectator expects will happen, and he anticipates it on the basis of other, non-linguistic factors. In other words, it is precisely the juxtaposition of seemingly suspense-devoid obscene expressions and non-linguistic suspense-laden elements that creates a particular type of suspense in Tarantino's films. Moreover, suspense via the usage of obscene expressions can be interpreted from an additional point of view. Linguistic repertoires of hard-core criminals are abundant in such expressions. Usage of obscene language is most frequently associated with physical aggression and acts as its replacement (Henderson 1991: 10). Since a high frequency of obscene language is often interpreted as expression of aggression towards others (Jay 2000: 81), suspense can be interpreted in terms of the spectator expecting or anticipating the physical type of aggression as well on the part of the character who uses them.

What follows are examples from *Pulp Fiction* in which obscene expressions appear as parts of objective and relative clauses creating suspense [*our emphasis*]:

(14)
–Forget **it**, it's too risky. I'm through doin' **that shit**.

(15)
–Vietnamese, Koreans, they can't **fuckin' speak English**... and they don't know **what it fuckin' means**.

(16)
–...and your ass ain't **talkin' your way outta this shit**.
(17)
–I just want you to know how sorry we are **that things got so fucked up with us and Mr Wallace**.

(18)
–...that's pride **fuckin' with ya**.

(19)
–Why do we feel it's necessary **to yak about bullshit** in order to be comfortable?

(20)
–It's the one **that says Bad Motherfucker on it**.

The same usage is identified in *Reservoir Dogs*. In describing the nature of the dialogue, Pratt (2011: 28) focuses on the opening scene where viewers are presented with a "macho world" and emphasizes that "the dialogue is peppered with obscenities and jibes". Here are some of the examples from the film in which obscene expressions appear as parts of objective clauses [*our emphasis*]:

(21)
–Learn **to fuckin type**.

(22)
–First I was just trying **to get the fuck outta there**.

(23)
–I came this close **to taking his ass out myself**.

The following are examples of obscene expressions functioning as direct objects [*our emphasis*]:

(24)
–Shoot **this piece of shit**, will ya?

(25)
–They make **shit**.

(26)
–I paid for your **goddamn** breakfast.

(27)
–Hey, just cancel **that shit** right now!

(28)
–Say **the goddamn words**!

Besides functioning as a means of creating suspense, obscene expressions perform another important function which can be identified in *Reservoir Dogs*. As Robson (2006: 81) notes, such expressions have an important role "in both an individual's affirmation of his membership of a group and also in his initiation into it: the group may be joined as long as he agrees not to be offended by the use of obscene language". Mr Orange is a character in the film who is actually a policeman working undercover and who has spent a lot of time trying to assimilate himself into the criminal group under investigation. One of the most important means of his access to the group is language, and the dialogues reveal that his speech is full of obscene expressions, just like the criminals' speech.

4.3. Lack of correlation between the content of dialogues and different contexts of the two plots and / or individual characters

In *Pulp Fiction* time is expanded in the memorable and suspense-laden 'adrenaline shot' scene and it does not appear in correlation with the content of the dialogue. While preparing to save Mia with an adrenaline shot, Vincent counts out the three seconds before giving her the shot. The counting from three to one would have taken three seconds in real time, but it is stretched to forty seconds of screen time (Van Sijll 2005: 74).

Lack of correlation between the content of dialogues and different contexts of the two plots has already been hinted at in the discussion on how suspense is created by using obscene expressions in small talk, exhaustive, but communicatively relatively empty dialogues in relation to other, non-linguistic elements that create suspense. In the two films, there are examples of lack of correlation between the content of dialogues and different contexts of the two plots. In *Pulp Fiction*, the dialogue between the characters of Jules and Vincent in one scene revolves around unimportant discussion on what Big Macs, Quarter Pounders with Cheese, and Whoppers are called in France, about the pop band Flock of Seagulls, TV pilots, etc. The scene precedes a violent encounter where Vincent and Jules murder a group of young boys. It may be argued that, instead of functioning as a comic relief for subsequent violence, such content of the dialogue represents a means for the characters to make sense of their lives (Conard 2006: 127). However, such lack of correlation between the content of meaningless, small-talk-type of dialogues and subsequent aggressive behavior creates additional suspense.

There is also the lack of correlation between the content of dialogues and other, both linguistic and non-linguistic features of characters used in their overall portrayals. For example, Jules, a hard-core criminal who has no problems with committing murder, supposedly quotes a passage from the Old Testament –Ezekiel 25: 17– immediately before killing a young man. Such utterances are highly strange for a hardened criminal, as the content of the rest of his utterances is full of obscene expressions. Such juxtaposition also adds to the creation of suspense. Furthermore, there is a lack of correlation between the criminals' and murderers' usual speech, full of vulgarities and swear words, and usage of formal expressions.

The following are Jules' utterances in the dialogue with the young man he is about to murder shortly after the dialogue and utterances of other characters of similar criminal portrayal and verbal repertoire [*our emphasis*]:

(29)
–Mind if I have some of your tasty **beverage** to wash this down with?

(30)
–Well, allow me to **retort**.

(31)
–Trying to forget anything as intriguing as this would be an **exercise in futility**.

(32)
–It's unfortunate **what we find pleasing to the touch and pleasing to the eye is seldom the same**.

(33)
–Jesus Christ!
–Don't **blaspheme**!

(34)
–I've **grasped** that, Jules. All I'm doin' is **contemplating** the "ifs".

5. Conclusion

Quentin Tarantino has shown a unique ability to blend traditions as diverse as the classical Hollywood film, Italian spaghetti westerns and French crime thrillers. His style has been influenced by all these traditions, ranging from the thematization of the code of honor similar to the films of Howard Hawks or Jean-Pierre Melville, camera movements similar to Sergio Leone's films, and the violent pacing of films by Sam Peckinpah or Hong Kong action masters.

Although influenced by the classical Hollywood, Tarantino has managed to subvert one of its fundamental principles –the linearity of the story. His first two films juxtapose the linear structure and flashbacks, and represent extremely complex, but nevertheless very effective narrative puzzles. The most notorious element of his films, the use of violence, in fact has a completely different dimension than has usually been perceived. Although sometimes brutal, violence in Tarantino's films proves to be a realistic portrayal of criminal life, and can even be perceived as the foundation of contemporary morality plays, and his films can be described in such a way as well.

Perhaps the most recognizable characteristic of his style is a very inventive use of dialogue, making him an ideal research project for the intersection of film and linguistic studies. Although analyses of suspense creation may refer to different film genres, the most valuable source for such investigations includes thrillers. As it is primarily used to prolong the dialogue, repetition seems to be the most productive linguistic means for creating suspense. An equally prominent and powerful linguistic device used to create suspense has been identified in objective clauses and direct objects containing obscene expressions. Although seemingly devoid of suspense because of lack of ambiguity, when combined with non-linguistic suspense-creating elements, obscene language actually creates suspense as it serves as a replacement for physical aggression and symbolizes acceptance to particular social groups where such aggression might be expected. Lack of correlation between the content of dialogues and the different contexts of the two plots and / or individual characters as a suspense-building device is identified in the juxtaposition of the triviality of dialogues and subsequent physical aggression, but also in the juxtaposition of excessive obscenity and formality identified in the speech of the characters.

---

[1] For detailed analyses of Tarantino's style, compare Barlow 2010, and Page 2005.

[2] Although *Reservoir Dogs* can be generically described as a heist movie, the heist is never shown in the film and we only see its aftermath. The unusual organizational structure has its polar opposite in *H-8...*, one of the most important works of Croatian cinema. Based on a true story of an accident involving a hit-and-run driver, the film begins with the climax, showing the accident, and then gradually builds tension, focusing on the events preceding the tragedy.

[3] Sam Peckinpah and Martin Scorsese, especially his *Mean Streets*, are of vital importance for understanding Tarantino's style and his depiction of violence.

[4] The image of Mary holding the body of Christ. Cf. also Brintnall 2004: 72-75.

[5] False quotations are another element shared by Melville and Tarantino. Both *The Samurai* and *The Red Circle* begin with a false quote.

Bibliography

Primary Sources

Avary, Roger & Bender, Lawrence (Producer), & Tarantino, Quentin (Director). 1992. *Reservoir Dogs*. United States: Miramax Films

Bender, Lawrence (Producer), & Tarantino, Quentin (Director), 1995. *Pulp Fiction*. United States: Miramax Films

Secondary Sources

Barlow, Aaron. 2010. *Quentin Tarantino: Life at the Extremes*. Santa Barbara, CA: Praeger.

Bell, James Scott. 2011. *Elements of Fiction Writing: Conflict and Suspense*. Blue Ash, OH: Writer's Digest Books.

Berg, Charles Ramirez. 2006. 'A Taxonomy of Alternative Plots in Recent Films: Classifying the "Tarantino Effect"' in *Film Criticism* 31 (1/2): 5-61.

Bidwell, Duane R. 2001. '"Let's Get Into Character": A Narrative / Constructionist Psychology of Conversion in Quentin Tarantino's *Pulp Fiction*' in *Pastoral Psychology* 49(5): 327-340.

Brintnall, Kent L. 2004. 'Tarantino's Incarnational Theology: *Reservoir Dogs*, Crucifixions and Spectacular Violence' in *Cross Currents* 54(1): 66-75.

Conard, Mark T. 2006. 'Symbolism, Meaning, and Nihilism in Quentin Tarantino's *Pulp Fiction*' in Conard, Mark T. (ed.) *The Philosophy of Film Noir*. Lexington, KY: The University Press of Kentucky. 125-136.

Derry, Charles. 1988. *The Suspense Thriller: Films in the Shadow of Alfred Hitchcock*. Jefferson, NC: McFarland & Company.

Friedmann, Anthony. 2010 (3rd ed.). *Writing for Visual Media*. Burlington, MA and Kidlington, Oxford: Focal Press.

Henderson, Jeffrey. 1991 (2nd ed.). *The Maculate Muse: Obscene Language in Attic Comedy*. Oxford: Oxford University Press.

Hopper, Dennis and Quentin Tarantino. 1994. 'Blood Lust Snicker Snicker in Wide Screen' in *Grand Street* 49: 10-22.

Jay, Timothy. 2000. *Why We Curse: A Neuro-Psycho-Social Theory of Speech*. Amsterdam and Philadelphia: John Benjamins Publishing Company.

Johnstone, Barbara. 1996. *The Linguistic Individual: Self-Expression in Language and Linguistics*. Oxford: Oxford University Press.

Loker, Altan. 2005. *Film and Suspense*. Victoria, BC: Trafford Publishing.

McKinney, Devin. 1993. 'Violence: The Strong and the Weak' in *Film Quarterly* 46(4): 16-22.

Noble, William. 1994. *Conflict, Action and Suspense*. Cincinnati, OH: Writer's Digest Books.

Page, Edwin. 2005. *Quintessential Tarantino: The Films of Quentin Tarantino*. London and New York, NY: Marion Boyars Publishers.

Peary, Gerald (ed). 1998. *Quentin Tarantino: Interviews*. Jackson, MS: University Press of Mississippi.

Pratt, Mary K. 2011. *How to Analyze the Films of Quentin Tarantino*. Edina, MN: ABDO Publishing Company.

Robson, James. 2006. *Humour, Obscenity and Aristophanes*. Tübingen: Gunter Narr Verlag.

Rogers, Robert. 1978. *Metaphor: A Psychoanalytic View*. Berkley and Los Angeles, CA: University of California Press.

Skakov, Nariman. 2012. *The Cinema of Tarkovsky: Labyrinths of Space and Time*. London and New York, NY: I. B. Tauris & Co Ltd.

Van Sijll, Jennifer. 2005. *Cinematic Storytelling: The 100 Most Powerful Film Conventions Every Filmmaker Must Know*. Los Angeles, CA: Michael Wiese Productions.

Webster, Joan Parker. 2002. *Teaching through Culture: Strategies for Reading and Responding to Young Adult Literature*. Houston, TX: Arte Público Press.

Chapter 3: The voices of suspense and the French detective novel: Alain Demouzon's *Melchior*

Soledad Díaz Alarcón

Abstract

Suspense is one of the most powerful ways to capture the attention of the reader of detective novels, whether it be the suspense inherent in a particular situation or the type of suspense that leaves the reader wondering what will happen next. A suspenseful narrative is one which creates a feeling of uncertainty and anxiety in the reader about the outcome of an action, which the author strategically delays through formulas involving textual reticence such as ending the chapter, slowing down the action, the sequencing of events, or dialogue techniques. In literary texts, the speakers communicate directly and consciously with each other through dialogue and indirectly and unconsciously with outside interlocutors. This paper presents a pragmatic study of the articulation of dialogue in the French detective novel, specifically in Alain Demouzon's *Melchior*. Following a short introduction in which we provide a theoretical framework for oral discourse in French-language detective stories, we analyse the dialogue in this author's work to reveal how the fictional dialogue heightens the suspense, builds and interrelates the characters, and serves as a stylistic device to create realistic or verisimilitudinous effects.

Keywords: Suspense, French detective novels, dialogue in fiction, oral discourse

1. Introduction

It is an undeniable fact that the pleasure we feel for stories and what draws us to them is the way in which the plot arouses and holds the reader's interest. Impatience becomes an everyday experience for the reader, who is unable to put down a book that he is passionate about, yet fully assumes the uncertainty of an unfinished story. The reader relishes the temporal indeterminacy of stories and the surprises that they hold, and it is precisely this tension interwoven with the story that grips the reader, who awaits an uncertain outcome sustained by the hopes and fears that emerge from it.

Narrative tension, as Raphaël Baroni (2007: 17) explains, can be defined as the phenomenon that begins when the reader of a story is motivated to wait for an outcome; a wait characterized by anticipation tinted by uncertainty, thus conferring passion upon the act of receiving.

In his analysis of this uncertainty, Meir Sternberg (1990: 901-948) distinguishes, among the thymic functions of a story, three main modalities, each of which is linked to specific textual effects of the narrative situation, called "expositional modes" of presentation. These modalities are curiosity, which is caused by delayed exposition; surprise, when information that was previously unknown is suddenly revealed; and finally, suspense, which depends on the chronological order in which the events are presented. Readers experience suspense when faced with the uncertainty of a narrative situation whose outcome or resolution they desire to know, and there is a strategic delay in the response arising from forms of textual reticence (the end of a chapter or episode, a sudden unexpected event, the slowing down of the action, etc.). Indeed, suspense leaves the reader wondering: What is going to happen next?

The term 'suspense' has traditionally been linked to crime fiction, and has come to constitute a sub-genre, the thriller, whose origins can be found in the hard-boiled detective novels of Dashiell Hammett and Raymond Chandler in the twenties in North America. This sub-genre takes the viewpoint of the victim, who becomes disoriented when faced with danger. The threat, the wait, and persecution are three components of thrillers, which also offer a psychological analysis or a behavioural study of a complex character. The reader inquires into both the future (what will happen to the characters) and the past (the causes that have led to the situation).

Suspense, however, is also a discursive resource that keeps the reader expectant and attentive to the development of the conflict or the crux of the narrative, and for which the author uses a range of specific textual strategies characteristic of narrative tension as Umberto Eco explains in the following quote:

> Un texte narratif introduit des signaux textuels de différents types pour souligner que la disjonction qui va être occurrente est importante. Appelons-les signaux de suspense. Ils peuvent, par exemple, consister à différer la réponse à la question implicite du lecteur. (Eco 1985: 144)

One such strategy is the discursive mode of speech acts, understood as direct speech, 'discours direct', indirect speech, 'discours indirect', free indirect speech 'discours indirect libre' or narrative report of speech acts, 'discours narrativisé' (Adam 1999: 50-74). While it follows that one of the functions of dialogue is to create suspense, uncertainty, anxiety or excitement, the dialogue also permits readers to establish a close relationship with the characters by defining them, and especially with the action, in that it sets the scene, provides information, acts as a thread of the main event, indicates the crux of the plot, replaces or represents the action (in the novels of Raymond Chandler, the characters use dialogue as a weapon when they do not have one at hand), drives the story, complements the action, and provides the reader with clues. Dialogue is therefore a communicative situation with its corresponding frameworks of rewriting such as the metalinguistic function, which focuses on the linguistic register used; paralinguistic elements, which describe the gestures; question forms and the interlocutive relationship. Through these references, we can identify the dialogue, that is, as a way of representing the linguistic behaviour in the relationships between characters.

In line with the above, we will analyze the discursive mode of the novel *Melchior* by Alain Demouzon, taking into account aspects such as orality, the interactive dimension of the dialogues or response and counter-response, and the manner in which the dialogues are represented.

2. Discursive modes in *Melchior*

Alain Demouzon (1945) soon became an important figure on the literary scene thanks to the reinterpretation and revival of a detective genre with outstanding novelists such as A.D.G., Manchette and Vautrin. Demouzon's work spans several fields including the "roman blanc", "polar", "reportages of faits divers" or "énigmes 'à résoudre vous-même'", which have been published in several volumes. He is also a screenwriter for film (*Stress*, Jean-Louis Bertuccelli) and television (*Les Cinq Dernières Minutes; Inspecteur Puzzle; Ferbac*).

In 1994, his novel *Dernière station avant Jérusalem* was published in *La Série Noire* collection. This first season of the *Melchior* series marked Demouzon's comeback to crime fiction in print and confirmed the success of the existential adventures of an atypical and particularly original Commissioner in a publishing world where stereotypes triumph. Through this key character, Demouzon attempts to merge the usual ingredients of hard-boiled thrillers with elements of classic novels in six stories,[1] with each of the author's novels differing from the previous ones. Like Tarpon (the detective created by Jean-Patrick Manchette), Melchior leaves the police force to become a private detective. The method of this new *privé* is to unravel the threads of intrigue in search of his own truth, beyond the official story. The character of Melchior allows Demouzon to explore, in his own way, the cliché of Simenon; a classic (at least in appearance) police commissioner working in the outskirts of Paris, but whose personality is wholly original. That is, the author, in the manner of Alfred Hitchcock, makes use of a stereotype to then rid himself of it.

In *Melchior*, Police Commissioner Jean-François Melchior of the central brigade of Fontenay receives a call informing him that the emergency services have found a young woman on the quays of the River Marne whose belly has been sliced open and from whose womb a baby has been extracted. After arriving at the scene, Melchior is told that he will not be assigned the case, but that the criminal brigade of Paris will take charge. However, out of compassion for the victim and to duly complete his report, he visits the woman in the hospital and interrogates the doctors who are attending to her. This first crime is, in turn, interwoven with a second one: the search for the rapist who left Jessica, the 16-year-old daughter of one of Melchior's old friends, Madeleine, pregnant. Thus the first phase of the plot gets underway: the interrogation that will trigger the action.

Detective fiction is a strongly coded genre, which is subject to very precise thematic, structural and narrative rules. These rules have permitted classifying detective fiction into three main types: *mysteries* 'récit d'énigme', *hard-boiled fiction* 'roman noir', and *thrillers* 'roman de suspense'. Two narrative forms predominate in hard-boiled fiction in particular: the first is to tell the story through the words of the main character, whether it be the investigator, the criminal or the victim. Thus, the narrative can be homodiegetic or heterodiegetic with an internal focus. In any case, as Uri Eisenzweig (1986: 53) indicates, the observer has a limited outsider's view of the objects described. The reader knows only what the characters know, hence the importance that the reader identify with these characters. The second form is to use a neutral, heterodiegetic narrator, who limits himself to "filming" or observing outside actions and characters, giving the impression that he knows less than they do.

In *Melchior*, the narrator tells the story in the third person; he presents and watches the events unfold and is able to express the interiority of the characters; moreover, he passes judgment and has complete knowledge of the past and present of the events in the narrative. He is, ultimately, an omniscient heterodiegetic narrator. However, the focal point cannot be defined as "zero focalization" because the narrative is subtley / cleverly interwoven with the chronological development of the events. Thus despite the omniscience of the narrator, the action adapts to the movements of the main character without prolepsis, guarding at all costs the effect of surprise and showing, in chronological order, every step, every adventure, and every predicament in which the main character finds himself, or which he faces. In the story, the events unfold in a detailed and very limited chronological order of only four days, thus giving the eight parts, into which the novel is divided, their names: *Mardi soir, Mercredi de l'aube jusqu'au soir, La nuit du deuxième jour, Jeudi matin, Jeudi après-midi, La nuit du troisième jour, Vendredi dans la matinée, Quatrième jour de midi à minuit.*

The narrative begins *in medias res,* at an intermediate point of the story to then recount events that took place later than the beginning of the story, but with the necessary analepsis to define the personality of the characters, particularly that of the protagonist. While numerous descriptive pauses are made in the action scenes, they do not hinder the rapid pace of the events. Indeed, the chain of events fuels the reader's sense of urgency to know the outcome, which in turn heightens the tension and thus the reader's interest. This tension will be relieved, as we shall see, by satisfying the reader's intellectual curiosity, that is, all the enigmas will be resolved at the end of the book.

Parallel to the narrative, focalization occurs on different levels. Just as the narrator can give the floor to another, the localizer can also change the point of focalization. These changes permit playing with the relationship between total knowledge, perceived appearances, or a subjective view; changes that are multiplied by the direct, indirect and free indirect styles. In the work analysed here, there is a clear predominance of the direct form to reproduce words, namely the direct style of narration. The chapters are organized around structures containing dialogue full of rhythm, irony, insinuations, innuendos, and complicity, which the reader interprets and which will allow him to build the framework that will gradually give shape to the story, as well as construct the physical and psychological profile of the characters. In what follows we will explore some of the functions these dialogues perform in the story.

Informative function. Despite the presence of the narrator whose function is to inform the reader, the dialogues in the story also have an informative function. At times, however, the narrator hides behind his characters, allowing them to talk and argue, reveal their story and their characteristics, as well as providing clues, evidence, and small pieces of the puzzle that the reader can pick up and put in place. During these dialogues, the narrator becomes a mere assistant to the action, intervening only when necessary. The narrator guides us towards one or another part of the scene, watches over it and observes the reactions of the characters.

Advancing the action. In this story, it is essential that the action move forward through dialogue as the events occur quickly and the action lasts a mere four days. The words advance the action and produce mental movements that change the course of events in a particular direction.

Scenic function. The scenes are those spaces of the story in which, once the situation presents itself, the narrator withdraws to allow the readers to witness the events without intermediaries. It is the moment when we hear the voice of the characters accompanied only by the narrator's remarks about their tone of voice, gestures or movements. The dialogues appear in important parts of the text at moments which require a more detailed examination of the events or dramatization. Whether presented in a clear and direct form or embedded in the text, the dialogues are always a respite for the reader. Moreover, they ensure that the reading of the text coincides with the action: we hear and see the characters in a live and direct manner.

3. Orality

As Genette indicated in his essay on style (1991: 137-138), in the nineteenth century, writing was essentially viewed as being intentional, as the effect of a choice or a commitment, rather than having a social or ethical function. Oral communication presents a number of specific features as a result of particular spatiotemporal parameters. The co-presence of interlocutors means that communication is not only established on a verbal basis, but also on a physiognomic, gestural and behavioural one. Similarly, production time, and the spontaneity of the speech act or utterance entails particular verbal features of a syntactic and pragmatic nature. Nonetheless, all these features of spoken communication are not found in an oral style due, in part, to the fact that the author has to present the information in a linear form and choose those features that are "real". The dialogue convinces the reader that what he has read is plausible, that it is actually occurring as he recognizes realistic elements in it, that is, real spoken situations. As Genette (1991: 35-52) explains, the novelist is producing a reality from fiction. The following are some examples of these features of orality in Demouzon's novel *Melchior*:

Phonic features: These refer to the phonetic reproduction of a particular form of pronunciation. In the first example they denote a humble social class and a very low educational level.

(1)

On né pas des voleurs. Je rens ses bijous à S. Le bébé va bien. La police, ne cherché pas, laissé nous, c'es mon bébé! (Demouzon 1995: 314)

The following example reproduces the speech of the police officer, Bertrand, who is always eating and whom we perceive to be unprofessional.

(2)

On a rechu cha! proclama l'inspecteur à travers une bouchée de Marshmallows. Ch'est arrivé au comptoir. (Demouzon 1995: 313)

Prosodic features: These features are related to intonation, stress, rhythm, cadence or pauses. Ellipses, exclamations, and interrogations are used to indicate indecision or silence, tension or surprise and curiosity. In the first example, the ellipsis points denote the silences, with which the character attempts to justify himself, while they accentuate the character's collusion with the reader:

(3)

−Bien sûr que oui! Dès quatorze ans. Une môme toute seule dans la cité… Tu sais comment c'est?... Et puis, elle a quand même traîné ici. L'ambiance… C'est peut-être contagieux? Elle n'a pas connu son père… Les garçons l'intéressaient, bien sûr… mais… merde! (Demouzon 1995: 47)

In the following example the exclamation marks are a clear sign of tension.

(4)

−Ailleurs! Les mettre ailleurs!... Dans mon bureau et sur mon bureau, et sous mon bureau! Tel que je le connais! Le roi du boxon (burdel)!... Droit y en avoir partout. (Demouzon 1995: 117)

66

Here, the fast pace of the dialogue piques the reader's curiosity.

(5)
–J'ai été violée! dit-elle d'une voix bizarre, comme une mauvaise élève avouant une note
    catastrophique.
–Tu n'as rien dit à ta mère?
–À elle? Surtout pas!
–Et c'est cet homme que tu recherches?
–Oui.
–Tu l'as vu?
–Oui.
–Cette nuit?
–Oui.
–Et tu as eu peur... très peur... Il t'a fait mal?
–Non... il ne m'a rien fait (...) (Demouzon 1995: 72)

word structure / syntactic structure

Morphosyntactic features: The most widely used morphosyntactic structure in
the story is the incomplete construction of a sentence by elision (of the verb,
preposition or initial negation).

(6) *elision of verb*
–Dans quel état, la victime? interrogea Melchior. Vivante? (Demouzon 1995: 17)

(7)
–La pilule, connaît pas? (Demouzon 1995: 288)

Likewise we find interrogative structures which reproduce the word order of a
spoken register.

(8)
–T'es enceinte? (Demouzon 1995: 19) /–C'est quoi, le nom de cette Clinique? (Demouzon 1995:
34)

The syntactic constructions based on juxtapositions speed up the pace, facilitate
our comprehension and permit a large amount of information to be conveyed.

(9)
–Je préviens la Criminelle. Ils seront saisis du dossier. Restez sur les lieux. Faites la jonction.
(Demouzon 1995: 24)

The enumeration technique, in which the complement is repeated, highlights the
importance of the concept over the action, while reducing speaking time.

(10)
Melchior admit la remarque. Son regard fit un nouveau tour de piste. Il y avait là quelques petits
revendeurs de drogue à la dose, rarement plus de deux ou trois paquets sur eux–et qui ne pesaient
rien dans le creux de la main. Des mange-merde! Et d'autres encore, des voleurs à sacs à main et

de pneus, des casseurs de cabines téléphoniques, des dépouilleurs de coin de rue, des bastonneurs de HLM… De la poussière de délinquance, de la limaille de la criminalité, mais insupportable et cruelle quand on l'avait dans l'œil. (Demouzon 1995: 45)

Lexical features: As regards the language, we see how Demouzon exercises his mastery of linguistic registers, from the most classical to slang, although he makes it clear that he prefers spoken language, personal turns of phrase, sarcastic formulas, and plays on words; thus at times revealing his most cynical side.

(11)
–Qu'est-ce que je fous de ce truc, oui! rouspéta l'inspecteur.
–C'est quoi, ce que tu trimballes ?
–Le placenta.
–Quoi ?
–Le toubib me l'a refilé en partant. Il dit que ça peut intéresser la justice. (…)
–Balance-moi cette merde aux Martiens! dit-il… (Demouzon 1995: 22)

In the same reply we find changes in register.

(12)
–Merde, vous déconnez! Faut quand même qu'on boucle un minimum! C'est une procédure de flagrant délit ça, et on ne pourra pas s'en tirer sans un chouia d'enquête préliminaire. Juste un petit rapport comme il faut!... Et on ne peut pas conclure par un: «Monsieur le procureur, ayant estimé devoir confier l'affaire à la Brigade criminelle parisienne, nous avons estimé de notre côté ne plus en avoir rien à foutre.» (Demouzon 1995: 27)

(13)
–Cutter ?
–Vous savez, ce truc à lame rétractable, pour couper le plastique ou la moquette…
–À ce propos, dit Melchior, vous devriez faire recoller des dalles sur votre revêtement de sol. (Demouzon 1995: 37)

(14)
–Si monsieur l'inspecteur désire prendre quelque chose…
–Donnezmoi un sac de graines, dit Chemineau. Je veux dire: des cacahuètes! (Demouzon 1995: 45)

The author also borrows and adapts words from English terms.

(15)
–J'ai mon bizness. (Demouzon 1995: 42)

(16)
–(la jeune classe de la criminalité montante avait son verlan relooké; Melchior rechignait à l'assimiler). (Demouzon 1995: 44)

Demouzon uses sayings and idioms such as

(17)
–"Si tu ne vas pas à Lagardère, Lagardère ira à toi!" tenta de plaisanter Melchior. (Demouzon 1995: 333) (in clear reference to the saying 'If the mountain will not come to Muhammad, then Muhammad must go to the mountain')

as well as affective terms. *emotional*.

(18)
–Pourquoi ça, mon vieux? (Demouzon 1995: 137) / –C'est la crise, mon pote! (Demouzon 1995: 228)

Puns are another frequent element in Demouzon's narrative. In this particular example the author plays with the use of the same verbs which appear in a chiastic structure. *symmetrical patterns in structure*

(19)
–Quand même, ce type, tu l'as reconnu ! Tu peux le reconnaître !... Tu le connais !
–Je ne le connais pas, mais je peux le reconnaître. Cette nuit, je l'ai bien reconnu. (Demouzon 1995: 81)

Semantic features: An essential characteristic of Demouzon's novel is the density of its images (comparisons, metaphors, metonymies, etc.). Obviously, the more popular the characters, the more rhetorical devices we find, as in the case of our story.

(20)
–Balance-moi cette merde aux Martiens! (Demouzon 1995: 23) (metaphor: crime scene investigators)

(21)
–Bon, tu vois! Confirma Melchior. On aura bien une surdose de drogue, ici ou là. Une poignée d'ivrognes en travers de la chaussée, un casse de magasin de télévisions et un mari qui bat se femme… Par ici, tout est calme, c'est pas l'Amérique! (Demouzon 1995: 45) (comparison)

(22)
–… Pas si cinglé que ça, d'ailleurs. Cette manière d'agir est un signe d'intelligence et de compréhension. Si j'étais dans la merde, ma dernière ideé serait de sonner les flics! Et puis, ce que ce gars-là envisageait, c'est qu'on vienne en vitesse recoudre la fille qu'il venait de chacuter… Jack l'Éventreur, version droits humanitaires! (Demouzon 1995: 20) (metaphor in clear reference to this mythical English serial killer)

(23)
–Fatima… Il paraît qu'elle a "perdu la pudeur" (Demouzon 1995: 280) (euphemism)

alliterative ↓

[handwritten: in context]

Pragmatic features: Through this lens, we understand the dialogue as a semiotic process in which verbal signs appear simultaneously with signs of kinesthetic, proxemic and paralinguistic codes, which actively intervene in the dialogue. We *[handwritten: gestures]* also perceive changes in tone through the inclusion of ironic and satirical nuances.

(24)

[handwritten: kinesthetic]

–Mon bébé? Comment va mon bébé? murmura la femme en dodelinant sur son empilement d'oreillers. (Demouzon 1995: 116)

(25)

[handwritten: paralinguistic]

–(…) Des fins limiers de la Criminelle doivent s'en occuper. Le commissaire prit sa mine boudeuse, la plus empâtée, avec triple menton. (Demouzon 1995: 117)

(26)

–Et il est où, ce Zerbib? insista Chemineau.
–Le docteur Zerbib est retourné à la clinique. Il n'était pas de service ici, ce soir. Comme l'affaire éstait inhabituelle, j'ai préféré l'appeler. Le professeur Zerbib a d'autres accouchements à contrôler (…) (Demouzon 1995: 33) (ironic tone)

(27)

–Donnez (moi une fourchette!... Aux légistes, je demande toujours une fourchette.
–Je ne suis pas légiste.
–J'entends bien… D'ailleurs, on n'enseigne plus la médecine légale à la faculté. Nos légistes vont apprendre en Suisse ou au Canada, vous le saviez? (Demouzon 1995: 32) (satirical tone)

4. Replication and attributive discourse

[handwritten: Response - counter response] *[handwritten: he said, she said.]*

Replication, or response and counter-response, is simply the discursive exchange between two or more characters who alternate their voices, their role as senders and receivers, and in which the written language is perfectly marked by graphical features such as dashes, quotation marks or changes of line. In most cases, the narrator intervenes in these replies; he is a witness to or a participant in the dialogue, giving rise to interpolated clauses or attributive discourse. These clauses typically introduced by *verba dicendi* allow the narrator to reveal extralinguistic elements relating to the sender such as gestures, glances, movements, etc. In what follows we highlight three structures in the story that, in our opinion, are the most representative of this type of discursive exchange.

a. Dialogue consisting of the rapid succession of responses and counter-responses in which the narrator does not intervene.

b. Dialogue with interpolated clauses introduced by *verba dicendi*. There are very few of these clauses, with most of them serving as a reference for the reader, so that after a long succession of responses, the reader will remember who intervened in the dialogue. All are expressed in "passé simple". According to the classification of Strauch (1972: 229-236), these clauses can be grouped into different types: *contextual* (rectifia, constata, renauda, intervint, etc.), *elocutive* (grogna, s'écria, hurla, marmonna, etc.), and *notional and affective* (informa, avoua, promit, etc.).

c. Dialogue where the information provided by the narrator is an attempt to create a certain density in the utterance, to show the complexity of the speech act, whose meaning is also conveyed by the intonation, gestures or gazes that accompany it. The attributive discourse therefore supplants replication and is instead a remark with psychological content made by the narrator. In some of these cases, these interventions are presented in a separate paragraph without a dash that makes them dependent on direct style. Some examples are shown below.

(28)

Replication.

–J'ai essayé d'appeler, dit Chemineau (referencia al interlocutor del protagonista)
–J'ai oublié de rebrancher. Ma fille m'est tombée dessus. Je suis de repos, théoriquement.
–Théoriquement, moi aussi.
–Du nouveau sur cette affaire des docks?... Que dit la Crim'?
–Ils sont discrets, pour le moment. Ils analysent tous leurs petits flacons. Ça prendra du temps…
–Et sur le terrain?...
–Justement… le proc' voudrait que vous vous en occupiez.
–Il ne disait pas ça, hier soir.
–Il aimerait vous en parler… au téléphone… ou si vous pouvez passer. Il dit que votre connaissance du terrain est meilleure. Il s'est emballé. C'est pas un dossier pour la Criminelle.
–Mais si!
–Criez pas comme ça, vous allez réveiller le petit! On dirait que cette affaire vous déplaît…
–Elle me déplaît!
–Vous avez passé toute la nuit et la matinée à vous en occuper, alors qu'on vous demandait de ne pas le faire…
–Justement!
–Justement pour justement, c'est peut-être la raison pour laquelle le procureur a opéré ce revirement… Il y a quelque chose… (Demouzon 1995: 93)

In the following example, we show a routine interpolated clause spoken by the narrator.

attributive with pyscholog. content

(29)
–C'est des gens que vous ne connaissez même pas, murmura Chemineau sur un ton de reproche.
(Demouzon 1995: 113)

Likewise, we note that some clauses are more extensive than the interventions themselves.

(30)
–Comment vous appelez vous, madame? demanda le commissaire en recalant le prote-fiche métallique de façon à ne pas le cogner désagréablement contre les barreaux du lit. (Demouzon 1995: 116)

(31)
–[…] Ce viol d'abord, comment ça s'est passé? demanda stupidement Melchior, gâchant toute chance d'avancer, et le sachant aussitôt, et s'en voulant à mort, mais ça ne servait à rien, c'était trop tard. (Demouzon 1995: 82)

Despite being less frequent than the above examples, in this work we also find several cases of dramatic monologue, where only the voice of one of the interlocutors is heard, often coinciding with phone call scenes. This technique serves to lighten the narrative discourse and add to the intrigue.

(32)
–Fontenay-Central, j'écoute!... Vous êtes en ligne avec le commissaire Melchior… C'est moi, en effet… Puisque je vous le dis, conclut-il avec un calme apaisant (Demouzon 1995: 13)

(33)
–Oui, oui, monsieur le procureur, je comprends bien, dit Melchior. Venir maintenant, c'est un peu difficile… Je… (nouveau crépitement accéléré). Non, je ne me retranche pas derrière les nécessités du service et la multiplicité des tâches… puisque je suis de repos! Ne vous excusez pas, c'est sans importance… Si, si je vous assure!... Non, le problème, c'est Benjamin, mon petit-fils… j'ai promis à ma fille de le garder. Elle a des examens… Des examens de DROIT! (Il amplifia le mot droit comme s'il s'agissait d'une chose effroyable.)… (Crépitement)… C'est une heureuse proposition, (…) (Demouzon 1995: 97)

The indirect discourse style or transposition of the characters' speech in the narrator's own language is also present in this story by Demouzon, but obviously to a lesser extent. However, it is interesting to highlight some examples. In the first, the narrator uses declarative verbs to reproduce a telephone conversation and the reaction of Commissioner Melchior.

(34)
Le brigadier-chef était effectivement de service. On lui expliqua la situation et il proposa aussitôt en riant qu'on monte chez lui, il n'était pas si tard que ça, des gens regardent encore la télé à ces heures-là! Si Mme Lacacia était couchée, elle aurait tout loisir de se rendormir…
Melchior estima qu'il serait plus correct de téléphoner pour avertir de cette intrusion. Le brigadier promit de s'en occuper immédiatement. Il rompit la conversation, sur un grand rire. (Demouzon 1995: 146)

In the following example, we hear, in the form of an echo, the comments of the people that throng the corridors of the police station; comments which Commissioner Melchior also hears as he walks to his office.

(35)
Dans leur dos, il y eut des remarques. Un jeune à tête rassée estima que c'était pas discret, pour une "balance", de s'afficher comme ça. Une ménagère persifla que "ces gens-là" passaient toujours devant, y en a que pour eux, c'est comme à l'hôpital. Un vieil homme très calme estima que le tutoiement et le vous-soiement n'étaient pas à leurs places légitimes. (Demouzon 1995: 166) (corridor of the police station)

In this third example, we are struck by how the narrator suddenly interrupts the indirect discourse to summarize the most relevant information.

(36)
Il appela l'hôpital intercommunal. Rodier lui donna de bonnes nouvelles de Sylvaine Valentin, le fait qu'on lui ait retrouvé son nom facilitait le retour de la mémoire. Ils en avaient discuté avec le docteur. Conclusion: amnésie lacunaire, comportant un déficit antérograde et un déficit rétrograde, liée à la commotion cérébrale concordante au traumatisme psychocphysiologique subi para la madade, (…) (Demouzon 1995: 192)

Finally, it is interesting to note this extract in which there is a change from the indirect to the direct style to again return to the indirect style.

(37)
Melchior téléphona. Il composa le numéro des Anciens établissements Morinceaux, marbrier funéraire. Il rappela qu'il avait demandé cent fois une gravure sur la tombe de sa femme, qu'il devait y avoir quelque part –probablement aux Archives nationales, vu la date!– un bon de commande en bonne et due forme. Devait-il communiquer le numéro du reçu des arrhes qu'il avait versées?.../Qui il était lui? Le commissaire principal de Fontenay-Central!... Oui, ça rime. Ça vous fait rire? Dans votre boulot, je ne suis pas sûr qu'il soit bien venu de s'esclaffer au nez des clients… À quelle date la défunte a-t-elle été inhumée?.../Melchior indiqua le jour et l'année, on lui répondit bientôt que tout était maintenant sur ordinateur et qu'aucune commande au nom de Wirtz ou Melchior ne figurait sur nos listes. (…) (Demouzon 1995: 186)

The discursive variety of this narrative reveals the importance of the free indirect style. This narrative mode allows the narrator to gain access to the character's conscious in the form of interior monologue. It is an attempt not only to economize when introducing a character, but to lessen the importance and presence of the narrator. By eliminating language barriers –the features of syntactic dependency– the rendering of the stream of consciousness is lightened, but still influenced by the presence of the narrator, who refuses to leave the reins of the discourse in the character's hands. The result is an ambiguous statement in which we do not always know who is actually speaking or to whom to attribute the discourse.

(38)
Melchior envisagea de mettre tout le monde au travail: chacun son contigent de sacs à éventrer, à épandre sur les bureaux et à trier… À la recherche de quoi? Un objet singulier? Ou bien la vérité devait-elle naître de la coïncidence des évidences, de l'accumulation des trivialités?... Ne valait-il pas mieux constituer d'abord un protocole d'investigation, une hypothèse de travail? Coller toute l'équipe à l'autopsie d'un monceau d'ordures, sur une recommandation du genre: "Cherchez! Quoi? je n'en sais rien… trouvez-le!", aurait par trop des allures de brimade. Pourtant, le commissaire savait que cette méthode aléatoire pouvait être bonne (…) (Demouzon 1995: 170)

(39)
Il avait sûrement déjà rencontré la femme de Lacacia dans une cérémonie officielle, un pot amical de flicards; mais c'était resté sans souvenir. Ce qu'il savait, c'est qu'il avait peur –car il

avait toujours peur, au moment de frapper à une porte opaque qui pouvait s'ouvrir sur un inattendu bouleversement du destin. Souvent, il avait été le messager impitoyable de ce bouleversement qui, jusque-là, n'avait atteint que la vie des autres sans fracasser trop la sienne… Qui peut dire ce qui attend l'homme derrière une porte close? (Demouzon 1995: 148)

5. Conclusions

As we have seen, suspense is one of the most powerful means of capturing the attention of the reader of detective stories, whether it is inherent in a situation or leaves the reader wondering what will happen next. From the point of view of the audience, the narrative sequence is not fully realized as conceived by the author, but is instead "in progress" and plays out in successive parts or portions. This is achieved through specific textual strategies or elements of suspense such as the division into chapters, episodic narrative, inserting a time lapse between questions and answers, the abrupt introduction of new characters, the presentation of a new action to pique the reader's curiosity, and, of course, dialogue techniques. These techniques allow the interlocutors of the dialogues of literary texts to directly and consciously communicate among themselves, and to indirectly and unconsciously communicate to external receivers through the words of the narrator.

Through our analysis of Demouzon's story *Melchior*, we have attempted to demonstrate that textual polyphony is one of the strategies used in "polar" narratives to build tension through curiosity, surprise and suspense. Thanks to the different voices in the discourse, specifically those of the principal character and the narrator, the reader progresses through the action that they mark. These voices allow us to know and recognize each of the characters involved in the action as they report the movements of the different actors, describe the scenes and settings, provide clues, reveal evidence and recognize failures; all of which is framed in a lively, rapid and realistic discourse that kindles a burning desire in the reader to know the outcome.

---

[1] *Melchior* (1995), *Melchior et les innocents* (2000), *La Promesse de Melchior* (2000) (Prix polar 2000 du salon de Montigny-lès-Cormeilles - Prix Mystère de la critique 2001), *Melchior en automne* (2003), *Agence Melchior* (2006), *Un amour de Melchior* (2008).

Polyphony = simultaneity of pts. of view within narrative.

Bibliography

Primary Sources

Demouzon, Alain. 1995. *Melchior*. Paris: Calmann-Lévy.
——. 2000. *Melchior et les innocents*. Paris: Calmann-Lévy.
——. 2000. *La Promesse de Melchior*. Paris: Calmann-Lévy.
——. 2003. *Melchior en automne*. Paris: Calmann-Lévy.
——. 2006. *Agence Melchior*. Paris: Fayard-Noir.
——. 2008. *Un amour de Melchior*. Paris: Fayard-Noir.

Secondary Sources

Adam, Jean-Michel. 1999. *Linguistique textuelle. Des genres de discours aux textes*. Paris: Natham.
Baroni, Raphael. 2007. *La Tension narrative*. Paris: Éd. du Seuil.
Eco, Umberto. 1985. *Lector in Fabula*. Paris: Grasset.
Eisenzweig, Uri. 1986. *Le récit imposible*. Paris: Christian Bourgois éditeur.
Garrido Domínguez, Antonio. 1993. *El texto narrativo*. Madrid: Editorial Síntesis.
Genette, Gérard. 1991. *Fiction et diction*. Paris: Seuil.
Sternberg, Meir. 1990. Telling in time (I): "Chronology and narrative theory" in *Poetics Today* 11: 901-948.
Strauch, Gérard. 1972. "Contributions à l'étude sémantique des verbes indroducteurs du discours indirect" in *RANAM* 5: 229-236.

[handwritten note: Looked at on Amazon UK in t/lation – didn't seem particularly relevant.]

Chapter 4: Reconstructing suspense: Borges translates Faulkner's *The Wild Palms*

Leah Leone

Abstract

With *The Wild Palms* (1939), William Faulkner critiques commercial literature through the treatment of pulp-fiction themes with high modernist literary style. Through experimental prose, metafictional uses of pulp literature, and complex, non-traditional representations of gender, Faulkner complicates the experience of suspense traditionally associated with the sex, crime and violence featured in the novel. On the part of Faulkner's various publishers and his translator, famous writer and critic Jorge Luis Borges, there has been a concerted effort to reformulate and repackage *The Wild Palms* as a thriller. *Las palmeras salvajes* (1940) diverges from the English in manners suggesting a conscious attempt to reconstruct suspense in both the prose and the storyline –most strikingly through the exchange of fictional dialogue between the novel's female and male protagonists.

Keywords: Jorge Luis Borges, William Faulkner, *The Wild Palms*, pulp-fiction, hard-boiled

1. *The Wild Palms*: Pulp-fiction or high art?

The Wild Palms (1939) is generally considered one of William Faulkner's minor works. Overshadowed by his modernist masterpieces such as *The Sound and The Fury* (1929), *As I Lay Dying* (1930) and *Absolom, Absolom!* (1936), the novel is also excluded from bibliographies citing Faulkner's crime fiction, with works such as *Sanctuary* (1931), *Intruder in the Dust* (1948) or *Knight's Gambit* (1949) (Hubin 1979: 142; Reilly 1985: 305-307). Notably, this exclusion from Faulkner's crime fiction canon occurs despite *The Wild Palms*' action centering around a prison break, the performance of illegal abortions by an unlicensed doctor and a murder trial. The problem, it seems, is not that the novel cannot be considered high art or commercial fiction, but rather that it is the synthesis of both. Unlike *Sanctuary*, which –out of financial necessity– Faulkner modeled on the pulp novels that were bringing his contemporaries financial success, *The Wild Palms* rather constitutes a deconstruction of pulp fiction.[1]

Toward the end of the 1930s, Faulkner was anxious to distance himself from mass culture after "whoring [himself] with short stories", an economically motivated stint in Hollywood, and in the wake of the notoriety he garnered with *Sanctuary* (Faulkner 1978: 59). *The Wild Palms* instead became the site for a critical modernist engagement with the commercial literature on which Faulkner had reluctantly been earning a living (King 1998; Earle 2009: 204-206).[2] *The Wild Palms* deploys complex prose and formal experimentation in the exposition of pulp themes –crime, sex, violence– in such a way that he dismantles the experience of suspense traditionally achieved through the consumption of pulp fiction.[3] Rhetorically, the narrative devices through which Faulkner complicated suspense in *The Wild Palms* had the effect of both exposing and undermining the values underlying commercial fiction –particularly hard-boiled crime narrative– namely, the commodification of art and the mystification of gender. Despite the novel's lofty intentions, its failure to conform to either genre appears to have made a negative impression from the start. From the time of its initial release, there was a concerted effort on the part of publishers, through editing, censorship and marketing, to repackage *The Wild Palms* as precisely the kind of suspenseful thriller Faulkner attempted to critique.

The novel's Spanish translator, Jorge Luis Borges, whose *Las palmeras salvajes* was published by Sudamericana in 1940, can be counted among those who sought to recast *The Wild Palms* as a thriller. Despite, or possibly because of the kinds of transformations Borges effectuated in the translation (among them the mere inclusion of his name on the book cover!) in the Spanish speaking world, *Las palmeras salvajes* has come to be considered one of Faulkner's most important and influential works. In stark contrast to *The Wild Palms'* scant recognition among English language readers, *Las palmeras salvajes* has been personally mentioned as a significant influence by such celebrated writers as Mario Vargas Llosa, José María Arguedas, Juan Carlos Onetti, Ricardo Piglia, Manuel Puig and Guillermo Cabrera Infante (Leone 2011). It is impossible to definitely establish whether it is Borges's name, his translation style, or merely the condition of the Latin American polysystem that motivates *Las palmeras salvajes'* initial and ongoing success in the Hispanophone world. Regardless, study of the translation and its legacy is well worth undertaking –be it a polysystems approach as suggested by Even-Zohar (1978), a descriptive study as originally proposed by Toury (1995), considerations of literary manipulation as discussed by Hermans (1985) and Lefevere (1992), or a gendered approach as taken by Simon (1996) and von Flotow (1997). From any angle one approaches *Las palmeras salvajes*, one may discover the surprising expense at which creating the desired effect of suspense may come. In what follows we will examine the literary techniques by which Faulkner destabilized suspense in *The Wild Palms*, historical evidence of publishers' attempts to recast the novel into the very style it satirized, and then employ comparative analysis to reveal the ways in which Borges turned Faulkner's most subversive tactics on their heads.

2. Strangeness and suspense in *The Wild Palms*

2.1. Two novels in one

Reading Borges's rather scathing review of *The Wild Palms*, published in *El Hogar* in 1939, one is almost surprised he accepted the commission to translate the novel. Annoyed –as many U.S. critics were– with Faulkner's formal experimentation in the novel, he wrote:

> En las obras capitales de Faulkner –en *Luz de agosto*, en *El sonido y la furia*, en *Santuario*– las novedades técnicas parecen necesarias, inevitables. En *The Wild Palms* son menos atractivas que incómodas, menos justificables que exasperantes. (Borges 2007: 527)

Chief among critics' complaints about *The Wild Palms* was its consisting of two alternating short novels.[4] In "The Wild Palms", considered the primary story, Charlotte Rittenmeyer abandons her husband and two daughters to run away with her lover, a medical student named Harry Wilbourne; after Charlotte becomes pregnant, and at her insistence, Harry performs but botches an illegal abortion, killing Charlotte and landing himself a life-sentence in prison. "Old Man" relates a convict's unintentional flight from and desperate attempts to return to prison during a Mississippi flood, during which he saves a pregnant woman who gives birth in the midst of the storm. As Borges states in his review, "[e]sta segunda historia, admirable a veces, corta y vuelve a cortar el penoso curso de la primera, en largas interpolaciones" (2007: 527).

While somewhat missing the thematic confluence of the two stories, in a 1939 review of *The Wild Palms*, critic Paula Snelling certainly noted the effect of their intermittent juxtaposition:

> [Faulkner] tells two unrelated stories which have been placed in the same volume for little other discernible purpose than to afford him the pleasure, after engrossing you in one story to the point where you have forgotten what occurred in the other and have lost all interest in its characters, of transporting you to the other, there to remain until the same disinterest has arisen concerning the first set; then back again. (Cited in Inge 1995: 202)

In other words, a primary strategy by which Faulkner interrogated commercial genres was splicing the two pulp-inspired stories precisely at moments of high drama. While in a typical thriller, there may be cuts to other scenes as a way to provide background information, or provide alternative sources of details perhaps unknown to protagonists; these devices generally serve to enhance the primary narrative. In *The Wild Palms*, these cuts rather detract from each story, going on long enough after interrupting the experience of suspense as to obliterate the previous story from the reader's mind.

2.2. Prose as an obstacle to suspense

Faulkner's technical experimentation also extended to his prose, which was at times so wrought, dense, and often ungrammatical, it was simply described as "impudence... a cynical disregard of ordinary politeness" by one reviewer (Robinson [1939] cited in Inge 1995: 191). Suspense in the novel was often curtailed by intrusions into the narration of dramatic exposition through character interruptions into extended dialogue, a third-person narrator's interjection of details, a first-person narrative, and the mid-sentence placement of descriptive parentheses consisting of several paragraphs. Fast-moving scenes are often cut up and spliced with characters' reflections on the events, and even more intrusively, the narrator's supplementation of character motives, events from their past that are directly impacting current events, hints at what a character *would* think, were her or his intellectual or spiritual faculties better developed, and personal guesses about what a given character *might* be thinking, as if the narrator, at some points, is barred from omniscience. Indeed, rather than occlude details from readers in order to keep them engaged and guessing about what will come next, Faulkner saturates them, slowing them down, as another reviewer noted, "as if one were inside a miasma" (March [1939] cited in Inge 1995: 197).

2.3. Metafictional uses of pulp-fiction

The novel's interrogation of commercial literature can also readily be seen in the disastrous consequences that result from reading it as a truthful representation of reality. In "Old Man", the convict blames his imprisonment on "the writers, [...] the paper novels", who put the idea in his head that he could successfully rob a train, just like the fictional characters in his dime-store paperbacks (1939: 19).[5] In "The Wild Palms", Charlotte has so internalized romance novels that she abandons her husband and children, demands an abortion of her unwilling lover, and then later refuses to seek medical attention for the toxemia it produces because she learned in books, "that love and suffering are the same thing and that the value of love is the sum of what you have to pay for it" (1939: 43). Harry, for his part, is not unduly influenced by pulp-fiction (except as the victim of Charlotte's credulous reading), but rather must bear the weight of Faulkner's irony, as he –like the author at varying points in his career– must write pulp-fiction to make a living.

2.4. Subverting heteronormative gender representations

2.4.1. Critical reception of Harry and Charlotte

In addition to the metafictional uses of pulp-fiction in the novel, it is in Faulkner's treatment of gender that the subversion of popular literature, particularly hard-boiled crime fiction, truly reveals itself. More troubling to critics than the experimental format of the novel were the protagonists of "The Wild Palms", Harry and Charlotte, whose characterization made them virtually unrecognizable as possible people with whom readers could identify.[6] Reviewer William McFee claimed that Faulkner "outrages the intelligence of his readers and admirers with such preposterously distorted characters" ([1939] cited in Inge 1995: 193), while Mary-Carter Roberts argued, "[t]he poignancy of the adventure itself naturally suffers from the unnatural quality of the adventurers. The hero is pallid and the heroine is chromo" ([1939] cited in Inge 1995: 191). She went on to add:

> [T]he heroine is one of those awful monsters which male novelists from time to time create when they decide to forgo nature as a source of material and rummage about instead in the old grab-bag of desire, bringing up a half dozen or so isolated traits and arbitrarily shoving them together, making such a creature as has haunted a good many dreams since the world began but which nobody has ever yet met in the flesh —or could endure. ([1939] cited in Inge 1995: 191)

In effect, the terms "unnatural" and "distorted" refer euphemistically to the feminization of Harry and masculinization of Charlotte. These traits are particularly jarring, as they occur within the framework of a hard-boiled plot, which traditionally hinges upon male dominance over the female.

2.4.2. Moving beyond mere gender role inversion

Deborah Clarke has asserted that "Faulkner consistently questions cultural definitions of gender, and in ... (*The Wild Palms*], in particular, reveals their tenuous nature" (1995: 112). Nevertheless, as a genre, hard-boiled fiction has also consistently questioned cultural definitions of gender –but as an anxious response to social and economic changes occurring over the first half of the 20th century, which include the permanent entrance of women into the workforce, immigration, corporate capitalism and the new market system's rendering impossible the fulfilment of an individualistic masculine ideal. Yet rather than offer an alternative to the debilitating gender expectations whose impossibility fuelled the darkness and tragedy that often characterizes the noir genre, hard-boiled fiction presented a reactionary version of masculinity: brute strength, violence and either the absence of, or opposition to, women. As Christopher Breu defines it,

[T]he hard-boiled male was characterized by a tough, shell-like exterior, a prophylactic toughness that was organized around the rigorous suppression of affect and was mirrored by his detached laconic utterances and his instrumentalized, seemingly amoral actions. (2005: 1)

"The Wild Palms", however, rather than reify, often undermines hard-boiled representations of masculinity as it is the "awful monster", Charlotte who performs them: she is aggressive, violent, sexually dominant and the independent breadwinner in her extra-marital relationship. Harry, despite his role as the male protagonist, cooks, cleans, writes confessional erotica from a female point of view, and openly admits that Charlotte is a "better man" and a "better gentleman" than he (Chatto and Windus 1939: 123, 129). Character discourse in "The Wild Palms" is especially suggestive of the text's complex relationship with both pulp-fiction and the hard-boiled style of masculinity it projects; for as Faulkner breaks down normative representations of gender he also complicates the associations that produce reader anticipation, and hence, suspense. Language is a defining aspect of hard-boiled masculinity, which can be located in cool detachment, threats, cursing, slang, orthographic markers of pronunciation. The power and control present in hard-boiled language traditionally contribute to a sympathetic identification with the male protagonist, whom readers desire to see rise victorious from verbal conflict (Nyman 1997: 142). Again, when such language is deployed in "The Wild Palms", it is almost exclusively uttered by Charlotte: she is dry and ironic, curses, gives Harry orders, berates and belittles him.

The preservation of male power though its exertion over the feminine, a core value of hard-boiled fiction, is thus unravelled in the novel (Nyman 1997: 55). Notably, "The Wild Palms" is not merely an inversion of gender stereotypes that effectively uphold traditional masculinist values even as they are being performed by a woman.[7] For at other times, the values underlying hard-boiled language are ironically undercut by Harry's insight into the motivations behind tough-guy speech: fear, isolation, powerlessness, and the masking of pain. In the following example, Charlotte's husband, Rittenmeyer, has accompanied the couple to the train, should his wife decide at the last minute not to leave him. This is one of the few scenes of homosocial triangulation in the novel, ripe for conflict in a classic competition for a woman's love.[8] Rittenmeyer's tough talk nevertheless fails to create the suspense it might in a traditional hard-boiled novel as a result of its framing by Harry's direct thought:

(1)
Why, he's suffering, he's actually suffering, thinking how perhaps it is not the heart at all, not even the sensibilities, with which we suffer, but our capacity for grief or vanity or self-delusion or perhaps even merely masochism. "Go on", Rittenmeyer said. "Get out of the aisle". His voice was harsh, his hand almost rough as he pushed her into the seat and set the bag beside the other one. "Remember now. If I don't hear by the tenth of each month, I'm going to give the detective word. And no lies, see? No lies".... "I want to talk to you", he said in that seething repressed

voice. "Come on"... [Wilbourne]... thought again: *He is suffering; even circumstance, a trivial railroad time table, is making comedy of that tragedy which he must play to the bitter end or cease to breathe*. (50)

Harry's sensitivity, his ruminating on causes of suffering, make a caricature of the husband's toughness, intimating that it is nothing more than a shallow veneer to cover his pain. "The Wild Palms" thus moves beyond simply switching gender attributes between the male and female protagonists while still aligning itself with hard-boiled values regardless of who enacts them. The reader still identifies with Harry, even as he not only fails to speak and perform hard-boiled masculinity but effectively mocks the actors who do.

3. Repackaging *The Wild Palms*

3.1. Extraction

In direct conflict with the author's subversive approach to pulp-fiction, various stakeholders in the publication of *The Wild Palms* ironically pushed the novel into the very models of literary consumability Faulkner had originally set out to interrogate. When the New American Library of World Literature, Inc. published *The Wild Palms* as its first paperback title in 1948, they extracted –with Faulkner's express permission– the "Old Man" sections of the novel entirely (Schwartz 1988: 59). Not only did they assess the illicit love story as the more marketable aspect of the text, the foreclosure of suspense that "Old Man" had exacted on "The Wild Palms" was eliminated, producing a smoother, faster read. The paperback cover featured a bikini-clad woman with a parasol behind her; across the bottom a red banner announced, "From the author of 'Sanctuary'", Faulkner's most salacious novel.

3.2. Omission

Previously, in 1939, Chatto & Windus, Random House's counterpart in the UK, not only localized the novel to conform to British orthographic conventions and regional word use, but censored the text extensively. Intentionally or not, the British Charlotte was pushed back in line with the heteronormative standards, as her coarseness was softened by the omission of her most vulgar comments. In the Chatto & Windus edition, gone –in addition to most of her cursing and sexual innuendos– are her accusation of Harry working as a crossing guard "...so you can rape little girls in parks on Saturday afternoons!" (1939a: 220, 1939b: 202); her explanation for how she became pregnant: "...when the stove went out, my douche bag was hanging behind it. It froze and when we lit the stove again I forgot it and it burst" (1939a: 205, 1939b: 188); and her crude joke just before Harry performs the abortion: "We've done this lots of ways but not with knives, have we?" (1939a: 161, 1939b: 203). Crucial to the legacy of *The Wild Palms* in Spanish, when Borges translated the novel, he used the censored British version –whether or not he was aware of this censorship is still a mystery.[9] Yet, as we will see, even the pairing down of Charlotte's vulgar language, which pushed her into more traditional standards of femininity, appears insufficient to produce convincing enough suspense for the author of *Ficciones*.

3.3. Recreation

Borges was not exactly a fan of hard-boiled fiction, preferring instead puzzle-style detective novels such as those by C.K. Chesterton and Robert Louis Stevenson.[10] Yet, as indicated in numerous essays and book reviews, the plodding pace and extraneous details –which, as mentioned above, abound in both stories in *The Wild Palms* as integral parts of Faulkner's project of deconstructing pulp-fiction– Borges found practically insufferable. Given the Argentine's translation aesthetic of creative infidelity,[11] it is perhaps no surprise that, wherever possible, Borges picked up the pace and increased elements of danger and suspense through the elimination of the very stylistic details Faulkner had employed to distinguish *The Wild Palms* from traditional crime fictions. Interruptions in character dialogue, experimental discourse strategies, narrator interjections, parenthetical asides lasting several paragraphs were all eliminated or standardized in the translation through added punctuation, quotation marks, and italics.[12] Yet the most notable instances of increased suspense and danger in the text are carried out through Borges's exchanging of roles between Charlotte and Harry, confirming a foundational, cross-cultural assumption about the relationship between gender and genre in the 1930s and 40s: stable relations between a hard-boiled male and *femme fatale* being the necessary conditions for convincing suspense. In the examples that follow, it is clear that a deliberate choice has been made to alter the feminized characterization of Harry to bring him more in line with traditional, hard-boiled masculinity, and likewise, to push Charlotte back into heteronormative representations of femininity.

3.3.1. Shifting line breaks, shifting power

Continuing from the train scene above (see section 2.4.2.), one stop before the station at which Rittenmeyer intends to depart the train, Charlotte asks Harry if she may go speak with him. Harry is confused by the question, finding it absurd that she should ask permission to speak to her own husband. He imagines

Charlotte may be thinking of going back to him, and that if she turns to look at Harry, she is actually saying goodbye:

(2)
ST. "Can I go back and speak to him a minute?"
"Can you go? –"
"Hammond is the next station".
Why, he's your husband, he was about to say but caught himself. "It's the men's room", he said. "Maybe I had better–" But she had already risen and passed him; he thought: *If she stops and looks back at me it will mean she is thinking, 'Later I can always know that at least I told him good-bye'* and she did stop and they looked at each other, then she went on. (Faulkner 1939: 52)

In the Spanish version, a very different scene occurs. When Charlotte asks permission to see her husband, Harry coldly grants it, his question transformed into a reluctant concession. But in a displacement of Charlotte's words to his mouth, he then reminds her that the next station is the one at which Rittenmeyer will be leaving the train, as if warning her not to get off the train with him. When Charlotte walks away, Harry does not imagine *what* she is thinking, but merely *that* she is thinking:

(3)
TT. –¿Puedo ir un momento a hablarle, un minuto?
–Puedes… Hammond es la próxima estación.
Pero es tu marido, estuvo a punto de decir, pero se contuvo.
–Está en el compartimiento de los hombres –dijo–. Tal vez sería mejor que yo… Pero Carlota se había levantado y seguía adelante; él pensó: *Si se para y me mira querrá decir que está pensando. Más tarde sabré que al menos le dije adiós,* y se detuvo y se miraron y ella siguió. (Faulkner [1939]1940: 54)

Here, dominance is asserted as Harry is now in a position of power in which he may grant Charlotte permission to speak with her husband, and violence comes into play as he holds back anger rather than confusion when containing his, "pero es tu marido". Whether the removal of the quotation marks surrounding Charlotte's imagined dismissal were intentional or mere carelessness, the effect on Harry's characterization is a fatalistic attitude typical of hard-boiled males. He nonchalantly notes that at least *he* said goodbye, staunchly bracing himself for Charlotte not to return.

Charlotte does not get off the train with Rittenmeyer but follows through with her intention of running away. In the conversation that ensues, Charlotte concedes that she has returned, but admits that "it's not finished"; she might not be strong enough to resist the urge to return to her husband, should he purchase another ticket and get back on the train to allow her a few more stops to change her mind:

(4)

ST.   "So you came back", he said.
      "You didn't think I was. Neither did I".
      "But you did".
      "Only it's not finished. If he were to get back on the train, with a ticket to Slidell—"
      She turned, staring at him though she did not touch him. "It's not finished. It will have
      to be cut". (Faulkner 1939: 53)

The "cut" to which Charlotte is referring is a break to her emotional ties to Rittenmeyer. Knowing that only a passionate emotional experience will have the power to break those bonds, she demands that Harry book the couple a private cabin on the train, so they may make love for the very first time.

In the Spanish translation of this passage, Harry again takes on an air of authority and coldness more appropriate to hard-boiled fiction. Borges eliminates any sentimentality on Harry's part, and gives him one of Charlotte's lines to emphasize his dominant role.

(5)

TT.   –Así que has vuelto –dijo él.
      –Tú no lo creías, ni yo tampoco.
      –Pero no hemos concluido. Si vuelve al tren con un billete hasta Slidell.
      Se dio vuelta mirándolo pero sin tocarlo.
      –No hemos concluido. Hay que darle un corte. (Faulkner [1939]1940: 54)

Harry's "so you came back" takes on an ironic tone when his maudlin rejoinder, "but you did" is removed. Instead, Charlotte's line, "Only it's not finished" becomes his own. With Harry insisting that things are not finished, Charlotte's reply, "No hemos concluido. Hay que darle un corte", comes as the response to an order, rather than as her personal solution for dissolving the affective ties she still has to her husband. Thus, when she asks Harry to get a room for them, the full force of what she is asking for is lost. More in line with a typical *femme fatale*, Charlotte's request suggests her to be uncontrollably randy rather than to be making a rational decision about how to most effectively sever the emotional bonds that may hinder her life choices. What has become Harry's initial assertion that things are not over, that Charlotte's husband could get back on the train, also introduces the possibility for a showdown between the men in the narrative, adding an entirely new source of suspense to the story and bolstering Harry's toughness.

3.3.2. From virgin to potential murderer

The introduction of suspense through the suggestion of male competition occurs earlier in the translation as well. Prior to their running away together, when

Charlotte and Harry were deciding how to proceed with their love affair, Borges uses ambiguous line breaks to suggest an entirely new line of possible action:

(6)
ST.   "Can't you get the divorce?"
"On what grounds? He would fight it. And it would have to be here—a Catholic judge. So there's just one other thing. And it seems I can't do that".
"Yes", he said. "Your children".
For a moment she looked at him, smoking. "I wasn't thinking of them. I mean, I have already thought of them". (Faulkner 1939: 42)

The "just one other thing" that Charlotte cannot do is have an illicit affair, she refuses to sneak around. Harry naively understands that the one other thing she cannot do is run away, because she could not leave her children. Contrasting Harry's sentimentalism against Charlotte's cynicism, she corrects him, and makes clear that her children have ceased to be a factor in her decision making. In translation, however, the roles are again reversed:

(7)
TT.   –¿Y tú no puedes pedir el divorcio?
–¿Con qué motivos? Él pleitearía. Y tendría que ser aquí, con un juez católico.
–Sólo queda una solución. Y para ésa parece que yo no sirvo.
–Sí –dijo él–. Tus hijos.
Lo miró, por un momento, fumando. *cut off line*
–No pensaba en ellos. Quiero decir que ya he pensado en ellos. (Faulkner [1939]1940: 54)

In the English, Charlotte's comment, "[s]o there's just one other thing. And it seems I can't do that", is part of the previous section of her speech. In the translation, however, that line is cut off, and put in dialogue below, effectively becoming Harry's in normal turn-taking. Harry, thereby boldly and fatalistically states that only one other solution remains, seemingly implying homicide. Harry's next words remain a separate line of dialogue, yet also must be his, as the dialogue marker "dijo él" clearly indicates. In other words, though tough enough to murder Charlotte's husband, Harry is sufficiently benevolent not to do so for the sake of her children (who incidentally are two girls). Interestingly enough, in subsequent editions of the translation, this scene was amended to repair the double turn-taking that occurs from Borges's placement of Charlotte's "just one other thing" on a separate line. Rather than return the line to her, however, an entirely new line of dialogue was created! The following passage can be found in the one of the latest printing of *Las palmeras salvajes*, released by Delbolsillo in 2006:

(8)
TT.   –¿Y tú no puedes pedir el divorcio?

–¿Con qué motivos? Él pleitearía. Y tendría que ser aquí, con un juez católico.
–Sólo queda una solución. Y para ésa parece que yo no sirvo.
–**¿Qué no sirves?** *New line created*
–Sí –dijo él–. Tus hijos.
Lo miró, por un momento, fumando.
–No pensaba en ellos. Quiero decir que ya he pensado en ellos. (Faulkner [1939] 2006: 45, *my emphasis*)

The addition of the line for Charlotte, "¿Qué no sirves?", eliminates any ambiguity as to who is speaking –or to whom is in charge. Now without question, Harry proves his toughness as he boldly implies that were it not for his lover's children he would murder her husband. A revision of all the editions of *Las palmeras salvajes* remains to be conducted in order to determine the point at which this line was inserted into the translation. The fact that editors would take the target text farther away rather than closer to the source suggests that some heteronormative concepts regarding male and female roles are still firmly lodged in place.

4. Conclusion

The transformations to *The Wild Palms*, both at the hands of Faulkner's editors and his translator, strongly suggest that their visions of credible suspense hinge upon stable and traditional definitions of gender, and that increasing suspense was essential to its success with readers. Compared to censorship, the elimination of "Old Man" and provocative packaging, Borges's revisions in *Las palmeras salvajes* are perhaps the most creative, and certainly the most subtle. And possibly the most effective. In both the train ride and the plotting of their escape from New Orleans, Borges's inversions and inventions of Harry's and Charlotte's speech are directly tied to a transformation in the dynamics of the plot, creating possibilities for masculine aggression, and hence suspense, that were entirely absent from the source text.

While his attempt to masculinize Harry and feminize Charlotte are impossible to maintain for the length of the novel, Borges appears to use individual passages from the text to create fragments of the sort of story he would have chosen to write. Upon reading Borges's version, José María Arguedas wrote of *Las palmeras salvajes*, "es una maravilla, la mujer me parece superextraordinaria" ([1940] cited in González Vigil 2000: 88). Yet who might the Peruvian author have encountered had Charlotte not been censored by Chatto & Windus and then subdued by Borges? The words stolen from her mouth and put into Harry's made him more of a hard-boiled man, one better fit for the role of renegade lover and potential murderer. Rather than pliant and pleading as he is in the English, Harry becomes dominant, calculating and cold, exhibiting exactly the kind of toughness Faulkner sought to undermine with *The*

Wild Palms. While the kinds of changes Borges exacted upon both the plot and the characterization are surprising, we may do well to avoid assuming that they are unique. The oft-lamented invisibility of the translator is the perfect cloak *Venuti* behind which one may hide the creative introduction of her or his own literary aspirations into any translation.

---

[1] For more on Faulkner's anxiety over and creative response to his association with pulp-fiction, see Wenska (1999-2000), King (1998), Earle (2009) and Breu (2005).

[2] In *Hard-Boiled Masculinities* (2005), Christopher Breu finds this same mass vs. high culture dynamic in Faulkner's *Light in August* (1932).

[3] One reviewer of *The Wild Palms* even asked: "What prevents Faulkner from perceiving that his subject matter isn't adequate to the demands of his theme?" (Hart 1995: 202)

[4] Ted Robinson (1939): "And perhaps we are lucky to get two novels for the price of one. But I can't see the point in mixing them" (Hart 1995: 192); William McFee (1939): "*The Wild Palms* is a curious production likely to confuse the average reader because it presents, intertwined, two separate themes" (Hart 1995: 192).

[5] All quotations are from the Chatto & Windus edition of *The Wild Palms* unless otherwise noted.

[6] This essay will deal primarily with "The Wild Palms" sections of the novels. For more on Borges's translation of "Old Man", see Leone (2011).

[7] Nyman sees a less successful questioning of gender through Horace McCoy's use of role reversal between Robert and Gloria in his 1935 thriller, *They Shoot Horses, Don't They?*: "Although McCoy's novel points to the possibility of new constructions of gender, it is not extremely radical in this respect. It implies that the only way to cope with the world is to adopt a masculine stance, as can be seen in the significance of the issues of power and domination [...] Thus the novel remains obedient to the genre, as can also be seen in its way of understanding woman as Other" (1997: 133).

[8] All references to homosocial desire and homosocial triangulation derive from their treatment in Sedgwick (1985).

[9] Unaware that Borges based his translation upon the censored Chatto & Windus version, a number of scholars have erroneously compared Borges's translation to the Random House edition and come to the conclusion that he censored the text himself –venturing that curse words, and the issues of sex and abortion, were distasteful to him, and possibly, to his mother. See Leone (2011) for an extended discussion of this debate.

[10] In a talk he gave on the subject of crime fiction, Borges stated: "Actualmente, el género policial ha decaído mucho en Estados Unidos. El género policial es realista, de violencia, un género de violencias sexuales también. En todo caso, ha desaparecido. Se ha olvidado el origen intelectual del relato policial" ("El cuento policial" OC IV 2007: 239)

[11] For an excellent analysis of Borges's aesthetic of creative infidelity, see Waisman (2005).

[12] The impulse to include clear distinctions between character and narrator is an impulse found ubiquitously across Borges's translations of English language fiction. See Leone (2011) and Willson (2004).

Bibliography

Primary Sources

Borges, Jorge Luis. 1999. *Jorge Luis Borges in Sur, 1931-1980*. Buenos Aires: Emecé.
———. 2007. 'The Wild Palms' in *Obras completas* IV. Buenos Aires: Emecé. 527-528.
Faulkner, William. 1939a. *The Wild Palms*. New York: Random House.
———. 1939b. *The Wild Palms*. London: Chatto and Windus.
———. 1940. *Las palmeras salvajes*. Translated by Jorge Luis Borges. Buenos Aires: Sudamericana.
———. 2006. *Las palmeras salvajes*. Translated by Jorge Luis Borges. Buenos Aires: Delbolsillo.
Inge, M. Thomas. 1995. 'The Wild Palms' in William Faulkner: *The Contemporary Reviews*. Cambridge: Cambridge UP.

Secondary Sources

Blotner, Joseph (ed.). 1978. *Selected Letters of William Faulkner*. New York: Vintage.
Borges, Jorge Luis. 2007. 'El cuento policial' in *Obras completas* IV. Buenos Aires: Emecé. 229-240.
———. 2007. 'Emma Zunz' in *Obras completas* I. Buenos Aires: Emecé. 677-682.
Breu, Christopher. 2005. *Hard-Boiled Masculinities*. Minneapolis: U of Minnesota Press.
Clarke, Deborah. 1994. Robbing the Mother: Women in Faulkner. Jackson: University of Mississippi Press.
Earle, David M. 2009. *Re-Covering Modernism: Pulps, Paperbacks, and the Prejudice of Form*. Surrey: Ashgate.
Even-Zohar, Itamar. 2000. 'The Position of Translated Literature Within the Literary Polysystem' in Venuti, Lawrence (ed.) *The Translation Studies Reader*. New York and London: Routledge. 192-197.
GonzálezVigil, Ricardo. 2000. 'Introducción' to *Los ríos profundos*. José María Arguedas' Madrid: Cátedra. 9-108.
Hermans, Theo. 1985. *The Manipulation of literature: studies in literary translation*. London and New York: Routledge.
Hubin, Allen J. 1979. *The bibliography of crime fiction, 1749-1975: listing of all mystery, detective, suspense, police, and gothic fiction in book form published in the English language*. Del Mar: Publisher's Inc.
King, Vincent Allan. 1998. 'The wages of pulp: The use and abuse of fiction in William Faulkner's *The Wild Palms*' in *Mississippi Quarterly* 51(3): 503-26.
Lefevere, André. 1992. *Translation, Rewriting, and the Manipulation of Literary Fame*. London and New York:Routledge
Leone, Leah. 2011. *Displacing the Mask: Jorge Luis Borges and the Translation of Narrative*. PhD thesis. The University of Iowa.
Nyman, Jopi. 1997. *Men Alone: Masculinity, Individualism, and Hard-Boiled Fiction*. New York and Amsterdam: Rodopi.
Reilly, John M. (ed.). 1985. *Twentieth-Century Crime and Mystery Writers*. New York: St. Martin's. Publications
Sedgwick, Eve Kosofsky. 1985. *Between Men: English Literature and Male Homosocial Desire*. New York: Columbia UP.
Schwartz, Lawrence H. 1988. *Creating Faulkner's Reputation: The Politics of Modern Literary Criticism*. Knoxville: University of Tennessee Press.
Simon, Sherry. 1996. *Gender in Translation: Cultural Identity and the Politics of Transmission*. London and New York: Routledge.
Toury, Gideon. 1995. *Descriptive Translation Studies – And Beyond*. Amsterdam and Philadelphia: John Benjamins.

von Flotow, Luise. 1997. *Translation and Gender. Translating in the 'Era of Feminism'*. Manchester: St. Jerome.

Waisman, Sergio. 2005. *Borges and Translation: The Irreverence of the Periphery*. Lewisburg: Bucknell UP.

Wenska, Walter. 1999-2000. "'There's a Man with a Gun over There": Faulkner's Hijackings of Masculine Popular Culture' in *Faulkner Journal* 15(1-2): 35-60.

Willson, Patricia. 2004. *La constelación del sur, traductores y traducciones en la literatura argentina del siglo XX*. Buenos Aires: Siglo XXI.

Jorge Luis Borges
(1899 - 1986).

Part II

Translation of language variation and foreign language use

Chapter 5: Chester Himes's *For Love of Imabelle* in Spanish: Josep Elias's "absurdly" overcompensated slang

Daniel Linder

Abstract
In order to prevent the standardization of slang, Josep Elias i Cornet, Spanish translator of Chester Himes's *For Love of Imabelle* (1957) overcompensated. So much additional slang was included in his *Por amor a Imabelle*, published in Editorial Bruguera's classic Libro amigo series in 1980, that a translator's prologue and glossary were introduced. Elias composed his version with the help of local underworld figure, Manuel Sánchez Torres, a.k.a. "el Palomo", Curiously, Elias's translation seems perfectly matched to the "absurdity" of the conditions under which Himes wrote the novel. Commissioned to write it by Gallimard's Série Noire editor, Marcel Duhamel, Himes created Harlem cops, Coffin Ed Johnson and Grave Digger Jones, and certainly exaggerated their slang lexicon for the benefit of a French audience who only stereotypically envisioned black Harlem characters. However, the speech of main character Jackson, a prudish and devout "square" who only speaks in his "native dialect" when he is nervous and frightened, reveals some of the complexity of the speech universe of Himes's characters. The article reveals that some cases of compensation of slang likely stemmed from the French version which Elias certainly consulted. The 2009 retranslation by Mª Dolores Ábalos is also discussed.

Keywords: Compensation, novela negra, Série Noire, slang, translation

1. Introduction

Translating sociolinguistic varieties of language such as African American English Vernacular (AAEV) and specialized non-standard lexis such as underworld slang challenge both the limits of translation studies theory and professional practice (Brodovich 1997; Rabadán 1991; Mattiello 2009; Zauberga 1994). When faced with a literary passage, typically a dialogue, laden with the specific features of the non-standard language variety used in a fictional portrayal of the urban streets of Harlem, for instance, translators often substitute variety for variety, seeking to use in their target texts comparable target-culture equivalents. Seeking such a target text variety may actually be possible, as there are urban sociolects in Spanish, for instance, that share many of the features and functions of the source text variety, however the use of these very target-culture specific varieties can trigger undesirable connotations and associations unique to the target language and so the variety-for-variety solution tends to be unsatisfactory. AAEV in films is often replaced with southern peninsular

Spanish dialects or the dialects of ethnic gypsies that mimic some of the features of the source text variety though these dialects are not specifically urban. Black characters in films are often given Cuban accents when dubbed into European peninsular Spanish. However, the accents stir up new associations of Spanish target-text culture that jar with the film's image content (see Mayoral 1999).

In the case of slang, i.e. specialized non-standard lexis used typically to signify belonging to a group and referring to the group's activities and interests, similar solutions are often taken. The lexicon of the criminal underworld in Harlem, for instance, is often replaced in literary texts with slang terms from a target language city with an established criminal milieu. As with the variety-for-variety solution, slang-for-slang translation is also possible, as large urban centers such as Barcelona have local criminals and gangs who use local lexis. Slang-for-slang translation that is too specific of a particular country or city can draw up new connotations and associations in the target text which the source text did not have, and translated slang that is extremely contemporary at the time of publication can quickly age and soon make the target text unacceptable to future readers. In order to avoid such negative effects, standard language equivalents of slang are often used. Slang-for-slang translation can only exist where there are equivalents in the target language with which to replace them, but there is not a target text slang term available. In these cases, translators of literary slang must also replace slang terms with standard equivalents. There are a number of studies which have found evidence of standardization in novel translation (Glewwe 2012; Matiello 2007; Stolt 2010). There are two articles that examined slang in J.D. Salinger's *The Catcher in the Rye*, with similar findings (Ulvydienė and Abramovaitė 2012; Andújar Moreno 2009). These studies unearthed not only evidence of standardization of slang translation, but also evidence of omission of slang, mistranslation and other specificities. Standardization, i.e. the replacement of non-standard language varieties or lexis with standard language forms, is often in the interest of target text stakeholders, such as publishers, who lengthen the marketable life of their published works in inverse proportion to how much local, time-anchored slang they contain.

A promising case to analyze slang in translation is the Harlem cycle of novels by Chester Himes, which feature the tough New York City detectives Gravedigger Jones and Coffin Ed Johnson. These novels were written in a style that conscientiously emulated Dashiell Hammett, who used slang liberally in his novels. Slang in the detective fiction novel is defined as non-standard specialized lexical units which refer to criminals and criminal activities, detection and pursuit of criminals, and prosecution of crime, and also general non-standard lexical units typically associated with detective fiction and referring to such things as alcohol, money, tobacco, cars, and so on (Linder 2001). It should be noted that use of substandard language (incorrect usages often indicating a sociolect) and non-standard vocabulary (regionalisms, colloquialisms and vulgarisms), also contribute to the overall effect of slang in fiction. Himes's novel *For Love of Imabelle* (1957), the first in the series, contains an abundance of slang, which posed the challenges described above to the novel's French (1958) and Spanish (1980) translators.

There is a technique which can counteract the loss of slang through standardization which is called compensation. In places where the source text contained no slang, but where it exists in the target language, compensation can be used to create a similar effect. Harvey (1995) defines compensation as "a technique for making up the loss of a source text effect by recreating a similar effect in the target text through means that are specific to the target text language and / or target text." (1995: 66). Though not an extremely common practice, because it involves a translator's direct intervention in the target text rather than the more customary invisible role, compensation is indeed used in target texts (Linder 2013, 2011, 2000). Less common still are cases of overcompensation, when the amount of slang terms in the target texts exceeds the number of slang terms in the source text.

2. *For Love of Imabelle* has line upon line of cryptic slang… but not here

Josep Elias i Cornet's *Por amor a Imabelle*, the first Spanish version of Himes's novel, clearly contains overcompensation of slang, as even a cursory reading of any page at random reveals. Perceptive Argentinian literary critic, Pablo Sapere (Buenos Aires), in an online article entitled "Sepulturero, Ataúd y el policial muy negro", commented on how indecipherable portions of the Spanish version are, pointing to the particular difficulty of the emphasized sentence in TT2 (the French translation, TT1, is included here because it will be referred to in section 5 below):

(1)
ST. "Listen, Marshal, I swear to God I didn't have nothing to do with that. I don't even know how do it. The little man called Hank who got away is the counterfeiter. He's the only one who got the paper."
"Don't worry about them, Jackson. I'll get them too. But I've already got you, and I'm taking you down to the Federal Building. So I'm warning you, anything you say to me will be used against you in court." (Himes 2011/1957: 21-22)

TT1. –Ecoutez, monsieur l'Officier de Police. Que le bon Dieu me confonde si je mens. Le faux-monnayeur, c'est le p'tit mec qu'a filé. C'est lui seul qu'avait le papier pour.
–T'casse pas la tête pour les autres, Jackson. Je les choperai en temps voulu. Mais toi, je te tiens et tu vas me suivre à la police fédérale. Te voilà donc prévenu -- tout ce que tu me diras sera utilisé contre toi au moment du procès. (Himes 1958: 14)

TT2. –Oiga, inspector, se lo juro por Dios que yo no tengo nada que ver con todo esto. Si ni siquiera sé cómo se hace. El canijo que se llama Hank, el que se ha largado, ése sí que falsifica. Es el único que entiende con el papel.

–No me llores por ésos, Jackson. *También los atorigaré. Pero a ti te atorigué ya, y te voy a llevar al gobi.* Con que te aviso, todo lo que me puches puede servir de marrón contra ti en el juicio. (Himes 1980: 19)

Sapere mentions how useful the glossary at the end of the book is for resolving such cryptic slang, as the wordlist contains atorigar=detener (arrest) and gobi=cárcel (jail). With the aid of this resource, the sentence can be understood. In my English back translation: "I'll nab them, too. But I have already nabbed you, and I am going to take you to the clink." Surprisingly, however, there is absolutely no slang in the source text.

What I will attempt to do is understand how so much slang could have been introduced in places where *For Love of Imabelle* (later published as *A Rage in Harlem* 1965) contained none, and under what circumstances a translation such as *Por amor a Imabelle* (Bruguera 1980), so overcompensated in very local Spanish slang, could have been produced. Very uniquely, the Spanish translation by Josep Elias attributes expert lexical consulting to Manuel Sánchez Torres, "el Palomo", and also contains a prologue and a glossary by the translator. I will also be discussing the French translation entitled *La Reine des Pommes (The Five-Cornered Square)* (Gallimard 1958) and its very special relationship with the English source text.

The ways in which slang is used in the novel and the ways in which it was translated into French and Spanish will be analyzed. Slang is used by virtually all characters except for the novel's main character, Jackson, who only uses it when nervousness and fright make him slip into his "native dialect" and when he is trying to dupe white police officers. In the study which follows, slang usage in the source text is identified then traced in the target text versions. Instances of compensation in the French target text by Minnie Danzas are identified and compared with the Spanish version. Instances of compensation in the Spanish version by Josep Elias i Cornet are also identified and compared with the preceding French translation and with the subsequent 2009 Spanish retranslation by Mª Dolores Ábalos.

3. Chester Himes to Marcel Duhamel: "OK, I'll write for the Série Noire"

The writing of the originally titled *The Five-Cornered Square* is virtually insepararable from the production of the French translation by Minnie Danzas entitled *La Reine des Pommes*. Himes, who had never written detective fiction before 1957, was approached by Marcel Duhamel, the Éditions Gallimard Série Noire editor who had translated *S'il braille, lâche-le* [*If He Hollers, Let him Go*] in 1948 for another publisher. Duhamel suggested Himes read Peter Cheney and Raymond Chandler, but especially Dashiell Hammett, and write a novel for the Série Noire using his own curt, short sentence style which was not dissimilar to

Hammett's. After Himes agreed, and received an advance from Duhamel, he started writing and agreed to show what he had written after he had produced about 80 pages. Upon submitting the first instalment, Duhamel said that he needed to introduce some police officers, which Himes then did by introducing his Harlem series characters, Coffin Ed Johnson and Grave Digger Jones. Minnie Danzas, Duhamel's head translator and also a literary advisor, confirmed that the novel could indeed be translated successfully into French, and she began translating the finished parts as quickly as Himes delivered them. The novel was completed on January 18, 1957 (Himes 1976: 111). This novel was first translated into French, then published in English, after which it was published in French; however, the remaining novels in the Harlem series featuring Coffin Ed and Grave Digger appeared in French first (Polito 1997: 883).

In order to grasp Chester Himes's mindset during the writing process, and understand my use of the word "absurd" in the title, consider the following very famous quote from the second volume of Himes's autobiography, entitled *My Life of Absurdity,* in which he describes how he felt as a black ex-patriot fleeing racism trying to live off his "serious" writing but being commissioned to write stereotypically of black Americans within a formulaic genre typical of whites:

> I would sit in my room and become hysterical thinking about the wild, incredible story I was writing. But it was only for the French, I thought, and they would believe anything about Americans, black or white, if it was bad enough. And I thought I was writing realism. It never occurred to me that I was writing absurdity. Realism and absurdity are so similar in the lives of American blacks one cannot tell the difference. (Himes 1976: 109)

Himes, in his autobiography, further clarified that he was not writing realism, though he made it perfectly clear that in being absurd he had the ulterior motive of making Harlem "his" literary space, i.e. a black literary space, much like Hammett's was San Francisco, and Chandler's was Los Angeles.

> I didn't really know what it was like to be a citizen of Harlem; I had never worked there, raised children there, been hungry, sick or poor there. (…) The Harlem of my books was never meant to be real; I never called it real; I just wanted to take it away from the white man if only in my books. (Himes 1976: 126)

The main character, Jackson, is a square, a completely atypical character. A "square" is defined in the American Dictionary of Slang as "one easy to deceive, trick or victimize because of his lack of worldly wisdom or knowledge of modern attitudes" (Wentworth and Berg 1975 [1960]: 513). For a good visual image of "five-cornered square" Jackson, one must see Forrest Whitaker as Jackson in the film *A Rage in Harlem* (1991); devoutly religious and slightly pudgy, Jackson wears a bowtie, round glasses and hugs his belongings in front of him when he walks down the dangerous Harlem streets. Jackson falls into the unscrupulous clutches of Imabelle, his "high-yellow" woman", defined by the

New Dictionary of American Slang as "a light-skinned black person, esp. an attractive young woman" (Chapman 1986: 207), who suckers him into losing fifteen hundred dollars, or fifteen Cs in a confidence trick called "The Blow". Jackson willingly contributed his fifteen Cs because he believed the men Imabelle introduced him to could raise the value of his fifteen one-hundred-dollar bills to one-thousand-dollar bills, in other words fifteen Gs. In order to catch the confidence tricksters later, Jackson agrees to act as the sucker again in "the lost gold mine pitch" and lead Coffin Ed Johnson and Grave Digger Jones to the thieves' lair, where they find Imabelle. Because Jackson is such a square, he refuses to believe even then that Imabelle is involved in any wrongdoing.

La Reine des Pommes (The Five-Cornered Square) was published in 1958 as number 419 in Gallimard's Série Noire collection; the French text was "traduit de l'americain par Minnie Danzas". The book contained a number of praiseworthy comments on the jacket flaps, including one blurb by Jean Giono that, translated into English, said "I give you all of Hemingway, Dos Passos and Fitzgerald for this Chester Himes" (Himes 1976: 181). This was incredibly high acclaim for a black writer of any stature, and for the first black writer to publish in the Série Noire the praise led to further acclaim. *La Reine des Pommes* won the Grand Prix de la Littérature Policière in 1958, and Chester Himes continued writing the Harlem series of detective novels featuring Coffin Ed Johnson and Grave Digger Jones, though many of the remaining novels in the series were published first in French, then in English (Polito 1997: 883)

4. Josep Elias, translator, and "El Palomo", urban underworld slang expert: We'll translate Himes like never before ... with paratexts

Now, let us look at the Spanish translation by Josep Elias i Cornet. This version was published as volume 48 in the Novela negra series in the Libro amigo collection of Barcelona-based popular publisher, Bruguera; the text was produced with the acknowledged lexical expertise of Manuel Sánchez Torres, "el Palomo", and the text is preceded by a prologue entitled "Sobre la traducción" and followed by a three-page "Glosario".

Elias makes a string of assumptions about the source text that determine his decision-making. First, Elias assumes Himes is realistically portraying the way people speak in Harlem. In the prologue, it becomes very clear that this is true: "On the face of it, the language used by black people in Harlem, where all the novels featuring Coffin Ed and Grave Digger Jones take place, is absolutely untranslatable, both because of its lexical peculiarities and its syntactic structure." (*my translation*, Himes 2003: 9)

Secondly, Josep Elias chooses a real Spanish cultural equivalent, i.e. the slang used in the Spanish urban underworld, namely "the slang of our so-called urban underworld" to represent "the language of the blacks in Harlem" in the translation (*my translation*, Himes 2003: 9). This equivalence, in his view, is established based on the common denominator of "picaresque, sordidness, imposed violence as the only permissible ways of life in marginalized cultures". (*my translation*, Himes 2003: 9)

Thirdly, Elias chooses a real-world lexical advisor, Manuel Sánchez Torres, a.k.a. El Palomo, who he acknowledges in the prologue: "Lastly, I would like to thank Manuel Sánchez Torres, formerly known in his barrio as "El Palomo", for the explanations and revelations about slang usage that he has provided me with". (*my translation*, Himes 2003: 10)

Finally, he chooses to include a glossary "for the benefit of uninitiated readers", though the glossary "sounds" so very local that for the Spanish reader it could hardly be expected to trigger anything suggestive of black Harlem speech at all (*my translation*, Himes 2003: 9). Consider this list of equivalents:

Ahuecar: Marcharse
Birlar: Hurtar
Camelar: Engatusar, Engañar
Currar: Trabajar, Pegar una paliza
Currelar: Trabajar
Enchiquerar: Encarcelar
Famurria: Familia

Guita: Dinero
Mogollón: Botín. Cantidad de algo
Pringar: Actuar: Salir mal las cosas
Remanflinflar: Importar poco
Trinca (nuevo de): Recién estrenado
Viaje (atizar un): Golpear
(Himes 2003: 221-223)

One biographical item may explain how Josep Elias i Cornet (1941-1982), Catalan-language poet and (mostly) French-Spanish translator, may have chosen to use excessive compensation. In 1972, Elias translated Raymond Chandler's *Farewell, My Lovely*, which for nearly thirty years was the "classic" version of Chandler's second novel. About that translation we know:

- Elias's version is critically acclaimed, particularly regarding its rendering of slang (Morán 1975: 38)
- It contains intensified colloquial language (Abio 2004; Franco and Abio 2009)
- It contains intensified local, criminal slang (Linder 2012)
- Elias used his own inventiveness to stray from the ST meaning entirely in a number of instances (Linder 2011)
- It was translated from the English, though portions of the text were certainly translated in conjunction with or with some support from the French target text. (Linder 2011: 285)

Perhaps based on the success of his previous experience with Chandler, Elias wanted to go one step beyond, and he may have been encouraged by a certain amount of intensification and compensation he found in the French version.

5. The French connection: compensation using substandard language and nonstandard vocabulary

Let us examine one example of how the French version contains compensations that Elias may have used as his source text or which may have inspired him. In example 2 below, the same two characters as in example 1 above are speaking. Main character Jackson is speaking to a fake U.S. Marshal who has caught him trying to raise the value of U.S. currency with Imabelle and other conspirators. Jackson is extremely nervous, and it is very important to note what the narrative voice tells us of his control over substandard language use: "Jackson attended a Negro college in the south, but whenever he was excited or scared he began talking in his native dialect." (Himes 2011: 21) There was proof of such substandard usage in example 1 above ("didn't have nothing to do with that") and there is further proof in example 3 below ("I've done lost" and "Ain't that punishment enough?"). The phony Federal Marshal, however, avoids any such use of substandard language (incorrect usages often indicating a sociolect), and he also avoids using any non-standard vocabulary (regionalisms, colloquialisms and vulgarisms), as these would provide clues of his illegitimacy and lead Jackson to suspect him.

In the Spanish translation below we notice that Jackson uses no substandard language; the U.S. Marshal uses no substandard language but he does use an exorbitant amount of slang, i.e. non-standard vocabulary (*andoba, enchiquerar, menda, currelo, chorizo*). The amount of slang used by Elias in this segment prompted prologuist Juan Eslava Galán to make the following comment on the stark reality Himes is reflecting in the example: "This is Himes: the underworld slang, the crude and atrocious reality" (*my translation*, 2003: 7). The language used by these two characters seems reversed in the Spanish translation, with Jackson using standard language and the U.S. Marshal using non-standard lexis.

When we examine the French version which Elias certainly looked at while preparing his Spanish version, we see that both Jackson's and the U.S. Marshal's speech contain substandard language (for instance, the misuse of the negative by Jackson, who says "vous croyez pas" instead of "vous ne croyez pas", but also by the Marshal, who twice misuses the negative, first saying "t'es pas le premier" instead of "tu n'es pas le premier" and then "je tarde pas" instead of "je ne tarde pas"). We also see that Jackson's speech contains non-standard French in the form of slang terms (pognon=argent, taule=prison). In the French version, therefore, both Jackson's and the U.S. Marshal's speech contain substandard language, and Jackson's speech also contains non-standard vocabulary. Both the Spanish and French versions have compensated with respect to the U.S. Marshal's speech, which in the source text was completely standard and in the target texts is now loaded with substandard language (French version) and non-standard vocabulary (French and Spanish versions).

(2)
ST. "You could have a little mercy," he said. "Just a little of the milk of human mercy. I've
done lost all my money in this deal already. Ain't that punishment enough? Do I have to
go to jail too?"
"Jackson, you're not the first man I've arrested for a crime. Suppose I'd let off
everybody. Where would I be then? Out of a job. Broke and hungry. Soon I'd be on the
other side of the law, a criminal myself." (Himes 2011/1957: 23-24)

TT1. –Vous pourriez avoir un brin d'pitié, tout d'même! dit-il. La pitié, ça soulève les
montagnes! J'y ai déjà paumé tout mon pognon, dans c'bizness. Vous croyez pas que
j'suis assez puni comme ça, dites? Faut-y vraiment que j'aille en taule, par-dessus le
marché?
–Jackson, t'es pas le premier que j'arrête pour acte d'iniquité. Supposition que je
relâche tous les malfaiteurs que j'appréhende… qu'est-ce que je deviens? Chômeur! Le
ventre creux et les poches vides. Et, du coup, je tarde pas à passer de l'aut'côté de la
barrière. Je me fais malfaiteur, comme vous aut'. (Himes 1958: 16)

TT2. –Podría tener un poco de piedad –dijo–. Sólo una pizca de piedad humana. He perdido
todo mi dinero en este lío. ¿No he recibido ya suficiente castigo? ¿Y encima he de ir a
la cárcel?
–Jackson, no eres el primer andoba que enchquero por tocar teclas. Supónte que suelto
a todos los que cojo. ¿Y qué del menda, entonces? Que de currelo, nanay. Gasusa y
miseria. Pronto me tiraría al otro lado de la ley y el chorizo lo sería yo mismo. (Himes
1980: 21)

The French translation of example 1 above also contains substandard language
("t'casse pas" instead of "ne te casse pas") and non-standard vocabulary
(mec=homme) in both Jackson's and the U.S. Marshal's speech, whereas in the
source text there is only substandard language in Jackson's speech.

French translator Minnie Danzas used substandard language and non-
standard vocabulary in all dialogues, regardless of when they intentionally
contained standard speech (for instance, Jackson, unless he was excited and
scared, and the U.S. Marshal, as he wanted to avoid suspicion). The Spanish
translator, who on a previous occasion had used a French translation as a source
text, may have transferred some of the solutions in the French translation to the
Spanish version, though he was careful to leave Jackson's speech completely
devoid of substandard features and non-standard vocabulary (even when he did
use them, as in examples 1 and 2). However, going beyond the compensation of
the French translator, he highly exaggerated the nonstandard and substandard
features of all other dialogues, even when they contained none of these features
(for instance, the U.S. Marshal).

6. Overcompensation in Spanish, with a touch of French

In what follows, I am going to study specifically the slang in one more example
from the *For Love of Imabelle*, *La Reine des Pommes (The Five-Cornered
Square)*, and *Por amor a Imabelle*. Using a three-code identification scheme I
am going to illustrate slang usage in the English source texts and how some of

those instances were preserved in the French and Spanish versions. Other types of nonstandard vocabulary such as colloquialisms, regionalisms and vulgarisms, clearly present in all of the examples, are not analyzed.

The next step in the analysis was to identify how compensation for slang was used in the French text then possibly preserved in the Spanish text, which are in italics. Instances of compensation in French were identified, with recourse to the *L'argot de la Série Noire, Vol. 1: L'argot des traducteurs*, a very unique dictionary that traces the slang used by the Série Noire translators, and two native-speaking expert informants, Danielle Dubroca and Chloé Signès, for whose generous help and enthusiastic support I am grateful.

The instances of slang in the source text are identified using *italics*, as are the instances of slang preservation in the French and Spanish target texts. Instances of slang compensation in the French target text which were preserved in the Spanish target text were identified using ***bold italics***. The instances of slang compensation which occurred solely in the Spanish target texts are identified using **bold underlining**.

In example 3 below, Jackson is speaking with a fellow customer at a bar in Harlem where he is supposed to show his "phony roll" of money and be led to Gus Parsons, who will treat him as a sucker in the "lost-gold-mine pitch". As in example 1, Jackson is "excited and scared" and begins "talking in his native dialect" ("You're name ain't Gus Parsons, is it?"); the other man also uses substandard language, though much more intensely ("Everybody in here lookin' for something, ain't they?" and "See them ...?") and he also uses non-standard vocabulary (*a trick, roll a drunk*).

(3)
ST. "Everybody in here lookin' for something, ain't they?" the man next to him said. Jackson gave a start. "Looking for something?"
"See them whores, they're looking for *a trick*. See them muggers ganged around the door, they're looking for a drunk *to roll*. These *jokers* in here are just waiting for a man *to flash* his money."
"Seems like I've seen you before," Jackson said. "You're name ain't Gus Parsons, is it?"
The man looked at Jackson suspiciously and began moving away. "What you want to know my name for?"
"I just thought I knew you," Jackson said (...) (104) (Himes 2011/1957: 104)

TT1. –Ici tout le monde a l'air d'être à l'affût, pas vrai? fit le voisin de Jackson. Jackson sursauta.
–A l'affût ? articula-t-il.
–Vous les voyez, *les **tapineuses***? Eh bien, elles sont à l'affût d'*un flanche*. Et *les cravateurs*, là, près de la porte ? Ils comptent bien *faire un pionnard*. Tous ces *tocards*, ils sont à l'affût, des fois qu'*un mec* oublierait de planquer son *fric*.
–J'ai comme une idée que je vous ai déjà aperçu quelque part, dit Jackson. Vous vous appelleriez pas Gus Parsons, par hasard?
L'homme lança à Jackson un regard soupçonneux et fit mine de s'éloigner :
–C'est pourquoi faire que vous voulez savoir ***mon blase***? demande-t-il.

–J'ai cru que je vous connaissais, c'est tout, dit Jackson (…) (88) (*my emphasis*, Himes 1958: 88)

TT2. –**Acoqui** parece que todos **marcan**, ¿eh ? –le dijo el tipo que tenía al lado.
–¿**Marcan**?
–**Dica** *las manús*, están **roneando** *un jambo*. **Dica** esos *enteraos* bacilando alrededor de **la burda**, están **semando** algún **morao. Acoqui** todo Dios anda a la caza del primer *andoba* que se despiste con *la tela*.
–Creo que yo le he visto a usted antes —dijo Jackson—. ¿No se llama por casualidad Gus Parsons?
El tipo miró a Jackson con desconfianza y comenzó a apartarse.
–¿Pa qué quiere **ficharme** *el peta*?
–Sólo pensé que le conocía –dijo Jackson (…) (*my emphasis*, Himes 1980: 100)

TT3. –Aquí todo el mundo andan buscando algo, ¿verdad? –dijo el hombre que tenía al lado.
–¿Buscando algo?
–Sí, las putas, *echar un polvo*; los estafadores que se arremolinan alrededor de la puerta, algún borracho al que *esquilar*. Todo dios parece estar a la espera de que alguien se despiste y enseñe **la pasta**.
–Creo haberle vista antes –dijo Jackson–. ¿No se llama usted Gus Parsons?
El hombre miró a Jackson con recelo y se apartó un poco.
–¿Para qué quiere saber mi nombre?
–Por nada; es que creía que le conocía –dijo Jackson (…) (*my emphasis*, Himes 2009: 84)

All in all, the source text contains 4 instances of slang, the French target text has 8, the Elias Spanish target text has 13, and the Ábalos Spanish text has 3. The 4 instances of compensation which occurred in the French target text were preserved in the Elias version (in ***bold italics*** above). The Elias version has 5 additional instances of compensation (in **bold underlining** above). Of these five instances, 3 are repeated (*acoqui, marcar, dica*), so in total the Elias target text has 12 instances of slang more than the source text. The most recent Ábalos translation contains 2 preserved slang terms and 1 instance of compensation; this is within a comparable range to what was found in a previous study (Linder 2013). Notice how the use of substandard language and non-standard vocabulary also contribute to the overall effect of the slang in this passage.

The French target text contains a number of interesting slang compensations that may have been an inspiration for the first Spanish source text. In particular, the French "ils sont à l'affût, des fois qu'un mec oublierait de planquer son fric" [they are on the lookout for a guy to forget to put away his dough] seems to have directly inspired "anda a la caza del primer andoba que se despiste con la tela" [are on the hunt for the first guy to lose track of his dough]. The structure of the sentence, the usage of verbs implying "lose control" of money rather than "show" it flashily, and of course the compensation of two slang words, both included in *L'argot de la Série Noire, Vol. 1: L'argot des traducteurs* (Giraud and Ditalia (eds) 1996: 197 & 152, respectively) prove the connection.

The amount of compensation in Spanish is noticeably overcompensated, to the extent that some passages are absolutely cryptic ("Dica esos enteraos bacilando alrededor de la burda, están semando algún morao" [Check out those jokers hanging out by the slammer trolling for a drunk]). It should be noted that the word "morao" is not in specialized Spanish slang dictionaries in that exact form, though *El Tocho Cheli: Diccionario de jergas, germanías y jerigonzas*, by José Ramón Julio "Ramoncín" Márquez Martínez contains "ponerse morado", which in Spanish slang means to eat or drink something to the point of excess, (Ramoncín 1993: 162). Again, in this example, as in examples 1 and 2, the exaggerations seem to revolve around Jackson, as if they were staged in order to make his voice contrast with the voices of others, even when Jackson uses substandard English (You're name ain't Gus Parsons, is it?=¿No se llama por casualidad Gus Parsons?) and the voices of others contain no slang or little slang (What you want to know my name for?= ¿Pa qué quiere ficharme el peta?).

By way of contrasting the Elias translation with the most recent effort, the 2009 translation by Mª Dolores Ábalos for AKAL (Madrid) is offered, and the slang has been highlighted using the same manner as above. The segment shown contains slang which has been preserved (in *italics* above) and one term which has been compensated (in **bold underlining** above). It is very interesting to note that the the Ábalos translation of "These jokers in here are just waiting for a man to flash his money" is "Todo dios parece estar a la espera de que alguien se despiste y enseñe la pasta", which apparently contains a remnant of the previous Spanish translation (se despiste) and also contains an instance of compensation (money-pasta). What is entirely missing from the Ábalos translation are any potential links to the compensation from the French version, as Ábalos purportedly did not consult it.

7. Conclusions

Josep Elias overcompensated for the presence of slang in the English source text to such an extent as to need paratextual support in the form of the prologue and glossary. The French translation often used substandard and non-standard French in places where the source text contained none. Because Elias consulted the French translation while crafting his Spanish version, a number of his overcompensations may have been taken directly from the French version, or at least they were inspired by decisions taken by the French translator Minnie Danzas.

A number of the overcompensations in the Spanish version (examples 1, 2, and 4) were instances in which the speech of other characters involved in conversation with the main character Jackson were overinflated with slang so as to exaggerate Jackson's unworldliness and gullability by contrast. This was purportedly done for the sake of facilitating the Spanish readers' identification of Jackson's "square" character, despite the fact that those other characters used little or no slang.

I have shown that the French translation used substandard language and non-standard vocabulary in all sample dialogues involving the black inhabitants of Harlem, even when these dialogues contain only standard speech, such as when Jackson speaks without the strain of excitement or fear (example 3), and all instances when the U.S. Marshal speaks to Jackson (examples 1 and 2). Nonetheless, a complete study of the French translation would be compelling to undertake, as it would indicate that the translator "heightened" the speech of all Harlem inhabitants regardless of the immediate conversational situation, the educational background of each individual speaker and other intervening factors, perhaps indicating the application of an ethnic or racial stereotype to Himes's Harlem characters, who are in actual fact quite differentiated and complex.

I have also shown that the first Spanish translator was careful in leaving Jackson's speech devoid of substandard features and non-standard vocabulary in the samples studied (even though Jackson indeed used them), though he overcompensated the nonstandard and substandard features of other speakers, even when they contained none of these features (for instance, the U.S. Marshal) or few of them (for instance, the fellow bar customer who speaks with Jackson). Nonetheless, a complete study of Jackson's speech in the Elias translation would reveal whether this pattern holds true in cases when Jackson intentionally used substandard language and non-standard language as a ploy with white characters (which he does, for instance, in chapter 14 to escape from two white police officers by pretending that he is a lowly Harlem junkman ("speaking in dialect to impress the cop that he was the rightful junkman": 155).

I have shown that the most recent translation of Chester Himes's *For Love of Imabelle* by María Dolores Ábalos (2009) contains more customary ratios of preservation of slang (3 instances of slang, of which 1 is preserved) and compensation of slang (1; thus of 3 instances of slang in total, 2 are present in the final target text), though it shows one case of dependence on the previous French / Spanish version (se despiste). Nonetheless, a complete study of the Ábalos translation would reveal to what extent the most recent translation preserves slang in the source text and avoids overcompensation, and to what extent this translation is dependent on the French / Spanish preceding texts in terms of originality.

Whenever I could not find a word I needed in order to understand the Elias translation –for instance "morao" in example 4, which means "borracho" [drunk]– I found Ramoncín's *El Tocho Cheli* very useful (1993: 162). Ramoncín's dictionary initially started as a novel, but it ended up in a drawer, incomprehensible and unpublishable, when he decided to use the language of the Madrid underworld where he grew up as his vehicle of literary expression: "There was only one solution, either rewrite it, or –insanely– add a dictionary as an appendix in order to help readers to understand the novel. The problems started when the appendix became longer than the novel and attracted more interest than my literary opera prima" (*my translation,* 10). Today our interest in Josep Elias i Cornet's translation is certainly in its value as an exaggerated sample of Spanish underworld street slang from the late 1970s perhaps more than it is as a translation of Chester Himes's *For Love of Imabelle,* for it is indeed virtually impossible to read without the support of the prologue and glossary, and even additional dictionaries such Ramoncín's *El Tocho Cheli.*

Bibliography

Primary Sources

Himes, Chester. 1958. *La Reine des Pommes (The Five-Cornered Square)*.Translated by Minnie Danzas. Paris: Librarie Gallimard (Série Noire).

————. 1980. *Por amor a Imabelle* Translated by Josep Elias. Con el asesoramiento léxico de Manuel Sánchez Torres (a) el Palomo). Barcelona: Bruguera. (Libro amigo; 750 Novela negra; 48)

————. 2003. *Por amor a Imabelle*. Translated by Josep Elias. Con el asesoramiento léxico de Manuel Sánchez Torres. Barcelona: MDS Books / Mediasat (Biblioteca El Mundo, Las mejores novelas de la literatura universal contemporánea; 79)

————. 2009. *Por amor a Imabelle*.Translated by Mª Dolores Ábalos. Madrid: Akal (Serie básica de bolsillo; Serie Negra, 191. Madrid: Akal.

————. 2011 [1957]. *A Rage in Harlem (For Love of Imabelle)*.New York: Penguin Books.

Secondary Sources

Abio Villarig, Carlos. 2004. *Manipulación de elementos ideológicos y censura en las traducciones al castellano de la novela Farewell, My Lovely, de Raymond Chandler*, Universidad de Alicante, Unpublished Master's dissertation.

Andújar Moreno, Gemma. 2009. 'La representación del discurso individual en las traducciones castellanas y catalanas de *The Catcher in the Rye*: el caso de la unidad léxica crap' in Alsina, Victòria, Gemma Andújar and Mercè Tricàs (eds) *La representación del discurso individual en traducción*. Frankfurt am Main: Peter Lang. 65-83.

Brodovich, Olga. 1997. 'Translation Theory and Non-Standard Speech in Fiction' in *Perspectives: Studies in Translatology* 5(1): 23-31.

Chapman, Robert. 1986. *New Dictionary of American Slang*. New York: Harper & Row.

Eslava Galán, Juan. 2003 'Prólogo a *Por Amor a Imabelle*' in Himes, Chester. 2003. 5-8.

Franco Aixelà, Javier and Carlos Abio Villarig. 2009. 'Manipulación ideológica y traducción: Atenuación e intensificación moral en la traducción de la novela negra norteamericana al español (1933-2001)' in *Hermeneus* 11: 109-144.

Giraud, Robert and Pierre Ditalia (eds). 1996. *L'argot de la Série Noire, Vol. 1: L'argot des traducteurs*. Paris: Joseph K.

Glewwe, Eleanor. 2012. *Translating French Slang: A Study of Four French Novels and Their English Translations*. 1-55. On line at: http://triceratops.brynmawr.edu/dspace/handle/10066/10115 (consulted 10.03 2013). Senior Honors Thesis.

Harvey, Keith. 1995. 'A Descriptive Framework for Compensation' in *The Translator*. 1(1): 65-86.

Himes, Chester. 1976. *My Life of Absurdity: The Autobiography of Chester Himes, Volume II*. Garden City, NY: Doubleday.

Linder, Daniel. (2012). 'Translating Hard-boiled Slang: Specialized Underworld Terms in Spanish Versions of Chandler's *Farewell, My Lovely* (1940)' in Pérez Veneros, Miriam, Izaskun Elorza, Ovidi Carbonell, Reyes Albarrán, and Blanca García Riaza (eds). *Empiricism and Analytical Tools for 21 Century Applied Linguistics: Selected papers from the XXIX International Conference of the Spanish Association of Applied Linguistics (AESLA)* (Colección: Aquilafuente, 185). Salamanca: Ediciones Universidad de Salamanca: 1029-1040.

————. 2000. 'Translating Slang in Detective Fiction' in *Perspectives: Studies in Translatology* 8(4): 275-287.

————. 2001. 'Hammett's *The Maltese Falcon* and Chandler's *The Big Sleep*' in *The Explicator* 60(1): 35-37.

————. 2011. *The American Detective Novel in Translation: The Translations of Raymond Chandler's Novels into Spanish* (Colección Vítor, 292). Salamanca, Ediciones Universidad de Salamanca).

————. 2013. 'La compensación del argot en traducciones al español de la novela negra norteamericana clásica' in Sánchez Zapatero, Javier and Àlex Martín Escribà. 2013. (eds). *Historia, Memoria y Sociedad en el Género Negro: Literatura, Cine, Televisión, Cómic.* Santiago de Compostela: Andavira Editora.

Mattiello, Elisa. 2007. 'Keeping Lexical Complexity in Slang Translation' in Bertuccelli Papi, Marcella, Gloria Cappelli and Silvia Masi. 2007. (eds). *Lexical Complexity: Theoretical Assessment and Translational Perspectives.* Pisa: Edizioni Plus Pisa University Press. 121-140.

————. 2009. 'Difficulty of slang translation' in Chantler, Ashley and Carla Dente (eds). *Translation Practices. Through Language to Culture. Proceedings of the 8th Leicester-Pisa Collaborative Research Colloquium, Leicester, 11-14 September 2003.* Amsterdam and New York: Rodopi. 65-83.

Mayoral Asensio, Roberto. 1999. *La traducción de la variación lingüística.* Soria: Diputación Provincial de Soria.

Morán, Carlos Alberto. 1975. 'Lectura latinoamericana de Raymond Chandler' in *Imagen* 103/104: 34-39.

Palimp (Cuchitril Literario). 2005. 'Chester Himes. El gran sueño de oro. Por amor a Imabelle. Algodón en Harlem'. On line at: http://lepisma.liblit.com/2005/07/26/chester-himes-el-gran-sueno-de-oro-por-amor-a-imabelle-algodon-en-harlem (consulted 02.02.2012).

Polito, Robert. 1997. 'Bibliographical Notes' in Polito, Robert (ed.) *Crime Novels: American Noir of the 1950s* (The Library of America). New York: Library Classics of the United States: 879-883.

Rabadán Álvarez, Rosa and María José Álvarez Maurín. 1991. 'La traducción del sociolecto criminal en *Red Harvest* de Dashiell Hammett' in *Atlantis: Revista de la Asociación Española de Estudios Anglo-Norteamericanos* (AEDEAN): 209-220.

Sante, Luc. 2011. 'Introduction to *A Rage in Harlem*' in Himes, Chester. 8-14.

Sapere, Pablo. 'Sepulturero, Ataúd y el policial muy negro'. On line at: http://www.pasadizo.com/index.php/archivo-de-articulos/949-34. (consulted 21.01.2012).

Stolt, Robert. 2010. *The Translation of Slang: Within the Bounds of Possibility?* Grin Publishing.

Ulvydienė, Loreta and Abramovaitė, Brigita. 2012. 'Literary Style in Translation: Slang in J. D. Salinger's *The Catcher in the Rye*' in *Studies about Languages* 20: 100-108. On line at: http://www.kalbos.ktu.lt/index.php/KStud/article/view/1776/1448 (consulted 11.03.2013).

Wentworth, Harold and Stuart Berg Flexner. 1975 [1960]. *Dictionary of American Slang.* Second Supplemented edition. New York: Thomas Y. Crowell.

Zauberga, Ieva. 1994. 'Pragmatic aspects of the translation of slang and four-letter words' in *Perspectives: Studies in Translatology*, 2(2): 137-145.

Bonnevg — no dialect, yet shd. be Jewish/Dutch as in previous book

Dialect — a stylistic choice beyond the geographical.

Chapter 6: "Se so' sparati a via Merulana": Achieving linguistic variation and oral discourse in the French and Spanish versions of *Quer pasticciaccio brutto de via Merulana* (chapter 1)[1]

José Luis Aja Sánchez

Abstract   *Italian*

Gadda's *Quer pasticciaccio brutto di via Merulana* (1946-1947) is the story of a sordid murder related from police inspector Ciccio Ingravallo's point of view. The use of slang and vernacular becomes a stylistic choice that transcends the mere replication of regional voices: it is an author's resource to produce a baroque and flowery style, with a profusion of rhetorical, phonetic and symbolic nuances. This paper describes the processes in Juan Ramón Massoliver's and Louis Bonalumi's translations, analysing the different ways in which both translators deal with dialects, regional variations, and paralinguistic elements, by focusing on the spoken discourse represented in written language. An interdisciplinary method of study is suggested, giving outlines of functional, textual, pragmatic, and other translation strategies (House, Chesterman, Venuti).

Keywords: Oral strategies and linguistic variation in translation, paradigmatic elements contrast in SL and TL, equivalence, canon function in literary translation

1. Style and meaning of the novel

It is hard to define the writer, Carlo Emilio Gadda (1893-1973), whose work embraces the influences from so many literary eras, with its abundance of philosophical and aesthetic references from both the 19th and 20th centuries, as belonging to any one literary period.

A great admirer of the work of Alessandro Manzoni, whose influence on Gadda's work is keenly felt, Gadda proclaimed the need to defend a moral dimension in political life. Like Manzoni (author of *I Promessi Sposi and Storia della colonna infame*), he shared the same revulsion towards institutional violence and uttered the same outcry against man's vulnerability in times of war and tyranny; indeed, Carlo Emilio Gadda's life had been dramatically influenced by his personal experience during World War I.

The despair that underscores Gadda's choice of narrative style, and the language he uses, is his response to the incompetence of the mechanisms of power to understand the reality of the individual, and this is reflected in Gadda's characters, who continually question their own perceptions of reality.

La considerazione della realtà nella sua complessità di sistema e il concetto di conoscenza come deformazione guidano le riflessioni gaddiane, che spaziano dall'etica alla gnoseologia, dalla poetica alla lingua. Appare sempre più evidente come la scrittura gaddiana, tutt'altro che giocosa e superficiale, costituisca un modo di esplorare il mondo attraverso l'uso consapevole e meditato degli strumenti espressivi. (Pecoraro 1998: 34-35)

It is precisely these two themes, the futility of our perceptions and the arbitrary nature of power, which lead Carlo Emilio Gadda to adopt this genre of mystery / detective novel or *giallo*; a choice to which can also be adduced a political explanation:

La scelta del genere giallo, dato il divieto, negli ultimi anni del regime, di pubblicare gialli, è la prima tessera di un orientamento globale antifascista. Non più un giallo in contumacia, come succedeva per la *Cognizione del* dolore [...] ma un giallo poliziesco esplicito. (Pecoraro 1998: 133-134)

As well as the evident political undertones, Gadda has deliberately chosen to imbue the language of the witness statements, gathered by Inspector Ingravallo in the wake of the crime, with dialectal flavours, thus adhering to a stylistic strategy:

Anche l'invasione delle forme dialettali, data l'avversione del fascismo per i dialetti in generale e per il romanesco in particolare, rafforza una strategia antifascista. (Pecoraro 1998: 133-134)

The reasoning behind this is that Gadda believed that standard language was too coldly academic and that dialects were far more expressive (Gadda 1956). In his novel, *Quer pasticciaccio brutto di via Merulana*, dialect is used to convey subjective truth: the characters express themselves in the dialect of their region: an elementary but sincere language whose underlying meaning is lost further on in the novel, as reality, and a confusion concerning the facts, combine to devalue the real meaning of the characters' words. This narrative confusion is due in part to Gadda choosing to let his characters express themselves in flashback, with the author adopting the narrative voice to describe events through the detective character, Inspector Ingravallo. However, two different perspectives, the diegetic and the extradiegetic, cross over at various points during the novel, intercalating examples of metalepsis (Genette 2007: 243-244) which endow the narrative with an oral quality.

In reproducing the dialect oral quality, Don Ciccio, Ingravallo's assistant, plays an interpreting role which tends to contaminate the style:

La parole prise par le narrateur reatrace, sans rien y changer, les diverses langues des ayants droit non pas à la parole, mais à l'idée de parole réélaborée par le narrateur. Refaire la langue des autres, dans le sens d'une mimésis féconde pour l'écriture: c'est là qui réside la nouveauté de ce texte, qui s'écart du naturalisme par le fait même que, tout en semblant le copier pas après pas, il l'envoloppe en réalité d'une grande distance critique, par l'ingérence de la parodie, de l'humour et de l'ironie. (Manganaro 1994: 108)

The witness statements repeat themselves, cross over and contradict each other, giving way to a series of microstories which detract the reader from the police investigation, from its detective essence, and emerge as a nuance or suggestion, within which we can appreciate a most appealing linguistic ebb and flow:

Élaborant à la fois les notions d'ordre et de désordre, de fonction et de dysfonction, il aboutit à l'enchevêtrement (groviglio), car, chez Gadda, les entrechocs, qui sont constitutif de l'intrigue-intreccio, ne sont, en fait, au bout de la chaîne insoluble des séries, que le groviglio d'une trame ou l'on perd toute raison, comme dans l'oxymore [...]; la vie est un songe. (Manganaro 1994: 108)

From this, we can appreciate that the greatest obstacle in this novel is not only the presence of several different dialects but also the narrative construction and the way Gadda has woven the plot, which, given the bitter existential background, is not able to move towards the more typical ending of a detective story, that is to say, towards finding out who the murderer is. The narrative, a meandering narrative, advances and recedes in a perpetual movement and Manganaro (1994) sees a resemblance to the narrative style in the short stories of Jorge Luis Borges. If we were to borrow a metaphor from the world of art, we could also say that Gadda's narrative is akin to the style adopted by Giovanni Battista Piranesi in his engravings.

2. Methodological strategies. The French and the Spanish editions

In this article, we are going to comment on a small fragment taken from Chapter One, at the moment when Inspector Ingravallo learns that there has been a violent break-in at number 229, of the via Merulana (Gadda 1982: 16-40) and he arrives on the scene to take the witness statements. We shall examine how the translation conveys the aspect of orality and how the element of suspense is maintained.

The only Spanish translation of the novel, entitled *El zafarrancho aquel de vía Merulana* (TT1), was undertaken by Juan Ramón Masoliver, and published in 1965 by Seix Barral (Barcelona), being republished on a number of occasions without any major changes. The only French version (TT2), was translated by Louis Bonalumi, and published by Éditions du Seuil (Paris) in 1963 under the title, *L'affreux Pastis de la rue des Merles.*

The translation study of orality which we are going to examine in this article will centre on two very significant aspects of the fragment analysed:

a) The way dialect is introduced and the relationship between diatopic (regional) and diastratic (social) language

b) Paradigmatic contextual elements and oral discourse

3. How dialect is translated

The Italian linguistic reality, studied from a variety of different perspectives (Cortelazzo 1969; De Mauro 1995; Berruto 1997, etc.) has always posed a problem for the translation of orality, given the complex coexistence between standard language and dialect. Indeed, several experts have already studied the way dialect has been translated, almost wholly in terms of the stylistic features involved. This linguistic diversity is frequently present in literary works and covers every possible range of emotion and sentiment, broadly summarised in the two definitions below:

a) Dialect which is used in order to indicate the regional or social origin

b) Dialect which is used as a stylistic device in those works which reveal an overlapping of vernacular and standard register

In the case of Italian, both dialect and vernacular use of language have a symbolic value and using them gives rise to many contextual interpretations. Two authors, Fogazzaro (1842-1911) and Verga (1840-1922), believe that dialectal use is a sociological referent which creates a more intimate framework, whereas Pasolini (1922-1975) believes that dialectal use is a spoken testimony to a stratum of society that is dying out and a cry of resistance against the imposition of a standard language (*koiné*), whose real purpose is to bind an industrial society together (Pasolini 1991: 5-24).

Antoine Berman deals at length with the subject of translating dialect in his book, *La traduction et la lettre ou l'auberge du lointain*. He describes this as a deformation strategy and outlines the different steps in translating dialect into the SL (Berman 1999: 64-64):

a) Translation of the phrases in italics

b) Intensification of the vernacular

c) Substitution of the SL vernacular for a TL vernacular

None of Berman's above proposals has been used systematically to analyse the translations of this novel, although they are helpful in evaluating certain aspects of both the Spanish and the French translations.

Other critics, such as Juliane House (1981), place importance on the use of dialect in order to understand the significance of the diatopic dimension in a specific translation and, in particular, to gauge the difference between American

English and British English. We do not believe that this differentiating strategy is very helpful in our analysis from the methodological point of view. The broad range of vernacular tongues used does not always coincide comfortably within the different linguistic and cultural realities; however, House's functionalist theory, with its macrostructural vision over the relationship between the original text and the translated work, is applicable in the evaluation of other parameters of the translations.

Indeed, the very peculiarities of the expressions used in the novel make us think that the two translators, Juan Ramón Masoliver and Louis Bonalumi, have had to invent a new translation strategy in order to recreate a parallel communicative and aesthetic system to that offered by Carlo Emilio Gadda in the original. This is because we can see that, embedded in Gadda's novel, there exists a network of diverse systems (linguistic, aesthetic and cultural) which puts it beyond any literary canon and which constitutes its own cultural polysystem (Even-Zohar 1990). The underlying subsystems which coexist in the novel are ruled by a series of norms which the translator must decodify correctly during the translating process. Once these norms have been identified, the mechanism for recreating the ST version will involve the translator in a series of decisions relating to the distance-proximity dynamic and the linguistic difficulties of the novel (Toury 1980). Undoubtedly, both Juan Ramón Masoliver and Louis Bonalumi have had to dig deeply into the Spanish and French literary patrimony in order to translate linguistic references at a more cultured and educated level, as well as those which correspond to the more colloquial or vulgar level of the vernacular tongue. As we shall see in the conclusions, both the Spanish and the French versions have many points in common, despite their different linguistic premises and concepts.

[handwritten margin note: Note unspecific referencing]

3.1. How dialect is managed in the Spanish and French translations of the original text

One of greatest challenges found in this translation is how the translators have dealt with the problem of the many different dialectal varieties coexisting in the novel.

Let us look at the strategies employed by the two translators in the translation of the most widespread dialect: urban Roman Italian, the language spoken by the majority of the characters.

(1)
ST. «A polizzia,» disse qualcuno. «Fa' passà lo Sgranfia, a maschié... Addio, Pompé! Che, l'hai agguantato er ladro?... Mo' c'è er bionno... (Gadda 1983/1946-1947: 19)

TT1. «La poli», profirió alguien. «Dejar pasar al Garras, tú, chaval... ¡salve, Pompé! ¿Qué, ya le has echao el guante al caco?... y ahora, con el Rubianco...» (Gadda 1990/1965: 18)

TT2   "Les flics!", lança quelqu'un. "Place au Grap' eh, jeunesse... Salut, Pompée! Tu l'as piqué ton monte en l'air?... Tiens, v'la Beau Blond, ça va barder!" (Gadda 1963/1957: 24)

Juan Ramón Masoliver (TT1) has used two fundamental strategies to deal with all the lexical and morphosyntactical features, which are framed within the diatopic variation, at the diastratic level:

a) Colloquial register: *poli* for 'policía', *echar el guante* for 'detener', *caco* for 'ladrón'

b) Morphological incorrections: incorrect participle with the missing intervocalic 'd', *echao* for 'echado'

The same can be seen in the French translation (TT2):

a) Colloquial register: *flics* for 'agents de police', *piquer* for 'arrêter', *monte en l'air* for 'voleur' (see *Bob dictionnaire argotique*).

c) Elision to reproduce oral quality: *v'la* for 'voilà'.

Reading the two translations, we can see a contradiction of one of the principles relating to the strategies of deformation as proposed by Antoine Berman (1999: 63-64): the register of the vernacular language does not coincide at the diastratic level, nor does it coincide with the colloquial register, so the effect produced by the SL can never be replicated exactly in the TL.

This loss of dialectal connotation is felt more intensely in the speech given by one of the characters, Signora Menegazzi. Victim of a robbery, Signora Menegazzi, compared to the other characters in the same scene, is considered a lady of somewhat questionable moral character; this disreputable quality being explained in *una tenutaria od ex-frequentatrice d'una qualche casa d'appuntamenti un po' scaduta di rango*. Here, her Venetian dialect ironically conveys a thwarted attempt at upward social mobility:

(2)
ST.   «Ah! signor commissario [...] ci auiti lei: lu ch'el pol giutarne. Ci aiuti lei, per carità, Mària Vergine. Una vedova! Sola in casa, Mària Vergine! Che brutto mondo ch'el xe questo!» (Gadda 1983/1946-1947: 22)

TT1.   «¡Ah! señor comisario [...] ayúdenos usted: el que nos puede ayudar. Ayude, por favor, Virgen Santa. ¡Una viuda! Y sola en casa, Virgen Santísima! ¡El acabóse! Es que no son ni cristianos, ¡demonios coronados, almas de satanases!» (Gadda 1990/1965: 22)

TT2   "Monsieur le Commissaire, faut nous aider! Y a que vous qui pouvez.! Faites quelque chose, Zezus-Marie, une pauvre veuve sans défense! Ah, c'est plus un monde, Monsieur le Commissaire, c'est l'Apocalysse!" (Gadda 1963/1957: 24)

In this particular excerpt, the two translators have chosen different tactics. Juan Ramón Masoliver has identified the Venetian register with an elevated register in the TT, and this produces a clear dichotomy between the way the other characters speak (Roman dialect), and the way Menegazzi speaks. It is an efficient differentiating strategy, despite revealing, yet again, the diastratic and diatopic dimensions.

The French translation, however, has maintained a phonic quality to codify the lisping speech of this character (*Thethus-Marie*). Compared to the Spanish translation, where the characters speak in an educated tongue, the French translation combines colloquial speech patterns, thus making Menegazzi's speech virtually the same as the speech of all the other characters.

One final point on the dialectal level which we shall examine is the vernacular usage of Inspector Ingravallo. Ingravallo is a native from the south of Italy and speaks with a southern accent when he is thinking out loud or speaking to himself. En route to the *via Merulana* to start his investigation, Ingravallo says:

(3)

ST.   «Jàmmoce,» disse Ingravallo, e poi borbottò: «Jamecenne». (Gadda 1983/1946-1947: 22)

TT1.   «Andando» —dijo Ingravallo, y luego rezongó—: Vámonos ya». (Gadda 1990/1957: 18)

TT2.   «Allonzi» fit Ingravallo. Puis il marmonna: «Lon-nouzan». (Gadda 1963/1947: 25)

The second part of his speech, preceded by a brief aside, indicates a change of register: Ingravallo is speaking to himself and uses his native dialect: *Jamecenne*, rather than the previous offering, *Jàmmoce*, which indicates that he is using the same Roman vernacular as his work colleagues. This dichotomy shows how important dialect is as the means of expression, especially when characters want to be shown thinking, or in more intimate contexts.

The two forms, *jamecenne* and *jàmmoce*, have, once again, different forms in the Spanish and French translations. Juan Ramón Masoliver has chosen to reproduce both phrases in standard language, which is similar to his treatment of Signora Menegazzi's speech, whereas Louis Bonalumi has preferred to keep the two registers quite different, using the lisping voice *Allonthi* in the first case, and a play on words, as a solution for the second: *Lon-nouzan*.

4. Strategies for translating orality

The fragment under analysis reveals, by virtue of a confusing and multivoiced dialogue, a segment of life in which each participant attempts to give their own personal and very varied vision of exactly what happened.

In order to understand the translation process of the fragment in Spanish and in French we obviously have to consider what criteria the original author used in order to create this oral dimension in the scene described. This is because all examples of created orality in a written text, and especially in the case of a narrative text, follow a carefully planned reformulation which is absent in any spoken discourse. As Lakoff points out:

> Truly spontaneous discourse has an immediacy, an emotional directness, that is truly exhilarating: at the same time, it carries the burden of immediacy, lack of the clarity, use of the wrong word or phrase, hesitation, repetition, and so on. [...] Planned discourse avoids these pitfalls; but at the same time, it necessarily lacks warmth, closeness, and vividness. But print — more than oral non spontaneous media— exacerbates these difficulties because it lacks many of the devices oral present discourse utilized as carriers of emotional tone: intonation, pitch, gesture, eyes and so on. (Lakoff 1993: 242)

Unquestionably, the written medium does not offer the same resources as the phonic medium for the reproduction of spoken discourse. According to Lakoff, writing is characterised by careful planning and the absence of spontaneity, compared to spoken language, which is wholly spontaneous, and relies on extralinguistic communication signals, such as non-verbal language and direct eye-to-eye contact. Other authors who have explored the somewhat arbitrary differences between spoken and written language and, in its more diluted variation, between colloquial and formal register, have also examined the dichotomy between spontaneity and planning, and concluded that a continuum between the two extremes does exist (Bazzanella 1994: 29-30; Berruto 1997: 12; Koch and Oesterreicher 2007: 21).

Given the idiosyncratic nature of this novel, the hermeneutic process of recreating the development of the translation process must of necessity resort to cognitive reformulation following certain key cultural and expressive ST norms. Then the strategies employed to create the feeling of orality in the original are reinterpreted in order to replicate the effect in the translated text.

> A printed narrative text is, first of all, something we perceive through our eyes, and the "intellectualize" in a process conditioned by series of factors, mainly personal (socioeducational status), cultural (specific interpretation of certain interactive silences), and situational. (Poyatos 1997: 19-20)

4.1. How to reproduce the conversational parameters of the story

The language of the fragment we are going to comment on is characterised by parameters which, within the written framework, give a feeling of communicative immediacy, according to the terminology employed by Koch and Oesterreicher (Koch and Oesterreicher 2007: 34), or the complicity of the speakers (Chafe 1993), as can be seen in the following examples which have been classified according to Koch and Oesterreicher's terminology:

a) Features of communicative immediacy depending on the conditions of the conversation and which are strongly linked to a situation of suspense: familiarity, emotion, engagement with the communicative situation.

b) Features of communicative immediacy following the strategies of verbalization: extratextual contextualisation (gesture and mimicry), partial or total absence of prior planning, aggregate structure.

4.2. Paralinguistic elements which frame the development of the conversations

Gadda has made use of two key elements, visual and acoustic, to recreate the confusion that reigns throughout the investigation at number 219 of the via Merulana. Both of these key elements are powerful factors in the transmission of orality despite the fact that they are often used at the contextual level. Since the story is essentially discursive with occasional use of flashback, the narrator's voice is the essential mechanism for reproducing the communicative process, conferring valuable information about the behaviour and attitude of the other characters, clarifying the often ambivalent nature of their speech and guiding the reader through the setting of the dialogues. As Poyatos explains:

> The writer, therefore, will exercise his or her ability, once that initial presentation has been done, to maintain kinesic and paralinguistic repertories that correspond precisely to those characters. (Poyatos 1997: 23)

Fernando Poyatos speaks of the importance of both of these two elements, visual and acoustic, in oral discourse. However, given the importance of the acoustic elements in the fragment we are examining, and the lack of space, we shall confine our examination exclusively to these elements, which, according to Poyatos (1997: 23), are repeated in the oral framework and can be categorised in two groups.

a) Bodily-related sounds. Paralinguistic elements which give rise to primary qualities such as the voice: talking loudly or softly, whispering, spelling out words, an affected voice, an ironic laugh, exclamations of surprise, disappointment or fear, coughing, doubt, irony etc. These paradigmatic acoustic elements also include a wide range of sounds reproduced in the following contexts: the speakers interacting with themselves, such as drumming their fingers, smacking their forehead with the palm of their hand; the speakers interacting with their listener (punching someone); or the speakers interacting with a series of objects, such as kicking the table or banging on the door. These do not appear in the fragment under analysis.

b) Background noises. These can have a parallel significance between the conversation and the respective bodily-related sounds:

Environmental sounds can also acquire, as in real-life interaction, an impressive speech-like quality related to the character's behaviors, interwoven with the other verbal and non verbal elements in the experience of reading. (Poyatos 1997: 33)

Background noise is akin to being considered a further conversational element in this fragment, as it is a resource used by the author to emphasise the confusion surrounding the jewellery theft and, besides, it fulfils a symbolic function by expressing doubt about the possibility of ever being able to exact the truth of this crime.

Let us now take a look at the mechanisms that the two translators, Juan Ramón Masoliver and Louis Bonalumi, use in the reproduction of the acoustic elements within the conversational developments.

(4)

ST. [Don Ciccio] omise i «Gesù mio bello! Sor commissario mio!» e le altre **interiezioni-imprecazioni** di cui la «signora» Manuela Petacchioni non tralasciava d'inzeppare il suo referto. (Gadda 1983/1946-1947: 20)

TT1. Don Chito omitió los «¡Jesús, Jesús de mi corazón! ¡Querido comisario mío!» y demás **interjecciones-invocaciones** con que la señá Manuela Pettacchioni atascaba de continuo su relato. (Gadda 1990/1965: 20)

TT2. Don Ciccio se mit donc à l'oeuvre [...] non sans laisser de côté les "Sante-Vierge Maire" et el "mon cher Commissaire" **longs comme les bras**, dont la "femme" Manuela Petacchioni n'arrêtait pas de farcir son histoire. (Gadda 1963/1957:24, *my emphasis*)

The French translation has omitted the paradigmatic reference associated with the acoustic element, in this example related to bodily expression (the tone of voice), which is very important when referring to the expressive intensity and the communicative proximity which is characteristic of the neighbours and their declarations: the terms *interiezioni* and *imprecazioni* describe the register and the tonal intensity of the speakers and their yelling and clamouring. According to Chesterman's translation criteria of semantic strategies (Chesterman 1997: 105), this is a metaphorical or trope change. By adopting the metaphor 'longs comme les bras', the comparative element is forced on to the visual level, and the acoustic element of the SL is not reproduced (Chesterman 1997: 110-115).

(5)

ST. Il patema testimoniale, appiccato il foco delle anime, **deflagrava ad epos.** Parlavano tutte in una volta. (Gadda 1983/1946-1947: 26)

TT1. La pasión testimonial, prendiendo fuego a las almas, **deflagraba en ellos.** (Gadda 1990/1965: 26)

TT2. Ayant mis le feu aux âmes, la ferveur des témoins oculaires explosait d'un seul coup **en chanson de geste.** (Gadda 1963/1957: 29, *my emphasis)*

The expression *deflagrava ad epos* is an educated register which demonstrates the novel's habitual strategy of combining different registers, dialect, *epic poem, medieval narrative*

colloquialisms and elevated speech, all at the same narrative level. The register of lower social levels of speech, as seen in their declarations, take on epic tones, and this connotation is clearly appreciated in the French translation with the association between the *epos* and the 'chanson de geste'. This adaptation, which reveals a clear tendency to domestication of the language, (it becomes hard not to think in terms of the French literary tradition) suffuse the hybrid stylistics of the original but is not found in the Spanish version.

The word *epos* means a 'fable' or a 'fable with epic tinges'. The word *epos* is a key word in the original: it is an explicit nod to deferred discourse proffered through the mouths of those being questioned, so that the phonic element is present through the use of indirect speech. Besides which, it is also a rhetorical element with nuances of irony, because it is indeed difficult to imagine some of the shabbier neighbours, with their uneducated use of language, as befits the communicative immediacy, and their high dialectal content, regaling their listener with an epic tale.

(6)
ST. Domandò ancora se fossero rimaste delle tracce... o impronte, o altro... dell'assassino. (Quel termine della **collettività fabulante** gli si era ormai annidato nei timpani: gli forzò la lingua a un errore). (Gadda 1983/1946-1947: 30)

TT1. Preguntó además si por ventura quedaban trazas... o huellas, o cualquier otra cosa... del asesino (aquel término de la colectividad **fabulante** ya se le había metido en los tímpanos; y le forzó la lengua al error). (Gadda 1990/1965: 29)

TT2. Il demanda une fois de plus si on avait relevé des traces, empreintes, ou autre... de l'assassin (ce terme, issu de **l'imagination collective**, s'était logé dans ses oreilles et il le prononça malgré lui). (Gadda 1963/1957: 32-33, *my emphasis*)

Our third example shows how the acoustic element forms part of the context. It is produced by the speaker and it is not a strategy of a bodily-related sound. Nonetheless, it is a strategy or a resource used to give the idea of orality because it alludes to the noisy clamouring of the neighbours. In this case, the French translation uses the strategy of modulation/generalisation, thereby diminishing the hyperbolic perception of the discourse which is channelled through the word *fabulante*, an adjective which makes a clear paradigmatic reference to these raucous neighbours and their shouting, and their unreliable witness statements.

5. Conclusions

From this analysis of the fragments taken from the Spanish and the French translations, we can see that the process of translation has been dealt with from different perspectives.

Juan Ramón Masoliver's Spanish version prefers the creation of a flowing prose with expressions that remind one, on numerous occasions, of examples from Spanish classical literature, in particular in the narrative.

That being said, we can also appreciate that at times the colloquial register and the occasional use of more classic phrases set off a domestication process whose result is certainly questionable from the point of view of the effect produced, probably due to the typically Spanish touch of the register which undoubtedly awakens feelings in the Spanish reader. This particular strategy in translation has been widely criticised by Antoine Berman, who acknowledges that it is most unusual to be able to reproduce the vernacular in a translation without it sounding like a pastiche or a parody of the original text (Berman 1999: 63-65), as we can see in the following example.

(7)
ST. «Ecché macché! Macché un cavolo, sora Teresa mia! Che avrò li occhi pe nun vedecce? Staressimo bene.» (Gadda 1983/1946-1947: 28)
TT1. «¡Qué hablar ni hablar! Ni hablar un cuerno, seora Teresa mía. ¿O es que tengo los clisos pa no ver? Estaría una fresca...» (Gadda 1990/1957: 27)

Borrowing words like 'clisos', from the Spanish gypsy dialect *caló* (see Corominas 1973), or, as is documented in classical literature, abbreviating 'señor' or 'señora' to *seor* or *seora*, produces a strange effect on the reader. Masoliver, in trying to mimic the diatopic and diastratic registers of the original, uses words which conjure up a completely different reference for the Spanish reader, than do the original words for the Italian reader. It is indeed questionable whether the text functionality and adaptation, to use House's terminology, have been correctly discharged.

Another of Juan Ramón Masoliver's strategies is to link the dialectal tongue to a morphological or lexical incorrection. So we might come across words like *entoavía* and *mismamente*, or imperative forms such as, *me deje que lo piense*, which all point to the distratic aspect, that is to say, to the cultural register of the speaker, but not to the diatopic or regional register.

The French version that Louis Bonalumi proposes is, in many ways, similar in the strategies employed to differentiate dialect and standard language:

(8)
ST. «Gesummaria! Prima aveva sonato alla sora Liliana...» «Chi?» «Ma l'assassino...» «Ma qua' assassine si nun ce stà 'o muorto? La sora Liliana (Ingravallo trepidò), sola in casa, non aveva aperto. «Era nel bagno... sì... stava facendo il bagno.» (Gadda 1983/1946-1947: 20)
TT2. «Juste ciel, il avait sonné d'bord chez Ma'me Liliane». «¿Qui donc?» «Mais l'assassin!» «Quel assassin, puisqu'y a pas de cadavre? «Bref, se trouvant seule chez elle, Mam'Liliane (Ingravallo s'agita) n'avait pas ouvert. **Pasque** elle était dans son bain... **Voui,** elle s'prenait un bain.» (Gadda 1963/1957: 25, *my emphasis*)

However, in other instances, Bonalumi reflects the diatopic register by using elision and writing out the common spoken-French contractions:

(9)

ST. «Ma sor commissario mio... un'emozzione così! Chi ce pensa ar beretto, in queli momenti? Che ve pare?... Diteme voi, quanno che spareno tutti sti córpi, si ve pare che una signora po pensà ar beretto...» (Gadda 1983/1946-1947: 22)

TT2. «Mon cher m'sieu l'Commissaire! Qui qui s'occupe encore d'casquettes à des moments pareils? C'pas votre avis? Quand ça tire tous ces coups de revolvers, dites, vous croyez qu'une dame, elle peut penser aux casquettes?» (Gadda 1963/1957: 26, *my emphasis*)

Louis Bonalumi prefers this means to reproduce diatopic variation, whereas Juan Ramón Masoliver's version in Spanish reveals a profusion of slang and defective constructions.

Where the French version also differs from the Spanish version is in the handling of improvised discourse, such as one might find in real-life. The Spanish translation adopts a distant communicative approach in order to recreate a different type of syntactical structure, whereas the French version alternates between communicative immediacy and proximity (Koch and Oesterreicher 2007: 34), as it tends to erase any improvised discursive markers which, in the deferred story, try to demonstrate the spontaneous nature of the oral expression. The syntax used by Louis Bonalumi tends to elevate the register of the narrative, and this is repeated in various contexts throughout the translation. The Spanish translation, however, is more receptive to a more frequent use of strategies of orality.

The tendency to normalise the features of spontaneous communication demonstrates a predisposition, on the part of the French translator, to elevate the register, as can be seen in the following context:

(10)

ST. Il commendatore non si dava pace. Quel tic tac del maledetto orologio della stanza, di tocco in tocco gli aveva scavato le orbite [...]. A interrogarlo, nel primo pomeriggio, fu lo stesso Ingravallo, che alternò blandizie e amabilità varie a fasi un po' più grevi. (Gadda 1983/1946-1947: 38)

TT2. Il Commendatore, lui, **était sur le gril**. D'heure en heure, le tic-tac de la maudite horloge suspendue au mur lui avait taraudé les orbites [...]. Ingravallo en personne entreprit de l'interroger, au début de l'après-midi, **faisant alterner main de velours et gant de crin**. (Gadda 1963/1957: 38, *my emphasis*)

The use of stylistic figures of speech and proverbs which are not available in the ST is frequent in the French version. Nonetheless, these changes can be justified as a compensation strategy, given the number of educated speech patterns which appear in the original.

We would like to end our conclusion with a brief comment about the methodology: the final reading of the two translations has been undertaken with special attention being paid to the effect in the ST, in particular, to the way in which the suspense of the scene has been recreated. Thus, we have analysed the criteria of adaptation of the two versions with respect to the original, and have paid less attention to a microtextual analysis and criteria of equivalence; we have not carried out a quantitative study of the domestication of terms in the Spanish version, as we believe that the use or abuse of colloquial language and the introduction of typically Spanish linguistic elements has been undertaken according to the needs of the dialogue and the sensitivities of the translator. Our process has been similar to the one carried out in the French edition which, on the whole, manages to achieve, as does the original Italian, a complex harmony between educated and colloquial language, despite the final effect veering more towards the former.

The applications of concepts such as domestication and foreignisation, which have been used frequently during our analysis, are equally applicable to both translations. The combination of the two opposite terms in the same text might seem contradictory or paradoxical, but we believe that this contradiction is due to the absence of a specific canon (Venuti 1995: 43-147) for a novel such as *Quer pasticciaccio brutto di via Merulana*. The impossibility of being able to transfer the communicative and cultural dimension of the Italian dialects into the Spanish and French versions has led the translators to create their own system which borrows from both Spanish and French literary canons in order to reproduce the colloquial tone of the speakers and the rhetorical style of the narrator, without forsaking, in certain contexts, the few Italianate features which are the essence of the novel.

So we can only conclude by applauding the two translators, Juan Ramón Masoliver and Louis Bonalumi. By accepting the challenge to deal with the difficulties present in this novel, they have overcome one of translations' greatest hurdles: dealing with a work which, like many of its kind, is branded untranslatable. If we allow ourselves to be guided by the Benjaminian concept of the translating process, we can even detect certain complicity between the two translators and the original text. The fruits of this collusion are two translations which, despite our asymmetric findings, enable us to sense and enjoy the emotions produced in the original through the transmission of oral discourse.

---

[1] The original Spanish version of this paper has been translated by Susan Jeffrey, Universidad Pontificia Comillas, Madrid.

Bibliography

Primary Sources

Gadda, Carlo Emilio. 1956. "Perché cinema radio e scrittori ci parlano in romanesco?" in *Epoca* 281.
——. 1963 [1957]. *L'affreux Pastis de la rue des Merles*. Translated by Louis Bonalumi. Paris: Editions du Seuil.
——. 1983 [1946-1947]. *Quer pasticciaccio brutto di via Merulana*. Milano: Garzanti.
——. 1990 [1965]. *El zafarrancho aquel de vía Merulana*. Translated by Juan Ramón Masoliver. Barcelona: Seix-Barral.

Secondary Sources

Bazzanella, Carla. 1994. *Le facce del parlare*. Firenze: La Nuova Italia.
Benjamin, Walter. 2004 [1921]. 'La tarea del traductor' in Vega, Miguel Ángel (ed.). 2004. *Textos clásicos de teoría de la traducción*. Translated by H. P. Murena. Madrid : Cátedra.
Berman, Antoine. 1999. *La traduction et la lettre ou l'auberge du lointain*. Paris: Editions du Seuil.
Berruto, Gaetano. 1997. "Le varietà del repertorio" in Sobrero, A (a cura di). 1997. *Introduzione all'italiano contemporaneo. La variazione e gli usi*. Roma-Bari: Laterza.
BOB dictionnaire argotique. On line at: http://www.languefrancaise.net/#bob_dictionnaire_fam_pop_arg (consulted 21.10.2012).
Chafe, Wallace L. 1993. 'Integration and Involvment in Speaking, Writing and Oral Literature' in Chafe, Wallace L. (ed.). 1993. *Spoken and Written Language. Exploring Orality and Literacy.* Norwood, New Jersey: Ablex Publishing Corporation.
Chesterman, Andrew. 1997. *Memes of Translation*. Amsterdam: Benjamins.
Corominas, José. 1973. *Diccionario etimológico de la lengua castellana*. Madrid: Gredos.
Cortelazzo, Manlio. 1969. *Avviamento critico allo studio della dialettologia italiana*. 2 vols. Pisa: Pacini.
Coseriu, Eugene. 1983. 'La lengua funcional' in Coseriu, Eugene. 1983. *Lecciones de lingüística general*. Translated by José María de Azáceta. Madrid: Gredos. 302-315.
De Mauro, Tullio. 1995. *Storia linguistica dell'Italia unita*. Roma-Bari: Laterza.
Even-Zohar, Itamar. 1990. "Polysistem Studies" in *Poetics Today. International Journal for Theory and Analysis of Literature and Communication.* 11: 1.
Genette, Gerard. 2007. *Discours du récit*. Paris: Editions du Seuil.
House, Juliane. 1981. *A Model of Translation Quality Assessment*. Tübingen: Narr.
Lakoff, Robin F. 1993. 'Some of My Favorite Writers and Literate: The Mingling of Oral and Literate Strategies in Written. Communication' in Deborah Tannen (ed.). 1993. *Spoken and Written Language. Exploring Orality and Literacy.* Norwood (NY): Ablex Publishing Corporation.
Manganaro, Jean-Paul. 1994. *Le Baroque et l'Ingénieur. Essai sur l'écriture de Carlo Emilio Gadda*. Paris: Editions du Seuil.
Oesterreicher, Wulf and Peter Koch. 2007. *Lengua hablada en la romania. Español, francés, italiano*. Tanslated by Araceli López Serena. Madrid: Gredos.
Pasolini, Pier Paolo. 1991 [1964]. 'Nuove questioni linguistiche' in Pasolini, Pier Paolo. 1991. *Empirismo eretico*. Milano: Garzanti.
Pecoraro, Aldo. 1998. *Gadda*. Roma-Bari: Laterza.
Poyatos, Fernando. 1997. 'Aspects, problems and challenges of nonverbal communication in literary translation' in Poyatos Fernando (ed.) 1997. *Nonverbal communication and translation. New Perspectives and challenges in literature, translation and the media*. Amsterdam and Philadelphia: Jonh Benjamins.
Steiner, Georg. 2001. *Después de Babel*. Translated by Adolfo Castañón y Aurelio Major. Madrid: FCE.
Toury, G.ideon. 1980. *In Search of a Theory of Translation*. Tel Aviv: Porter Institute.

Van Leuven-Zwart, Kitty. 1989. 'Translation and Original: Similarities and Dissimilarities I' in *Target* 1:2: 151-181.

Venuti, Lawrence. 1995. *The Translator's Invisibility. A History of Translation*. London: Routledge.

Chapter 7: Bringing home the banter: Translating "empty" dialogue in exotic crime fiction *2014*

Jean Anderson

Abstract

This study explores some of the issues and strategies related to the use of foreign language terms in dialogue in the context of "exotic" crime fiction, meaning crime fiction set in a country where an *exotic language* is spoken, a language other than that of the author (and presumed original reader), as opposed to the local or *narrative language* which is the main language of the original text, or featuring an "exotic" character. It surveys patterns of usage adopted by authors to create exotic atmosphere and language use (*exoticisation*), before analysing some of the strategies used by translators whose task it is to move such works into the formerly exotic language of the original (*repatriation*). Considering the English-French language pair, examples will be drawn from classic Agatha Christie and two more recent authors, Canadian Louise Penny and American Cara Black, who all choose French-speaking detectives, although in quite different contexts.

Keywords: Exotic language, exoticisation, repatriation, Agatha Christie, Louise Penny, Cara Black

1. Writing and reading exotic crime fiction

Even a quick glance along the shelves of the Mysteries section of a public library will provide evidence of the recent proliferation of exotic detective stories, that is, thriller writing across a range of subgenres set in locations other than the writer's and source readers' own. This is not a new phenomenon: the text often cited as the first example of crime fiction in English, Poe's *Murders on the Rue Morgue* (1841), is already cross-cultural, exploiting the fact that an unfamiliar setting can add significantly to the reader's sense of derailment, thereby increasing the suspense, at the same time as it offers a certain comfort, the idea that such things do not happen "here". Creating crime fiction with an exotic setting, or reading crime fiction from exotic countries, appears to be a growing trend: in the words of Jason Goodwin, historian and travel writer turned crime writer, "Crime fiction is the new travel writing" (Goodwin 2011). To cite only a few current examples, Briton Michael Dibdin and American Donna Leon set their detective series in Venice; Scotsman Peter May's China series takes place in Beijing and Shanghai, and his Enzo McLeod books, featuring a half-Italian, half-Scots detective, are set in France; British author John Burdett's Bangkok series consists of five novels to date. Goodwin is the creator of the

Yashim the Ottoman Investigator series set in 1830's Turkey. Perhaps the most blatant example of this equation of the foreign with the lethal is the Michael Pearce series, *A Dead Man in...* which consists of seven novels to date, each adding a different city to the title (Trieste, Istanbul, Athens, and so on): Londoner Pearce is also the author of the Egyptian-based Mamur Zapt series. There are in fact far too many examples to name them all. The majority of these exotic crime works date from the late twentieth century and reflect a growing globalisation of crime fiction, which also entails a rising interest in translated crime fiction. As Geherin (2012: 4) states, discussing the greater presence of foreign crime writing in the USA, traditionally an environment hostile to translations, "[...] the borders are coming down, and the size of the Atlantic Ocean is shrinking". It is timely to reflect on the presence of exotic elements in crime fiction and some of the challenges these pose to translators.

While this trend is by no means restricted to the English-speaking world,[1] the present analysis will necessarily be limited to a small number of examples written in English: these are taken mainly from the early work of Agatha Christie, to establish a baseline for comparisons that will then be made with two contemporary writers, Canadian Louise Penny and American Cara Black. These three writers have in common their choice of a French-speaking detective, and all three have been translated into French. We will consider here how these writers create an impression of foreignness, mainly, but not only, through dialogue, and how translators might cope with translating such exoticisms when the target language is the same as the original's exotic elements: in other words, when fictive dialogue containing exoticisms is *repatriated* through translation and thereby loses part of its purpose, how does the translator maintain the author's characterisation choices and the separation between narrative and exotic languages?

2. Writing foreign-inflected dialogue

Students of creative writing are often caught in a dilemma: how to write natural-sounding dialogue without boring the reader, a topic dealt with by many "how-to" manuals. As Hall (1989: 94) puts it, "Dialog takes pains to appear totally realistic without being so at all, for it is very much the product of conscious craft". Although advice is offered on the writing of dialogue generally, few guidelines are given for dealing with foreign language. Exceptions include Elizabeth George, who points out that James Clavell's *Shōgun* (1975) features Japanese statements followed immediately by translations, which cease once the reader may be assumed to have understood the meaning (George 2004: 143). She suggests a "less awkward" solution of using the foreign language followed by a contextual explanation, and gives the example of unappetising *frijoles* named in Spanish in the dialogue then described in the narrative as cold beans topped by a puddle of congealed cheese (George 2004: 143-144). Here George moves without comment from a dialogue example to one found in the narrative, thereby obscuring some important issues, as will be shown later. Quick considers the treatment of dialect to belong in the same category as foreign-inflected and historical variants of English, again preferring a light touch, through the use of interlanguage calques in the second case and more frequent subordinate clauses in the third, adding: "These sorts of tricks enable you to give a flavour of speech [...]" (George 2004: 141).

Referring to what he calls "Foreign Speech", Hall proposes Ernest Hemingway's *For Whom the Bell Tolls* as a model, explaining that "Clarity can be gained by context and ensuing locutions, but most simply by repeating the phrase a second time, in translation" (Hall 1989: 108). In referring to this practice of glossing, Hall fails to note other strategies deployed by Hemingway, such as the use of simple expressions or single words of unglossed Spanish, relatively "empty" of meaning, such as *"Hola* Santiago! *Qué tal?"* or *"Guapa"* (Hemingway 1999: 151-152), or the use of Spanish-calqued English, as in: "'Is the same to me,' Sordo said simply and not boasting. 'Better four good than much bad. In this war always much bad, very little good. Every day fewer good. And Pablo?'" (Hemingway 1999: 157). Hemingway makes very extensive use of this technique, by means of which he allows his characters to communicate directly among themselves, but also with the reader, while at the same time maintaining the pretence that they are speaking Spanish.[2]

For Whom the Bell Tolls has been acclaimed as a great work, although Hemingway's strategies are clearly intrusive and result in text that can be difficult to decipher.[3] This would seem to be in conflict with the writing strategies suggested above, which share an assumption that the foreign must not impede the reader's understanding, and that the exotic must be made transparent. For transparency to exist, an author may rely on factors other than dialogue, as in George's *frijoles* example: it is important to acknowledge that a novel's exotic environment relies on a combination of elements, including description and action as part of the narrative, where foreign language terms are also found as part of a network of factors that localise the events of the text: names of people and places, foods, flora and fauna cross between these different aspects. While the following analysis will focus on dialogue, we should bear in mind that this is only a part of a larger picture.

2.1. Agatha Christie's Poirot

According to her autobiography (2010: 256-257), Christie (1890-1976) was influenced in her creation of Hercule Poirot by two main factors: the presence of Belgian refugees in England, and the journalist detective, Joseph Rouletabille, in Gaston Leroux's *Mystère de la chambre jaune*, first published in serial form in

1907, and which she had recently read.[4] She chose to depict Poirot as an idiosyncratic, fussy individual, distinctly and firmly foreign: Grossvogel (1983: 9) describes his behaviour as revealing "[...] an unBritish propensity for exuberance and exaggeration [...]" underscored by "[...] sentences [...] marred by Gallicisms, even though they became more probable over a lifetime".[5] Both these behaviours are highlighted on Poirot's first ever appearance, in *The Mysterious Affair at Styles* (1920), as recounted by Hastings: "[...] he clasped me in his arms and kissed me warmly. '*Mon ami* Hastings!' he cried. 'It is indeed *mon ami* Hastings!'" (Christie *Styles*: 34).[6]

As well as French expressions, marked here through italics which underline their foreignness,[7] there are a number of Gallicisms, or non-native uses of English: "'What have you, my friend?' he cried, 'that you remain there like – how do you say it?– ah yes, the stuck pig?'"[8] (*Styles*: 63). Christie uses brief instances of French throughout, generally as salutations ("*mon ami*", "*messieurs, mesdames*") or as exclamations, such as "*voyons!*", "*eh bien!*", "*voilà!*", "*bon!*", "*allons!*", "Oh *là là!*"[sic], "*Mon dieu!*", all invariably followed by exclamation marks: she occasionally has Poirot express himself more fully in French. When this happens, for example with "'*En voilà une table!*' cried Poirot" (*Styles*: 63) and "*Ne vous fâchez pas!*" (88), the meanings are clear from their respective narrative contexts –a cheap table that falls over and a cold response on the part of Hastings. The use of an unexplained "*mauvais quart d'heure*" (273) may speak to its being a commonplace saying among Christie's anticipated readers at the time, although it too can be safely ignored or interpreted in the light of the rest of the dialogue that follows in English: "[...] there is no doubt that for one terrible moment she must have feared [...]" (273).

While some knowledge of French is of assistance to the reader, the overall principle of relatively empty dialogue in the foreign language has clearly been followed in Christie's first novel. The number of calqued expressions is, despite Grossvogel's claim, low: Poirot's English, once past the early pages of the book, contains only a handful of French-inflected expressions.[9]

This is however not the case with the second of Christie's crime novels, *Murder on the Links*,[10] inspired by a real-life case in a small French town (Christie 2010: 281). Here the author makes extensive use of calqued English for her numerous French characters, including a more foreign-sounding Poirot: compare the two novels' treatment of Poirot's fussiness in respect of Hastings's tie: "'Excuse me, *mon ami*, you dressed in haste, and your tie is on one side. Permit me.' With a deft gesture, he rearranged it." (*Styles*: 59); and from the second novel: "It is a marvel, almost you are exact this morning. *Pardon*, but your tie is not symmetrical. Permit that I rearrange him" (*Links*: 10). Although the situation is the same, Poirot's English is noticeably less standardised in the later work.[11]

In this second detective novel, then, exoticisation is more widely used, although it follows similar principles on the whole. While Christie sometimes gives Poirot entire sentences in French, for the most part she has recourse to three principal strategies:

1) The vocabulary is relatively basic, and therefore likely to be understood; or it is, semantically speaking, relatively empty, i.e. it has a semiotic purpose (that of signalling foreignness) rather than a semantic one (of communicating specific meaning);

2) These examples of code-switching are positioned in a particular way: in a majority of cases, the French is pre-positioned, at or near the start of the line of dialogue,[12] rather than the middle or end of the character's intervention, although there are instances of all three options;

3) French-speaking characters –principally Poirot– use French-inflected English.

2.2. Translation challenges

Since the point of these language elements in the dialogue is to signal Frenchness, when the texts are translated into French (*repatriated*), this purpose is necessarily lost. Just as the inflected syntax of Hemingway's resistance fighters would, where these are accurate calques, blend into a Spanish translation which normalises them, so too do the majority of the signifiers of Frenchness disappear when Poirot is translated into French. To take the example of the tie adjustment cited above, these two episodes become, respectively: "'Pardonnez-moi, mon bon ami, mais je vois que vous êtes venu en hâte. Votre cravate est de travers. Si vous le permettez...' D'une main preste, il l'arrangea [...]" (Christie *Affaire*: 50);[13] and "'C'est extraordinaire, vous êtes presque à l'heure, ce matin. Ah! Pardon, mais votre cravate est légèrement de travers. Laissez-moi vous arranger ça' [...]" (Christie *Golf*: 240).[14] Instead of signalling fastidiousness and Frenchness, these statements now present only fastidiousness and a degree of (still unBritish) courteousness. Poirot's faintly ridiculous behaviour underlined by his foreign way of expressing himself is gone: in other words, the distinctive character of Christie's detective is inexorably altered by the linguistic repatriation of the text.[15] Arguably, his apparently Belgian characteristics are replaced by more personal idiosyncracies.

The translators have preserved what they can, however, notably the formality and sometimes pomposity of Poirot's speech.[16] For example, both opt to translate "*mon ami*" by "mon bon ami", and both refrain from giving him more oral structures such as "Est-ce que ..." for asking questions: Poirot almost invariably uses verb inversion, for example, "n'y a-t-il pas une autre issue à ce cabinet de toilette?" or "sans doute votre montre avance-t-elle, madame?" (Christie *Golf*:

268, 271). To some extent, however, this stylistic distinction is lost in that the whole text is translated in a relatively formal style, as befits a novel from this period.

One further challenge facing the translators warrants comment here: Christie's knowledge of French was not that of a native speaker. Her attempts at creating calqued English are therefore sometimes based on erroneous assumptions. This has been shown in the examples of the *cravate* treated as masculine, and of the "stuck pig", as well as the placement of "*Hein*". As we have seen, the gender error resolves itself in the repatriation process –what reason could there possibly be for Poirot to mistake the gender of the word in his own language? The pig is necessarily converted by the translator into a normal French collocation –"planté comme un ...– comment dit-on déjà?– ... comme un épouvantail!" (Christie *Affaire*: 53).[17]

Elsewhere, Christie has given Poirot other distinctly non-French usages, quietly corrected by the translators. His recurring exclamation "*Sacré!*" (*Styles*: 143 and 1999: 52, 207)[18] is translated as "Sacré nom!" (*Affaire*: 113), "Sapristi!" (2009: 611), and "Sacrebleu!" (2009: 631).[19] These are all rather old-fashioned terms and serve not only to correct Christie's error, but also to heighten Poirot's characterisation.

To sum up, then, the repatriating translator faces inevitable loss of one dimension of the original text, and takes on new responsibilities in ensuring other dimensions are authenticated. The changes made by the translators are in response to a logical necessity that goes much deeper than a simple standardisation according to differing source and target text norms. It is not a question here of the imposition of repertoremes (Toury 1995: 268) but the result of a fundamental shift in the functioning of textual elements within the new language context.

2.3. Louise Penny (1958–)

Penny is an English-speaking Canadian author who has set her eight detective novels, featuring the francophone Inspecteur, Armand Gamache, in the French-speaking countryside close to Montreal. These choices are not without their political implications in a region and country where language conflict has a long history: it is unlikely that the quirky behaviour and mannered speech of a Quebecois Poirot would be acceptable to a local readership.[20] Gamache's exoticness is in fact linked to a strong measure of *gravitas*, and other than their language, the two detectives have little in common, something which has not prevented reviewers from comparing Penny with Christie.[21] There are certainly a number of similarities in the writing, particularly the exoticisation strategies noted in Christie's novels which are by and large replicated in Penny's work. A combination of greetings ("*Bonjour*", "*Salut*", "*Bonsoir*") and salutations

("*Monsieur*", "*Madame*", "*patron*") is used with very high frequency in dialogue throughout the novels, thereby underlining the Frenchness of the setting. Within the narrative, references in French to the policing system, "la Sûreté du Québec", are a further reminder, and a limited number of items relating to food –some of the lead characters run a bistro– are also found repeatedly. For example, characters frequently drink "*café au lait*", referred to thus in all the novels presumably to distinguish it from the "bottomless cup" watery brew that is the usual fare in many Canadian diners and restaurants. Other usages, however, are less clearcut: why the term "*confitures*" (Penny 2008: 46, 186) is preferred to "preserves" or "jam" other than as an additional exoticism, is unclear.

For the most part, these more denotative items rarely figure in the dialogue, where French terms are essentially limited to greetings and salutations, usually in combination and positioned at the start of a line of dialogue, as befits such formulae. Penny occasionally gives her detective a line of the more sustained French speech that Poirot produces from time to time; she also employs some of the other exoticisms found in Christie's work, notably exclamations / expletives. Although several of her characters use the international French "*merde!*" the typically Quebec expression "*tabernac*" is used in *Still Life* (2005), with added commentary.[22] In *The Brutal Telling* (2009) she makes more use of this Quebec-specific system of swearing, known as "*les sacres*", which uses words from the religious rather than the sexual or organic domain for their shock value: both "*tabernac*" and "*calice*" highlight Quebec French. "*Calice*", sometimes written "*câlice*" to represent the back "a" sound also a distinguishing feature of local pronunciation, is here spelled "*Chalice*" in error (Penny 2009: 228). This is not unlike Penny's attempt to use the Quebecois term that designates anglophone bigots, or "*têtes carré*" and "*tête carré*" (Penny 2010: 47), where she fails to make the adjective agree, or her use of "*pointe finale*" (Penny 2005: 110, 192) in place of the appropriate "*point final*" or "*un point, c'est tout*".[23]

[handwritten margin note: imitates in French.]

Again like Christie's, Penny's usage of French within both dialogue and narrative is relatively limited, and when she ventures into more colourful areas of dialogue she encounters some of the same pitfalls. This is also the case with the third author in this study.

2.4. Cara Black (1951–)

American crime novelist Cara Black, inspired by Frenchman Léo Malet's project of writing one novel for each of Paris's twenty *arrondissements*, released *Murder Below Montparnasse*, her thirteenth in the series "Aimée Leduc investigates", in 2013.[24] Well-known for her painstaking research into locations and their historical associations, Black chooses to insert French sporadically, both in dialogue and in the narrative itself, as a further exoticisation strategy.

[handwritten: narrative as reoralisation — hard-boiled style.]

[handwritten margin note: note referencing]

Here we should mark one of the principal differences between Christie and Penny, on the one hand, and Black on the other. The narrative in the latter's work is close to the dialogue in tone, because it is focalised principally by Leduc. This strategy on the author's part can be seen as "reoralisation" of the novel form, as discussed by Cadera citing Nänny (1988) and Marcone (1997) (Cadera 2012: 36). It is often found in "hard-boiled" detective fiction and has the advantage of creating greater suspense than third-person omniscient narrative precisely because it limits knowledge as the investigator puzzles her way through events.

As a "chick dick" in the unconventional style of V.I. Warshawsky and Kinsey Milhone, Leduc recounts her adventures in a tough and sometimes humorous tone that belongs to an informal and oral register. For example, she refers in the narrative to "*flics et taxes – la double morte*" (Black 1998: 28).[25] Notwithstanding this and other examples, Black's novels are predominantly like Christie's and Penny's, that is to say, the French insertions consist chiefly of pre-positioned greetings and salutations. Here Black encounters some difficulties: calling a cautious inquiry into an apparently empty apartment, Leduc uses the word "*Allô?*" (1998: 11), whereas a native speaker would reserve this for answering the telephone. Again because of the repatriation, the French translator has no choice but to select a target text-appropriate formula, "Bonjour?" (Black 2009: 14).

[handwritten margin note: mistakes]

As was the case for Christie and Penny, colloquialisms are problematic for Black, particularly expletives. "*Cochon l'assassin*" (1998: 147) is corrected to "Cochon d'assassin" (2009: 175). When an elderly bigot denouncing the easy life of ethnic minorities favoured by the government shouts "*Salopes!*" out of frustration (1998: 207), the translator, bemused by this usage ("bitches") modifies it to the singular (2009: 242), when in all likelihood the less gender-specific "*salauds*" (bastards) is what is intended.

3. Repatriation and repair

This is by no means an exhaustive analysis, but we may draw some conclusions from the examples considered. The authors have all endeavoured to create an exotic atmosphere and build exotic characters through code-switching. These usages can be found in both the dialogue and the narrative, in the latter case usually in a more denotative, neutral situation. However they rarely occur in the dialogue in large blocks of text that might be obscure, and are usually confined to very basic vocabulary and functions, such as greetings. Thus Quick's "flavour of speech" is achieved, and the author signals foreignness without creating obstacles to understanding.

The positioning of such exoticisms at the beginning of lines of dialogue arguably allows the eye to slide past them, noting their semiotic function as their meaning, rather than being interrupted mid-sentence to decipher any deeper sense that might be important for the plot. In terms of characterisation, code-switching within the dialogue again serves to reinforce other exoticising elements in the narrative, such as proper names, or references to cultural practices.

When exoticised writing is translated into the originally exotic language, the effect is a repatriation, a normalisation of the previously exotic. The translator's task is then complicated by the necessity of ensuring these former exoticisms are, or at least pass as, authentic within the target readership. There is no longer any reason, and therefore no place, for quaint calques, errors in placement or personal names, or incongruencies such as Black's puzzling menu item, "*cul de lapin au basilic*" (1998: 113).[26] The normalisation practised here by translators is a necessity.

Colloquialisms, in particular expletives, appear to be especially problematic, as in the example of Poirot's exclamation "*Sacré!*", Penny's misuse of Quebecois expletives, and Black's "*salope / salaud*" confusion.

When repatriated through translation, instead of signalling foreignness in a way which does not in fact require authenticity, merely a simulacrum of it, texts of this kind require absolute target culture and language accuracy. The emptiness of the original exotic terms must now convey meaning in a quite different way, and this is an important part of the translator's responsibilities, requiring loyalty rather than faithfulness (Nord 2006).

Writers, then, create exoticisms in what may seem a relatively superficial way, using a small number of strategies that create a flavour of the foreign, by signalling foreignness generally. Translators must give these much more weight and ensure that these items have meaning that is appropriate in the new context. A case might well be made for eliminating some of this empty dialogue, on the grounds that its purpose no longer exists.

But what of translations (which are *ipso facto* from exotic languages) of texts which are not being repatriated in the process? What is happening for example in respect of the so-called "Nordic slaughterfest" (Craven 2012)? If authors of exoticised thrillers make use of expressions in a foreign language to signal foreignness,[27] then surely translators of genuinely exotic writing might do the same? While detailed analysis of these translations falls outside the limits of the present study, it would seem, from a cursory survey that this is not the case. Reg Keeland's *The Girl with the Dragon Tattoo* contains little Swedish other than proper names; the same is true of Neil Smith's rendering of Kallentoft's *Autumn Killing*, and (looking to French) of David Bellos's version of Vargas's *Seeking Whom He May Devour*.[28] While we can only hypothesise at this point, there are likely to be two reasons for this. The first is that the original authors, having no need to signal foreignness, have not inserted the kind of empty dialogue we have examined here: it is after all, empty. The second reason is likely to be that translators translate: they convert a text from one language to another. While personal and location names survive this transition unaltered, greetings and commonplace sayings generally do not, and calques are avoided in the interests of creating a "smooth" and "natural" translation, the invisibility Venuti condemns. Perhaps it is time to revisit some of these considerations, and to give thought to ways in which the foreignness that is clearly tolerated by readers of exoticised thrillers might also be reflected in translations, which, if more foreignised, would simply reflect an established tradition in crime writing.

---

[1] In France, for example, Caryl Férey's exotic thrillers set in New Zealand, Africa and Argentina have received several prizes and attracted a wide readership; most of Maud Tabachnik's more than thirty books are set outside France.

[2] His most noticeable calque is the use of "thee", "thou" and "thy" to represent a second person singular still in use in Spanish, but archaic in English.

[3] These texts are not translations *sensu stricto*, but there is clearly a "foreignisation" principle at work reminiscent of the translation approach recommended by Venuti (1995, 1998). I refer to this strategy on an author's part as *exoticisation* to distinguish it from *foreignisation*, which will designate a translatorial choice.

[4] Christie does not state whether she read it in English or French. It appeared as a novel in 1908, the same year as the first English translation. She also credits this same work with influencing the way she wrote her second crime novel (see below).

[5] Grossvogel gives sparse evidence for this assertion of improvement: this warrants further research outside the bounds of the present study.

[6] To avoid confusion, Christie's works will be referred to by an abbreviated title instead of the date of the source work quoted, since these are not the original editions. *The Mysterious Affair at Styles*, published in 1920, but consulted in a 2001 edition, will be referred to as *Styles*.

[7] We must assume that decisions about italicisation remain with the editorial staff: however, this is an area that also warrants further study. In Louise Penny's books "croissant", for example, is not italicised, while "*confiture*" is. The degree to which foreign words are considered foreign and the point at which they cross into another language and are therefore not italicised may impact on the reader's perception of foreignness within the text as a whole. In quoting from both original texts and translations I have reproduced their use of italics.

[8] Grossvogel (1983: 9) comments on this example, but fails to note that it is not just a Gallicism ("What have you my friend?" for "Qu'avez-vous mon ami?") and may even be a joke: the French expression is "être planté là comme un poireau" (Poirot); in the English idiom, "stuck pigs" either bleed or squeal, and are stabbed rather than trapped.

[9] The reader may, nonetheless, as a consequence of the primacy effect, have a lasting impression of the little detective's foreignness. For a list of French expressions used in all 66 of Christie's detective novels, see Zemboy (2008), who does not, however, comment on their authenticity.

[10] Henceforth *Links*. Christie (2010: 282) describes the second novel as having "[…] that high-flown fanciful type of writing […]" that she had just read in Leroux's novel. Whether this is in fact Leroux's style or the translator's is a moot point.

[11] There seems no obvious linguistic reason for Poirot to refer to the tie (*la cravate*) as "him" in the second example. Despite the realism implied by the story's inspiration, the language forms used in the dialogue remain very much the author's invention rather than being convincingly mimetic.

[12] Incorrectly, on occasion, as with "'*Hein*, it is a good sight this!' murmured Poirot" (*Links*: 14), translated as "'Quel spectacle!' murmura Poirot" (Christie *Le Crime du golf*, 2009: 556; henceforth *Golf*). *Hein* would normally be found in post-position, following a statement, and the translator has

corrected this by removing the word.

[13] Translated as *La Mystérieuse Affaire de Styles*, henceforth *Affaire*.

[14] While these translations are by different translators, Thierry Arson for *Affaire* and Françoise Bouillot for *Le Crime du golf* (henceforth *Golf*), they adopt some of the same strategies in dealing with Poirot's dialogue.

[15] In Poirot's case it is perhaps more accurate to consider this an exoticisation of the whole text, I maintain the terminology here to refer to the language transfer.

[16] Although outside the scope of this study, it could be enlightening to compare the choices of these contemporary translators in 1991 and 1990 with those made in the 1932 translations.

[17] The "comment dit-on déjà", which is, in the original, a reminder that Poirot is not always certain of his English, is slightly odd here, but may perhaps be read as an indication of hesitation and avoidance of the more usual collocation of "planté comme un poireau" – an unwanted pun.

[18] In the short stories "The Disappearance of Mr Davenheim" and "The Case of the Missing Will" (Christie 1999: 41-52, 202-209).

[19] "Une étrange disparition" and "L'Affaire du testament disparu", (Christie 2009: 595-611, 623-634). Translation by Laure Terilli.

[20] Five of the novels have now been published in French by Flammarion Québec, and four by Actes sud in France.

[21] See for example Girard (2010): 'Une sorte d'Agatha Christie des Cantons-de-l'Est'.

[22] "Her impeccable French had disappeared as well, replaced by street French, twangy and harsh, the words covered in grit" (Penny 2005: 59). The spelling "tabarnak", used by some other writers, is arguably grittier.

[23] It is not my intention here to criticise Penny's (or her editors') command of French, but rather to recognise the difficulties that arise in these attempts at exoticisation.

[24] Two titles have been translated and published in France: *Murder in the Marais* (1998) and *Murder in the Sentier* (2003).

[25] Revised in the translation to "policiers et taxes – la Double Mort" (Black 2009: 31).

[26] "Corrected" by the translator into "rable de lapin au basilic" (Black 2009: 135).

[27] Not all authors exoticise to the same extent: Leon includes very little Italian other than proper names, and Cruz Smith limits Russian and Spanish similarly.

[28] Bellos does make some exceptions, for example the word "flic" is retained, rather than being replaced by "cop".

Bibliography

Primary Sources

Black, Cara. 1999. *Murder in the Marais*. New York: Soho.
———. 2002. *Murder in the Sentier*. New York: Soho.
———. 2009. *Meurtre dans le Marais*.Translated by Michèle Zachayus. Paris: City.
———. 2013. *Murder Below Montparnasse*. New York: Soho.
Christie, Agatha. 1990 [1923]. *Murder on the Links*. London: Collins.
———. 1999. *Hercule Poirot: the Complete Short Stories*. London: HarperCollins.
———. 2001 [1920]. *The Mysterious Affair at Styles*. London: HarperCollins.
———. 2009. *Hercule Poirot: Agatha Christie l'intégrale*. Vol. 1. (tr. Various). Paris: Le Masque.
Clavell, James. 1975. *Shōgun*. New York: Atheneum.
Cruz Smith, Martin. 2008. *Stalin's Ghost*. London: Pan Macmillan.
Hemingway, Ernest. 1999 [1941]. *For Whom the Bell Tolls*. London: Vintage.
Kallentoft, Mons. 2012. *Autumn Killing*. Translated by Neil Smith. London: Hodder & Stoughton.
Larsson, Stieg. 2008. *The Girl with the Dragon Tattoo*.Translated by Reg Keeland. London: Maclehose.
Penny, Louise. 2005. *Still Life*. New York: Headline.
———. 2009. *The Brutal Telling*. New York: St Martin's Press.
———. 2010. *Bury Your Dead*. New York: Minotaur Books.
Vargas, Fred. 2005. *Seeking Whom He May Devour*.Translated by David Bellos. London: Vintage.

Secondary Sources

Cadera, Susanne M. 2012. 'Translating Fictive Dialogue in Novels' in Brumme, Jenny and Anna Espunya (eds). *The Translation of Fictive Dialogue*. Amsterdam, New York: Rodopi. 35-51.
Craven, Peter. 2012. 'Books' in the *Sydney Morning Herald* (30 December 2012). On line at: http://www.smh.com.au/entertainment/how-much-is-too-much-20121227-2bx02.html (consulted 31.12. 2012).
Geherin, David. 2012. *The Dragon Tattoo and its Long Tail*. Jefferson, NC: McFarland.
George, Elizabeth. 2004. *Write Away: One Novelist's Approach to Fiction and the Writing Life*. London: Hodder and Stoughton.
Girard, Marie-Claude. 2010. 'Louise Penny: des polars qui font du bien'. On line at: http://www.lapresse.ca/arts/livres/romans-quebecois/201008/28/01-4310631-louise-penny-des-polars-qui-font-du-bien.php (consulted 12.12.2012).
Goodwin, Jason. 2011. On line at: http://www.criminalelement.com/blogs/2011/06/crime-fiction-is-the-new-travel-writing (consulted 12.10.2012).
Grossvogel, David I. 1983. 'Death Deferred: The Long Life, Splendid Afterlife, and Misterious Workings of Agatha Christie' in Benstock, Bernard. 1983. *Art in Crime Writing: Essays on Detective Fiction*. New York: St. Martins Press. 1-17.
Hall, Oakley. 1989. *The Art and Craft of Novel Writing*. Cincinnati, OH: Story Press.
Nord, Christiane. 2006. 'Loyalty and Fidelity in Specialized Translation' in *Tradução Cientifica e Tecnica 4*. Tradução e localização: 29-41.
Quick, Alex. 2012. *102 Ways to Write a Novel: Indispensable Tips for the Writer of Fiction*. Brecon: Old Street Publishing.
Toury, Gideon. 1995. *Descriptive Translation Studies – and Beyond*. Amsterdam and Philadelphia: Johns Hopkins.
Venuti, Lawrence. 1995. *The Translator's Invisibility: A History of Translation*. London and New York: Routledge.
———. 1998. *The Scandals of Translation: Towards an Ethics of Difference*. London and New York: Routledge.

Zemboy, James. 2008. *The Detective Novels of Agatha Christie: A Reader's Guide.* Jefferson, NC: McFarland.

Chapter 8: The semiotic implications of multilingualism in the construction of suspense in Alfred Hitchcock's films

Giuseppe De Bonis

Abstract
This paper aims to shed some light both on the role that multilingualism plays in Alfred Hitchcock's films and on the semiotic implications it has in the construction of the distinctive feature of his filmography, namely suspense. Through a diachronic analysis of the evolution that multilingualism undergoes from the director's early production of the 1930s to the end of the 1960s, when the universally acknowledged "master of thrill" directed *Torn Curtain* (1968), his most well-structured multilingual film, three main functions of multilingualism in Hitchcock's films will be identified and discussed: realistic rendering, conflict, and confusion. If realistic rendering is intended as a means to enhance viewers' perception of the reality depicted on screen, particularly if the story has an "international" setting with characters coming from different parts of the globe, conflict as well as confusion of languages and lingua-cultural identities both become strategies to produce the distinctive feature of Hitchcock's films: suspense. The presence of so-called "secondary languages" will also lead to the analysis of the different translational solutions and techniques used to handle them in the original version of the fourteen films taken into consideration in this study.

Keywords: Multilingualism, suspense, conflict, confusion, contextual translation

1. Preliminary remarks

This study has two main goals. Firstly, it aims to shed some light both on the role that multilingualism plays in Alfred Hitchcock's films and on the semiotic implications it has in the construction of the distinctive feature of his filmography, namely suspense. From his early sound films shot in the 1930s, before moving onto Hollywood, to the end of the 1960s when Hitchcock directed *Torn Curtain* (1966), which can undoubtedly be considered one of his most well-structured multilingual films, Hitchcock resorted to multilingualism and 'played' with languages on several occasions, and for different purposes. A diachronic analysis of the evolution that multilingualism undergoes from his early production of the 1930s to the end of the 1960s will be carried out, to then explore the semiotic role that the presence of different languages on screen has in Hitchcock's multilingual production, particularly as far as the construction of suspense is concerned.

Out of the 53 films directed by the universally acknowledged "master of thrill", fourteen films can be rated as multilingual. The term "multilingual" in Hitchcock's production refers to those stories which have an "international" setting with characters coming from different parts of the globe and thus speaking, or at least supposed to speak, different languages. In other words, these films portray on screen a multilingual situation in which a primary language is present along with one or more secondary languages. The primary language is the prevailing language, the one which is most significant in terms of quantitative presence throughout the film. From a narrative viewpoint, the so-called "dominant language" can be considered as the film's main language of communication (Heiss 2004), in the sense that most of the dialogues are uttered in this language. In Hitchcock's films, the primary language is always English. Secondary languages are, conversely, those languages which are less present in the film from a quantitative perspective. Nonetheless –as it will be shown in this article – these languages may have a decisive function in the film, if considered from a wider qualitative standpoint, be it either narrative or semiotic. In Hitchcock's films, secondary languages very often operate as a vehicle for suspense.

Before moving onto the detailed analysis, some preliminary observations are required in order to clarify the theoretical framework whereby the role and the meaning of multilingualism in film will be interpreted. Generally speaking, multilingualism in film appears to have three main functions: realistic rendering, conflict and confusion (see De Bonis forthcoming). With regard to realistic rendering, multilingualism seems to be a means to enhancing viewers' perceptions of the reality depicted on screen, particularly if the story has an "international" setting with characters coming from different countries and thus speaking different languages. Diversely, multilingualism expresses conflict, mainly in dramatic films, when lingua-cultural identities are sharply depicted and strongly maintained on screen, giving rise to communicative problems which become hard to solve. Finally, when lingua-cultural identities are mixed up on screen in a somewhat disorderly fashion, the result is confusion, a feature commonly found in comedies in which multilingualism generally produces a humorous effect.

The second purpose of this study is to consider the translational implications present in Hitchcock's films by analysing the different techniques used to deal with so called "secondary languages" present in the original version of the films taken in consideration. More precisely, special attention will be paid to the cases of interpretation performed by a character, on the one hand, and to what is defined as "contextual translation" (Baldo 2009a, 2009 b), on the other.

Whereas the former case is a clear example of what can alternatively be described in terms of "translation provided directly on screen", in the latter, viewers are helped by the images and by the overall context from which they can draw the meaning of what they see on screen. In other words, contextual translation[1] "exploits" the polysemiotic nature of audiovisual texts (Chiaro 2009), that is, their distinctive feature of conveying the overall meaning through the combination of different semiotic codes interwoven one another: verbal, non verbal, visual and acoustic. Films always require a multimodal or multimedia type of reading (see Zabalbeascoa 2010; Zárate 2010) in which the overall meaning is understood through the integrated interpretation of their different semiotic components.

2. The multilingual production of the 1930s

The first film in which Hitchcock resorts to multilingualism is *The Man Who Knew Too Much*[2] (1934). Multilingual situations are present in the first part of the film, which has an international setting, the ski resort town of Saint Moritz. Multilingualism is meant both as a means to achieve a realistic effect and as a narrative device to help the story unfold. English is the primary language, while German, Italian and French are the film's secondary languages: German is spoken by the hotel staff where the Lawrences are vacationing; Italian is spoken by the hotel manager. In the first part of the film, languages become an important resource, a vehicle for producing and increasing the suspense, for instance, when the Lawrences first meet a foreigner, Mr Abbot (Peter Lorre), who claims to have a poor command of English. But, as the story unfolds, viewers will learn that this is far from being true: not only is Mr Abbot's English much better than he has pretended it to be, but the man also turns out to be the leader of the terrorists.

Multilingualism is also present in the scene set at the hotel during Jill Lawrence's interrogation by the local police. In this case, employing different languages is meant to create confusion between characters and to increase suspense. There is even a funny attempt made by Bob Lawrence to utter some words in French in order to communicate with a member of the staff, who appears not to speak English. Interestingly enough, this contributes to producing a slightly humorous effect, making the sequence, to some extent, not as dramatic as one would expect, considering that the couple has just learnt about their daughter's kidnapping. The overall result is thus what Hitchcock used to define in terms of "understatement" (Truffaut 1966), that is representing a situation in a less dramatic fashion through a combination of both drama and humour, leading both characters and viewers to feel "mixed emotions". Multilingualism is an integral part of this process.

The Secret Agent[3] (1936) is a spy story combined with romantic elements.[4] Although most of the film's events occur in Switzerland, English is the primary language in the film. German, French and Spanish are the secondary languages. German is present throughout the film both for a more realistic representation and for producing conflict between characters (as happens, for instance, in the scene at the casino). It also plays a crucial role in the film's narrative development, as the plot pivots around the identification of the German spy that the British secret agents, the film's main characters, are meant to murder. In this sense, language and lingua-cultural identity both become vehicles for suspense leading to decisive happenings.

In the scene in which Mrs Caypor gives Elsa and Marvin a little lesson in German, multilingualism operates as a clear semiotic device to increase suspense, as the lesson takes place at the same time as her husband, the mistaken target, is being cold-bloodily murdered by "the General": the combination of the "alternating cut" and multilingualism, along with some close-ups of the dog who is manifestly nervous, all play a part in raising emotional tension. Moreover, during the lesson, Marvin ironically claims: "I don't understand a single word of German, but I speak it fluently", showing "bad pronunciation" of German, as the lay teacher immediately remarks.

Robert Marvin (Robert Young) is the antagonist in the film: his unfamiliarity with foreign languages has already been revealed in a previous scene, the only one which contains some French. Differently from German, French is meant to create confusion by aiming at a slightly humorous effect: Elsa and Marvin are riding in a coach at night, with the man constantly courting the girl. In an attempt to favourably impress her, Marvin even tries to speak some French to the coach driver, but with awful results. Eventually he is obliged to ironically admit that he is "a well-equipped young man at home in every language." Marvin's ostentation of his limited linguistic skills is a capital semiotic marker, a decisive "clue", since in the end the man turns out to be the real German spy.

Some Spanish words are often uttered by "General" Pompilio Montezuma de la Villa Something (Peter Lorre), who speaks his own idiolect, a combination of broken English and Spanish, which could be labelled as "Spanglish." In this case language is a key device to accurately define and connote this 'peculiar' character: in other words, it is an important means of characterisation (Wahl 2005, 2008; Sanz Ortega 2011). As a consequence, this aspect has considerable implications not only on a semiotic level, but also from a translational point of view,[5] since the character's own idiolect has to be somehow maintained and conveyed to the audience of the translated version as well –be it subtitled or dubbed.

Typical features of the spy story also characterize *The Lady Vanishes*[6] (1938). The film has an international setting with its characters, passengers on a trans-European train, coming from different countries. English remains the film's main language of communication, while German, French, Italian and Bandrikian are the secondary languages. Bandrikian is the imaginary language of a small fictional country in the Balkans called Bandrika –governed by a dictator– in which the first part of the story takes place. Its being acoustically similar to German is not accidental, since, along with the reference to the dictator, it clearly alludes to Nazi Germany. Something similar happens also in the film *The Great Dictator* directed by Charlie Chaplin in 1940, in which the dictator's imaginary language explicitly imitates German's intonation and contains German words put together nonsensically.

Besides a more realistic representation from a linguistic standpoint, secondary languages aim either at conflict or at confusion between characters. Sometimes multilingualism shows a sort of "duplicity" as it seems to lead both towards conflict and confusion simultaneously within the same scene. The secondary languages' main goal, however, remains suspense. Although Iris Henderson, the main character in the film, persists in saying that she has really met Miss Froy, the missing lady to whom the film titles refers, both the train staff and her compartment companions appear rather reluctant in answering her direct questions, with some of them even using a foreign language (namely Italian) in order to evade them This overtly reticent behaviour persuades the young woman –and consequently the audience– that something suspicious is occurring on that train.

3. Multilingualism as a semiotic device

In this paragraph, three films will be analysed in which Hitchcock resorts to minimum multilingualism, in the sense that the presence of secondary languages is reduced to one or two scenes alone. The films are *Rebecca* (1940), *Strangers on a Train* (1951) and *The Wrong Man* (1956). From a narrative point of view these films can easily be considered monolingual films, since all their salient dialogues are in English. At first glance, these films thus appear multilingual only from a merely formal perspective. Nonetheless, as audiovisual products are polysemiotic texts in their essence, it goes without saying that multilingualism is there for a reason and plays a part in the construction of the film, in its textuality. In these films, multilingualism operates as a semiotic device to increase the suspense either of the scene in which it occurs, or of the film's overall narrative design.

In the film *Rebecca*[7] the multilingual situations are not numerous, being essentially concentrated in the first part set in Monte Carlo. French is always in the background: it is spoken by secondary characters (waiters in restaurants and hotel staff)[8] and it consists only of short phrases and sentences, mainly terms of address such as *Monsieur*, *Madame* or *Mademoiselle*. There is only one scene in which French comes more to the foreground. The couple have just got married. As they are leaving *la salle des mariages* ('the registry office'), the employer looks at the window and calls them back saying: "*Monsieur, vous avez oublié votre carnet de mariage!*". The bride immediately asks the groom: "What did he say?" and he answers: "He said I forgot the proof that we are married." If we consider this bilingual sequence from both a narrative perspective and a translational one, nothing particularly relevant seems to happen: the linguistic sense is not left ambiguous as we face a case of interpretation performed by a character. Multilingualism, hence, appears not to pose any significant problems for viewers' understanding. Yet, if a wider semiotic perspective is embraced, it immediately becomes clear that employing multilingualism is far from being meaningless or accidental, but it is rather a deliberate choice made by the director: it functions as an enunciative marker, a semiotic device which allusively preannounces that the newlyweds' marriage will not exactly be a fairy tale romance. *a sign that st will be wrong with the marriage*

Something similar also happens in the other two films directed by Hitchcock later in the 1950s: *Strangers on a Train* and *The Wrong Man*. From a narrative standpoint, *Stangers on a train*[9] may be considered a monolingual film, since English remains the main language of communication throughout the film. There is one scene alone which presents some French, precisely the one showing the first tennis match played by the main character, Guy Haines. After the match, the man catches up with his fiancée Anne and her sister Bárbara, who are in the company of the Darvilles and Bruno, the psychopath who is harassing him. Bruno is introduced to Guy as a friend of Monsieur and Madame Darville. Both the men pretend not to know each other. Part of the conversation takes place in French: they are telling jokes and "funny stories" as Madame Darville explains to Guy.

Resorting to French has two important meanings. Firstly, on a narrative level, it is used to socially distance the two men, underlining Bruno's high social standing and education. Thus multilingualism operates as a means of characterisation. Secondly, moving onto a wider perspective, the verbal code (French) becomes a crucial semiotic device that, combined with the turning up of the volume of the music in the background (acoustic code) and the close-up of Bruno's tie pin (visual code), increases the suspense of the scene, producing a sense of confusion and dismay in both Guy and the viewer.

As Hitchcock himself claims at the very start of the film, *The Wrong Man* is the true story of an innocent man, Christopher Emmanuel Balestrero (Henry Fonda), who is mistaken for a criminal. From a narrative standpoint, English is the main language of the film as practically all the salient dialogues are in English. Yet there is also some Italian (mainly terms of address and greetings) utilised as a means of characterisation, since the protagonist is Italian-American. Once again the verbal code, along with the visual code —we see Manny praying with a rosary as he is sent to jail— contributes to defining the character's identity: not only is Manny a faithful husband and a devoted father, but also a practising Roman Catholic.

With his wife's support, Manny starts his odyssey to prove his innocence by accurately reconstructing his alibi. In an attempt to find possible witnesses, he

146

goes with Rose (Vera Miles) to look for Mr Molinelli at his apartment. In this scene we have a brief dialogue in Spanish with one of Mr Molinelli's neighbours: since the woman claims not to speak English, Manny thus speaks in broken Spanish to her. The woman comments: "El señor Molinelli? Hace mucho tiempo que muriò!". Vera asks Manny: "What did she say?" and he answers: "Molinelli is dead". The volume of the background music starts to turn up and simultaneously Vera bursts into tears exclaiming: "That's perfect!".

In this sequence, Spanish is not only meant to accentuate conflict and tension, but it is also employed to slow down and dilate the pace of the story. The translation is provided directly on screen with Manny doing the interpreting for both Vera and the audience. Multilingualism, linguistic conflict, time dilation are all decisive elements to stress Manny's difficulty in finding witnesses, as one by one, every single person who could help him is no longer available to do so. Multilingualism is once again a crucial semiotic device to achieve the overall result.

4. Postcarding multilingualism and the homogenising convention

In this section, three of Hitchcock's films will be briefly discussed which, similarly to the ones analysed in the previous section, may be seen as multilingual only from a formal perspective. In these films not only is multilingualism present to the minimum, but, moreover, it never operates as a vehicle for suspense. These films are *Notorious* (1946), *I Confess* (1953) and *Topaz* (1969). They should be better rated as "multicultural films" in the sense that, although they have an international setting with characters coming from different areas of the world, the different lingua-cultural identities are simply hinted at rather than being clearly expressed through different languages. English always remains the main language of these films, while the secondary languages are recalled through an "indirect" procedure, that is to say through means such as the actors' accents, the terms of address and greetings, or even a limited number of foreign-language utterances. In other words, these films appear to resort to multilingualism as a "postcarding method" (Wahl 2005), which is utilised only to signal the national origin of a character, or the country where the story is set. This type of strategy has been defined in terms of "linguistic homogenisation" (see Strenberg 1981; Cronin 2009; O'Sullivan 2011): characters who should speak different languages, because they are supposed to come from different countries, actually turn out to speak one language alone (say English), while their "real" languages are evoked through the aforementioned devices.

This is the case of *Topaz*, whose characters are American, Russian, French and Cuban. They all speak fluent English throughout the film, while their lingua-cultural identities may be easily drawn both from the terms of address –

such as *Monsieur* and *Madame* for French or *Señor* and *Señora* for Spanish–
and from the actors' accents.[10] In this regard, it is worth noticing that Hitchcock
cast mainly mother tongue actors for each nationality present in the film.

The homogenising convention also operates in *Notorious*. The film is mainly
set in Brazil. The two protagonists Alicia Huberman (Ingrid Bergman) and T.R.
Devlin (Cary Grant) are both American. Although the antagonist Alex Sebastian
(Claude Rains) and his mother are both supposed to be French, they always
speak English throughout the film, even in private conversations while plotting
against Alicia. Nonetheless, their foreign origin may be easily inferred from the
slight foreign accent that Sebastian's mother has as she speaks English, this role
being played by the Austrian actress, Leopoldine Konstantin.

Although most of the story is set in Rio de Janeiro, the presence of
Portuguese is minimal and restricted to barely a few sequences: it always
remains in the background and appears to aim at enhancing a more realistic
perception of the situation on the part of the viewer. Only on one occasion does
Portuguese come more to the foreground, precisely when a few words are
uttered by Gary Grant's character as he orders something to drink from a waiter
in a café. The film also contains some French, which can be clearly heard in the
party scene at Sebastian's house. It gives a sense of realism, stressing the
"international" origin of the guests.

Not very different from *Notorious* is the case of *I Confess*. The story is set in
Quebec City, in French-speaking Canada. Even though the main characters
always speak English throughout the film, a little French is, however, used on
several occasions through the common procedures of the homogenising
convention. Firstly, the film presents some brief examples of code-switching, as
is the case when a child wants to confess to Father Michael Logan (Montgomery
Clift), the film's main character. Secondly, the terms of address (*Madame*,
Monsieur) as well as some other expressions and utterances are sometimes in
French. Finally, there is a short sequence[11] in which Ruth (Anne Baxter), Father
Michael's former fiancée, speaks to her maid in French. Since this scene has a
reduced impact on the unfolding of the story, it has not been subtitled into
English.

The antagonists Otto and Alma Keller (O.E. Hasse and Dolly Haas), escaped
from Nazi Germany and both have clear and credible German accents.
However, they always speak English, even during their private conversations.
There is only one word in German at the end of the film, when Alma Keller is
shot to death and asks for "*Verzeihen*" ('forgiveness'), with a translation
provided on screen by Father Michael himself.

5. Multilingualism as a vehicle for suspense

In this section the analysis will focus on five films from Hitchcock's production in which multilingualism plays a more crucial role in the overall narrative design, contributing to sustaining and to increasing the suspense. The secondary languages, though restricted in quantitative terms, are, however, essential. The films are *Foreign Correspondent* (1940), *Lifeboat* (1944), *To Catch a Thief* (1955), *The Man Who Knew Too Much* (1956) and *Torn Curtain* (1966). They all have an international setting. Their leitmotif is generally related either to World War II, or to the Cold War and the Iron Curtain.

This is exactly the backdrop against which the events of *Foreign Correspondent*[12] take place, a spy story set on the eve of World War II. English is the main language of the film, while Dutch and Latvian are the secondary languages. Dutch is present in the part of the film set in Amsterdam. Multilingualism becomes a means of increasing the suspense in particular in the scene at the windmill, where the main character, John Jones, discovers that the diplomat, Van Meer, is being kept hostage by some Nazi spies. The relevant role played by Dutch as a vehicle for suspense lies in the fact that Jones does not understand Dutch. Nonetheless, he clearly comprehends that something suspicious is happening. So do viewers, who are helped by the images and the context in general, exploiting what has been defined as "contextual translation". Jones has some problems in convincing two Dutch policemen to follow him to the old mill, until he meets a little girl who mediates between the two parts. An example of interpretation performed directly by a character on screen, but for the benefit of the film's characters alone, since viewers already know what is happening.

In addition to Dutch, the film has two sequences displaying some Latvian, spoken by a funny character. Firstly, during the party taking place in London, when Jones first meets Carol Fisher (Laraine Day): Latvian, meant to create confusion, becomes the pretext for Jones to go and introduce himself to the girl. The second sequence occurs in Jones' hotel room when two spies disguised as Dutch policemen arrive to kidnap him: as the man immediately suspects who they really are, he rushes out through the window and escapes into Carol's bedroom. The scene turns into a humorous *pastiche*, as the Latvian man knocks at Carol's door: he immediately misinterprets what he sees, clearly alluding to a romance likely to develop between the two. The confusion produced by Latvian (verbal code), combined with the amused facial expression shown by the man (visual code), manages to effectively convey the sense of both sequences. In other words, multilingualism is a semiotic device which contributes to drawing viewers' attention to emotions, even before the two people concerned become totally aware of what is happening.

Lifeboat is set during World War II. In the North Atlantic, several British and American civilians are stuck in a lifeboat after their ship and a U-boat sank each other in combat. The survivors are from a variety of socio-cultural backgrounds: an international journalist, a rich businessman, a radio operator, a nurse, a steward, a sailor and an engineer with communist tendencies. Troubles start when they pull aboard a German survivor, Willy (Walter Slezak), who denies being an enemy officer. The real protagonist of the story is actually conflict: conflict between social classes (each character respectively representing one); conflict between languages (English *vs.* German) and, mostly, conflict between cultural and political identities (on the one hand, the Western World and the Allies and, on the other, Nazi Germany represented by the German survivor).

In this regard, not only is multilingualism a means to accentuate conflict, but it also becomes a vehicle for suspense, because all the shipwrecked people always look at the German man suspiciously, never trusting him, even when they reluctantly let him guide their lifeboat towards the Bermudas. Despite the interpreting performed by Connie‾ (Tallulah Bankhead), the barrier between Willy and the other survivors is never overcome. Actually he is indeed deceiving them: not only can he speak English fluently, but he is also hiding a compass in one of his pockets, which he regularly consults.

The film represents a very interesting example in Hitchcock's multilingual production, because not only does German –the secondary language– play a crucial role from a qualitative point of view, but it also has a significant presence in quantitative terms. As the German man seems unable to speak English, one of the characters takes charge of the linguistic mediation throughout the film. This is the only case in Hitchcock's multilingual filmography which massively resorts to the interpretation performed by one of the film's characters as a translational technique used to deal with secondary languages.

While the plots of *The Man Who Knew Too Much* and *Torn Curtain* are related, more or less explicitly, to the Cold War and the Iron Curtain, *To Catch a Thief*[13] is more of a romantic thriller, which has an international setting and thus presents some multilingual situations. Although the story is entirely set in France, English is the main language of the film. There is also some French, but it predominantly remains in the background just to give the viewer a more realistic "flavour" of the general atmosphere. Consequently, most of the front-page headlines (the verbal visual code) referring to the new wave of thefts are consistently in French.

French comes more to the foreground in two main scenes, when multilingualism functions both as a narrative element for the further development of the plot, and as a semiotic device to increase the tension. The first scene is set in the casino: John Robie drops an expensive chip down the cleavage of a French roulette player in order to overtly draw the attention of Jessie Stevens (Jessie Royce Landis), one of richest personalities vacationing on the Côte d'Azur at the time. As the French player does not seem to speak English, Robie asks another player to translate what he has just said in English into French. The confusion and linguistic incomprehension, as well as Robie's simulated embarrassment, immediately capture the bystanders' attention, arousing their curiosity.

The second case occurs during the funeral of Foussard, one of Robie's former associates. His daughter Danielle, played by the French actress Brigitte Auber,[14] insults Robie quite furiously, code-switching from English to French, and chases him away. Resorting to French has a double effect. Firstly, it achieves a more realistic rendering of a private situation such as a funeral disturbed by an intruder: Danielle's irritation, her increasing anger, and her deep sorrow definitely have an extraordinary emotional impact as she expresses them in her mother tongue. The sequence would not have achieved the same result, if the actress had said her lines in any other language. Cases of code-switching obviously pose a challenge to film translation, particularly to dubbing.[15]

Secondly, multilingualism functions as a vehicle for suspense. Danielle accuses Robie of being "*un ignoble assassin*" ('a vile killer') and "*un voleur*" ('a thief') and then she also repeats some of the previous insults in English. Multilingualism is meant to cast doubt on Robie's innocence, as Danielle has insinuated with her accusation, making the audience suspicious of him for the first time ever. French clearly accentuates conflict between characters ("horizontal dimension of communication", Sanz Ortega 2011), while it may lead viewers to confusion ("vertical dimension", Sanz Ortega, *id.*) if they do not understand French. This state of uncertainty in which viewers are left, however, lasts only for a while, as a rough translation is provided on screen by the character herself. This way, if linguistic incomprehension is partially solved, the meaning of the sequence is conveyed anyway, in the sense that multilingualism achieves what it was aiming at: throwing doubt.

The Man Who Knew Too Much (1956) is the American remake of the previous film with the same title shot in 1934 in the UK (see Chiaro Nocella 1999). The plot is almost unchanged, but the first part of the remake takes place in Morocco. In this new version, English is the prevailing language, while Arabic and French are the secondary languages. Compared to the first version, shot in 1934, Hitchcock shows greater awareness of the role which multilingualism may play in the development of the story. Arabic, and more precisely lingua-cultural mediation from Arabic to English, becomes the means through which Louis Bernard (Daniel Gélin) befriends Ben and Jo McKenna (James Stewart and Doris Day) on the bus to Marrakesh. As viewers will learn later on, Bernard is in reality a French Intelligence agent on assignment in Morocco: he has to spot an apparently "ordinary" couple, who are actually terrorists.

Compared to Arabic, French is quantitatively more present in the film. It functions as a vehicle for suspense on different occasions. Firstly, at the McKennas' hotel room in Marrakesh: Louis Bernard has just arrived for a drink before going out for dinner, when a stranger with a sinister look knocks at the door, claiming in French that he is looking for another guest's room. As the man realizes his mistake, he apologizes and takes leave of them. Bernard immediately asks the McKennas whether he may make a phone call. He speaks on the phone in French and, as he hangs up, he goes away with an excuse. Who actually was that man? Why did Bernard leave so unexpectedly? As will be clarified afterwards, that sinister-looking man is the killer hired to shoot an important diplomat in London. As the stranger leaves, Bernard soon understands that he has spotted the wrong couple on the bus, which is why he goes away so suddenly.

The couple that Bernard is looking for are actually the Draytons (played respectively by Bernard Miles and Brenda De Banzie). Ben and Jo McKenna accidentally meet them in a local restaurant the same evening. While the two couples are dining together at the same table, Bernard comes in, in company with a girl, apparently ignoring the group. Later, during dinner, the girl asks Bernard in French: *"C'est ça la couple que tu cherches?"* ('Is that the couple you are looking for?'), to which he answers: *"Oui, c'est ça"* ('Yes, exactly'). In both scenes, French has never been subtitled into English, thus leaving viewers in the dark to some extent. Nonetheless, employing multilingualism becomes a way of increasing the suspense as it clearly alludes at something suspicious happening, or about to happen.

The following morning, after Bernard is murdered, Mr Drayton offers to go with Ben to the local police station to interpret for him, as Ben speaks no French. On their arrival, Drayton explains to the police officer the reason why he is there with the American man. The officer tells him in English: "We won't need any interpreter, *Monsieur*". Later, as the story unfolds, we understand the reason why the man was so interested in being present during the interview: he is one of the conspirators who are planning the assassination in London. Similarly, when the McKennas arrive in London, Ben is questioned by a Scotland Yard officer at the airport. In order not to compromise what he knows, he tells the officer: "The man spoke in French. I don't understand a single word of French." Multilingualism is once again a fruitful resource to increase suspense, a device that leads the story to further narrative developments.

The analysis concludes with *Torn Curtain*,[16] probably Hitchcock's most well-structured multilingual film, because not only does it resort to multilingualism very frequently (quantitative standpoint), but it also uses it as a vehicle for suspense (qualitative perspective). While English is the prevailing language in the film, Norwegian, Danish and Swedish are the secondary languages. They are all restricted in quantitative terms and generally remain in the background for a more realistic representation of the different geographic situations in which the film's events occur: the story opens with a cruise on the North Sea aboard a Norwegian liner, then it moves onto Copenhagen, to set most of the film's events in East Berlin, and finally it concludes on the Swedish coast. On the contrary, German may be considered a "co-primary" language because of its significant presence in both qualitative and quantitative terms.

Besides a more realistic representation, with most of the film's events set in East Germany, German is used both to accentuate conflict between characters (diegetic level) and to produce suspense (viewers' perception). In other words, it both gives the plot a "boost" to further narrative developments and it functions as a semiotic device to increase suspense, very often simultaneously within the same scene. This happens, for instance, in the scene in which Michael Armstrong, the film's main character, kills Gromek, the East German security officer assigned to him, in the isolated farmhouse where his contact from Pi, an anti-communist organisation, lives. Later, it occurs again when the East German police go back to the farmhouse searching for Gromek's body.

Another exemplary case is the famous scene in which Michael and his assistant / fiancée Sarah escape from Leipzig travelling on a fake bus towards East Berlin, an operation organized by the escape network related to Pi, and led by Mr Jacobi. Time is deliberately dilated so as to increase suspense: roadblocks, highway robbery by Soviet Army deserters, bunching with the real bus, anything seems to happen; even multilingualism seems to further accentuate the tension. One of the passengers on this bus, Fräulein Mann, insistently complains about having the two Americans with them, stressing the point that it may seriously endanger their enterprise. She continuously code-switches from English to German. Multilingualism is a semiotic device which contributes to producing the emotional tension involved in this scene, and even to accentuating it: as a result, viewers feel a growing sense of anxiety as the journey proceeds.

To conclude, it is worth considering the final sequence of the film, when the two main characters reach the Swedish coast travelling on a freighter hidden in two big baskets. The two baskets are about to be dumped ashore, when a German ballerina[17] begins to suspect something. Suddenly she starts to shout out something in German. Though no subtitles are provided, what she is saying is self-evident: the visual code, combined with the understanding of the overall context, helps the viewer to draw the meaning of the verbal code. Once more, the suspense is increased by multilingualism.

6. Concluding remarks

This study has analysed the semiotic role that multilingualism plays in Alfred Hitchcock's films, focusing on the implications it has in the construction of

Giuseppe De Bonis

how lang. develops thru time

suspense. A diachronic analysis of the evolution that multilingualism has undergone from the director's early production of the 1930s to the end of the 1960s has been carried out showing how so-called "secondary languages", though restricted in quantitative terms, have, however, a crucial function in qualitative terms. The analysis has defined and discussed three main functions that the presence of different languages on screen has in the films directed by the universally acknowledged "master of thrill", namely realistic rendering, conflict and confusion. If realistic rendering aims at enhancing viewers' perceptions of the reality depicted on screen, particularly if the story has an "international" setting with characters coming from different countries, conflict as well as confusion of languages and lingua-cultural identities all become effective semiotic strategies to produce the distinctive feature of Hitchcock's films: suspense. Embracing a wider semiotic perspective has led to the need to stress the "delicate" role played by multilingualism in the director's production, which has turned out to be important for the unfolding of the film's story.

Multilingualism in Hitchcock's filmography has thus to be carefully evaluated and studied not only from a semiotic standpoint, but also from a translational one. The latter consideration leads us to pose further questions, as we move from the original version of the film which has been taken in consideration in the study, to its translated version, whether it is subtitled or dubbed. In particular it will be interesting to carry out a similar diachronic analysis of the different solutions adopted by audiovisual translators in the dubbed version of Hitchcock's multilingual films. The aim would be to verify how a complex phenomenon such as multilingualism has been managed in translation (See Heiss 2004; Dwyer 2005; Wahl 2005, 2008; Sanz Ortega 2011, De Bonis forthcoming), particularly in dubbing, which appears to be more oriented towards linguistic flattening and homogenisation and thus more "vulnerable" to the challenge that multilingualism represents.

---

[1] "Embedded translation" and "cushioning translation" (Baldo *id.*) are alternative labels for contextual translation. The two concepts were originally used by Camarca (2005) to refer to literary texts, but they can easily be applied to audiovisual texts as well. Cases of embedded translation occur when, during a conversion, the meaning of a question is drawn from its answer resorting to code-switching strategies, while in case of cushioning translation, a single foreign word is inserted into a dialogue or conversation in the dominant language so that the words that accompany it explain its meaning, operating as a sort of vocabulary or thesaurus.
[2] Jill and Bob Lawrence (Edna Best and Leslie Banks) are spending a winter holiday with their daughter Betty in Saint Moritz, Switzerland. One night, while Jill is dancing with their friend Louis Bernard, a secret agent, the man is shot to death. Before dying, Bernard manages to tell Bob of an assassination about to take place in London, planned by some terrorists. Fearing that their plan would be revealed, the conspirators kidnap Betty and carry her off to London with them. The couple thus goes back to London, searching for their daughter.
[3] During the First World War, the English novelist Edgar Brodie (John Gielgud) is sent to Switzerland

154

by the British Intelligence Service to kill a German agent. During the mission he meets first a fake general and then his colleague Elsa Carrington (Madeleine Carroll). After mistakenly targeting an innocent old man –amed Caypor– as the German operative, both Edgar and Elsa start questioning the morality of the mission.

[4] The combination of thriller and romance is a very common feature throughout Hitchcock's filmography, far beyond the multilingual films taken in consideration in this study. See Truffaut 1966.

[5] The written messages in the film represent an interesting case of "cushioning translation" (Baldo 2009a; 2009b): all the notes and telegrams which are in German are first shown in the original language and then replaced with their English translation. Translation is thus provided directly in the film's images as the verbal part of the visual code.

[6] Travellers on a trans-European train are delayed for a night due to bad weather conditions in a small fictional country somewhere in the Balkans called Bandrika, which is governed by a dictator. The passengers are hosted in a small village hotel, where socialite Iris Henderson (Margaret Lockwood) meets an old woman named Miss Froy (Dame May Whitty). Shortly after the journey restarts, Miss Froy mysteriously vanishes from the train.

[7] The film is based on the novel of the same title written by Daphne du Maurier in 1938. A naive paid-companion (Joan Fontaine) meets the wealthy widower Maxim de Winter (Laurence Olivier) in Monte Carlo. They fall in love, marry and return to Manderley, the man's large country estate in England. The second Mrs de Winter clashes with the housekeeper, Mrs Danvers (Judith Anderson), and discovers that the memory of the first wife Rebecca still maintains a strange grip on her husband and the servants.

[8] As will be discussed in more detail in the next section, this turns out to be quite a common strategy aiming at a more "realistic" portrait of what occurs on screen: resorting to some expressions or words in a different language from the film's main language of communication is a way of enhancing viewers' perception of the linguistic reality in which the story takes place.

[9] The film is an adaptation from the 1950's novel of the same title by Patricia Highsmith. Tennis star Guy Haines (Farley Granger) meets a stranger on a train who proposes a "criss-cross murder". The man, named Bruno Anthony (Robert Walker), will kill Guy's estranged wife on condition that Guy kills Bruno's hated father. Guy does not take Bruno seriously until his wife is found murdered in an amusement park. When Bruno, who is a psychopath, understands that Guy does not intend to kill his father, he begins to harass Guy, determined to persuade him to maintain "their deal".

[10] The homogenising convention is still a very common practice in the Italian dubbing of multilingual films, which tends to reduce the different languages present in the original version to one language alone (Italian), resorting to "stereotypical" accents to differentiate the characters' nationalities (see De Bonis forthcoming). Interestingly enough, in the Italian dubbed version of Topaz all the characters speak a standardised Italian showing no traces of different accents, although it could have been quite feasible to make them speak with a slight foreign accent.

[11] The main function of the sequence is to give the viewer a "flavour" of the linguistic reality in which the story should actually occur, a French-speaking community. This turns out to be quite a common strategy as the homogenising convention operates on screen.

[12] The American reporter, John Jones (Joel McCrea), is sent to Europe to find out what is really occurring on the eve of Second World War. While in Amsterdam to attend a peace conference, where the Dutch diplomat Van Meer (Albert Bassermann) is expected to give an important speech, Jones witnesses the "apparent" murder of the man. He immediately sets off after the gunman only to find that the real Van Meer has been kidnapped and is being held by some enemy agents. Jones does his best to get to the bottom of the matter and to set the diplomat free.

[13] The story is set on the French Riviera where the American expatriate John Robie (Cary Grant) has moved, after retiring from his occupation as a "cat burglar". As a new series of jewel robberies leads the police to suspect him, Robie makes every effort "to catch" the real thief in order to prove his innocence.

[14] Danielle is the daughter of Foussard, one of Robie's former associates. The Foussards are French,

but they speak English almost all the time in the film. They both have a clear French accent as they speak English. See the aforementioned considerations on the homogenising convention made in the previous paragraph.

[15] The Italian dubbed version of this scene, for instance, does not have the same force as the original, because both English and French have been adapted into Italian, with the consequent neutralisation of this multilingual situation.

[16] American Professor Michael Armstrong (Paul Newman) defects to Eastern Germany, followed by his reluctant assistant/fiancée, Sarah Sherman (Julie Andrews). In reality, his defection is not genuine: his real mission is to steal a secret mathematical formula from a renowned scientist in Leipzig and to escape back to the West as soon as he obtains it.

[17] This German ballerina was flying on the same plane to East Berlin as Armstrong. She is also the lead ballerina in the crowded theatre, from where Michael and Sarah escape after being spotted by the woman. Humorously, she is never the "star" whose arrival is anxiously awaited by the press. As she arrives in East Berlin, she mistakenly believes that the journalists are there to greet her rather than Armstrong. Something similar happens on her arrival in Sweden.

Bibliography

Primary Sources

Balcon, Michael and Ivor Montagu (Producers) and Alfred Hitchcock (Director). 1936. *The Secret Agent*. United Kingdom: Gaumon British Distributors.

Black, Edward (Producer) and Alfred Hitchcock (Director). 1938. *The Lady Vanishes*. United Kingdom: Metro-Goldwyn-Mayer.

Chaplin, Charles (Producer and Director). 1940. *The Great Dictator*. United States: United Artists.

Hitchcock, Alfred (Producer and Director). [1934]1956. *The Man Who Knew Too Much*. United States: Universal Pictures.

————. (Producer and Director). 1934. *The Man Who Knew Too Much*. United Kingdom: Paramount Pictures and Universal Pictures.

————. (Producer and Director). 1946. *Notorious*. United States: RKO Radio Pictures.

————. (Producer and Director). 1951. *Strangers on a Train*. United States: Warner Bros.

————. (Producer and Director). 1953. *I Confess*. United States: Warner Bros.

————. (Producer and Director). 1954. *To Catch a Thief*. United States: Paramount Pictures.

————. (Producer and Director). 1956. *The Wrong Man*. United States: Warner Bros.

————. (Producer and Director). 1966. *Torn Curtain*. United States: Universal Pictures.

————. (Producer and Director). 1969. *Topaz*. United States: Universal Pictures.

Macgowan, Kennet (Producer) and Alfred Hitchcock. 1944. *Lifeboat*. United States: 20th Century Fox

Selznick, Davod O. (Producer), and Hitchcock, Alfred (Director). 1940. *Rebecca*. United States: United Artists.

Wanger, Walter (Producer), and Alfred Hitchcock (Director). 1940. *Foreign Correspondent*. United States: United Artists.

Secondary sources

Baldo, Michela. 2009a. 'Subtitling Multilingual Films. The Case of Lives of the Saints, an Italian-Canadian TV screenplay' in Federici, Federico M. (ed.) *Translating Regionalised Voices in Audiovisuals*. Roma: Aracne. 117-135.

————. 2009b. 'Dubbing multilingual films. La terra del ritorno and the Italian-Canadian immigrant experience" in Giorgio Marrano, Michela, Giovanni Nadiani and Christopher Rundle (eds) *The translation of dialects in Multimedia*. Special issue of *InTRAlinea*.

Camarca, Silvia. 2005. 'Code-switching and textual strategies in Nino Ricci's trilogy' in *Semiotica* 154-1 (4): 225-241.

Chiaro Nocella, Delia. 1999. 'The Man Who Knew Too Much: Hitchcock remakes Hitchcock' In Bussi, G. Elisa and Delia Chiaro (eds) *Letteratura e Cinema. Il remake*. Bologna: CLUEB. 161-174.

————. 2009. 'Issues in audiovisual translation' in Munday, Jeremy (ed.) *The Routledge Companion to Translation Studies*. London: Routledge. 141-165.

Cronin, Michael. 2009. *Translation goes to the movies*. London and New York: Routledge.

De Bonis, Giuseppe (forthcoming) 'Commedia in scompiglio: One, Two, Three. Il multilinguismo come veicolo di umorismo'. To appear in *Translating Humor in Audiovisual Texts*.

Dwyer, Tessa. 2005. 'Universally speaking: Lost in Translation and polyglot cinema' in Delabastita, Dirk and Rainer Grutman (eds). *Fictionalising translation and multilingualism. Linguistica Antverpiensia New Series 4*: 295-310.

Heiss, Christine. 2004. 'Dubbing Multilingual Films: A New Challenge?' in *Meta. Translator's Journal* 49 (1): 208-220.

O'Sullivan, Carol. 2011. *Translating Popular Film*. Basingstoke: Palgrave Macmillan.

Sanz Ortega, Elena. 2011. 'Subtitling and the Relevance of Non-verbal Information in Polyglot Films' in *New Voices in Translation Studies* 7: 19-34. URL: http://www.iatis.org/images/stories /publications/new-voices/Issue7-2011/article-sanz-2011.pdf (consulted 10.12.2012)

Sternberg, Meir. 1981. 'Polylingualism as Reality and Translation as Mimesis' in *Poetics Today* 2(4): 221-239.

Truffaut, François. 1966 (1983). *Le cinéma selon Hitchcock*. Avec la collaboration de Helen Scott. Paris: Gallimard. Italian translation: 2009. Il cinema secondo Hitchcock. Milano: Il Saggiatore.

Wahl, Chris. 2005. 'Discovering a genre: the polyglot film' in *Cinemascope* (1).

———. 'Du Deutscher, toi français, you English: beautiful! – The polyglot film as a genre' in Christensen, Miyase and Nezih Erdöğan (eds) *Shifting Landscapes. Film and Media in European Context*. Newcastle: Cambridge Scholars Publishing. 334-350.

Zabalbeascoa, Patrick. 2010. 'Translation in constrained communication and entertainment' in Díaz Cintas, Jorge, Anna Matamala and Josélia Neves (eds) *New Insights into Audiovisual Translation and Media Accessibility – Media for All 2*. Amsterdam and New York: Rodopi. 25-40.

Zárate, Soledad. 2010. 'Bridging the gap between Deaf Studies and AVT for Deaf children' in Díaz Cintas, Jorge, Anna Matamala and Josélia Neves (eds) *New Insights into Audiovisual Translation and Media Accessibility – Media for All 2*. Amsterdam and New York: Rodopi. 159-174.

Part III

Transferring narrative structure, plot and semiotic elements in translation

Chapter 9: The narrator's voice in translation: What remains from a linguistic experiment in Wolf Haas's Brenner detective novels _2012_

Jenny Brumme

Abstract

The aim of this article is to study the translation of fictive orality in the specific genre of suspense. Crime fiction has experienced some substantial innovations in recent years. We find that contemporary thrillers tend to use highly differentiated language to enhance character portrayal and also employ more realistic conversational style in everyday dialogues. The challenges deriving from this new crime fiction are briefly outlined by some examples from Wolf Haas's novels featuring Detective Brenner. Attention is paid to how suspense is generated in the Austrian source text and its translation into the target texts (English, French and Spanish). More specifically, the language awareness of the writer is related to the characteristics of the narrator's voice (informal T-form and dialogue with the reader). The different empirical data observed in the ST and the TTs highlight the interplay between the devices of spoken language (truisms, telegraphic style) and strategies used in order to bolster the suspense (holding-up of the showdown, allusions, play on words).

Keywords: Style (and translation priorities), fictive orality, suspense, detective novels, translation (of stylistic features), character portrayal

1. Introduction

Crime fiction has experienced some substantial innovations in recent years. For example, we find that contemporary thrillers tend to use highly differentiated language to enhance character portrayal and also employ more realistic conversational style in everyday dialogues. An interesting example can be found in Wolf Haas's Brenner detective novels. This enormously successful series of detective stories combines the structure and argument of the well-known hard-boiled thriller with a generous dose of dark humour and satirical criticism of Austrian society. However, one of the novels' striking features is language. The style created by Haas seems to imitate Austrian spoken language use, but this "linguistic hallucination" (Fludernik 1993: 453) consists of an ingenious amalgam of two aspects. On the one hand, there are characteristics found in the language of communicative immediacy and, on the other, language of distance. This extremely elaborated language gives support to two outstanding voices. There is the voice of private eye Brenner himself and also a narrator's voice, which presents certain parallels to the traditional omniscient narrator, but differs from it in some ways, as we will see when examining the translations.

Therefore, the title of my article directly refers to Nindl's study of Wolf Haas's literary style; she describes his style in terms of a linguistic experiment in crime fiction (2010). Naturally, there are always problems while translating; but it is supposed that a new experimental style will increase problems for translators. In the Brenner detective novels language and style become protagonists of the plot.

The aim of my article is to briefly outline the challenges deriving from this renewed crime fiction written by Haas and its translation into English, French and Spanish. In order to highlight the importance of language while translating, Haas's acute awareness of language is characterized by two of his statements on this point (see Nindl 2009; Schwitalla 2009). This will enable me to argue for maintaining certain traits of Haas's narrative language as a priority of translation. Then I will focus on the peculiarities of the narrator's voice and its function for creating suspense. In a last step I will briefly present some of the different devices and their reflection in the English translation (allusions, dialogue with the reader, truisms, anticipation, etc.). On this basis I will finally argue for considering the importance of style and language in a genre which is often seen as a minor one belonging to the popular culture of entertainment and therefore not so powerful as "serious literature" (Schreckenberger 2010).

2. The Brenner novels and their translations into English, French and Spanish

Wolf Haas was born in 1960 in a little village (Maria Alm) in the Austrian province of Salzburg. As he stated in a very extensive interview with *Die Welt am Sonntag* (2 January 2011), his parents worked as waiters and growing up in a Catholic boarding school, his life and his parents' lives diverged over time, particularly when he went on to study psychology, German philology and linguistics. He gained his PhD on *The linguistic foundations of concrete poetry*, published in 1990. After university he worked as an advertising copywriter.

Between 1996 and 2003 he wrote six of the seven detective stories which feature detective Simon Brenner. In 2009 Wolf Haas published the seventh and last one *Brenner and God*. This was the first to be translated into English. As the following table shows, a systematic analysis of a homogeneous corpus of the translations is impossible for the three target languages I have chosen:

Table 1. The Brenner novels in English, French and Spanish

ST	ENGLISH TT1	FRENCH TT2	SPANISH TT3
1996: *Auferstehung der Toten.* Roman.		2007: *Quitter Zell.* Traduit de l'allemand (Autriche) par Marie Reygnier.	2011: *La resurrección de los muertos.* Traducido por María Esperanza Romero.
1997: *Der Knochenmann.* Roman.	2013: *The Bone Man.* Translated by Annie Janusch.		2011: *El triturador de huesos.* Traducido por María Esperanza Romero.
1998: *Komm, süßer Tod.* Roman.		2002: *Vienne la mort.* Traduit de l'allemand (Autriche) par Marie Reygnier.	2012: *Ven, dulce muerte.* Traducción de María Esperanza Romero.
1999: *Silentium!* Roman.		2004: *Silentium!* Traduit de l'allemand (Autriche) par Marie Reygnier.	
2001: *Wie die Tiere.* Roman.			
2003: *Das ewige Leben.* Roman.			
2009: *Der Brenner und der liebe Gott.* Roman.	2012: *Brenner and God.* Translated by Annie Janusch.		

It goes without saying that the novels have won several prizes for crime fiction, and in Austria there is a real Brennermania.

3. Language awareness and language use

3.1. Language awareness

Before I analyse some aspects of the narrator's voice, I would like to focus on the writer's language awareness. In the interview with *Die Welt am Sonntag* newspaper, Haas confessed that he started late with reading and it was writing that motivated him to read. He emphasised that his language always has a strong rhythm, a so-called "Brenner-Sound". He cannot write without a formal idea, that is to say, he needs a certain mannerism, mostly an experimental form, in order to convey the plot. Given that, for 15 years, no publishing house wanted to publish his novels, one day he started writing in a new, unorthodox way.

ST. Welt am Sonntag: Wie sind Sie überhaupt auf den Brenner-Sound gekommen?
Wolf Haas: Den ersten Brenner-Roman habe ich aus einer starken Trotzhaltung heraus geschrieben. Bis dahin hatte ich 15 Jahre lang keinen Verlag gefunden. Irgendwann habe ich einfach so geschrieben, wie man angeblich nicht schreiben darf, wie es mir aber am meisten Spaß gemacht hat. [...]
Wenn man als Kind unstudierter Eltern auf einmal studieren darf, ist das ja grundsätzlich schön für einen. Aber es entfernt einen auch von seinen Wurzeln. Die Sprache ist für mich offenbar ein Trick, meine Herkunft und die durch Bildung entstandene Gegenwart miteinander zu vereinbaren. (Lochbihler 2011)

TT1. *Welt am Sonntag*: How did you actually come up with the Brenner-Sound?
Wolf Haas: I wrote the first Brenner novel out of a strongly rebellious attitude. For fifteen years I had been unable to find a publisher. One day I simply wrote the way you supposedly mustn't write and for the most part I had more fun.
If you're suddenly allowed to study as a child of parents without any university studies, it's undoubtedly wonderful for you. But it takes you away from your roots. For me, language is evidently a trick to reconcile the two: my past and the present that has come from education. [*my translation*]

This quotation shows that an author's language awareness and his or her statements are particularly interesting not only for critics, readers and linguists, but first and foremost for translators. In our recent studies we have paid little attention to this point,[1] which needs an in-depth insight in order to relate our linguistic and cross-linguistic approach to translation studies.

In our research project,[2] we started from the assumption that fictive orality has to be described considering the interplay between two elements. On the one hand there are the selected features which evoke a spoken context in a written text, and their functions in fictional dialogue. On the other, there are the reflections on language and language use adduced by the authors and translators of fictional texts, the so-called metalinguistic thought. Both of these elements are essential for an inner-linguistic and cross-linguistic approach to the ST and the different TTs.

In the case of the Brenner novels, the author's awareness of language also suggests some priorities in translation. A very important one is to elaborate the immediacy of the narrator's voice and to maintain as many as possible of the oral features. Once more, the metalinguistic reflections highlight the need to consider language peculiarities in translation:

ST. Wolf Haas: Ich glaube, sie hat viel mehr damit zu tun, wie man als kleines Kind die Sprache der Erwachsenen wahrnimmt. Wenn man als Kind Sprache schon ein wenig versteht, aber noch nicht richtig beherrscht –etwa mit zweieinhalb Jahren–, hört man dauernd Erwachsene reden. Dabei bekommt man allerdings mehr den Gefühlsgehalt des Geredeten als das Rationale mit: 'Pass auf! Du, hör mal zu!' und solche Sachen. Ich glaube, dass meine Erzählsprache damit viel zu tun hat. Auch dass man manches nur halb versteht und den Rest selbst ergänzen muss. (Lochbihler 2011)

TT1. Wolf Haas: I believe that it [this way of speaking] has to do much more with the way you as a child perceive the language of the adults. If you as a child already understand the language a little but you haven't mastered it correctly yet –for instance when you are two and a half years old– you permanently hear adults talking. In this case, however, you catch more the emotional meaning of what is said than the rational meaning: 'Mind out! Hey, listen to me!' and such things. I believe that my telling-language in this way has to do a lot. Also that one understands only half and must make up the rest oneself. [*my translation*]

It becomes clear by this quotation that Wolf Haas's way of telling the Brenner stories is connected with the language heard in his childhood. But there is also another feature mentioned: the hearer or reader of the stories has to construct the meaning like in an oral telling situation; the reader must infer details and must complete the meaning. This is essential for translators, because they often tend to explain the hidden signs and make the cues clearer.[3] However, the different translation strategies can try to observe these intentions, but naturally this purpose is limited by the specific devices each of the target languages uses in order to evoke spokenness in written texts.

3.2. Allusions and playful use of language

Another main feature of Wolf Haas's novels can be appreciated even by the title of the first Brenner story, translated into French and Spanish: *The Resurrection of the Dead*. All the Brenner novels are characterised by the very frequent allusions or reference to other texts or cultural facts (Nindl 2010: 269-271).

Related to this feature is the playful use of language and language ambiguities. This is also the case with the title *Auferstehung der Toten*. Suspense is created because of the grammatical ambiguity of German (see Table 2). The allusion to the New Testament, which is the most obvious, sets the reader off on the wrong track, while the other interpretation of the grammatical form leads to the denouement and solution of the case.

Figure 2. Ambiguities of the German title

Auferstehung der Toten (Resurrection of the Dead)	
der Toten (New Testament): genitive, plural (of the dead persons)	*der Toten* (novel): genitive, singular (of the dead woman)
Suspense	*Dénouement*
Tension (the wrong track): two murdered Americans	Eutension (the right track): the murderer

This ambiguity is maintained throughout the whole novel and there are several cues in the text, which are a real problem for translation. The French title *Quitter Zell* (the place where action happens) changes completely and the allusion is ignored. The translator into Spanish, María Esperanza Romero, decided to keep the closest solution to the original text and the allusions to the New Testament. Naturally, in Spanish there is no grammatical ambiguity. So, the title sets the reader off on the wrong track (*la resurrection de los muertos*, 'the resurrection of the dead people' which means 'the resurrection of the dead' vs. *la resurrección de la muerta*, 'the resurrection of the dead woman'):

(1)
ST. «Auferstehung der Toten.»
«Jajaja, obwohl gar nicht Ostern gewesen ist.»
«Wie hast du das damals eigentich gemeint?»
«Ja, wenn die Parsons nach ihrem Tod noch Schecks ausstellen. Müssen sie ja fast auferstanden sein. Bei Jesus ist das auch nicht anders gewesen.»
«Also Plural: die Toten. Genitiv: der Toten.»
«Ja, sag einmal, Brenner!»
«Aber bei Jesus, da hätten wir Singular: Auferstehung des Toten.»
«Ja, sag einmal, Brenner, zu was fragst du mich das alles?»
«Wozu, Mandl, man sagt: wozu! Und wie heißt es richtig, wenn die Vergolder Schwester auferstanden ist?»
«Da heißt es, aha! Wieder: Auferstehung der Toten.»
«Genau. Weil zu was haben wir eine Grammatik.»
«Der Duden-Detektiv!› [...]»   *The grammar detective*
(Auferstehung 2012: 150-151)

TT2. –«Résurrection».
–Oui. Pourtant, nous ne sommes pas à Pâques.
–Qu'est-ce que tu entendais par là?
–Que les Parson rédigeaient des chèques après leur mort. Qu'il fallait bien pour cela qu'ils soient sortis de leur tombe. Jésus ne s'y pas pris autrement.
–Donc, tu parles de deux résurrections, même avec un mot au singulier.
–Mais qu'est-ce qui te prend, Brenner ?
–Si tu avais voulu parler de la résurrection de Jésus en particulier, tu aurais utilisé le même terme au singulier. Pour être précis, tu aurais dû dire : « Résurrection du mort ».
–Mais dis-moi, Brenner, c'est quoi ça, toutes ces questions ?
–On dit: *Qu'est-ce que c'est que ces questions*, Mandl, voilà ce que l'on dit quand on s'exprime correctement. Et si tu avais voulu parler de la résurrection de la sœur d'Anstretter en particulier ?
–J'aurais dit: «Résurrection de la morte».
–Exactement. Le génitif, ce n'est pas fait pour les chiens. C'est quoi ça, cette façon de dire les choses à moitié?
–Le détective grammairien! [...] (Quitter Zell 2007: 170)

TT3. –«La resurrección de los muertos.»
–Jo, jo, jo. Y eso que aún no estábamos en Pascua.
–¿Se puede saber a quién te referías con esa frase?
–Pues a los Parson. Si podían girar cheques, es que tenían que haber resucitado. Que con Jesucristo pasó lo mismo.
–¿O sea que pensabas en los americanos?
–A ver, Brenner, ¿en quién si no?

–Pero en el caso de Jesucristo habría que decir la resurrección de entre los muertos, ¿verdad?
–Córtala ya, Brenner. ¿Pa qué me preguntas esas tonterías?
–«Para qué», Mandl, se dice «para qué». ¿Por qué cómo hay que decir si la resucitada es, por ejemplo, la hermana del orfebre?
–Pues igual… Ahora caigo… La resurrección de entre los muertos…
–Eso mismo, porque pa qué tenemos la gramática.
–El detective gramático. […]
(Resurrección 2011: 164)

But, the real difficulty is at the end of the novel, when Brenner and the journalist, Mandl, sum up the evidence. Brenner tries to explain that it was the grammatical ambiguity of an article written by Mandl which gave him the key. The French translator, Marie Reygnier, tried to explain the ambiguity, as we can see in quotation (2). She maintains the opposition singular-plural with *deux résurrections* 'two resurrections'. So, she can play with *Résurrection du mort* 'resurrection of the dead man' and *Résurrection de la morte* 'resurrection of the dead woman' (Metz 2011: 76-79). But, strictly speaking, the reference to the genitive is not coherent with the French grammatical system (*Le génitif, ce n'est pas fait pour les chiens*).

In the Spanish translation, the cue is clearer because of the two prepositions: *la resurección de entre los muertos* 'the resurrection from among the dead people'. This could even have been the title *La resurección de entre los muertos*, but the combination of the two prepositions is inconvenient; the cue is clearer, the allusion is less strong.

We can find another example in the third Brenner story, also translated into French and Spanish. The novel incorporates a quotation from the St Matthew Passion by Johann Sebastian Bach (BWV 244), *Komm, süßes Kreuz* (Come, Sweet Cross), a song for solo bass voice and viola da gamba. But Brenner is wrong and sings *Komm, süßer Tod* (*Come, Sweet Death*), a song for solo voice and basso continuo from the *69 Sacred Songs and Arias* by Bach (BWV 478). The title and the cues in the text (Nindl 2010: 273-276) set the reader on the path to the murder act (injecting insulin to diabetics), while Brenner unconsciously anticipates the correct solution of the case. Therefore, the whole text works by interwoven allusions and hidden cues, which should be taken into account in its translations.

This novel and two others were made into films. *Come, Sweet Death* (2001) is available with English subtitles; but I should mention that the film was also broadcast with subtitles in order to transfer Austriacisms and coarse language into standard German (Nindl 2010: 49).[4] In France, some of the publishing houses consequently chose to distribute the novel in a way that highlighted its origin: «*traduit de l'allemand (Autriche)*» ('translated from German (Austria)'; Daran 2010: 41-50).

4. Characteristics of the narrator's voice and their translation into English

We can claim that the main attraction of the Brenner detective novels is the narrator's voice. All the plots are narrated through this unmistakeable voice. This first-person narrator apparently shares aspects of the omniscient narrator: he tells the story, he knows the scene and the events and he knows Brenner and the other characters. Nindl, who studied the language of the first six novels, states that 83% of the total text corpus belongs to the narrator's voice (Nindl 2010: 189). In comparison with the character of Watson in Conan Doyle's Sherlock Holmes novels, the narrator's voice does not belong to the narrated world. This "Austro-Watson", as Haas calls him, tells and comments on the story from a position outside of the reported events. And the narrator seems to be a professional at his job of keeping the listener or reader engaged with the story and with himself.

As we have already seen (3.1.), the language of the narrator connects with the language Haas heard in his childhood and home village. This spoken dialect is the emotional link to his past, and the narrator's voice exploits this link in order to keep the reader engaged and to direct his or her attention. I think that this highly emotional language, full of everyday expressions, subjective points of view, humour, playful distortions of ordinary phrases, dialect, and down to earth remarks, explains its success. I do not believe it is that important to the reader if he or she, in fact, understands all the words. The overall feel of the language, rather than a precise grasp of its meaning, seems to be what readers find attractive.

Below are some examples mostly taken from the last novel because there is an English translation.

4.1. Informal T-form, dialogue with the reader and "omniscient" narrator

First of all, the narrator's voice is clearly different from the voice of the private eye Simon Brenner. Brenner's investigations are told, commented on and judged by this voice. In order to reduce quotations to a minimum, I will analyse several features in the same extract. I will centre on the last chapters of *Brenner and God*, because what is apparently the main intrigue has been resolved, that is to say, the kidnapped two-year-old girl has been found. But Brenner's investigations go on to discover political corruption, sexual exploitation and extortion by Viennese politicians, bankers, and real estate magnates, all implicated in the kidnapping.

(2)
ST. **Der Brenner** ist ein bisschen ins Schwitzen gekommen, wie er das gelesen hat. **Ob du es glaubst oder nicht**, von den vier Leuten auf dem Foto hat er drei gekannt: [...] Und der Vierte war ein hoher Wiener Politiker, mit dem hab ich mir ausgemacht, dass ich ihn

nicht namentlich nenne. **Das musst du verstehen**, weil Quelle. (Gott: 166, *my emphasis*)

TT1.   **Brenner** started sweating a little when he read that. **Believe it or not**, of the four people in the photo, he knew three: [...] And the fourth was a high-ranking Vienna politician, who I have an agreement with not to identify him by name. **You'll have to take my word on it** because—sources. (God: 160, *my emphasis*)

In quotation (2) we can identify the following features: The narrator and the protagonist are two different people: the narrator tells the story and introduces Brenner from his point of view. His behaviour towards the reader is as towards a peer. He addresses the reader as someone he knows well with the informal T-form (Brown and Gilman 1960), a feature not shared in the English address system, but evoked by the way of speaking.

The narrator uses a restricted set of formulae for establishing the fictive dialogue with the reader and to inspire confidence in the narrated story. He apparently knows more than the reader and even Brenner, as remarks such as "who I have an agreement with not to identify him by name" show. In this regard he is similar to an omniscient narrator.

4.2. Truisms and plays on words

One of the most prominent features of the narrator's discourse is his use of idioms, sayings, proverbs and pseudo phrasal expressions. As Nindl (2010: 196-200) states, these devices help to evoke the naturalness of speech and the colloquial register. By using this type of generalization, the narrator underlines the validity of his story. As we can see in quotation (3), the narrator often sets up truisms and expressions which seem to be fixed, but which are created during the fluent discourse of telling. So, *der Mensch ist unbelehrbar* seems to be a maxim, because of its form starting with *der Mensch*, which often introduces a generalization.

(3)
ST.   Aber in dieser Hinsicht ist **der Mensch** unbelehrbar. **Er** versucht auch in der ausweglosen Situation noch vorherzusehen, wie es weitergeht. Weil **er** gar nicht anders kann. Und der Brenner natürlich immer noch fieberhaft überlegt, während er in der größten **Lebensgefahr** war, oder sagt man **Todesgefahr**? Siehst du, das weiß ich jetzt nicht mehr, **Lebensgefahr** oder **Todesgefahr**, jedenfalls war der Brenner mitten drin, ... (Gott 2009: 176)
TT1.   But **people** are stubborn in this regard. Even in a hopeless situation, **a person** will still try to predict what's going to happen next. Because there's nothing else to be done. And Brenner, of course, was feverishly doing just that while **his life was at its greatest risk**—or would you say while **his death was at its greatest risk**? You see, I don't know anymore, **life at risk** or **death at risk**. Anyway, Brenner was in the middle of it,... (God 2012: 169, *my emphasis*)

This kind of generality can easily become superficial and tiring. The narrator, as a professional storyteller, knows how to keep the reader or listener engaged. A powerful trick is humour, often created by plays on words or puns. In quotation (3) we can find a play with *Leben* (*life*) and *Tod* (*death*) starting with *es besteht Lebensgefahr* (literally 'there is a risk of life'). For the translation, this can be a problem, but in this quotation the translator could resolve the difficulty as we can see by the same play between *death* and *life* but in reversed order: *there is a risk of death.*

4.3. Comparisons, anticipation and information mentioned in passing

In quotation (4), we can identify some other features of the narrator's voice:

(4)
ST.   Ein bisschen komisch hat das schon ausgesehen, der Baustellenwärter muskulös wie ein Ochse, keine Haare auf dem Kopf Tätowierungen auf seinem breiten Hals, aber am Nikotinpfeifchen hat er gesogen wie ein Säugling. **Nur im Nachhinein muss man sagen**, es hat schon auch etwas Tragisches, wenn sich einer **in den letzten Lebensstunden** noch damit quält, sich das Rauchen abzugewöhnen. (Gott 2009: 178)

TT1.   It looked a little strange, the construction-site guard, muscular as an ox, not a hair on his head but twenty-five tattoos on his thick neck to compensate, and he was sucking on the nicotine pipe like an infant. **You can only say this in retrospect**, but there's something tragic about someone still struggling to quit smoking **even in the last hours of his life**. (God 2012: 171-172, *my emphasis*)

In this case the narrator anticipates the future events: *Nur im Nachhinein muss man sagen...* (*You can only say this in retrospect...*). Repeatedly he mentions some highly important information in passing: *in den letzten Lebensstunden* (*even in the last hours of his life*). In this scene Brenner is kidnapped by the perpetrator and interrogated by the security guard while the perpetrator is observing them. The reader learns that the security guard will die and Brenner will probably be freed from the perpetrator. The suspense of the situation is reduced by this information, although not eliminated. The reader needs to know how.

As you can see from the two comparisons underlined, once more humour is called on to keep the reader engaged. The description of the security guard is highly suggestive and contrasts with the information about the predicted death of this character.

4.4. Holding-up of the showdown, countdown and repetitions

As we have seen, several devices are used in order to create and maintain suspense. For example, in *Brenner and God* the showdown is slowed down by the narrator's way of telling. In contrast to the other Brenner novels, the slowing down in this novel is made explicit by a countdown. The perpetrator counts down to calm himself, while the narrator continues telling the story.

The events told in quotation (5) seem to imitate the panning movements of a camera. Repetitions help the reader to imagine the search and the subsequent disappointment. The translation follows the text in minute detail and maintains the expectation of the reader.

(5)
ST. »Vier.«

Du musst schon entschuldigen, wenn ich es dir so ausführlich erzähle, aber es ist einfach immer wieder beeindruckend, dass zwischen einem ganz normalen Ficus Benjamin, zwischen einem ganz normalen Türaufsperren, zwischen einem ganz normalen Blick ins Schlafzimmer, Blick in die Küche, Blick ins Badezimmer, Blick in die fünfundzwanzig Blumenzimmer, Blick in die Abstellkammer, zwischen **dieser** ganz normalen Enttäuschung, dass du nicht findest, was du suchst, und einem enttäuschten Täter, der dir in den Kopf schießt, oft nur ein paar Sekunden liegen.

»Drei.«

Und die Erde dreht sich in aller Ruhe weiter. (Gott 2009: 206, *my emphasis)*

TT1. "Four."

You'll have to excuse me for going into such detail, but it just never fails to amaze me how between a perfectly normal *ficus benjamina*, between perfectly normally unlocking the door, between a perfectly normal look in the bedroom, look in the kitchen, look in the bathroom, look in the twenty-five rooms filled with plants, look in the closet, between **the** perfectly normal disappointment of not finding what you're looking for, and a disappointed perp shooting you in the head—often a matter of just a few seconds.

"Three."

And the earth turns quietly on. (God 2012: 200, *my emphasis)*

This quotation once again shows some characteristic devices: the dialogue with the reader, here apologizing, for example, for going into detail. Then we can find truisms that make us smile because they are platitudes contrasting with the thrilling situation: *Und die Erde dreht sich in aller Ruhe weiter (And the earth turns quietly on).*

4.5. Telegraphic style and joker word *quasi*

Before concluding this brief overview of fictive orality, character portrayal and suspense in the Brenner novels, I would like to mention a real translation problem. We have seen that a large proportion of the features in the source language have been preserved in the target text. But the so called telegraphic style causes several shifts in the target texts, as we can see in quotation (6):

(6)
ST. **Der Brenner super getanzt**, so was hat man noch nicht gesehen, dagegen ist alles, was sich jemals zwischen New York und Jugodisco zur Musik bewegt hat, nur ein

schwachbrüstiger Vogerltanz, **weil der Brenner Urgewalt**. Aber die Jugokinder haben das nicht verstanden und haben nach und nach die Tanzfläche verlassen, **quasi Protest**. (Gott 2009: 170)

TT1.   **Brenner was a terrific dancer**, the likes of which you've never seen—everything that has ever moved to music between New York and the Yugo-disco is just a limp-chested chicken dance by comparison, **because Brenner was an elemental force**. But the Yugo-kids didn't understand and started leaving the dance floor one after another—**in protest, if you will**. (God 2012: 164, *my emphasis*)

The elision of the verb such as *Der Brenner* (hat) *super getanzt...* and *weil der Brenner* (war) *eine Urgewalt* can be judged as quite normal in spoken German (*Duden Grammatik* 1225). We see that the translator added the verbs in the two cases: *Brenner was a terrific dancer* and *because Brenner was an elemental force*.

The elision of the preposition *quasi* (aus) *Protest* is not so common and evokes some more informal registers, for example, the language of young people or the shortened forms of cyberspace. Nindl (2010: 140) characterises the use of *quasi* ('almost', 'more or less') as a feature of the narrator's idiolect, often used for adding a comment to an event already told. The translator added the preposition. There are other possibilities, as stated by Sylvine Muller (2001), for compensating the loss of these markers of orality. For example, the translation of *quasi* by the formula *if you will*, which takes up other devices used in the Brenner novels: *in protest, if you will*.

As you can observe in the two examples taken from the translations into Spanish and French (7), the study of these specific devices can indicate to what extent fictive orality is recreated in the three languages. The German sentence seems to be a spoken one, by word order and postposition of the part of sentence which should be placed in written language between the verbal bracket *hat sich ... bemüht*.

(7)
ST.   Die Lehrerin hat sich bemüht, **quasi** um Schadensbegrenzung. (Auferstehung 2012: 82, *my emphasis*)
TT2.   Kati Engljähriger s'efforça de limiter les dégâts et de calmer Mandl. (Quitter Zell 2007: 97)
TT3.   La profesora hizo lo que pudo para que la sangre no llegara al río. (Resurrección 2011: 93)

The translations tone down the spoken character and offer, syntactically speaking, standard sentences. The French translation explains the scene told by the narrator (also by adding 'for calming down Mandl'); and the Spanish translation keeps some oral features through the use of a colloquial phraseme *no llegar la sangre al río* ('not to go beyond that', which means 'to prevent things ending in disaster').

5. Final remarks

As we have seen through these few examples, Haas's Brenner novels tend to exploit the conventions of the genre. Haas combines linguistic experiment with innovative narrative strategies (Schreckenberger), social criticism, a generous dose of humour and sarcasm, as well as entertainment. The stylistic features of these novels evoke a spoken context that brings to mind an apparently immediate "telling" situation. The way of "speaking" used by the two main voices, the narrator and the protagonist, comprises a lot of devices typical of spoken language in Austria. But a more detailed study (Nindl) reveals that the use of these devices is exaggerated and the attraction of Haas's style consists of the tension between them and the written literary language.

Nevertheless, since oral markers help to generate and maintain suspense, it is important to preserve some essential features of this method of storytelling in the target texts. The writer's statements on language, which show an acute awareness of language, have been cited in order to underline the importance of oral markers for the translations. Despite this prioritising of the spoken context the language of the target texts is more standard than that of the source text. This general tendency towards standardisation is not a new insight in Translation Studies ("the law of growing standardization"; Toury 1995: 267-274).

As we have seen in our research project on the translation of fictional dialogue there are several reasons for the shifts of oral devices in the target texts. One factor is the specific range of devices each of the target languages possesses. Some devices of immediacy will not be available such as the informal T-form in English. Other factors are related to the flexibility of the written language, genre conventions and genre reputation in the different target cultures. Translators' abilities[5] and agility also influence, to a greater or lesser extent, the impression of immediacy. Retaining oral markers necessarily leads to a domesticated translation (Freunek 2007: 307). Last but not least, there are a lot of linguistic, literary and rhetorical resources which support the illusion of nearness and which are not restricted to a certain culture. These elements are carefully recreated in the translations, as we have seen through the English one. The target texts do not possess the same "power" of immediacy as the source text but they employ alternative devices in an attempt to generate a similar "feel" (Bosseaux 2007). The linguistic experiment gets lost, but the literary illusion and suspense keep on.

---

[1] See, for example, Brumme (2012) and Brumme and Espunya (2012).
[2] This chapter was written as part of the research project *The Translation of Fictional Dialogue. Literary Texts and Multimodal Texts* (TRADIF), reference number FFI2010-16783 (subprogramme FILO, 2010-2013), financed by the Spanish Ministry of Science and Innovation.

Jenny Brumme

---

[3] See, for example, Seago in this volume.

[4] "In Deutschland erfolgte die Ausstrahlung mit Untertiteln, um die Austriazismen und die teils recht derbe Lexik in die hochsprachliche Norm zu transferieren" (Nindl 2010: 49).

[5] This also comprises a high knowledge of spoken language frequently the main point while translating this type of experimental literature. Colloquial expressions are often a trap as for example in the following sentence: "My dear swan, Brenner hadn't been in a funk like this in a long time" (God 2012: 87-88). The expression *mein lieber Schwan* means 'my goodness!' or 'oh, damn!'. The ST is: "Mein lieber Schwan, mit so einem Grant hat man den Brenner schon lange nicht mehr gesehen." (Gott 2009: 92). So, the colloquial German expression caused a shift, while the Austrian *Grant* 'bad mood' (Ebner 1998: 131) is correctly translated.

Bibliography

Primary Sources[1]

Haas, Wolf. [1996]. 2000. *Auferstehung der Toten*. *Roman* (rororo, 22831). Reinbek bei Hamburg: Rowohlt-Taschenbuch-Verlag.
———. 2007. *Quitter Zell* (Rivages noir, 645). Traduit de l'allemand (Autriche) par Marie Reygnier. Paris: Payot & Rivages.
———. 2011. *La resurrección de los muertos*. Traducido por María Esperanza Romero. Madrid: Siruela.
———. [1997]. 2000. *Der Knochenmann*. *Roman* (rororo, 22832). Reinbek bei Hamburg: Rowohlt-Taschenbuch-Verlag.
———. 2011. *El triturador de huesos*. Traducido por María Esperanza Romero. Madrid: Siruela.
———. 2013. *The Bone Man* (Melville International Crime). Translated by Annie Janusch. New York: Melville House Publishing.
———. [1998]. 2000. Komm, süßer Tod. Roman. Orig. Ausg., 43-57. Tsd. Reinbek bei Hamburg: Rowohlt-Taschenbuch-Verl (rororo, 22814).
———. 2002. *Vienne la mort* (Rivages noir, 417). Traduit de l'allemand (Autriche) par Marie Reygnier. Paris: Payot & Rivages.
———. 2012. *Ven, dulce muerte*. Traducción de María Esperanza Romero. Madrid: Siruela.
———. [1999]. 2000. *Silentium!* *Roman* (rororo, 22830). Reinbek bei Hamburg: Rowohlt-Taschenbuch-Verlag.
———. 2004. *Silentium!* (Rivages noir, 509). Traduit de l'allemand (Autriche) Marie Reygnier. Paris: Payot & Rivages.
———. [2001]. 2002. *Wie die Tiere*. *Roman* (rororo, 23331). Reinbek bei Hamburg: Rowohlt-Taschenbuch-Verlag.
———. [2003]. 2011. *Das ewige Leben*. *Roman* (dtv, 21328). München: Deutscher. Taschenbuch-Verlag.
———. 2009. *Der Brenner und der liebe Gott*. *Roman*. Hamburg: Hoffmann und Campe.
———. 2012. *Brenner and God* (Melville International Crime). Translated by Annie Janusch. New York: Melville House Publishing.

Secondary Sources

Bosseaux, Charlotte. 2007. *How Does it Feel? Point of View in Translation. The Case of Virginia Woolf into French*. Amsterdam: Rodopi.
Brown, Roger and Albert Gilman. 1960. 'The Pronouns of Power and Solidarity' in Sebeok, Thomas A. (ed.). *Style in Language*. Cambridge: MIT press. 253-276.
Brumme, Jenny and Anna Espunya (eds). 2012. *The Translation of Fictive Dialogue* (Approaches to translation studies, 35). Amsterdam and New York: Rodopi.   Have ?
Brumme, Jenny. 2012. *Traducir la voz ficticia*. Berlin and Boston: de Gruyter (Beihefte zur Zeitschrift für romanische Philologie, 367).
Daran, Valérie de. 2010. *«Traduit de l'allemand (Autriche)». Étude d'un transfert littéraire*. Bern, Berlin, Bruxelles, Frankfurt am Main, New York, Oxford and Wien: Peter Lang.
Duden Grammatik. Dudenredaktion, Duden. 2006. *Die Grammatik. Unentbehrlich für richtiges Deutsch*, 7th ed. Mannheim, Leipzig, Wien and Zürich: Dudenverlag.
Ebner, Jakob. 1998. *Duden: Wie sagt man in Österreich? Wörterbuch des österreichischen Deutsch*. 3th ed. Mannheim, Leipzig, Wien and Zürich: Dudenverlag.
Fludernik, Monika. [1993]. 2006. *The Fictions of Language and the Languages of Fiction. The linguistic representation of speech and consciousness*. London and New York: Routledge.

Freunek, Sigrid. 2007. *Literarische Mündlichkeit und Übersetzung. Am Beispiel deutscher und russischer Erzähltexte* (Ost-West-Express. Kultur und Übersetzung, 2). Berlin: Frank & Timme.

Haas, Wolf. 1990. *Sprachtheoretische Grundlagen der konkreten Poesie*. PhD. Universität Stuttgart.

Lochbihler, Claus. 2011. 'Früher habe ich das Lesen gehasst' in *Welt am Sonntag* 2 January 2011. On line at: http //www.welt.de/11927288

Metz, Daniela. 2011. *Österreich nach Frankreich bringen. Eine Übersetzungsanalyse von Wolf Haas' Auferstehung der Toten*. Diplomarbeit, Karl-Franzens-Universität Graz, Institut für Theoretische und Angewandte Translationswissenschaft.

Muller, Sylvine. 2001. 'Traduire la syntaxe télégraphique dans les dialogues de romans anglais' in Ballard, Michel (ed.). *Oralité et traduction* (Traductologie). Arras: Artois Presses Universitaires. 181-208.

Nindl, Sigrid. 2009. '"Jetzt wird schon wieder was analysiert …". Der Linguist Wolf Haas und sein kriminalliterarisches Experiment' in Dannerer, Monika, Peter Mauser, Hannes Scheutz and Andreas E. Weiss (eds). *Gesprochen - geschrieben - gedichtet. Variation und Transformation von Sprache*. Unter Mitarbeit von Anne Betten. Berlin: Erich Schmidt. 103-115.

————. 2010. *Wolf Haas und sein kriminalliterarisches Sprachexperiment*. Berlin: Erich Schmidt.

Schreckenberger, Helga. 2010. 'Wolf Haas's Simon Brenner Novels: Austrian Adaptations and Transformations of the American Detective Story' in *TRANS. Internet-Zeitschrift für Kulturwissenschaften* (17).

Schwitalla, Johannes. 2009. 'Wortsuche, Wortkritik und Wortkampf in Wolf Haas' Dialog-Roman 'Das Wetter vor 15 Jahren' in Dannerer, Monika, Peter Mauser, Hannes Scheutz and Andreas E. Weiss (eds): *Gesprochen - geschrieben - gedichtet. Variation und Transformation von Sprache*. Unter Mitarbeit von Anne Betten. Berlin: Erich Schmidt. 116-130.

Toury, Gideon. 1995. *Descriptive Translation Studies – and Beyond*. Philadelphia: John Benjamins.

---

[1] Not in alphabetical order. Primary sources are organized by Wolf Brenner's novels.

Rhythmus of speech, indirect speech, footnotes

Chapter 10: Reducing distance between characters, narrator and reader. Fictive dialogue in Steinfest's *Nervöse Fische* and its translation into French

Guilhem Naro and Maria Wirf Naro

Abstract

The plot of *Nervöse Fische* is highly improbable and the culprit quickly found. Suspense arises from constant uncertainty about what will come next: either an unexpected turn of events or an outlandish association of ideas expressed by the narrator or the main character. Steinfest's narrator pokes fun at realism and presents his numerous digressions with self-irony and occasional playful allusions to the reader. He also adopts non-fictional forms like footnotes as if he were an author presenting real events and addressing himself directly to his reader. Whereas many crime novels introduce elements considered typical of orality to feign immediacy, Steinfest's narrator and his principal character exhibit aloofness. They accumulate complex formulations such as expanded participle constructions; consistently realize reported speech in the highly formal *Konjunktiv I*, and employ high-register vocabulary. However, the writer does imitate the flow of speech through the management of pauses, break-offs, inserts, verbless follow-up remarks, and blank lines which irregularly subdivide chapters. The French translation achieves a similar rhythm and an equivalent effect of highbrow formality, but does not imitate the innovative graphic choices through which the narrator of the original affirms his competence to fix rules and roles for himself and the reader.

Keywords: Digression, fictional orality / fictive orality / feigned orality, footnote, formality, typographic form

1. The distance of fiction[1]

To sum up the major events of *Nervöse Fische* in a few words:

A graphologist is found dead in the swimming pool of a Vienna apartment block, bitten to death by sharks (which are absent from the scene). Chief Inspector Lukastik, a disciple of Wittgenstein, finds out that the victim was murdered by Egon Steinbacher, a hairdresser who had taken his revenge on the graphologist (his ex-diving companion) for having accused him of plagiarizing a dedication by Hölderlin in a love letter. Steinbacher had arranged that he himself would also be thrown into the shark-infested subterranean pool underneath the apartment block, although in fact he commits suicide before. Lukastik presents himself in Steinbacher's name and is saved from the sharks at the very last moment by his assistant with whom he shares a relationship of mutual disdain.

In this concentrated summary, the absurdity of the plot becomes overwhelming. If an author strains the capacity of his audience for suspension of disbelief to this extent, all illusion of a natural communication with the author's speaker, his narrator, is excluded. Anyway, *per definitionem* the narrator of a novel cannot aspire to evoke a situation of communicative immediacy in relation to his readership. The very basis of the narrator-reader constellation is the exact opposite of social, referential and physical proximity between the communication partners, which Koch and Oesterreicher consider central elements of the prototypical situation of conceptual orality (1990: 8-9; Koch 1986: 117-119).

In fact, even if the medium is oral and the setting shared by all communication participants, the particular nature of the suspense story affects some of the factors that constitute the continuum of relative conceptual immediacy or distance. For example a certain degree of planning is necessary to build up suspense: the narrator deliberately withholds certain pieces of information and (partially) reveals others according to his design. As the architect of suspense, he clearly dominates the situation and leaves little space for cooperation in dialogical terms. He does, however, strongly solicit the affective participation of his public. When the medium is writing, the distance between the storyteller and the addressee is even greater. However, the narrator can resort to diverse stratagems to feign proximity.[2] Some of the choices of *Nervöse Fische* are atypical and therefore merit attention.

2. Macrostructure and typographic forms

The distance between narrator and reader is particularly evident in elements which reflect the physical making of the book: typographic form and structures like chapter headings which have no equivalence in orality. According to the local setting, *Nervöse Fische* distinguishes three unequal parts: "Zuerst Wien" (Steinfest 2004: 5), "Dann Zwettl" (Steinfest 2004: 97), "Wieder Wien" (Steinfest 2004: 250) and establishes a broad chronological macrostructure according to spatial unity. We often use *zuerst, dann, wieder* when we orally relate everyday sequences and the shortcut of the time adverb and the place name sounds like a spontaneously formulated working title. The respective part begins on a new page and the paratextual nature of the heading is highlighted through the use of a different font, but this organizing comment remains close to the body of the text, from which it is separated by a blank of only four lines.

The French translation makes more clear-cut separations than the original. The titles are written in larger capital letters in the same font. They are set apart on a special unnumbered page on the classical right-hand side, with a void verso before and after.

The chapters are simply numbered. The original leaves two lines blank after the end of the preceding chapter and places the figure (in the bigger font used for the headings) at the left border of the indented initial line of the following chapter.

In the translation, each chapter begins on a new page, the chapter number is centred and highlighted by significant blanks of seven and three lines respectively, cf. for example Steinfest 2004: 20 vs. Steinfest 2011: 31. Thus the paratext moves further away from the core text. The physical making of the book and the mediatedness of the narration become more evident in these traditional forms.

Within the numbered chapters the narrator introduces subdivisions by sometimes leaving a blank line between paragraphs. This break can correspond to a change in perspective (Steinfest 2004: 51), in location (Steinfest 2004: 256) or quality (Steinfest 2004: 260) of the scene, which would correspond to a cut in a cinematographic presentation. These pauses are of irregular frequency, short, unobtrusive, not arbitrary, but sometimes apparently unnecessary, as in the case of some one-paragraph units (Steinfest 2004: 60, 249). They do not seem to obey a pre-established overall structure, but to occur naturally, 'on the go', which can transmit the impression that we are assisting the elaboration of the narrator's draft. The French translation copies these one-line voids exactly. The visual interruption of the text flow also produces a break in the reception, which we logically associate with a pause in production: the narrator keeps silent for a moment –he takes a breath before he turns (or returns) to another point of the 'story'.

On the whole, the original uses the graphic possibilities of its medium in more innovative ways. When the murderer leaves a hand-written note for the inspector on two occasions (Steinfest 2004: 151; Steinfest 2004: 229), these are reproduced as an indented quote and in a font imitating handwriting. The narrator pretends to share evidentiary material in its original form with the reader. But this mock-copy is also a wink from the narrator to his reader: he endorses a role and invests his reader with the corresponding one.

The French translation introduces these notes like normal quotes (Steinfest 2011: 204, Steinfest 2011: 301-302), with inverted commas (whereas it generally opens the reproduction of direct speech with a dash). The little additional make-believe game which the narrator of the original proposes to his reader is lost.

The more extravagant the story becomes towards the end, the denser the signals of self-irony get. This narrator goes in for deviations and integrates numerous elements which are only loosely linked to the stream of narrative action. On several occasions he puts an entire paragraph into brackets (Steinfest 2004: 88, 164, 291; Steinfest 2011: 119, 220, 385), thus indicating to his reader a digression which can be theoretically skipped. He even alludes playfully to his reader:

(1)
ST.   (Für die, die es interessiert, er trug [...].) (Steinfest 2004: 289)
TT.   (Pour ceux que cela intéresse, il portait [...].) (Steinfest 2011: 383)

Later on he twice opts for a footnote (Steinfest 2004: 292, 302). Except for the asterisk instead of a footnote number, this narrator-organizer-author adopts non-fictional form conventions to comment upon his fiction and he solicits the reader to play the game and accept this mock-exposition: a procedure that we are used to in academic writing or informative texts in general. In order to concentrate on the main issue of an exposition, further elements or asides are banished, physically, from the core of the text and declared of secondary importance. The main string of communication is momentarily paralleled by another minor one: the author instructs his reader that he is giving additional, not indispensable elements. In literary texts we know footnotes mainly from translations, where they tend to be reduced to the strict minimum of necessary background information because they disrupt the fictional illusion. Usurping a non-fictional device, the narrator of *Nervöse Fische* gives another intertextual, metacommunicative comment: he is the text organizer and he assumes the right to behave as if he were the author, or as if the narrated events and he himself as the narrator were as real as the reader to whom he addresses the extra comment.

A footnote in published writing is certainly not a spontaneous utterance nor does it allow for a response, but it does create polyphony and a one-sided immediacy between the author and his reader. As brackets and footnotes belong to the classical form repertoire, the translation maintains them and even brings them closer to 'normal' standards: the italics are replaced by normal type, the asterisk is substituted by a number (Steinfest 2011: 386, 401).

Punctuation conventions can prompt certain adaptations. Short inserts (of just a proposition or a subordinate clause) or speech pauses are often marked by dashes in the German text. The French version tends to follow this use, except when these marks would be close to more dashes which open dialogue turns in the French text (for example Steinfest 2004: 22, Steinfest 2011: 34).

(2)
ST.   »Stimmt. Ich vergesse mich. – Also! Ich habe im Körper des Toten [...].« (Steinfest 2004: 22)
TT.   — C'est vrai, je m'égare. Donc, j'ai trouvé dans le corps du mort [...]. (Steinfest 2011: 34)

In comparison with the translation, in this example the original presents shorter speech units, longer pauses, and a verbless clause. On the whole this results in a very varied, lively, apparently spontaneous rhythm, whereas the French translation leaves the impression of a more regular speech movement.

On the other hand, the translation sometimes adds dashes to mark inserts, even when close to direct speech (e.g. Steinfest 2004: 119, Steinfest 2011: 161). A dash instead of a comma (cf. e.g. Steinfest 2004: 35, Steinfest 2011: 51; Steinfest 2004: 37, Steinfest 2011: 54; Steinfest 2004: 101, Steinfest 2011: 139; Steinfest 2004: 189, Steinfest 2011: 252) sets the insert more visibly apart, and its content receives greater weight as a consequence of this isolation. On the suprasegmental level, the dash lengthens the pause and creates a more clearly separate intonation unit: intonation rises in the preceding word and stays high during the insert, which normally fits easily into one breath. It becomes a kind of apposition, a statement of its own which links the propositional and the textual levels (Engel 1988: 806). The source behind the comment becomes particularly noticeable when the insert contains an evaluative or degree particle or when the speaker introduces his incidental remark with a coordinative marker. German syntax easily accepts the simple paratactical arrangement of verbs or other parts of a sentence; the French translation of *Nervöse Fische* sometimes introduces an additional *et*, often combined with the dash (cf. e.g. Steinfest 2004: 35, Steinfest 2004: 51):

(3)
ST.   Neben der »Freiheit der Kunst« existierte für ihn auch eine »Freiheit der Polizei«, und damit meinte er im Grunde sich selbst. [...] Ein Verbrechen, vor allem die vermeintliche Exklusivität eines Verbrechens, schien ihn persönlich zu beleidigen, so daß [...]. (Steinfest 2004: 35)

TT.   À côté de la « liberté de l'art » existait pour lui une « liberté de la police » — et par là il faisait en réalité référence à lui-même. [...] Il semblait voir dans le crime — et surtout dans son aspect prétendument unique — une offense personnelle. (Steinfest 2011: 51)

Thibaudet describes the different linking and disjunctive uses of *et* in Flaubert's writing (Thibaudet 1935: 265-269). Using *et* can lead in description or narration to a moment of higher tension, it is sufficiently strong to render consecutive elements like *also* (Steinfest 2004: 198, Steinfest 2011: 263) or *um* (Steinfest 2004: 198; Steinfest 2011: 263) or transmit some other logical relation.

What seems 'personal' (though not really individual) with the narrator and his main figures is the intellectual distance they display, their desire to seize things precisely, though according to their egocentric standards and intuitions. The original often casts this into a subordinate relative clause with *wobei* (e.g. Steinfest 2004: 12, 41), which is graphically presented as an independent unit: a comment which arrives after a time of reflection indicated by the full stop. The French translation tends to use *et*:

(4)
ST. Wobei wie so oft [...] die Feuerwehr – Mannschaft wie Material – einen vergleichsweise armseligen Eindruck machte, spielzeugartig. [Steinfest 2004: 225]
TT. Et comme à l'ordinaire [...] les pompiers — hommes et matériel — donnaient plutôt la piètre impression d'être des jouets (Steinfest 2011: 297)

Sometimes this after-thought takes the form of a simple noun phrase, after the pause of reflection:

(5)
ST. Er besaß – wie alle Künstler, wenn man Friseure denn als solche ansah – ein autistisches Gehabe. Einen alchemistischen Charakter. (Steinfest 2004: 161)
TT. Comme tous les artistes — à supposer que les coiffeurs en fissent partie —, il avait un comportement autiste. Une nature d'alchimiste. (Steinfest 2011: 216)

The management of pauses is also used to enhance suspense (and perhaps create suspicion in the first place). Pauses are used to delay information. Placing a piece of information at the end of a chapter makes it much more noticeable than if it had appeared in a less prominent position.

(6)
ST. Aber wirklich gut fühlte er sich dennoch nicht. (Steinfest 2004: 247)

Apart from these typographical features, there are the conceptual, lexical and syntactic ones in which the voice of the text organizer makes itself heard.

3. The voice of the text organizer: from narrator to reader

The narrator of *Nervöse Fische* accumulates digressions and comparisons, in an attempt to find the adequate words for a multitude of impressions and feelings. He seems to seek precision –and to give in to all his associations; self-assured he passes them on to his reader without further selection. This leisurely advance of the narrative discourse feigns spontaneity on the macrostructural level. Every now and then, however, the narrator raises his voice as the novel organizer to provide the reader with some orientation in this whirl. When the means is an inconspicuous structuring signal *nun*, followed by a comma, or a consecutive *also*, the French translation does not introduce a corresponding signal for the reader (e.g. Steinfest 2004: 14, Steinfest 2011: 22; Steinfest 2004: 9, Steinfest 2011: 17). But when the narrator makes more explicit comments on his presentation, these find an equivalent in the translation:

(7)
ST. Es muß noch gesagt werden, daß [...]. (Steinfest 2004: 6)
TT. Ajoutons que Lukastik [...]. (Steinfest 2011: 13)

(8)
ST. Wie gesagt, er fürchtete den Stumpfsinn der anderen. (Steinfest 2004: 119)
TT. Comme on l'a déjà évoqué, il craignait les esprits bornés. (Steinfest 2011: 161)

In the following example, the translation strengthens the ironical touch, when it has its narrator refer to his story-telling as if it were administrative writing:

(9)
ST. Und obgleich die erwähnte Kühle dieses Morgens […]. (Steinfest 2004: 10)
TT. Et même si la fraîcheur susmentionnée de cette matinée […]. (Steinfest 2011: 17)

This voice goes so far as to comment on its creative power: introducing declaredly invented elements, it ostentatiously pokes fun at realism and detracts from traditional modes of suspense:

(10)
ST. […] und in Richtung besagter Ortschaft fuhr. Einer Ortschaft, die nun doch einen Namen erhalten soll, freilich einen erfundenen, der weniger satirisch klingt als der tatsächliche […]. Der Ort soll *Nullpunkt* heißen, oder auch *Nullpunkt am Kamp*, […]. (Steinfest 2004: 175)
TT. […], roulant en direction de la localité que nous avons évoquée plus haut. Une localité qu'il nous faut à present nommer, d'un nom inventé qui soit moins parodique que le vrai […]. Ce village s'appellera Point Zéro, ou encore Point Zéro-sur-Kamp, […]. Comme on l'a déjà évoqué, il craignait les esprits bornés. (Steinfest 2011: 235)

In the French version, the narrator again steps back behind the rhetorical *nous* which feigns to include the reader.

This attitude is combined with the more traditional one of the narrator as a mediator between the reader and a reality that supposedly exists outside the book:

(11)
ST. Jenseits des Flusses erhob sich jener steile, bewaldete Hügel, der von den Nullpunkter Bürgern des Sanatoriums wegen »Krankenberg« genannt wurde. Es gab sogar welche, die vom »Grabhügel« sprachen, was übrigens eine ziemliche Übertreibung darstellte. Niemand kam hierher, um zu sterben. Woran sich die meisten auch hielten. (Steinfest 2004: 192)

The translation flattens off the ambivalence of the mediator's position: *übrigens*, which marks the ironical, if not sarcastic commentator's distance, remains untranslated, whereas *hierher*, with which the narrator situates himself, at the same time, at the place of action, is replaced by *là*, which dissociates the French narrator from the scene:

(12)
TT. De l'autre côté du fleuve s'élevait l'abrupte colline boisée, que les citoyens de Point Zéro avaient baptisée « la montagne malade » à cause de la maison de repos. Certains

même parlaient de colline funéraire, ce qui était passablement exagéré. Personne ne venait là pour mourir. Règle communément observée. (Steinfest 2011: 255)

Renaming is another easy way to create a distinct voice and to make the reader follow the narrator's (or a character's) thought. The narrator makes use of this power for example in *Nullpunkter Bürger* (Steinfest 2004: 192), *citoyens de Point Zéro* (Steinfest 2011: 255), but the same procedure is applied in what seem to be Lukastik's comments: after a more or less explicit comparison, the referent in the following text is not designated via the normal term, but through the object it is compared to (cf. *Felsen* (Steinfest 2004: 194) and *rocher* (Steinfest 2011: 258) for an armchair). In this case they serve to ensure the public's attentive reading and they help to evoke the particular cosmos of a character: a passage in which this personal usage appears is promptly recognized as the corresponding character's speech or thought. When the figure faces a potentially dangerous situation, the reader feels an association with his position and will identify more easily with the threatened hero. But beyond these moments of thrilling drama, in this crime story where the culprit is quickly found, it is above all the overflowing imagination of the narrator and his main character, with their ever new ideas, which represents the real source of suspense. In Hitchcock's famous distinction, surprise is caused by something unexpected; suspense is the more lasting expectation of a strong event whereby the spectator feels concerned due to empathy with the protagonists (Truffaut 1991: 57-59). Steinfest bases his suspense on the reader's constant expectation of the next surprise, caused by a turn in the plot, an association of ideas or a formulation.

On several occasions the narrator gives his reader a wink when he includes him / her in the group of those who share the narrator's or a character's assumed level of specialist knowledge:

(13)
ST.   [...] der Polizist [...] mißachtete also Beduzzis recht typische Laienphrase [...]. (Steinfest 2004: 149) (cf. Steinfest 2011: 202)

(14)
ST.   Es war eine der vielen Unarten in Fernsehkrimis, befreiten Opfern ihre Mundsperren herunterzureißen [...]. (Steinfest 2004: 155-156) (cf. Steinfest 2011: 209)

The reader finds him / herself in the position of reading remarks about common errors in crime fiction. At the same time this reader, presumably a non-specialist in crime detection, is part of the group of non-specialists alluded to. These 'insider remarks' are included to demonstrate the expertise of this novel above others, and to allow the reader to feel close to the standpoint of the narrating voice instead of that of the typical fiction addressee. The reader's status shifts to that of a peer and, without any address or signals of orality, a tacit, hidden exchange takes place, which the translation easily renders in the same way.

In order to create the empathy necessary for suspense, the original narrator also establishes contact with his reader through modal particles or *Abtönungspartikeln*, which allow him to introduce suppositions about his reader's attitudes, previous knowledge or probable reactions towards the respective element of narration (Liefländer-Koistinen 2004: 550). French does not always offer an exact correspondence for these modal particles, but this notorious translation problem has been widely discussed (cf. Wirf Naro 2012a) and so we will not go into it here.

Other evaluative elements in the form of adverbs are often, but not always rendered: looking at the length of just one page of German text, restrictive *freilich* (Steinfest 2004: 50) and *eigentlich* (Steinfest 2004: 50) remain without a correspondence (Steinfest 2011: 70), *offenkundig* (Steinfest 2004: 49) and *sicher* (Steinfest 2004: 50) are rendered through *visiblement* (Steinfest 2011: 70) and *sans doute* (Steinfest 2011: 70). On the whole, French as a language makes less use of modulation indices than German, and as a consequence, the intervention of the narrator through evaluative remarks is less prominent in the French text.

4. Modes and rhythms of speech

Like in any whodunit, the investigation evolves in part from the questioning of possible suspects, witnesses, experts, conversations with colleagues, superiors and staff. Reproducing these conversations and questioning sessions in direct speech is, as in any story, a way of interrupting the epic with more scenic elements and of introducing voices other than that of the narrator.

The French text highlights more strongly the dialogical aspect, beginning every turn on a new line with a dash instead of quotation marks. The visual blank between a remark and a following non-speech act (and the time which it takes the reader to jump this gap) will commonly be identified as a (short) lapse in time. The verbal exchange is physically isolated and brought into the foreground. Optically, the French edition thus bears more resemblance to a script than the German one does. In the original, the characters' speech, their thought and the description of situations and actions are more intimately interwoven. The importance of the *personae*'s voices is reduced, they are incorporated into the narrator's presentation or into what might be read as the perception of the main character (cf. e.g. Steinfest 2004: 106; Steinfest 2011: 145)

This once again increases the weight of the narrator, as well as his wilfully chosen *inquit formulae* which remind us of his orchestration. He is apparently reproducing, but also interpreting: the 'recommendation' of a superior to his staff (Steinfest 2004: 255), his 'order' to an equal (Steinfest 2011: 253)—such lexical choices also give a hint to the casualness or the emphasis with which these remarks are made. The French translation tends to flatten off these nuances and the surprise effect contained in the verbs (Steinfest 2011: 339, 338).

Both in direct and indirect speech the original makes extensive use of suspension points and italics in order to mark hesitations, stress, or the isolated accentuation of a quote, (e.g. Steinfest 2004: 253; Steinfest 2011: 337-338), and the French version mostly follows:

(15)
ST.　» […] Sehen Sie also bitte zu, daß Ihre … Mitarbeiter … keine relevanten Veränderungen im Haus vornehmen. «
»Keine Angst, meine *Mitarbeiter* sind nicht die Bauerntölpel, für die Sie sie halten.« (Steinfest 2004: 139)

TT.　— […] Je vous prierai donc de veiller à ce que vos… collaborateurs… ne dérangent rien dans la maison.
— N'ayez aucune crainte, mes *collaborateurs* ne sont pas les rustres que vous semblez croire […]. (Steinfest 2011: 188)

The habitual ingredients of (the representation of) dialogue, such as greetings, interjections, or phatic elements are missing in this novel, which aims to be anything but mainstream. It resorts to other evidence of realism, like marked cooperation efforts in the construction of dialogue (between Lukastik and his informants), and reduction in the professional exchange of information (between for example Lukastik and Dr. Paul; cf. Brumme 2012: 221).

Indirect speech occupies an important amount of space in the original novel, and it is normally realized in *Konjunktiv I*, a mode which is considered very formal and is normally limited to written (especially press) texts. As it marks indirectness, a speech verb or noun can be omitted, and *Konjunktiv I* on its own is sufficient to identify independent indirect speech or *berichtete Rede* as such (Duden 2006: 529, 530, 539-540). Especially in this case, but also when the reported speech is formulated as a main clause preceded by a *verbum dicendi*, the reported utterance forms an independent prosodic unit for which we easily imagine a phonic realization. On the one hand, the narrator using *Konjunktiv I* affirms his presence as a mediator and his aspiration at an elevated level of style. On the other hand, the management of pauses, break-offs, verbless follow-up remarks which furnish a complement of information maintain the illusion of a facsimile reproduction of the scene.

French does not possess a corresponding mode of indirectness. Verbs of indirect speech are subjected to the *consecutio temporum*: after an introductory verb in a past tense, the reported simultaneous, previous or following actions, events, or states are formulated in *imparfait, plus-que-parfait, futur du passé* or *futur antérieur du passé* respectively (cf. Grévisse 2007: 524). These are the basic tenses of narration. When additional signs of the reproduction of speech appear, the translation is clearly recognizable as reported speech; if not, the

French version can be interpreted both as reported speech or as narration (cf. Wirf Naro 2012b: 104-106).

5. Formal elements

The narrator and several of his main characters go in for a number of identical linguistic features. These are conspicuous because they are of a more formal, old-fashioned or 'academic' character than the novel, and especially the crime novel, normally opts for.

The relative refinement of a formulation makes itself particularly felt when a lower-register correspondence exists. This is the case in German with a combination of two determinatives as opposed to a simple determiner, for example, indefinite article plus *jeder*: "ein jedes Mal" (Steinfest 2004: 7) instead of *jedes Mal*. French cannot copy this ("chaque fois", Steinfest 2011: 13) and the formality of "in einem jeden Tun und Handeln" (Steinfest 2004: 5) is lost in the neutral French combination of *tout* plus definite article ("tous les faits et gestes", Steinfest 2011: 11). On the contrary, the French version transposes the higher degree of formality when it uses *tout* without article, formulating a more abstract and absolute value: "toute matière et toute lumière" (Steinfest 2011: 348).

The original also abounds in expanded participle constructions like "im von Blutschmieren aquarellartig verfremdeten Wasser" (Steinfest 2004: 11). Such highly condensed formulations are typical of written texts for specific purposes, since the delay of the nucleus of the noun phrase, and the left-hand ramification of the (often inflected) attributes, require time and preparation for both encoding and decoding. The translation often relieves this ponderousness, but even when it does not, the normal syntactical order in French is less marked in register because its arrangement of information –nominal referent first and attribute second– simplifies comprehension: "sous l'eau, étrangement aquarellisée par le sang", (Steinfest 2011: 19).

Present participle constructions are even more formal than past participles in German and the translation often opts for a more average level relative clause: e.g. "Abbilder jenes namensstiftenden goldenen Huflattichs" (Steinfest 2004: 193) vs. "l'image de ce tussilage d'or qui donnait son nom à hôtel" (Steinfest 2011: 256). The original indulges in accumulating indications of formality. The formulation "mit der Gelassenheit langjährig Leidender" (Steinfest 2004: 7) combines present participle, nominalisation, zero article and genitive; the French version prefers again the more verbal turn of demonstrative pronoun and relative clause: "avec le flegme de ceux qui souffrent depuis des années" (Steinfest 2011: 13). The following quote contains two genitives, the relative pronoun *welche* with its administrative ring, as opposed to *die*, the formal distal demonstrative *jene*, and an expanded infinitive construction which precedes the adjective it depends on; by contrast, the French translation could also appear in orality:

(16)
ST. [...] einer Stadt [...], die weitab des Lebensraums jener Fische lag, welche eine derartige Zerfleischung zu leisten imstande waren. [Steinfest 2004: 9]
TT. [...] une ville bien éloignée de l'habitat naturel de tous les poissons susceptibles de hacher menu qui que ce soit. (Steinfest 2011: 16)

Indefinite article, declined adjective and back-reference to a preceding noun instead of a simple undeclined adjective after copula verb cannot be copied in French:

(17)
ST. Ohnehin war ihre Begeisterung bei seinem Einzug eine geringe gewesen. (Steinfest 2004: 60)
TT. Du reste, elle avait montré peu d'enthousiasme à le voir emménager. (Steinfest 2011: 84)

Logically the translator wishes to avoid any possible parallelism which could be interpreted as clumsiness due to the mediator and she compensates by introducing elements which are generally accepted as typical of an educated, academic, conservative use of language: *ne explétif*, omission of the negation particle *pas* after a modal verb, *savoir* instead of *pouvoir*, recurrent use of *imparfait du subjonctif*:

(18)
TT. Et de fait, ça n'allait pas du tout, même si Lukastik n'avait pas à craindre qu'une insolence ne lui coutât le poste ou ne lui valût une mutation. (Steinfest 2011: 29) (cf. Steinfest 2004: 19)

(19)
TT. Et il n'aurait su dire où se situaient le haut et le bas, si tant est qu'ils existassent encore. (Steinfest 2011: 348) (cf. Steinfest 2004: 262)

On numerous occasions the translation falls back on *imparfait du subjonctif* and even *plus-que-parfait du subjonctif* (e.g. Steinfest 2011: 16, 81, 216). The former is a conventional mark of elaborate code (and its deliberate use), and nowadays the latter is hardly used even in writing because of its very high degree of formality. The criteria according to which the translation chooses one or the other or a mainstream *subjonctif du present* (e.g. Steinfest 2011: 402 for Steinfest 2004: 303) or a *conditionnel passé deuxième forme* (e.g. "la seule chose pour laquelle il eût valu la peine d'investir", Steinfest 2011: 355) are not clear: possibly the highly formal elements are meant to counterbalance a dramatization of speech (when for example dashes try to imitate the oral realization), or to render particularly formal expressions of the German source; and perhaps it is due to an involuntary or an intentional incoherence. Such incoherence is perfectly in line with the superposition of discourses arranged by the narrator.

Apart from these more systematic morphosyntactical features, a multitude of formal or high-register lexical items pervade the novel and its translation: *solcherart* (Steinfest 2004: 5), *selbige* (Steinfest 2004: 50), *gleichkommen* (Steinfest 2004: 7), *gleich* (Steinfest 2004: 127), *par suite* (Steinfest 2011: 54), *faute de* (Steinfest 2011: 399), *étioler* (Steinfest 2011: 399).

The repetition of this kind of choice results in a distinctive voice, which will be interpreted as the narrator's or a character's habit of speaking.

This narrator and his principal characters exhibit aloofness and sharp-mindedness and their discourse is full of surprises; what keeps the public reading even when the plot has become transparent is the expectation of the next surprise. The character whose individuality is most strongly elaborated is an intellectual who likes to demonstrate how knowledgeable or different he is. He cultivates understatement and distance, even towards himself, so that formality and formulations typical of deferred communication relying on complex encoding and decoding are natural to him.

6. Colloquial elements

The translation follows the same inspiration, though of course not every lexical element has a counterpart which is also of an equivalent register:

(20)
ST. »Rauch lieber nicht so viel, du dumme Kuh«, murmelte er vor sich hin. Es gab Momente, da er sich vergaß. (Steinfest 2004: 85)
TT. «Tu ferais mieux de ne pas fumer autant, espèce d'idiote », marmonna-t-il à part lui. Il y avait des moments où il s'oubliait. (Steinfest 2011: 116)

The youngsters around the shark lake are introduced with an element of youth language: "Ach Gott, wessen Papa ist das?" (Steinfest 2004: 294) –although the genitive interrogative is certainly (and deliberately) not in keeping with the rest. The narrator of *Nervöse Fische* is not trying to depict registers in a naturalist vein, but rather to choose a representative, evocative element and make himself heard at the same time, too. The French translation is more 'univocally' colloquial: "–Aïe, c'est le papa de qui?" (Steinfest 2011: 389).

On the whole, colloquialisms and other typical resources of oral discourse, like repetition, play a very subordinate role in *Nervöse Fische*, in comparison with other crime novels (cf. Brumme 2009: 153), and although the Viennese setting plays an important role, there are hardly any of the dialectal features which tend to complicate the translation task (cf. Cadera 2012: 291-295; 299-300).

7. Balance and perspectives

Fictive orality can be understood as 'would-be orality in fiction': the attempt to come as close as possible to a 'purified' version of real orality and to make this fiction look real. In *Nervöse Fische* the intention is apparently to give snatches of orality (together with moments of wit, erudition, local colour, etc.) and to highlight at the same time the fictiveness of these elements which, ironically, are normally used for authentification. The unusual use of orality is another element of surprise in this novel which creates its suspense less on the level of criminal action or its elucidation than by making its reader constantly expect the next astonishing turn. There is a polyphony of voices in which one and the same character can adopt different tones from one moment to the next and where different characters can sound alike and where the narrator makes himself constantly heard, even in direct and indirect speech. Polyphony is one of the ingredients in the mosaic that makes up this novel, a work characterized by the sheer number of its digressions and diverse elements.

In her translation Corinna Gepner on many occasions arrives at a decent compromise between the need to be faithful to the original and the wish to create an authentic ring in the meta text. Her introduction of footnotes (for example on *Krautfleckerl* (Steinfest 2004: 217; Steinfest 2011: 288) and *Biedermeier* (Steinfest 2004: 284; Steinfest 2011: 376)) is a less fortunate choice. In fact the use of footnotes is a general translation problem which acquires particular importance in the context of crime literature. Suspense depends entirely on the intensity of the fiction, its non-interruption and non-mitigation. Footnotes that explain culture-specific, 'untranslatable' elements in an encyclopaedic style are hardly beneficial to maintaining it. The discrepancy in tone and the sudden intrusion of the translator into the story remind the reader that the situation which s/he has felt absorbed in up to then is just an invention, a literary lie which was not even intended for him / her in the first place. Depending on the nature of the co-text, less invasive solutions will often be possible. Steinfest's writing –with all its digressions, verbose irony and self-irony, exposure of general culture with accompanying partial explanation, explicit remarks on the Viennese setting, narrator's footnotes, metalinguistic comments (e.g. Steinfest 2004: 11; Steinfest 2004: 292), conspiratorial winks to the reader etc.– opens various possibilities for integrating a complement of information more cohesively into the core of the translated text. In the case of crime stories, translation must also maintain suspense in order to be faithful.

The translation published by Gallimard in 2011 is certainly far from the "belles infidèles"-model which Robyns (1990) detects in the translations of its

requirement, need, prerequi-
site

Série Noire until at least the early seventies. The desideratum left concerns the
that's
respect of the original's typographical choices, which ought to be an easily
accessible aim since it hardly generates any financial costs, though it
presupposes of course the effort and the willingness to question and possibly
adapt form conventions. Admittedly, much crime literature is 'fast read' and will
only benefit from 'fast translation', but the popularity of the genre and the broad
public that good detective novels find across language borders ought to justify a
special effort of cooperation between author, translator, and publisher.

---

[1] This article was written as part of the research project *The Translation of Fictional Dialogue.
Literary Texts and Multimodal Texts* (TRADIF is its Spanish acronym), reference number FF12010-
16783 (sub-programme FILO, 2010-2013), financed by the Spanish Ministry of Science and
Innovation. Head researcher: Jenny Brumme.
[2] For a detailed discussion of the concepts of immediacy vs. distance and of feigned or fictive orality
(cf. Brumme and Espunya 2012: 7-14.)

*style, production, appearance
of printed matter.*

— History of a speech community

Bibliography

Primary sources

Steinfest, Heinrich. 2004. *Nervöse Fische. Kriminalroman*. München and Zürich: Piper Verlag.
———. 2011. *Requins d'eau douce. Une enquête de l'inspecteur Lukastik*. Translated by Corinna Gepner. Barcelone: Gallimard.

Secondary Sources

Brumme, Jenny and Anna Espunya (eds). 2012. *The Translation of Fictive Dialogue*. (Approaches to Translation Studies, 35). Amsterdam and New York: Rodopi.
———. 2012. 'Background and justification: research into fictional orality and its translation' in Brumme and Espunya (2012): 7-31.
Brumme, Jenny. 2009. 'La traducción de la oralidad en la novela negra. El caso de las traducciones de Juan Madrid al francés y al alemán' in Alsina, Victòria, Gemma Andújar Gemma and Mercè Tricàs (eds) *La representación del discurso individual en traducción*. (Studien zur romanischen Sprachwissenschaft und interkulturellen Kommunikation 53). Frankfurt am Main, Berlin, Bern, Bruxelles, New York, Oxford and Wien: Peter Lang. 149-166.
———. 2012. *Traducir la voz ficticia* (Beihefte zur Zeitschrift für romanische Philologie 367). Berlin and Boston: Walter de Gruyter.
Cadera, Susanne M. 2012. 'Representing Phonetic Features' in Brumme and Espunya (eds). 2012. *The Translation of Fictive Dialogue*. (Approaches to Translation Studies, 35). Amsterdam and New York: Rodopi. 289-304.
Duden. 2006. *Die Grammatik der deutschen Gegenwartssprache. Nach den Regeln der neuen deutschen Rechtschreibung 2006 überarbeiteter Neudruck der 7., völlig neu erarbeiteten und erweiterten Auflage*. Mannheim, Leipzig, Wien and Zürich: Dudenverlag.
Engel, Ulrich. 1988. *Deutsche Grammatik*. Heidelberg: Groos.
Grévisse, Maurice. 2007. *Le bon usage: grammaire française*. Fourteenth edition. Paris: Duculot; Bruxelles: De Boeck & Larcier.
Kittel, Harald et al. (eds). 2004. *Übersetzung - Translation - Traduction. Ein internationales Handbuch zur Übersetzungsforschung / An International Encyclopedia of Translation Studies / Encyclopédie internationale de la recherche sur la traduction*. Together with Juliane House and Brigitte Schultze. Vol. 1. Berlin and New York: Mouton de Gruyter.
Koch, Peter and Wulf Oesterreicher. 1990. *Gesprochene Sprache in der Romania. Französisch, Italienisch, Spanisch*. Tübingen: Niemeyer.
Koch, Peter. 1986. 'Sprechsprache im Französischen und kommunikative Nähe' in *Zeitschrift für französische Sprache und Literatur* 96: 113-154.
Liefländer-Koistinen, Luise. 2004. 'Modalpartikeln als Übersetzungsproblem' in Kittel rt al. (eds). 2004: 550-554.
Robyns, Clem. 1990. 'The Normative Model of Twentieth Century Belles Infidèles: Detective Novels in French Translation' in *Target* 2(1): 23-42.
Thibaudet, Albert. 1935. *Gustave Flaubert*. Paris: Gallimard.
Truffaut, François. 1991. *Hitchcock / Truffaut*. Con la colaboración de Helen Scott. Edición definitiva (tr. Rafael del Moral). Madrid: Akal.
Wirf Naro, Maria. 2012a. 'The translation of modalisers' in Brumme, Jenny and Anna Espunya (eds). 2012. *The Translation of Fictive Dialogue*. (Approaches to Translation Studies, 35). Amsterdam and New York: Rodopi. 251-268.
———. 2012b. 'Fictive orality and formality as a translation problem' in Brumme, Jenny and Anna Espunya (eds). 2012. *The Translation of Fictive Dialogue*. (Approaches to Translation Studies, 35). Amsterdam and New York: Rodopi. 101-118.

Chapter 11: Shifting points of view: The translation of suspense-building narrative style

Anna Espunya *Ariadne Oliver*

Abstract

Narrative point of view and the expression of uncertainty have been identified as successful means to build suspense at the discourse level. Speech and thought representation techniques favour the realisation of fictive orality, a variety characterised by a selection of elements from spontaneous speech, constrained by the graphic medium and filtered through planning and revision. In translated works in general, regardless of the acceptance of fictive orality by the target readership, there is an observed tendency to the loss of traces of spontaneity in favour of written-like cohesion mechanisms, a normalisation strategy where clauses are rearranged and repetitions avoided. The research question is how such translation decisions affect the construction of suspense. The stylistic analysis of a suspenseful episode from Agatha Christie's novel *Third Girl* presented here reveals that the protagonist character's inner thoughts gain in grammatical cohesion and economy, blurring the differences between the Reflector and the character. The reorganisation of clauses favours more explicit interpretations of the intentions of the antagonist as events unfold, changing the perception of danger and foreshadowing. Changes in the modality of the discourse and in the overall expression of uncertainty modify the source of suspense.

Keywords: Point of view, suspense, fictive orality, English-Spanish translation, Agatha Christie

1. Introduction[1]

Suspense is a term that designates an emotional response, related to anticipation of the outcome, of the viewer of a film or the reader of a book as they watch or read certain works and process the story that is narrated (see, e.g., Vorderer et al. 1996). It is generally accepted that certain textually and linguistically realised formulae are effective in arousing and increasing suspense, and that they can be identified through stylistic analysis (Toolan 2001; Iwata 2008).[2] *Note this*

Given that translation involves a reconstruction of the source text's content and style using the resources of a different language, it is to be expected that the building of suspense may be affected by certain translator and copy editor choices. The research question that this contribution aims to answer is which translation decisions affect the construction of suspense and how.

I take a case study approach, analysing a particular chapter, chapter 9, of the detective novel *Third Girl* (1966), by Agatha Christie. External as well as internal reasons support this choice. The external reason is that Agatha Christie is the most-widely translated individual author ever, according to *Index Translationum*. Her detective novels have been translated into Spanish by 16 different translators, and the subset of novels featuring one particular secondary character, detective novelist Ariadne Oliver, have been translated by five different translators. Such variety casts doubts on the possibility that Christie's style has been preserved consistently in Spanish.

The internal reason for this choice is that the chapter can be read as a metafictional exercise on the creation of a suspense scene within a detective novel. An earlier analysis of translations of this novel and of *Elephants Can Remember* (1972) into Spanish and Catalan reveals a tendency to the neutralization of markers of subjectivity (see Espunya 2009) which homogenizes the points of view presented in the novels: changes from Free Indirect Discourse to Indirect Discourse, less expressive syntax, loss of information packaging distinctions through the avoidance of non-canonical structures, lower frequency of discourse markers, etc. Normalization is a well-known tendency toward textual conventionality found in translation in many language pairs and text types. The fact that it improves the readability of the translated text has prompted different kinds of explanations, from the self-perceived role of the translator as a facilitator, preferably an "invisible" one, to the cultural dominance of the national literatures with respect to each other (see Laviosa-Braithwaite 1998 and references therein).

In the case of Christie's detective novels, normalization seems to be grounded on their consideration as popular fiction products, whose consumer readers will seek entertainment from the whodunit aspects, rather than appreciation of realistic mimesis of speech, character portrayal, social commentary or suspense. Ultimately, then, the goal is to vindicate a translation approach to Agatha Christie's works that preserves the heterogeneity of points of view, one of the narrative techniques that enrich the reading experience and build suspense.

The structure of this contribution is the following: section 2 frames the study within stylistic approaches to suspense in literary fiction, focusing briefly on point of view; section 3 offers an analysis of the role of point of view, including shifts in modality and the markers of uncertainty, in the building of suspense, both in the source text and in the translation. The analysis addresses particularly the contribution of fictive orality. Finally, section 4 summarises the main observations, focusing on the potential effects on the experience of suspense by the reader

2. Suspense and the role of point of view

2.1 The conditions for suspense in literary works

The approach taken here focuses on the techniques used in narrative genres in the written mode. Iwata (2008: 83), in her dissertation on suspense and surprise in short stories belonging to the literary canon, identifies a set of conditions for literary suspense on the levels of story and discourse (Chatman 1978). These conditions are not obligatory but optional. At the story level, the conditions are the following (Iwata 2008: 169-173): a) *bifurcation* –the notion that "suspense usually depends on clearly bifurcating plot lines, which may be either desirable or undesirable", mainly from the standpoint of the characters involved; b) *resolution* –the notion that suspense is resolved, either favourably or unfavourably, although Iwata found that suspense is left unresolved in some of the stories she analysed; c) a central *episode of interest*, "whether life threatening or non-life-threatening, that stem[s] from the protagonist's–or a character-sufferer's-*fear of losing someone or something important* in any given narrative situation", and d) *character*, since "suspense is mainly provoked by the protagonist's mental or physical reactions towards the trigger characters and narrative events / situations, rather than the difficulties directly hurting the characters".

At the discourse level (Iwata 2008: 173-175), the conditions are the following: e) *point of view*, as "suspense-provoking episodes in literary fiction tend to be narrated from a point of view restricted to that of the protagonist who is in trouble, or witnesses other characters in trouble", and f) *sustainment of a state of uncertainty*, or delay in showing the resolution, which can be "disproportionately extended" relative to the time spent on preceding events.

2.2 The role of point of view in building suspense

Point of view contributes to the arousal of suspense in different ways. The most obvious one is through the alignment of the narrator with the protagonist or the character undergoing events, which while not a necessary condition, "does seem to help to heighten suspense" (Iwata 2008: 108). Here the devices of inner speech and thought presentation are fundamental. As Leech and Short (1981: 338; 341) point out, the thoughts of a character an author chooses to represent invite the reader to see things from the point of view of that character. In parallel, Iwata argues that there must be a sense of detachment between the reader and the character *if suspense is to be enjoyed*:

> Rather speculative as it is, a sense of objectivity or detachment, that is, the sense that the reader is a 'spectator' of the ongoing narrative event needs to be implicated, or called to mind, for a feeling of suspense to be experienced as enjoyment. (Iwata 2008: 110)

[handwritten margin note: Barnevy's constant role as reflector tends to deflect suspense.]

deontic = duty / obligation:
boulomaic — what is possible / necessa
verba sentiendi — character's (naught /
emotions

The feeling of detachment can be enhanced specially through the choice of modality:

> As the narrative in neutral modality often gives more objective background information rather than psychological detail of the characters, the shift between the two modes can serve well to bring detachment into the story. (Iwata 2008: 110)

Iwata assumes the categorisation of modality by Simpson (1993), where *neutral* modality is characterised by an absence of modal expressions and by categorical, flat assertions, and *positive* modality includes deontic and boulomaic modal expressions, evaluative expressions and *verba sentiendi*, i.e., verbs that report "a character's thoughts, perceptions and reactions (*she noticed... it annoyed her that...*)" (see also Toolan 2001: 71-2). Negative modality corresponds to epistemic modality.

As far as the identification or detachment effects are concerned, positive modality is taken to reflect the perspective of the character, whereas neutral modality can reflect the perspective of either the narrator or the character. Iwata observes that in some of the short stories she analysed, whereas the narrator category remains the same in the story, the modality often shifts from the positive to neutral across the boundaries of sentences or even within a clause. This transition between positive and neutral modalities, she speculates, "should be one of the commonest ways of facilitating suspense, regardless of the narrative category" (Iwata 2008: 109).

Speech and thought presentation as well as modality are two stylistic techniques that help modulate the feeling of suspense; translation shifts that affect them should also affect the building of suspense.

3. A case study: chapter 9 of *Third Girl*

3.1. Summary of the plot and of chapter 9

Third Girl (Christie 1966) is a detective story of a special kind, since the murder that should trigger the investigation has not been committed when the detective starts working on the case.

A young woman (Norma Restarick) asks for Poirot's help believing that she may have committed murder; as there is no instance of one in her close circle, he must try to find out whether indeed murder has been committed, while watching the girl to prevent her from either committing murder, or becoming the victim of one. The uncertainty of the situation prompts *global* suspense (Iwata 2008: 81) as Poirot (and the reader) ignores the circumstances under which it will take place. Many scenes involve the investigation of significant people in Norma's life: her family and friends, including her flatmates (hence the allusion in the title). An eager participant in these investigations is the detective fiction writer Ariadne Oliver, a good friend of Hercule Poirot's. Initially the main suspect is Norma's boyfriend David. At one point, David and Norma meet in a cafe, and Mrs Oliver decides to follow him discreetly. The adventure is narrated in chapter 9.

Chapter 9 provides an instance of "local suspense", an adventure episode where the protagonist (here Mrs Oliver) is placed in a situation that might become life threatening. David catches Mrs Oliver following him and confronts her very politely. Two interpretations are possible for this situation: she may feel socially embarrassed by her having been caught, or she may feel truly threatened. She ponders both options but decides to pretend she favours the first one by producing a credible excuse. He accepts her explanations and invites her to visit his artist's studio, which is in the vicinity. She agrees to pay a visit and meets his friends, crucially including Norma's flatmate Frances, who eventually turns out to be the murderess. Mrs Oliver leaves the studio quite reassured that they are not dangerous, but as she tries to reach the main road, she is hit from behind and passes out. This is the only violent act that is described as it is happening; the two actual murders in the novel are presented *post hoc*.

As regards the plot, the chapter achieves two minor goals, namely a reinforcement of David's ambiguous nature as the charming antagonist, and the suggestion that one of the three youths sharing the studio (David, Frances, or their artist friend, Peter) is capable of an aggression.

The appraisal of David's character and potential for harm takes considerable space in the chapter. David is part of Norma's social network and has access to her father's house and to her flat. He is also a member of a generation of young people, the angry young men, indirectly evoked by the author through news and hearsay. The narrator conscientiously recreates Mrs Oliver's thought processes, her sources of knowledge, her inferences and her own constant re-evaluation of her conclusions. These are all mixed, indicating confusion in her mind, with ideas that she seems to discard only to reactivate them soon after.

3.2. Fictive orality and narrative modes

The narrator type is a third person narrator with access to the consciousness of Mrs Oliver, her perceptions and feelings, i.e. reflector-character (Stanzel 1984: 141) or Reflector (Simpson 1993: 51) providing an internal perspective. In addition, Mrs Oliver, as a character, is given a voice through Direct Speech and Free Indirect Thought representation. The latter technique is at some points virtually indistinguishable from the Reflector mode of narration.

Speech and thought representation instantiate fictive orality, a variety characterised by a selection of elements from spontaneous speech constrained by the graphic medium and filtered through planning and revision (see Brumme

[handwritten margin note: Bennery]

[handwritten note at bottom: represent s.t. abstract by s.t. concrete]

and Espunya 2012b for a review of the concept and the literature from different scientific traditions). The pool of linguistic resources varies individually and is constrained by the literary cannon and the dominant writing conventions in the author's society. Fictive orality is often used to set the non-standard uses and users against the standard, by foregrounding distinctive features of social and geographical dialects, slang or simply informal registers to achieve verisimilitude in character portrayal. For a brief discussion and literature review on fictional speech in British and American detective fiction, see Bönnemark (1997: 188-191).

In this chapter fictive orality is present in Reflector discourse and, more pervasively, in character speech and thought representation. Consider the following passage, which presents Mrs Oliver's reaction immediately after David has confronted her.

(1)

ST.   She turned sharply. Suddenly what had recently been almost fun, a chase undertaken light-heartedly and in the best of spirits, now was that no longer. What she felt now was a sudden unexpected throb of fear. Yes, she was afraid. The atmosphere had suddenly become tinged with menace. Yet the voice was pleasant, polite; but behind it she knew there was anger. The sudden kind of anger that recalled to her in a confused fashion all the things one read in newspapers. (Christie 1966/2002: 134)

Free indirect thought [handwritten annotation]

TT.   Se volvió, alarmada. De pronto, aquello que había resultado casi divertido, una persecución comenzada con un espíritu alegre y despreocupado, dejó de serlo. Lo que sentía ahora era miedo. Sí, estaba asustada. En el aire flotaba la amenaza. La voz era agradable, cortés, pero detrás se ocultaba una cólera que le hizo recordar todas aquellas cosas que se leían en los periódicos. (Christie 2003: 94-95)

See back Glosary (more) for meaning. [handwritten annotation]

After a first sentence narrating her physical reaction from an external perspective, the Reflector takes over, as signalled by the deictic 'now'. The passage displays traits of fictional speech, such as (a) the non-canonical focus construction ("What she felt now was"), (b) confirmation through rephrasing ("Yes, she was **afraid**."), (c) the "internal" argumentative move indicated by the connective 'yet', and (d) an aggregative clause connection style which simulates the lack of planning ("behind it she knew there was **anger**. The sudden kind of **anger** that"). These resources enhance the impression that the reader is given access to Mrs Oliver's internal dialogue with herself, as she zigzags between trust and apprehension.

In the translation, Mrs Oliver's inner discourse has been subjected to normalization: her thoughts are articulated in a written-like, economic, and cohesive manner, with hypotaxis instead of aggregation (vg. the relative clause *una cólera que* "an anger that"). Repetition is avoided, even of words that help construct suspense ('anger', 'sudden'). Her thought processes are less explicitly dialogic as the connective 'yet' is left out. For the Spanish reader, the Reflector is less anguished, more self-possessed.

The omission of the verb of knowledge "she knew" and of the modifier "in a confused fashion" enhances neutral modality, as the clues to her knowledge state are left out. In neutral modality, impressions are presented as bare assertions attributed to the Reflector. The only clue to Mrs Oliver's subjectivity is the use of the locative verb *ocultarse* 'hide' as a translation of "behind it [she knew] there was".

Mrs Oliver's thoughts are rendered also through Direct Speech, which is slightly more informal and expressive than Reflector discourse. The reader may feel closer to her and choose to sympathise with her –or reject her old-fashioned views altogether. Consider, as an example, the following passage with her thoughts after her visit to the artists' studio.

(2)

ST. 'Three perfectly nice young people,' said Mrs Oliver to herself. 'Perfectly nice and very kind. Left here, and then right. Just because they *look* rather peculiar, one goes and has silly ideas about their being dangerous.' (Christie 1966/2002: 143)

TT. Tres jóvenes muy agradables. Primero a la izquierda, después a la derecha. Solo porque tengan un aspecto peculiar, no puedes creer que sean peligrosos. (Christie 2003: 100) Back Translation […] Just because they have a peculiar look, you can't believe that they are dangerous.

In this very short fragment we can observe various resources: a *stair figure* (a pattern of spoken syntax in which a new sequence is anchored in the previous one by the repetition of lexical items), verbless clauses, the colloquial formulaic construction 'go and V' (where 'go' has a purely emotive role and the whole expression an overlay of disapproval, according to Huddeston and Pullum 2002: 1303), and the use of italics to render the prosodic focus accent on the distance between looking peculiar and being dangerous.

As in the previous example, translation involves normalization. Mrs Oliver's assessment of the three people she has just visited is shortened and the stair figure is lost, perhaps due to a general stylistic aversion to lexical repetition, in spite of the fact that stair figures are found in the literary recreation of speech by Spanish writers contemporary to Christie (see, e.g., López Serena 2012). As a result, her discourse is less aggregative, and hence less spontaneous, as shown also by the rendering of the spoken syntactic pattern "one goes and V" as the imperative no *puedes creer* 'you can't believe', which requires a sentential complement. We can also attribute to this strategy the arbitrary omission of the dialogue tag; paradoxically, this move foregrounds the character's perspective, particularly in the absence of quotation marks for Direct Speech when inserted in the running discourse of the narrator, which is not the translator's choice but the convention in Spanish.

Mrs Oliver is a privileged secondary character whose thoughts and conversations are presented in great detail. Bönnemark (1997: 168-171) discusses the love of external detail, such as precise renderings of actions and events, descriptions of objects and circumstances, the use of proper names and trademarks, technical acronyms, etc., as a feature of detective and suspense fiction. This phenomenon has been observed in fiction written by male writers and especially in Anglophone writers. I suggest that we can view detailed simulation of speech and thought in Agatha Christie's detective fiction in the same terms. According to Bönnemark (1997: 55), Christie "is considered a master at rendering dialogue". As a narrative technique, in the chapter analysed here, detailed rendering of thought and speech is a source of delay that increases the feeling of impending danger and, hence, of suspense. The editing strategies observed in this Spanish translation suggest, however, that it is underrated by the translator or by the copy editor.

3.3. Modality and reasoning patterns

In this section I explore the role of modality and particularly the move from positive to neutral modality, in building suspense. Consider the text immediately following (1) above:

(3)
ST.   Elderly women attacked by gangs of young men. Young men who were ruthless, cruel, who were driven by hate and the desire to do harm. This was the young man whom she had been following. He had known she was there, had given her the slip and had then followed her into this alleyway and he stood there now barring her way out. (Christie 1966/2002: 134)

TT.   Mujeres mayores atacadas por pandillas de gamberros. Jóvenes despiadados y crueles, animados por el odio y el deseo de hacer daño. Este era el joven al que había seguido. Había advertido que le seguía. La había conducido hasta el callejón para tenderle una trampa. (Christie 2003: 95)

In this passage Mrs Oliver –the character– evokes negative stereotypes of young men through intertextual references such as news reports (note the headline syntax of "Elderly women…") and the opinions of a section of society ("ruthless, cruel", "driven by hate"). Following these sentences characterised by positive modality, a categorical, neutral clause classifies David as a member of the group she has just evoked. In this new light, she reconstructs the sequence of recent events in a factual rather than a hypothetical mood, through the past perfect. The sequence of coordinated clauses lends an incremental rhythm to the reconstruction leading to a neutral but objective depiction of her current situation ("He stood there now barring her way out"). This is a suspenseful moment for an empathising reader.

In the Spanish translation, the positive modality and inter-textual allusions are maintained. The neutral modality of the reconstructed course of action is also maintained, but not so the incremental rhythm expressed by 'and' – coordination, as the clauses have been rearranged into an independent clause

Handwritten annotations at top:
unequal contructs in a sentence
—Some more important than others
e.g. a clause

Handwritten annotation: using conjunctions.

and a complex hypotactic sentence. Events are reorganised so that the resulting state is rendered as a purpose clause: David leads her to the alleyway in order to lay her a trap. Any ambiguity as to his conduct in the original situation is lost: verbs like *conducido* 'led' and *trampa* 'trap' explicitly attribute treacherous intention to the man. This modifies the origin of the reader's uneasiness from indeterminacy to definite and impending danger. It also renders the ensuing excuses produced by an embarrassed Mrs Oliver pragmatically inadequate. If he were leading her to the alley, then her admission that she had been following him is incongruous.

The reasoning pattern that goes from the general to the particular is especially effective in arousing suspense when it combines with the physical proximity of the antagonist, as illustrated in (4), which is the text immediately following (3).

(4)

ST. As is the precarious fashion of London, one moment you are amongst people all round you and the next moment there is nobody in sight. There must be people in the next street, someone in the houses near, but nearer than that is a masterful figure, a figure with strong cruel hands. She felt sure that in this moment he was thinking of using those hands... The Peacock. (Christie 1966/2002: 134-135)

TT. Como era habitual en Londres, un momento antes había gente por todas partes y, al instante siguiente, no había nadie a la vista. Sin duda, había gente en la calle siguiente, en las casas cercanas, pero se enfrentaba a una figura dominante con crueles y fuertes manos. Tuvo la impresión de que, en ese momento, el joven pensaba en utilizarlas. (Christie 2003: 95)

In the source text, the first sentence introduces a piece of common knowledge (through the use of the present tense for general truths and an arbitrary 'you') that contributes to a feeling of objectivity. The spoken quality of "one moment you are ... and the next moment" is compatible with the perspective of the Reflector, through "the colloquialization of the narrator's language" (Stanzel 1984: 195), cited in Bönnemark (1997: 144). Alternatively it can be interpreted as the perspective of the character in Free Direct Thought. The second sentence, also in the present tense, starts by introducing uncertainty by comparing the high degree of probability that there are people who might prevent an attack ("There must be") with the imagined reality ("nearer than that is"). The subjective perspective is realised in the deictic expressions 'next', 'near' and 'nearer', all of them with the victim as the deictic centre. In the second half, evaluative adjectives are introduced –'masterful', 'strong', 'cruel'–, and we seem to hear the thoughts of Mrs Oliver, the character. Iwata notes that "when narratives are dominated by FDT for some time, they begin to appear as if the character is talking to the reader directly, rather than through the narrator" (2008: 72). The change from neutral to positive modality, as well as the change from the general to the particular, express the materialisation of Mrs Oliver's fears through

Handwritten annotation: (Free Direct Thought

201

specific reference to the hands, first the "strong cruel hands" of an imaginary figure that become "those hands", i.e. David's, in the following sentence.

In the translation, there is no suggestion of Free Direct Thought, as the temporal anchor is narration time, as opposed to event time: note the use of relative temporal adverbs *antes* 'before', *siguiente* 'following' and the past tense of *se enfrentaba* 'faced', which translates 'nearer than that'. The passage is interpreted as event narration where David is presented directly as the evil antagonist, and as the evolution from an abstract 'masterful figure' to the particular cataphoric reference to David is lost. In translation, the reader must focus on a particular place and time and a particular character. The lexical choice *se enfrentaba* 'faced' for the presentational sequence "near than that is" clearly foregrounds the adversarial relationship. Somewhat paradoxically, however, the translation renders 'she felt sure', the moment of certainty for Mrs Oliver, as the much weaker *tuvo la impresión* ('she felt', literally 'she was under the impression'). The interplay of point of view and modality is reconstructed differently and so is suspense.

In this translation the source of suspense is altered owing to a coarser reproduction of Mrs Oliver's thought processes, and lower tolerance to indeterminacy and prolonged uncertainty. To a large extent, this can be attributed to the normalization strategy to make the novel conform to the Spanish norm for written prose (hypotactic syntax, avoidance of repetition, preference for full clauses, neutral or formal lexical choices, etc.). This affects the maintenance of ambiguity and uncertainty, as a shortened text means that content has to be abridged; however, to some extent, alterations in the presentation of David are due to the translator's lexical choices (such as *se ocultaba*, *se enfrentaba* and *tenderle una trampa*).

3.4. Markers of uncertainty

The main source of uncertainty is the speaker's lack of knowledge; its expression is related to the notion of epistemic modality, which Simpson (1993: 53-54) categorises as 'negative modality'. Among the linguistic expressions conveying certainty to various degrees are adjectives such as 'sure' in fragment (4) above ("she felt sure that"), and verbs such as 'must' in "there must be" expressing deduction, also in (4).

Knowledge is constrained by the stability of situations. Sudden changes in a character's immediate observable reality alter her knowledge state and introduce a feeling of uncertainty. In passage (1) above, for example, the Reflector explicitly renders the reaction of the character to the change of role from chaser to victim through the repeated occurrences of 'suddenly' and 'sudden', as well as the contrast between the previous and the current situation through 'now', 'recently' and 'no longer', with 7 such items in a 48-word passage.

In the translation there is an obvious reduction; only the first instance of 'suddenly' is translated (*de pronto*). The adverb 'now' is also reduced to one occurrence. The sequence in Spanish focuses on the new state of affairs (she was in fear, threat was looming or "floating in the air"). Notice also that Mrs Oliver presents the surge of emotion as physically perceptible –"unexpected throb", "tinged with"– which is not as clearly conveyed in the translation.

Uncertainty is related to the technique of foreshadowing. Toward the end of the episode, after her visit to the artist's studio, as David offers her directions to return to the main road, Mrs Oliver seems to be able to accept her own rational arguments that the youths are not dangerous. Still, she cannot overcome her irrational, ominous feelings. She will be proved right when she is attacked by surprise. The Reflector is very explicit in her use of the lexicon to anticipate the outcome of the episode.

(5)

ST. Curiously enough, as she walked across the shabby yard the same feeling of unease and suspense came over her. "I mustn't let my imagination go again."She looked back at the steps and the window of the studio. The figure of David still stood looking after her. "Three perfectly nice young people," said Mrs Oliver to herself. "Perfectly nice and very kind. Left here, and then right. Just because they *look* rather peculiar, one goes and has silly ideas about their being dangerous. Was it right again? or left? Left, I think –Oh goodness, my feet. It's going to rain, too." (Christie 1966/2002: 143)

TT. Una vez más, al cruzar el solitario patio, volvió a experimentar la sensación de inquietud. No debo dejarme dominar por mi imaginación, se reprochó. Volvió la cabeza para mirar hacia las escaleras y la ventana del estudio. David la vigilaba desde lo alto para comprobar que no equivocaba el camino. Tres jóvenes muy agradables. Primero a la izquierda, después a la derecha. Solo porque tengan un aspecto peculiar, no puedes creer que sean peligrosos. ¿Era otra vez a la derecha o a la izquierda? Creo que a la izquierda. Vaya dolor de pies. Me parece que va a llover. (Christie 2003: 100)

In the original, the adverbial phrase "curiously enough" is subjective: the adverb 'curiously' is evaluative (see, e.g. Huddleston and Pullum 2002: 771), and it is further modified by the degree expression 'enough' indicating sufficiency. The Reflector evaluates the return of the character's feelings of unease and suspense as strange. Combined with the repetition of "perfectly nice" (the adverb 'perfectly' defeats expectations of not being nice), followed by the mention of "silly ideas" about their being dangerous, the sequence is ominous.

In the translation the subjective adjunct is replaced by a temporal adjunct meaning "once again". As it is anaphoric, it preserves the meaning of "sameness" and "return", and the discursive topic-reactivation function; however, the Reflector offers a detached temporal frame instead of a glimpse into the subjectivity of the character. The feelings themselves are reduced to *inquietud* 'unease', with the loss of the explicit 'suspense', which is not a mere synonym but can be interpreted as a metafictional pointer. All this leads to the weakening of the foreshadowing effect.

[handwritten note: Anaphora – repetition of a certain word at beg. of successive lines]

In the translation the Reflector is more detached, acting less as the conveyor of the character's perspective than as the provider of the frame for action and interpreter of her thoughts for the reader (notice the introduction of the narrator tag *se reprochó* "reproached herself"). In contrast, the portrayal of the character through her direct thoughts preserves the spoken-like quality that enhances immediacy: note the intensifier *vaya* preceding the explicit *dolor de pies* (aching feet), pragmatically equivalent to the interjection "oh goodness".

4. Conclusions

In the analysis of chapter 9 of *Third Girl* we have been able to identify the mechanisms for suspense creation that Iwata identified in her analysis of short literary fiction, thus supporting the literary consideration for Agatha Christie's style. One of the main techniques is speech and thought presentation exploiting the resources of fictive speech, particularly through a wide variety of syntactic patterns. In the Spanish translation, syntax clearly complies with the norms of standard written (non-fiction) prose, and hence it is less realistic as a simulation of spontaneous thoughts. This hinders the illusion of direct access to the character's perspective. The loss of immediacy is also observed as a consequence of the alteration of tenses, from the present to the past, enhancing the role of the narrator as a teller rather than as a Reflector.

The downplaying of the character's perspective is observed in the manipulation of modality, illustrated by the suppression of the subjective modifier "in a confused fashion" and by the change from positive to neutral modality observed in the translation of "curiously enough" as "once again".

Another key element in suspense is the sustainment of uncertainty, achieved by repeated references to the suddenness of certain developments, the indeterminacy of new situations, and the presentation of characters as ambiguous (e.g. seductive but potentially dangerous). The translation exhibits a tendency to disambiguation and factuality, even at the cost of rendering David as more evil-minded than he is in the source text.

All these interventions by the translator affect the quality of experience of suspense by the reader, particularly that of foreshadowing. This is a relatively novel observation that needs to be confirmed by more studies of the translation of suspenseful scenes.

---

[1] The work reported in this paper has been supported by the Spanish Ministry of Science and Innovation through project TRADIF (reference number FFI2010-16783). The author belongs to the group CEDIT, financed by the Catalan government (reference number 2009SGR711).
[2] In literary studies the term 'suspense fiction' designates a category of fictional narrative works, i.e. a genre, which is set apart from other genres such as detective fiction on the basis of plot and discourse

characteristics identified by analysing a set of works *a priori* selected as representative of the genre. Suspense fiction can include spy fiction, the psychological thriller, etc. A thorough discussion of genres, and in particular of the differences between detective and suspense fiction, is provided in Bönnemark (1997).

Bibliography

Primary sources

Christie, Agatha. 1966 [2002]. *Third Girl*. Harper Collins, London.
———. 1972 [2002]. *Elephants Can Remember*. Harper Collins, London.
———. 2003. *Tercera muchacha*. Translated by Alberto Coscarelli. Barcelona: Random House Mondadori [Rights signed over from Editorial Molino; first edition from 1999]

Secondary sources

Bönnemark, Margit. 1997. *The Mimetic Mystery. A linguistic study of the genre of British and American detective fiction including a comparison with suspense fiction.* PhD Thesis. University of Stockholm.
Brumme, Jenny and Anna Espunya (eds). 2012a. *The Translation of Fictive Dialogue.* (Approaches to Translation Studies 35). Amsterdam and New York, NY: Rodopi.
———. 2012b. "Background and justification: research into fictional orality and its translation' in Brumme, Jenny and Espunya, Anna (eds). 7-31.
Chatman, Seymour. 1978. *Story and Discourse: Narrative Structure in Fiction and Film.* Ithaca: Cornell University Press.
Espunya, Anna. 2009. 'La simulación de la subjetividad en las novelas de Agatha Christie: análisis comparativo de traducciones' in Alsina, Victòria, Gemma Andújar and Mercè Tricàs (eds). *La representación del discurso individual en traducción.* Frankfurt am Main: Peter Lang. 127-148.
Iwata, Yumiko. 2008. *Creating Suspense and Surprise in Short Literary Fiction: A Stylistic and Narratological Approach.* PhD Thesis. University of Birmingham. On line at http://etheses.bham.ac.uk (consulted: 11.03.2013)
Huddleston, Rodney and Geoffrey K. Pullum. 2002. *The Cambridge Grammar of the English Language.* Cambridge: Cambridge University Press.
Laviosa-Braithwaite, Sara. 1998. 'Universals of translation' in Baker, Mona (ed.). *Routledge Encyclopedia of Translation Studies.* London: Routledge. 288-291.
Leech, Geoffrey N. and Michael H. Short. 1981. *Style in Fiction: A Linguistic Introduction to Literary Fiction.* London: Longman.
López Serena, Araceli. 2012. 'Recreating spoken syntax in fictive orality: an analytical framework' in Brumme, Jenny and Anna Espunya (eds). 167-183.
Simpson, Paul. 1993. *Language, Ideology and Point of View.* London: Routledge.
Stanzel, Franz K. 1984. *A Theory of Narrative.* Cambridge: Cambridge University Press.
Toolan, Michael. 2001. *Narrative: A Critical Linguistic Introduction.* Second edition. London: Routledge.
Vorderer, Peter, Hans J. Wulff, and Mike Friedrichsen (eds). 1996. *Suspense: Conceptualizations, Theoretical Analyses, and Empirical Explorations.* Hillsdale, NJ: Erlbaum.

Chapter 12: Red herrings and other misdirection in translation

Karen Seago

Abstract

Detective stories are structured around the conceit that, according to the Detection Club Oath of 'Fair Play' and SS Van Dine's 'Twenty Rules', the reader should be able to solve the crime on the basis of the clues made available to them. In order to maintain suspense and not to give the game away, legitimate clues are liberally mixed with misleading information, or are communicated only partially, in garbled form or are intentionally de-emphasised. As a result, the reader will only be able to reconstruct the detective's logical process of deduction in retrospect, when they are able to sort the important from the unimportant or misleading. But how does the translator approach such authorial misdirection? With reference to Marklund's *The Bomber* and German translations of Christie's *The Mysterious Affair at Styles* and *Mrs McGinty's Dead*, this chapter analyses how ambiguity, ambivalence, misdirection are achieved and considers to what extent these rhetorical strategies survive the process of translation.

Keywords: Detective fiction, fair play, cognitive poetics, rhetorical manipulation, crime fiction, translation, reader involvement, misdirection, Agatha Christie

1. Introduction

In 1928, Anthony Berkeley and other detective story authors founded the prestigious Detection Club. One of its first presidents was Dorothy L. Sayers and the membership reads like a Who's Who of Golden Age detective fiction and beyond. The club is still active and contemporary thriller writers such as Val McDermid, John Harvey and Ian Rankin are members. The club was founded as a forum for networking, in order for members to help each other with technical aspects of their writing and to develop a 'code of ethics'. On joining, new members had to take the oath of fair play, promising that they would not withhold information from their readers or resolve their mysteries in an unrealistic manner. The detectives in their stories would

> [...] well and truly detect the crimes presented to them using those wits which it may please [the author] to bestow upon them and not placing reliance on nor making use of Divine Revelation, Feminine Intuition, Mumbo Jumbo, Jiggery-Pokery, Coincidence, or Act of God. (Detection Club: online)

However, the authors' solemn oath "never to conceal a vital clue from the reader" (Detection Club oath) did not prevent them from engaging in ingenious forms of reader manipulation and misdirection. The golden age detective story lives on the battle of wits between author and reader, where the author attempts to lead the reader astray by providing partial information, foregrounding irrelevant clues and burying crucial evidence, giving facts out of context so that their relevance is not apparent or by suggesting associations and emphasising details which are later revealed to be misleading. Reader engagement –and entertainment– largely relies on the cognitive involvement of the armchair detective attempting to solve the puzzle despite authorial misdirection, to match their wits against the genius of the detective, to avoid and recognise the traps laid for them.

> The truth of the problem must at all times be apparent—provided the reader is shrewd enough to see it. By this I mean that if the reader, after learning the explanation for the crime, should reread the book, he would see that the solution had, in a sense, been staring him in the face—that all the clues really pointed to the culprit—and that, if he had been as clever as the detective, he could have solved the mystery himself without going on to the final chapter. (van Dine: online)

Of course, detective fiction lends itself to these cognitive games, to misdirection and rhetorical manipulation. The condition of all detective stories is that "the detective repeat, go over again, the ground that has been covered by his predecessor, the criminal" (Brooks 1984: 24). This retracing of steps makes crime fiction a double and discontinuous narrative, where the crime is presented (usually) at the beginning of the story initiating a double narrative moving backwards in time, retracing and uncovering the steps leading (usually) to the murder, and at the same time moving forward chronologically, charting the development, the growing understanding and knowledge of the detective towards resolution, the identification of the culprit. The crime is solved through rational deduction and logical thinking, where clues are uncovered, interpreted and causally related until ultimately the different layers of meaning and discontinuous narrative strands around hypotheses of cause, motive, manner and means are resolved into a linear narrative of cause and effect.

In addition to this fundamental structural discontinuity of crime fiction, the author further fragments the narrative by consciously manipulating the chronology, mis-associating time and place or characters, unsettling narrative perspective through shifting narrators and focalisers, scattering evidence through the text and across the different narrative strands and by giving differential treatment in terms of focus and emphasis to the various narrative components.

This manipulation of the reader is popularly referred to as red herrings. Strictly speaking, a red herring is a misleading plot line 'distracting the attention of the detective and reader away from the guilty and towards the innocent' (Dupriez 1991: 322) rather than the technical devices and manipulative strategies which the author deploys. In the following, I will focus on two broad categories: 1) the exploitation of inferences, that is the gaps in the text which the reader fills in on the basis of the knowledge they bring to the text, and 2) the use of rhetorical manipulation where plot-significant information is presented in such a way that the important is hidden, and the unimportant becomes prominent.

2. Exploiting genre conventions

Like all genre literature, detective stories draw on a set of typical tropes and topoi and it is these conventions that the author can exploit by playing a game of bluff and double-bluff with the reader's knowledge of and attentiveness to how typical settings, actions, conversations etc. may suggest a clue (or an attempt to divert attention from a clue). Similarly, the author can take advantage of shared assumptions what constitutes typical character behaviour or appearance and create character constructs which do not conform to the norm. Such departures from the conventional can function as a clue to moral deviancy and signal a potential suspect.

The following two examples show how the author exploits the reader's knowledge of genre conventions. In *Mrs McGinty's Dead* (1952), Agatha Christie's Poirot conducts an informal investigation to clear the suspect awaiting trial for the murder of the eponymous old woman and 'interviews' all the people who employed Mrs McGinty as a cleaner.

> (1)
> ST1   "I am investigating the murder of Mrs McGinty," said Poirot. "And I do not joke."
>   "Ouch," said Mrs Summerhayes. "I've cut my hand." (Christie 1952: 42)

The knowledgeable reader, on the look-out for potentially relevant clues, may interpret the fact that Mrs Summerhayes cut her hand as a guilty reaction to Poirot's announcement, an involuntary disclosure that she is implicated in the crime, rather than as an unrelated, accidental slip of the knife while chopping vegetables, and, as a result, will put her on the 'suspect list'. Similarly, in *The Bomber,* Liza Marklund exploits the convention that we assume the perspective presented in a prologue and interspersed first person reflections to be that of the perpetrator, giving the reader an insight into the mind of the killer, that it is their voice we are hearing.

> Sometimes I would put a lump of sugar on the hill. The ants loved my gift, and I smiled while they poured over it and pulled it down into the depth of the hill. In the autumn, when days grew colder and the ants slowed down, I would stir the hill with a stick to wake them up again. The grown-ups were angry when they saw what I was doing. They said that I was sabotaging the work of the ants and had ruined their home. To this day, I remember the feeling of injustice. I

meant no harm. I just wanted a bit of fun. I wanted to rouse the little creatures. (Marklund 2011:
10)

Here the inference is that this is the voice of the killer based on the assumption
that cruelty to animals in childhood is a marker for abnormal behaviour and
closely linked to (popular) psychological profiles of murderers. It also assumes
that the killer is a man, because it is 'understood' that it is little boys who torture
animals, that murderers are usually men, and that their victims are women –and
the reader knows that the victim in *The Bomber* is a woman who was killed by
brutal blows with a hammer to her head– described on the page immediately
preceding the first person reflection. As a consequence, the reader is guided
towards building up a construct of the killer as a man, potentially disregarding
any contextual clues implicating women. Throughout the novel, Marklund
ensures that any references to the killer are non-gendered, for example as 'the
figure' (Marklund 2011: 9) and that none of the first-person reflections contain
any unambiguously gendered indicators (clothes, behaviour patterns, absence of
pronominal references, etc).

In *The Mysterious Affair at Styles* Christie creates an inference-rich scenario
in which the characters and the reader develop a number of assumptions around
the identity of the male speaker in a quarrel which is overheard by the maid,
Dorcas, and reported to Poirot, who is investigating the poisoning of Mrs
Inglethorp in the night following the exchange.

(2)
ST2   "Well, sir, as I said, I happened to be passing along, when I heard voices very loud and
angry in here. I didn't exactly mean to listen, but—well, there it is. I stopped. The door
was shut, but **the mistress was speaking very sharp and clear**, and I heard what she
said quite plainly. 'You have lied to me, and deceived me,' she said. I didn't hear what
Mr Inglethorp replied. **He spoke a good bit lower** than she did—but she answered:
'How dare you? I have kept you and clothed you and fed you! You owe everything to
me! And this is how you repay me! By bringing disgrace upon our name!' **Again I
didn't hear what he said**, but she went on: 'Nothing that you can say will make any
difference. I see my duty clearly. My mind is made up. You need not think that any fear
of publicity, or scandal between husband and wife will deter me.' Then I thought I heard
them coming out, so I went off quickly." "You are sure it was Mr Inglethorp's voice you
heard?" "Oh, yes, sir, **whose else's** could it be?" (Christie 1920: online; *my emphasis*)

Dorcas takes it as read that the quarrel is between Mrs Inglethorp and her
husband and that she is accusing her husband of having an affair, on the basis of
the rather odd phrasing 'a scandal between husband and wife'. Any seasoned
reader of detective novels will of course realise that Dorcas's certainty is a fairly
obvious indicator that it is likely that the male speaker is not Mr Inglethorp and
that the third-person reference to husband and wife also points towards a scandal
between another couple in the household. However, the English leaves this

polysemy—word or phrase that has multiple meanings

entirely open to interpretation and the reader's sharpened awareness relies on knowledge of genre conventions.

The German translation however closes down on the possibilities of interpretation. The indeterminacy of 'whose' scandal Mrs Inglethorp is talking about is reduced by translating the word 'kept you' as *aushalten* which is only used to describe a sexual relationship where the (usually older) man pays for the upkeep of his (young) mistress. The English can have two meanings, either the sexual relationship or the situation where a relative or guardian pays for the upkeep of a dependent child or ward. In German, this word is *unterhalten* (although it would be more common to use a noun-verb construction *Unterhalt zahlen*). Because the German does not have the hyperonym containing both *more general* meanings of sexual and familial financial support but differentiates these meanings into the two hyponyms (*aushalten* and *unterhalten* / *Unterhalt* *more specific* *zahlen*), the translator had to make a choice and opted for the sexually connoted hyponym, clearly indicating that the quarrel is between Mr and Mrs Inglethorp, when, in fact, as is revealed at the end, the quarrel was between her and her stepson and she used the word in the sense of familial support and upkeep.

3. Assumptions about gender

So far, I have discussed two types of inference where the reader supplies meaning for a textual gap or decides on a preferred meaning for a polyseme on the basis of co-textual clues. As we have seen, the first type of inference, where two unconnected actions are linked by a motivated interpretation in the reader's mind, does not necessarily pose any problems in translation, while the choice of preferred meaning poses a problem, if the target language does not have a similarly polysemous or superordinate lexical item available. I will now turn to inferences which build on gender and identity role assumptions which are far more difficult to convey in languages which have explicit gendering strategies or where culturally-specific expectations are diverse. In the following examples, again taken from *Mrs McGinty's Dead*, the author exploits norms expectations around femininity –our understanding of what is especially in the fifties– normal behaviour and appearance. The attributes or characteristics which build up a cumulative image of an 'unwomanly' woman are highlighted in bold in the descriptions of Deirdre Henderson.

(3)
ST1   The **big** young woman with the **plain** face looked gratified. (Christie 1952: 160; *my emphasis*)

(4)
ST1   Deirdre Henderson came in. She looked pale and strained and, as usual, rather **awkward**. [...] Spence rose and pushed forward a chair. She sat down on it **squarely in an ungainly** schoolgirlish sort of way. (Christie 1952: 227; *my emphasis*)

211

(5)
ST1   "**No lipstick**," he said. "Or is that only this morning?" "No, it is not only this morning.
She never uses it." "That's **odd**, nowadays, isn't it?" "She is rather an **odd kind of girl**
–undeveloped." (Christie 1952: 230; *my emphasis*)

Deirdre is shown to be somewhat odd, unfeminine, big, and the knowledgeable
reader might use these apparent discrepancies in character presentation as
marking her out as deviant, potentially placing her on the suspect list. In
addition, some of her behaviour is described in such a way that it is suggestive
of masculinity making this a possible case of gender manipulation where
Deirdre could conceivably be unmasked as a man at the end of the novel.
Playing with gender, is, in fact, central to *Mrs McGinty's Dead* and is an
increasingly foregrounded theme in relation to a number of characters, but
Deirdre's non-conforming lack of femininity is a very clear red herring –she is
simply an awkward and not very stylish young woman. However, the German
translation foregrounds the gender theme in its choice of title *Vier Frauen und
ein Mord* (Four women and a murder), making the knowledgeable reader even
more susceptible to anticipating any potential twists in the tale based on gender.
Titles perform a number of functions in guiding reader expectation, from the
phatic (raising reader interest), informative (providing topic and content) and the
hermeneutic. It is the hermeneutic function which is most important for crime
fiction because it gives a clue for text interpretation (Iliescu 2001: 94) and in the
context of genre expectations, the reader will take the information contained in
the title as a heightened stimulus for interpreting any gender clues in the text.

3.1. The challenge of translating grammatical gender

So far, I have been addressing how an author can create ambiguity by
negotiating norms expectations and genre expectations revolving around gender
identity and gender norms. Grammatical gender, of course, adds a further
dimension to gender manipulation and poses particular problems for the
translator, especially if the author is consciously withholding linguistic clues by
using unmarked forms. We saw an example of this in Marklund's use of 'the
figure' to refer to the killer without disclosing whether this is a man or a woman.
English lends itself particularly to such masking of the biological sex of an
unknown character. Unlike inflected languages, it does not have gendered
endings or definite articles which disclose the gender identity of a character.

The following examples illustrate how the translation of grammatical gender
introduces (at times obligatory) shifts and makes explicit things that the source
text leaves, deliberately, open. Let us look at a number of instances taken from
The Mysterious Affair at Styles, where Christie was careful not to identify
whether the referent was male or female but the German translation rendered
these as explicitly feminine or masculine. The classic device of prolonging

suspense over the identity of the murderer even as s/he is revealed in the detective's final explanation of the crime to the assembled closed group of 'suspects', is also deployed by Christie in *Styles* when Poirot is about to name the suspect:

(6)
ST2   "We all know **this** hand-writing and——" A howl that was almost a scream broke the silence. "You devil! How did you get it?" A chair was overturned. Poirot skipped nimbly aside. A quick movement on his part, and **his** assailant fell with a crash. (Christie 1920: online, *my emphasis*)

TT1   'Wir alle kennen **seine** Handschrift und ...' Ein Aufheulen, das sich fast zu einem Kreischen steigerte, durchbrach die Stille. 'Du Teufel! Wie bist du daran gekommen?' Ein Stuhl fiel um. Poirot wich geschickt zur Seite. Eine rasche Bewegung **seinerseits** und **der** Angreifer stürzte krachend zu Boden. (Christie 2011: 295-6, *my emphasis*)

Christie was quite careful to avoid any gendered references –the handwriting is not modified by a gender-disclosing possessive (his / her) but by a demonstrative (this) pronoun, and 'the assailant', admitting his guilt by attacking Poirot, similarly leaves gender undetermined. In German, however, the use of gendered pronouns and articles cumulatively builds up a male identity: the possessive male pronoun (*seine*) identifies the handwriting as a man's and the use of the masculine definite article in *der Angreifer* (the [male] assailant) further spoils the suspense and removes immediately all female characters from the suspect list.[1]

While this occurs towards the end of the novel, and the main function at this point is to heighten (or diminish) the moments of suspense leading up to the imminent resolution, instances of gender explicitation in the middle of the novel have a more substantive impact on how effective the author's misdirection works. A central feature in *Styles* is signalled in the multiple meanings of 'affair'; the plot, and the shifting suspicions of who might be the murderer, revolves around a number of visible, suspected, concealed and surprising affairs of the heart between the members of the household at Styles (Mr and Mrs Inglethorp, Mrs Inglethorp's stepsons John and Lawrence Cavendish, her 'ward' Cynthia, her daughter-in-law Mary, her companion Evie Howard) and the visitors connected with Styles, Dr Bauerstein, Captain Hastings, and Mrs Raikes, the farmer's wife. The author creates a cumulatively tighter web of misdirection and confusion using the characters' jealousy, infidelity, suspected or concealed love affairs and love not acknowledged, recognised or admitted, to provide the motivation for the characters suspecting each other and for the reader –attentive to any suggestions of clandestine affairs– to place them on their suspect list.

3.2. Exploiting assumptions about gender in relationships

In the following two examples, Christie leaves it open whether the relationships referred to are opposite-sex ones. When Captain Hastings discusses the possibility that Dr Bauerstein, a frequent visitor at Styles, the home of the victim, might be the murderer and might not have acted on his own, his phrasing leaves open whether this accomplice is a man or a woman: 'Dr. Bauerstein might have had an accomplice'(Christie 1920: online). In the German translation, *Das fehlende Glied in der Kette* (The missing link in the chain), Nina Schindler makes the accomplice unequivocally female by using the feminine ending *-in*: *dass Dr Bauerstein eine Komplizin gehabt haben könnte*. (Christie 2011: 216) Similarly, in a fight between John and Mary Cavendish, Mary responds to her husband's jealous accusation over her inappropriately close friendship with Dr Bauerstein, challenging him 'Have *you* no friends of whom I should disapprove?' (Christie 1920: online). In the German, this again becomes explicitly feminine, the friends are women friends: *Hast du denn keine Freundinnen, die mir missfallen?* (Christie 2011: 210). The relationship between Mary Cavendish and Dr Bauerstein is one of the classic red herrings in *Styles*, ultimately revealed to be innocent on Mary's part, with her being used by Dr Bauerstein as an alibi for his spying for the Germans. But the fact that in the German version Hastings suggests a **female** accomplice, Mary is implicated far more explicitly, forcefully directing suspicion at her and placing her on the suspect list in a far more pronounced manner than in the English. Similarly, the exchange between Mary and John, explicitates her jealousy (which is revealed to be the explanation for a number of 'suspicious' actions which potentially implicate her in the murder) and foregrounds her suspicion that her husband is having an affair. Again, this is revealed to be the case at a much later point in the book, but it discloses a red herring which Christie very consciously and carefully constructs, by withholding and gradually revealing partial information. The German here closes down on the reader's cognitive enjoyment and interaction with the text –a clue is revealed rather than allowing the reader to deduce it by spotting the inferential gap.

4. Manipulation of information

I will now turn to an analysis of the rhetorical manipulation of plot-significant information, which strategies Christie deploys in *Styles*, and what implications these have for translation. Catherine Emmott and Marc Alexander have shown how cognitive poetics provides a theoretical framework which is particularly suitable to analyse reader manipulation in detective fiction (Alexander 2002; Emmott 2003; Emmott, Sanford and Alexander 2010). What is crucial here is the readers' ability to process, remember, and recall information. For example, research has shown that information in main clauses is more easily remembered than information in sub-clauses (Sanford and Sturt 2002: 386) and 'that false assertions in logically subordinate clauses are less likely to be noticed than they are in main clauses' (Sanford and Sturt 2002: 385). The opportunities for authors to misdirect their readers by hiding crucial clues in sub clauses and placing red herrings in main clauses are obvious. But this also has crucial relevance for translation strategies. In order to produce an idiomatic and stylistically fluent text, it is frequently necessary to reorganise sentence construction in the target language and such rearrangements frequently mean that units of meaning are shifted from their position in a subordinate clause to a main clause. In *Styles*, one of the very complex red herrings revolves around impersonation and disguise. Mr Inglethorp is implicated in the murder of his wife when he is identified to have bought a bottle of rat poison. However, he can provide an alibi for the time of the purchase and Poirot is attempting to find evidence of who could have carried out the successful disguise and posed as Mr Inglethorp. He has found a false beard, trimmed to the shape of Mr Inglethorp's beard in a dressing-up box in the attic and is interviewing the maid Dorcas about whether this box was used recently and who might have had access.

(7)
ST2   Well, sir, not very often nowadays, though from time to time we do have what the young gentlemen call 'a dress-up night.' And very funny it is sometimes, sir. Mr Lawrence, he's wonderful. Most comic! I shall never forget the night he came down as the Char of Persia, I think he called it—a sort of Eastern King it was. He had the big paper knife in his hand, and 'Mind, Dorcas,' he says, 'you'll have to be very respectful. This is my specially sharpened scimitar, and it's off with your head if I'm at all displeased with you!' <u>Miss Cynthia, she was what they call an Apache, or some such name—a Frenchified sort of cut-throat, I take it to be. A real sight she looked.</u> You'd never have believed **a pretty young lady like that could have made herself into such a ruffian**. Nobody would have known her. (Christie 1920: online, *my emphasis*)

Hidden in a sub clause, (identified in bold), is evidence of Cynthia's success at carrying off a male disguise in the past, which places her on the suspect list of having impersonated Mr Inglethorp. While the German translation has maintained the order of information in this instance, it has somewhat shortened Dorcas's long-winded narrative by summarising Cynthia's disguise (identified in italics) as *Miss Cynthia hat sich als Gangster verkleidet, die sah vielleicht aus!* (Miss Cynthia had disguised herself as a gangster; she looked a sight!). This tidying up on the part of the translator affects another feature of information processing which authors exploit. The more information is compressed into short text units, the shallower the reader processes this information – i.e. the reader skims over items, does not remember all details or does not differentiate between potentially relevant and irrelevant detail. Here are two examples where Christie has buried crucial information:

(8)

ST2   "I know what it is," she accused him, "you've been listening to the doctors. Never should. What do they know? Nothing at all—or just enough to make them dangerous. I ought to know—my own father was a doctor. That little Wilkins is about the greatest fool that even I have ever seen. Heart seizure! Sort of thing he would say. Anyone with any sense could see at once that her husband had poisoned her. I always said he'd murder her in her bed, poor soul. Now he's done it. And all you can do is to murmur silly things about 'heart seizure' and 'inquest on Friday.' You ought to be ashamed of yourself, John Cavendish. (Christie 1920: online)

In this long and excited rant, Mrs Inglethorp's devoted companion, Evie Howard, puts forward yet another tirade agitating against Mr Inglethorp, arguing that he is the murderer. Her pronounced dislike of Mr Inglethorp, articulated repeatedly by Evie, is another of the complicated red herrings Christie carefully devised. Mr Inglethorp and Evie are not only distant cousins but are actually in love with each other and they have planned the murder of Mrs Inglethorp in meticulous detail in order for Mr Inglethorp to inherit his wife's fortune. Exploiting the double indemnity feature of English law,[2] they had planned to implicate Mr Inglethorp in the murder by laying a trail of false clues (including buying the strychnine/rat poison), only for him to be cleared of the murder charge when he can demonstrate alibis for the (planted) evidence. The crucial clue which Christie has buried in the passage above is that Evie has sufficient medical knowledge (because her father was a doctor) to have executed the poisoning of Mrs Inglethorp through using a little-known interaction between sleeping powders and strychnine in a tonic which the murder victim was taking.

4.1. Maintaining ambiguity through redundant information

The challenge for the translator consists not so much in complex ambiguity but rather in maintaining a stretch of text containing substantial redundancy and not to falling into the trap of producing a more cohesive and coherent passage as the next example demonstrates. Here the translator has complied with the Gricean maxim of quantity[3] and has counteracted the intended effects of shallow processing (Emmott and Alexander 2010: 332) by removing apparently irrelevant detail and repetition in Poirot's description of his clumsiness.

(9)

ST2   **Is it possible?** Ah, but I am vexed with myself! **I am not usually clumsy.** I made **but a slight gesture**"—I know Poirot's gestures—"**with the left hand**, and over went the table by the bed! (Christie 1920: online, *my emphasis*)

TT1   Ich ärgere mich schrecklich über meine Ungeschicklichkeit. Stellen Sie sich vor, ich machte eine Handbewegung' – eine von Poirots Gesten – 'und schon fiel der Tisch beim Fenster um. (Christie 2011: 178)

The phrases in bold have been omitted in the German translation, and the sentence is far more focused, makes fewer demands on the reader's processing capacity, and as a result does not bury the relevant clue (knocking over the table by the bed which accounts for some of the evidence found at the scene of the crime). In addition, the translator mistranslated bed as 'window', completely confusing the reader who wishes to follow the deductive trail of the detective.

4.2. Repetition as a strategy for misdirection

Repetition is another strategy for misdirection which builds on the processing capacity of the reader and it can be used to confuse or to aid recall. We know that information which has been encountered more recently is more easily available for recall than less recent information. (Emmott and Alexander 2010: 331) Since clues and crucial information are broken up into small components and distributed across different narrative strands over potentially long stretches of text, the author needs to ensure that relevant details can be recalled by the reader at the conclusion so that they follow the argument and accept it without feeling that they have been misled or that information was withheld. In this balancing act of burying hints or fracturing evidence on the one hand, and complying with the fair play rules, repetition plays an important role.

Mrs Inglethorp has been poisoned and all evidence suggests that the agent was strychnine, although there are many factors which argue against it. The investigation into the properties, forms and occurrences of strychnine and its derivatives is a red thread throughout the narrative, and the question whether strychnine can have been the poison, or whether it is another poison, is complex and confusing, burying the 'identity' of the poison in the bewildering plots and turns, pros and contras. In the course of the English text, strychnine is mentioned six times –four repetitions of 'hydro-chloride of strychnine' and two minor variations 'strychnine hydrochloride' and 'Liq. Strychnine Hydro-clor'. These repetitions keep the name of the poison sufficiently active in the reader's memory to recognise it at the resolution and to realise that what had been suggested at the very beginning was proved to be right at the end. (This is quite important because it mirrors the underlying structure of the novel which is built on a double-bluff: the main suspect at the beginning turns out to be the real murderer and the method of poisoning is also shown to be the one initially suspected.)

4.3. Repetition in a German translation

In the German translation however, the repetition of the initially buried minor detail is not sustained. The name of the poison is mentioned only five times (one omission) and these five occurrences have two repetitions of *Strychnin,* and three variations of the name (*Chlorsäure-Strychnin-Mischung, Chlorsäure-Strychnin, Chlorsaures Strychnin*). Since it is not clear from the context whether these variations are synonyms, or refer to different forms of poison, this use of co-referents rather than repetition adds to the confusion and makes reader recall even more difficult.

Christie herself deploys repetition as a means to obscure meaning when she creates a passage where, again in a witness statement by the maid Dorcas, she repeats the pronoun 'it' seven times but links it two different referents 'salt' and 'tray'. The German translator clarifies the confusing repetition of cohesive devices by using the pronoun *es* (it) only four times and only when it refers to 'salt' (*Salz*). All references to the 'tray' (*Tablett*) are repetitions:

(10)

ST2   Yes. Coarse kitchen salt, **it** looked. I never noticed **it** when I took the tray up, but when I came to take **it** into the mistress's room I saw **it** at once, and I suppose I ought to have taken **it** down again, and asked Cook to make some fresh. But I was in a hurry, because Dorcas was out, and I thought maybe the coco itself was all right, and the salt had only gone on the tray. So I dusted **it** off with my apron, and took **it** in. (Christie 1920: online, *my empahsis*)

TT1   Ja, **es** sah aus wie grobes Küchensalz. Als ich das *Tablett* hochbrachte, hab ich **es** nicht gesehen, aber als ich dann später das *Tablett* in Mrs Inglethorps Schlafzimmer bringen wollte, hab ich **es** gleich bemerkt. Wahrscheinlich hätte ich das *Tablett* mit runternehmen und die Köchin bitten sollen, neuen Kakao zu kochen. Aber ich war in Eile, denn Dorcas war nicht da, und ich dachte, der Kakao selbst wäre in Ordnung, und irgendwer hätte Salz auf dem *Tablett* verschüttet . Deshalb wischte ich **es** mit meiner Schürze weg und brachte das *Tablett* hinein. (Christie 2011: 85-6, *my emphasis*)

Since *Salz* and *Tablett* are both neuter, they take the same personal pronoun *es* and it would have been perfectly possible to maintain the highly complex chain of referents in the German. The translator has tidied up and produced a fluent, clear and transparent passage but as a result has reduced the processing load, required, working against the intentional construction of reader confusion in the English.

5. Conclusions

Different linguistic structures and cultural contexts do not always permit the translator to maintain instances of ambiguity, allow for the same range of inferences, obscure identification of characters and events or to provide similarly misleading information as in the source text. As result, most translations of crime fiction will inevitably have instances of over –or undertranslation which remove some of the carefully constructed misdirection and rhetorical manipulations in the source text, and produce a text which is more coherent and explicit. This cannot be avoided; however, it is in those instances where explicitation or coherence are introduced even though the target language resources allow the translator to produce a comparably obscure text that an understanding of the specific rhetorical strategies of crime writing is necessary.

The analysis of *Das fehlende Glied in der Kette,* the translation of *The Mysterious Affair at Styles,* has demonstrated many instances where the German produces a far more reader-friendly, transparent and fluent text, in line with translational, or perhaps editorial, guidelines observing Grice's maxims, in particular those of quantity and manner. But this compliance with producing a well-constructed, clear, precise and non-redundant style actually works against the text function of crime fiction, obscures suspense and undercuts the author's intentional deployment of rhetorical devices to misdirect and manipulate the reader. The crime fiction translator –and editor– needs to be aware that repetition, redundancy, apparently badly constructed passages and a 'clumsy' style is not necessarily indicative of author incompetence but rather a feature of the genre-specific constraints of plot and the creation of suspense which a translation fit-for-purpose needs to maintain.

---

[1] It could be argued that the use of the masculine definite article is an instance of generic masculine usage into which the feminine is subsumed, allowing a potential female referent, and that it would have been difficult for the translator to render a similarly ungendered form in German without a class shift from noun to adjective or participle. However, the male (rather than potential female) interpretation of the attacker is reinforced by the masculine possessive pronoun identifying the handwriting, which could have easily been rendered in an ungendered demonstrative pronoun as in the English.

[2] Double indemnity means that a person cannot be tried for the same offence if they have been cleared of it in a prior trial.

[3] See Baker (1992: 225-226) for a discussion of Gricean maxims and their relevance for translation.

Bibliography

Primary Sources

Christie, Agatha. 1920. *The Mysterious Affair at Styles*. On line at: http://www.gutenberg.org/ebooks/863 (consulted 9.12.2012)
——. 1952. *Mrs McGinty's dead*. On line at: http://www.eslstudyguideresources.com/ pdf/Mrs%20McGintys%20Dead.pdf (consulted 9.12.2012)
——. 2011. *Das fehlende Glied in der Kette*. Translated by Nina Schindler. Frankfurt am Main: Fischer.

Secondary Sources

Alexander, Marc. 2008. "The Lobster and the Maid: Scenario-dependence and reader manipulation in Agatha Christie". *Online Proceedings of the Annual Conference of the Poetics and Linguistics Association* (PALA). http://www.pala.ac.uk/resources/proceedings/2008/alexander2008.pdf (consulted 9-12-2012)
Baker, Mona. 1992. *In Other Words*. London: Routledge.
Brooks, Peter. 1984. *Reading for the Plot*. Cambridge, Mass.: Harvard University Press.
Detection Club. On line at: http://www.detectionclub.com/ (consulted 31-8-2012)
Dupriez, Bernard. 1991. *A dictionary of literary devices: Gradus, A-Z*. Translated and adapted by Albert W. Halsall.Toronto and Buffalo: University of Toronto Press.
Emmott, Catherine and Marc Alexander. 2010. "Detective fiction, plot construction and reader manipulation". McIntyre, Dan and Beatrix Busse (eds). 2010. *Language and Style*. Houndmills: Palgrave Macmillan. 328-346.
Emmott, Catherine, Anthony Sanford and Marc Alexander. 2010. "Scenarios, characters' roles and plot status." In Jens Eder, Fotis Jannidis, and Ralf Schneider (eds). 2010. *Revisionen. Characters in Fictional Worlds*. Berlin: Walter de Gruyter. 377-399.
Emmott, Catherine. 2003. "Reading for pleasure". In Gavin, Joanna and Gerard Steen. (eds). 2003. *Cognitive Poetics in Practice*. London: Routledge. 145-159.
Iliescu, Catalina. 2001. "What's in a Title?" *Revista Alicantina de Estudios Ingleses*. 14. 93-109.
Marklund, Liza. 2011. *The bomber*. Translated by Neil Smith. London: Transworld Publishers.
Sanford, Anthony and Patrick Sturt. 2002. "Depth of processing in language comprehension". *Trends in Cognitive Sciences*. Volume 6, Issue 9. 382-386.
Van Dine, S. S. 1939. *Twenty Rules for Writing Detective Stories*. On line at:http://gutenberg.net.au/ ebooks 07/0700281h.html#ch17 (consulted 9-12-2012)

Chapter 13: Resonant voices: The illocutionary reconstruction of suspense in the translation of dialogue

Laila C. Ahmad Helmi

Arabic specific

Abstract

Though the subgenre of detective stories and thrillers is a well-established genre in Western literatures, it remains a virgin form of writing in Arabic literature. Thus the translator does not seem to have a secure repertoire of narratological conventions to fall back on when translating such novels into Arabic. At first glance, this may seem a confining obstacle but, in fact, it may allow for a wider scope of textual and discursive negotiation in the translation of both voice and dialogue. This is also significant when a major aspect of the suspense is built up through the verbal interaction and (indirect) intentionality of the characters. This paper sets out to examine how suspense is constructed through the narrative voice(s) and dialogue of the characters inhabiting the original text, and its subsequent reconstruction in the Arabic translation thereof. This will be conducted through the identification of a corpus of illocutionary forces in Dan Brown's work, and their corresponding TT in the Arabic translation.

Keywords: Illocutionary force / reconstruction, translation of dialogue, equivalence, thriller, English / Arabic translation

1. Introduction

Though the subgenre of detective stories and thrillers is a well-established genre in Western literatures, it remains a virgin form of writing in Arabic fiction[1]. Thus the translator does not seem to have a secure repertoire of narratological conventions to fall back on when translating such novels into Arabic. Though at first glance this may seem to be a confining obstacle, it may also be a blessing in disguise, for it may allow for a wider scope of linguistic, textual and discursive negotiation to become available to the translator. As Gideon Toury (1995: 268) points out, "in translation, textual relations obtaining in the original are often modified, sometimes to the point of being totally ignored, in favour of [more] habitual options offered by the target repertoire".

On the other hand, though translation is often defined in terms of the degree of equivalence established between the ST and the TT, in literary translation this relationship can be redefined into an equivalence of impact,[2] rather than that of content and meaning. Jean Boase-Beier (2011: 43) elaborates on this idea, stating that

> We ... need to see the sort of equivalence that literary translation aims for not in the preservation of meaning and implicatures, nor just implicatures, but in the preservation of open-endedness, the possibility of reader engagement and the recreating of the effects often triggered by formal elements.

This paper sets out to examine how suspense is reconstructed in the Arabic translation by Somaya Mohamed Abd Rabu (2004) of Dan Brown's *The Da Vinci Code*. As soon as it was published, the novel not only hit the bestseller list, and was translated into over 40 languages worldwide, but also triggered an endless controversy as to the religious and historical facts it fictionalizes and the overall discourse it creates. There is no doubt, then, that the translated text will be even richer in issues causing controversy.

The paper thus examines the strategies resorted to by the translator of the novel. Strategies[3] can be defined as "particular ways of translating, which relate to one's view of what translation is and how it works" (Boase-Beier 2011: 79). They are particular methods resorted to by the translator in an attempt to render both the propositional content, as well as the illocutionary impact of the ST in the TT.

> Utterances express propositions; propositions have truth conditions; but the meaning of an utterance is not exhausted by its own truth conditions. An utterance not only expresses a proposition but it is also used to perform a variety of speech acts. It can thus be said to encode two basic types of information: truth-conditional and non-truth-conditional, or propositional and illocutionary[4] –that is, information about the state of affairs it describes, and information indicating the various speech acts it is intended to perform. (Wilson and Sperber 1993: 1-2)

In other words, as Searle and Vanderveken (1985) argue, the illocutionary act of any utterance is the total sum of both the illocutionary force and the propositional meaning of the utterance. In addition, the illocutionary act varies due to the differences in either the illocutionary force or the propositional meaning in their combination together: "The distinction between illocutionary force and propositional content ... is motivated by the fact that their identity conditions are different: the same propositional content can occur with different illocutionary forces and the same force can occur with different propositional content" (Searle and Vanderveken 1985: 8).

To scrutinize these methods, the paper is divided into three sections which examine the translator's strategies on three main levels: *the linguistic equivalence* as observed in the translator's attempts at rendering linguistic units in the TT; *the textual / semiotic equivalence* as observed in the narrative techniques; and *the discursive equivalence* as observed in the set of discourses operating in each text, thus within their respective discursive / cultural universes.[5]

2. Linguistic equivalence

To start with, it is interesting to look into the various strategies adopted by the translator of *The Da Vinci Code* in rendering linguistic units, i.e. propositional content. It can be observed, for instance, that the translator uses *transliteration*, a strategy that uses transcription of a word into the TL, and as such retains the sound-image of the sign. The most immediate use of transliteration occurs for the names of entities such as "the Priory of Sion" and "Opus Dei", where the Arabic text provides a direct transcription of these words. The strategy is further used to represent an utterance in French in the ST: "مسيو لانغدون أه أريفه. دو مينيت" (Abd Raby 2004: 28) –"*Monsieur Langdon est arrive. Deux minutes*" (Brown 2003: 19). It is not clear why the translator opted here for such transliteration, since elsewhere similar utterances are rendered into Arabic. It may be that she intended to reflect the diversity of languages and voices inhabiting the text, or else intended this as an early form of encryption to evoke suspense.

Transliteration as a strategy, though, seems to also fulfil a functional aspect. A word like "cryptex", which is obviously a coinage in the ST, is retained in the form of the sound-image / signifier in which it occurs in the ST. The ST provides the necessary context for the reader to construct the mental-image / signified needed to bring the sign to wholeness:

(1)
ST.	The term *cryptex* possibly had been her grandfather's creation, an apt title for this device that used the science of *cryptology* to protect information written on the contained scroll or *codex*. (Brown 2003: 216)

TT.	وربما كان مصطلح كريبتكس من اختراع جدها. وهو اسم مناسب لهذه الأداة التى استخدمت علم الكريبتولوجيا – الكتابة بالشيفرة – لحماية المعلومات المكتوبة على لفافة الورق أو المخطوطة الموجودة داخله.
(Brown 2004: 223)

It should be noted here that a further strategy is introduced: glossing, i.e. a parenthetical explanation of the preceding word. *Cryptology* as a sign is qualified in Arabic with a parenthetical phrase elaborating on the signified / the mental-image: "encoding" or "encrypting".

An alternative strategy that also establishes what may be considered mirror equivalence between the ST and the TT is literal translation. Also termed as word-for-word translation, this strategy seems to adopt the TL signifier with an attempt at retaining the signified of the SL. Take for example, the translation of:

(2)
ST.	"After you, Mr Langdon," Fache said. (Brown 2003: 29)
TT.	"من بعدك، سيد لانغدون"، قال فاش. (Brown 2004: 37)

The ST obviously seeks to retain the subtle overtones of being a representation of the French expression (fully absent from both texts). In other words, the literal translation into Arabic seems to carry three layers of signification that the TT reader is intended to decode: the voice of the French Fache, the voice of the English ST, and the voice of the Arabic translation.

Another function of literal translation can be traced in the following example:

(3)
ST.   "I was looking forward to picking his brain".
      Fache glanced up. "Pardon?"
      The idiom apparently didn't translate. (Brown 2003: 24-25)

Conscious of the opaqueness of its structure, the translator resorts to the literal translation of the idiom to retain the functionality of it. Again there seems to be a third voice in the ST that seems to be dormant between the lines. However, it is not the relationship between the French and the English languages that is being explored in the Arabic equivalent:

(3)
TT.   لقد كنت أتوق إلى التقاط دماغه. (Brown 2004: 33)

The literariness of the rendering of the idiomatic expression is interesting since there is no such expression in the TL. When used in English in the ST, the expression exists in its natural habitat / context. When taken literally into Arabic though, it seems to lose an important condition of its very raison d'etre: it ceases to be an idiomatic expression.

Other interesting examples are expressions such as: "What the devil (is it doing on the floor)!" (Brown 2003: 35) or "What the hell (does this mean)!" (Brown 2003: 43);

(4)
TT.   ترى ماذا تفعل هذه اللوحة على الأرض **بحق الشيطان!** (Brown 2004: 43)
      ماذا الذى تعنيه هذه الكلمات **بحق الجحيم!** (Brown 2004: 51)

The translator again resorted to literal translation as a strategy. Yet it is interesting, that although بحق الجحيم or بحق الشيطان are not successful renderings of the speech act of cursing in Arabic, they cannot be said to be totally alien to the TT reader. There is no doubt that Hollywood subtitles have established these expressions as possible renderings of cursing in Arabic, even though one may still argue that they do not put across the full illocutionary force.

The tendency of the translator to resort to literal renderings can also be traced in the usage of speech act verbs and speech events. The following example is a sample to show how this strategy works in the TT:

(5)
ST. "Yes?" a male voice answered.
     "Teacher, I have returned."
     "Speak," the voice commanded ... (Brown 2003: 13)
TT. "نعم؟" أجاب صوت ذكرى.
     "أيها المعلم، لقد عدت".
     "تكلم" أمره الصوت ...
     (Brown 2004: 22)

There is no doubt that the conventions for representing speech in writing are very different in Arabic from what appears here in the TT. First, turn-taking is signified in Arabic with a short dash (-). Second, the interlocutor and the relevant speech act verb occur before the actual speech. Thus the structure of the speech event is rendered in a literal manner.

In the following structure, a further problem arises:

(6)
ST. The attacker aimed his gun again. "When you are gone, I will be the only one who knows the truth". (Brown 2003: 4)
TT. وجه مهاجمه مسدسه من جديد نحوه "عندما تموت سأكون أنا الوحيد الذى يعرف الحقيقة". (Brown 2004: 44)

The ST relies on punctuation marks and the implicit relationship between the two sentences. This does not work, however, in the TT, partly because Arabic depends more on explicit cohesion, but mainly because of the absence of the speech act verb from the surface structure.[6]

In other cases, the translator uses literal renderings of speech act verbs which do not seem to function equally in the TT. One such example is the verb "think" as used in such structures as:

(7)
ST. *Interpol,* thought Langdon. *Of course...* (Brown 2003: 11)
TT. الإنتربول، فكر لانغدون، بالطبع ... (Brown 2004: 26)

The use of italicization in the ST indicates a thought process, and hence that "thought" is used as a speech act. However, neither the literal translation of the structure, nor of the word "thought" into فكر is an adequate rendering of the illocutionary force of the ST. Though فكر is often deemed a lexical equivalent of "think", in context, the Arabic language expresses the "process of thinking" using يجول فى خاطره. In other words, Arabic requires an alternative lexical item to express the "act" or action of thinking.

The aim, however, as Hatim and Mason (1990: 77) point out, is "not at matching speech act for speech act but rather at achieving equivalence of illocutionary structure". In other words, "the cumulative effect of sequences of speech acts leads to the perception of a **text act**[7] ..., the predominant illocutionary force of a series of speech acts" (Hatim and Mason 1990: 78). This takes us to the next level addressed in this paper, namely the textual and / or semiotic level.

3. Textual / semiotic equivalence

If the novel is taken to be a text act intended to communicate with the reader, the first clear incident where the TT reader confronts a deviation is when the main character in the novel seems to address the reader directly:

(8)
ST. Langdon frowned. The French, it seemed, loved to ask Americans this. It was a loaded question, of course. Admitting *you* liked the pyramid made *you a tasteless American*, and expressing dislike was an insult to the French. (Brown 2003: 19; *my emphasis*)

TT. قطب لانغدون جبينه فالفرنسيون على ما يبدو يروق لهم أن يسألوا الأمريكيين هذا السؤال. كان هذا السؤال مفخخاً، فإذا **اعترفت** بأن الهرم **يعجبك** فإن ذلك يجعل **منك أمريكياً** عديم الذوق وإذا **عبرت** عن **عدم اعجابك** به فينذلك **تكون** قد **وجهت** إهانة للفرنسيين. (Brown 2004: 19; *my emphasis*)

The complication here is multiple. First, there is the context of the ST vs. that of the TT. The ST as a product was produced in the USA and is set in France and England. However, the TT is a translated text, in other words a displaced text. It is produced in the Arab World, and rather than being set in France and England, it becomes a text that is *about* France and England as a setting.

Second, there is the relation between the writer(s) and reader(s). Obviously, the ST was written by an American writer, and his intended reader was most probably the American reader. As for the TT, the translator / writer is an Arab whose intended reader is also an Arab. Thus the reader of the TT is most probably NOT an American which makes the phrase "يجعل منك أمريكياً / made *you a tasteless American*" lose its communicative value. As pointed out by Boase-Beier (2011: 111), "In the case of translated texts, the writer of the original and the reader of its translation almost always have greater cultural and linguistic difference from one another than writer and reader of a non-translated text".

Third, the actual rendering of the TT which seems to implicate the TT reader far more than the more "neutralizing" structure of the ST. In other words, the ST uses the direct pronoun "you" only twice, and structures the actions "admit" and "express" in the neutral(-izing) gerund form. The TT, on the other hand, uses seven incidences of the accusative pronoun, thus quantitatively implicating the addressee / the reader. Further, the gerund forms are transformed in the TT into active verb forms, such as "you admit, you like, you express, ..."

(9)
ST. If **you admitted** that **you liked** the pyramid, this **made you** a tasteless American, and if **you expressed** that **you did not like** it, **you thus aimed** an insult at the French. [*my back translation*]

In this sense it would seem as if the TT were seeking to compensate for the contextual distance between the original writer and the TT reader by forging stronger textual ties and illocutionary forces than exist in the ST.

In other incidences, the TT seems to collapse the signifiers of the SL and TL into each other. In such cases, the propositional content is brought across, but if tested by the reader may not hold in terms of truth-conditions because of the use of the TL signifier. One obvious example is the following:

(10)

ST. Once he had written the English word "planets" and told Sophie that an astonishing sixty-two *other* English words of varying lengths could be formed using those same letters.(Brown 2003: 106)

TT. ... قام بكتابة كلمة كواكب بالإنجليزية وقال لها إن هناك تسعة وتسعون كلمة مذهلة أخرى **بالإنلجيزية** يمكن أن **تتشكل باستخدام نفس أحرف كلمة كواكب.** (Brown 2004: 115; *my emphasis*)

Apart from the curious shift of "sixty-two" into "ninety-nine", there is a significant lack of the signifier "planets" in the TT. The TT text states that "99 other amazing words in **English** can be formed using **the same letters of the word kawakib**", where **kawakib** is the Arabic equivalent of "planets". Obviously, the statement fails to hold in terms of truth-condition, mainly because of the contradiction between "English" and "kawakib". Thus it seems that the TT seeks to retain the signified at the expense of the signifier, which is the more significant constituent in the construction of equivalence here.

As Munday (2001: 172) points out, "in Derrida's view, a relevant translation relies on the supposed stability of the signified-signifier relationship (it is 'what which presents itself as the transfer of an intact signified through the inconsequential vehicle of any signifier whatsoever' ..., and aims at total transparency". It is my claim, here, that the reconstruction of the ST in the TT not only destabilizes the Saussurean arbitrary relationship constituting the sign, but in fact forges new arbitrary links. This can be seen clearly in the following:

(11)

ST. For centuries, the symbol of the Rose had been associated with maps and guiding souls in the proper direction. The *Compass Rose* – drawn on almost every map – indicated North, East, South and West. (Brown 2003: 114; *my emphasis*)

TT. وعلى مر القرون كان رمز الوردة يترافق بخرائط ودلالات ترشد الناس إلى الاتجاه الصحيح. فالبوصلة أو **كما تدعى بالإنجليزية البوصلة الوردية** – ترسم على معظم الخرائط ... (Brown 2004: 122; *my emphasis*)

The TT provides an additional gloss stating that "the compass or **as it is called in English the Rosy Compass**". Apart from the fact that the rendering of "the Compass Rose" into Arabic is problematized by an inversion of the adjectival structure of the phrase, the interesting thing for this argument is the juxtaposition in the TT of "in English" and the Arabic signifier of البوصلة الوردية (or the Compass Rose). It would seem as if the syntagmatic structuring of the two is a reflection of the mental restructuring of the signifier-signified relation. In other words, the TT reader is intended to see the **Arabic signifier** as the **English one**.

There is no doubt, then, that the translation of the ST into Arabic has added a significant encoding layer. In its construction of suspense, *The Da Vinci Code* seems to rely to a great extent on a Foucauldian-like archaeological excavation of meanings and signs[8]. Passages exploring the etymological history of individual signifiers and the changing nature of their signified permeate the ST and often function as clues towards the unravelling of a mysterious point.

One example is the exploration of the word *hermaphrodite*:

(12)
ST. Langdon considered offering an etymological sidebar about the word *hermaphrodite* and its ties to Hermes and Aphrodite, but something told him it would be lost on this crowd. (Brown 2003: 129)

TT. فكر لانغدون بأن يقدم لهم معلومة جانبية تفسيراً **لكلمة** "خنثى" وعلاقتها بالإله هيرمس والإلهة افروديت **حيث أن** **أصل كلمة خنثى هو** "**هيرمافروديت**" إلا أن احساسه أنبأه بأن ذلك سيضيع هباء على هذه المجموعة. (Brown 2004: 136)

The textual reconstruction of the etymology does not seem to work in the TT. On the one hand, the equivalent signifier in the TL does not have the same derivational roots and as such a different historical development. Further, the Arabic signifier carries heavy negative connotations which cannot be ameliorated by the subsequent attribution to the god Hermes and the goddess Aphrodite. Third, the syntagmatic equation of the Arabic signifier with the English one in the TT gloss: "since the origin of the word khantha is "hermaphrodite"" [*my back translation*] is awkward and etymologically inaccurate. Obviously, the Arabic word does *not* derive from the Greek one, nor the latter's constituent parts.

In another example, the ST explores the etymology of the word "cross":

(13)
ST. Langdon was always surprised how few Christians who gazed upon "the crucifix" realized their symbol's violent history was reflected in its very name: "cross" and "crucifix" came from the Latin verb *cruciare* – to torture. (Brown 2003: 156 -7)

TT. والأمر الذى كان يثير دهشة لانغدون على الدوام هو أن قلة قليلة من المسيحيين الذين كانوا يتأملون **كلمة** **كروسيفيكس** "**الصليب**" أدركوا أن التاريخ العنيف لرمزهم ينعكس فى الاسم بحد ذاته **فكلمة كروس أو** **كروسيفيكس** اشتقت من الفعل اللاتينى كروشار أى يعذب.
(Brown 2004: 163; *my emphasis*)

The most prominent point here is the focus of the TT on the signifier, with full exclusion of the referent. In other words, where the ST uses "gazed upon 'the crucifix'", which obviously signifies both the sign and the referent, the TT specifies "contemplate **the word crucifix**". In the light of the rest of the extract, it would seem that the TT has a more intense focus on the etymological aspects of the signifier than the ST, a fact that again complicates the illocutionary force of the statement, since the Arabic signifier *saleeb* has a totally different derivational history.

A third interesting archaeological exploration can be seen in several passages that discuss the etymology of the Holy Grail.

(14)

ST. "Holy Grail is the literal meaning of Sanreal. The phrase derives from the French *Sangraal*, which evolved to Sangreal, and was eventually split into two words, *San Greal*". (Brown 2003: 175)

TT   "إن الكأس المقدسة هي المعنى الحرفي **للسانغريال**, وقد ترجع هذه اللفظة إلى اللغة الفرنسية **سانغرال** ــ والتي تم شطرها أخيراً إلى كلمتين **سان غريل** ــ Sangreal ــ التي تطورت لتصبح **سانغريال** ــ Sangraal San Greal." (Brown 2004: 182; *my emphasis*)

The first obvious phenomenon here is the difficulty of providing the same diversity of phonetic structures in Arabic as there are in the ST, partly because the ST derives its list of terms from different languages, which then converge into the one language of the TT. This is probably also the reason why the translator found it necessary here to provide the original terms combining thus the SL and the TL. A further possibility is added later in the ST when one of the characters (Teabing) suggests that the term was

(15)

ST. in its most ancient form, ... divided in a different spot". Teabing wrote on a piece of scrap paper and handed it to her.
She read what he had written.

Sang Real

Instantly, Sophie recognized the translation. *Sang Real* literally meant *Royal Blood*. (Brown 2003: 271)

TT. .... وقد قسمت إلى كلمتين قديماً لكن من مكان مختلف". كتب تيبينغ على قصاصة من الورق شيئاً وأعطاه إلى صوفي.
فقرأت ما كتبه.

Sang Real

عرفت صوفي الترجمة في الحال.
سانغريال كانت تعني حرفياً **الدم المقدس.**
(Brown 2004: 280; *my emphasis*)

The homophony is obviously lost in Arabic, which is partly why the translator retains the ST terms in their SL from. However, the impact of this new cue is lost in the TT, because "Sang Real" is translated into "Holy Blood" rather than "Royal Blood". The reader of the TT is thus directed into a slightly different direction in resolving the mystery of the Holy Grail, remaining locked in aspects of sacredness rather than royalty.

A further dimension introduced by the archaeological excavations of the etymology of signs is the cross-cultural and cross-religious nature of signifiers / signification. Again the stability of signs within the known boundaries of languages seems to be challenged by the ST. The reader of the TT is thus invited to examine the unifying origins of signifiers as opposed to the separating forces of signifying systems / languages. One example to highlight this point can be seen in Langdon's analysis of the etymological origins of the Mona Lisa's name.

(16)

ST. "It was Isis," Langdon told them, grabbing a grease pen. "So we have the male god, Amon". He wrote it down. "And the female goddess, Isis, whose ancient pictogram was called L'ISA".

Langdon finished writing and stepped back from the projector.

AMON L'ISA

"Ring any bells?" he asked.

"Mona Lisa … holy crap," somebody gasped. (Brown 2003: 130)

TT. "إنها إيزيس". قال لانغدون وقد أمسك بقلم شمعي. "لدينا الإله الذكر آمون" وكتب ذلك.
والإلهة المؤنثة إيزيس والتي كانت تكتب بحروف تصويرية ليزا "L'ISA ".
انتهى لانغدون من الكتابة ثم تراجع إلى الوراء مبتعداً عن جهاز عرض الصور.

AMON L'ISA

آمون ليزا

"هل يذكركم هذا بشئ ما؟"

"موناليزا ... ياللهول! " هتف أحدهم.

(Brown 2004: 137)

As Hatim and Mason (1990: 111) state, "The sign does more than simply elicit a concept. It is not an entity, but a correlation. That is the sign, as the 'associative' total of signifier and signified, is potentially greater than merely the sum of its parts".

The Mona Lisa does not only function as a sign that crosses cultural and religious borders in this novel. The sign becomes a significant clue in resolving the mystery, which takes us to the riddles upon which the major part of the suspense is based.

The first riddle appears in the TT as follows:

(17)

TT كتبت الرسالة كالتالي:

13-3-2-21-1-1-8-5

O, Draconian devil!

Oh, lame saint!

(Brown 2004: 55)

The first occurrence of the first riddle is kept in English. The implications for this for the TT reader are tremendous. It would seem that English, due to its different graphological nature and its very appearance in a *translation*, is set up as an encrypted code not just the SL that the reader believes to have "conquered" when reading the TT. This is supported by the fact that the very nature of the riddle requires the presence of the English letters, since the answer to the riddle is a reshuffling of the sequence of the letters into the keywords: "Leonardo Da Vinci" and "Mona Lisa". Thus it seems that what is important here is that the riddle deconstructs the signifier-signified relationship needed for the construction of meaning. The mental image / the signified is totally irrelevant. The riddle is not based on deducing the meaning of either "O, Draconian devil" or "Oh, lame saint", but rather the sequence of sound-images. In other words, the translation of the riddle into

(18)
TT.   أيها الشيطان المتوحش
       أيها القديس الضعيف

keeps the reader focused on the signifieds. At the same time, the sound-image sequences of the Arabic equivalents will never provide the solution to the riddle. This is also why the translator makes a point of delaying the appearance of the Arabic equivalents in the TT. However, when the Arabic translation does appear, the TT reader seems to attain a first revelation to the riddle. This compounding of the riddle in the TT no doubt enhances the illocutionary impact of constructing suspense: the first solution to the riddle is no solution at all, but rather a deviation into a mistaken deduction process.

This process is further complicated when a further line appears in the riddle. "P.S. Find Robert Langdon" (Brown 2004: 82). The next time this line appears only in Arabic without the English ST:

(19)
TT.   حملق لانغدون بذهول لعدة ثوان فى الصورة الفوتوغرافية حيث ذيل سونيير رسالته بجملة:
       بى. اس. آتوا بروبرت لانغدون.
       (Brown 2004: 83)

Again the TT presents the reader with only the phonetic representation of the ST, thus divorcing the signifier from its signified. The reader of the ST, like the character in the novel, has some clue at least as to what the possible signifier(s) of "P.S." may be. The reader of the TT is here fully disadvantaged. The riddle seems to be becoming a personal task for the TT reader to resolve! Take for example the following conversation between Langdon and Sophie, which attempts to resolve the issue of this signifier:

(20)
TT.
       "وعرفت ذلك من خلال لوحة الرجل الفيترونى؟".
       "نعم، ومن خلال الحرفين بى. اس. P.S. أيضاً".
       "تعنين حاشية الرسالة؟ **Post Script**".
       هزت راسها نافية." P.S. هما الحرفين الأولين من اسمى".
       "لكن اسمك صوفى نوفو".
       نظرت بعيداً وقالت: " P.S. هو اللقب الذى أطلقه علىّ عندما كنت أعيش معه". واحمرت وجنتيها خجلاً. "وهو يرمز إلى
       Princesse Sophie أو الأميرة صوفى".
       (Brown 2004: 85; *my emphasis*)

231

Langdon has the advantage of knowing the more immediate signified of P.S., namely Post Script. The TT reader, however, would be totally in the dark. Further, the more personalized signified –or "Princesse Sophie– would be totally inaccessible to the TT reader. Not only is it part of the twist in the tail, but it is also in French.

A few pages later, the TT brings the English signifiers of the riddle to life by transliterating the sounds and using the SL for glossing.

(21)

TT.
التفت فاش واجابه: "ليخبرونا أنهم لم يتوصلوا إلى أى أصل لدراكونيان ديفلز وليم سينتس"
(Draconian devils-lame saints)
(Brown 2004: 96)

It would seem as if the TT is enforcing upon its reader the fact that the riddle can only be solved by knowing the SL / English which seems to hold all the clues. Unlike the Arabic equivalents, the focus here is on the signifiers / the sound-images.

In the second riddle, the TT provides the translation prior to the English original:

(22)

TT.
بدت صوفى مرتبكة تحت بريق الرسالة المكتوبة على وجه الموناليزا
خداع الرجل كريه للغاية.
SO DARK THE CON OF MAN
(Brown 2004: 141; *my emphasis*)

This shift in order seems to examine the nature of the arbitrary relationship between the ST and the TT at large. Again the TT is incapable of capturing the full scope of signification: the ST is essential in resolving the riddle.

(23)

TT.
Madonna of the Rocks رمقها لانغدون بنظرة ذهول. "ماذا؟! لكن كيف عرفت أى لوحة؟ لماذا **سيدة الصخور** بالذات؟"
"خداع الرجل الكريه للغاية "So dark the con of man.
وابتسمت ابتسامة انتصار. "لقد فاتنى حل شيفرتين، روبرت. لم أكن أنوى أن أدع الثالثة تفوتنى".
(Brown 2004: 151; *my emphasis*)

The collapse of the signifiers onto each other is achieved a few pages later in the TT when we are made to follow Langdon's thoughts about the solution to this riddle:

(24)

TT.
So dark the con of man...فارتاح لانغدون فى مقعده وأخذ يتأمل ....
كان تفكير صوفى السريع مذهلاً.
Madonna of the Rocks

لقد قالت صوفي أن جدها قد ترك لها شيئاً خلف اللوحة. رسالة أخيرة؟ لم يستطع لانغدون اخفاء اعجابه الشديد باختيار جدها العبقري للمخبأ، فقد كانت لوحة **مادونا أوف ذا روكس** حلقة أخرى تضاف إلى سلسلة الليلة من الرموز المرتبطة ببعضها البعض.

(Brown 2004: 155; *my emphasis*)

The reader of the TT is to establish the link between the transliterated sounds and the English signifier. It is interesting that the previous use of the TL equivalent سيدة الصخرة disappears from the text here. The reader of the TT is expected to move into the series of symbols or signifiers, divorcing their perception from the more familiar sphere of the "wholesome" sign.

The riddles, however, are not all identical in their destabilization of the signifier-signified relationship. The pre-final riddle, for example, uses a signifier that may combine with several signified to construct meaning. The riddle is based on the ability to find the correct signified.

(25)
TT.

في لندن يرقد فارس دفنه بابا.
جلبت له أعماله عقاباً إلهياً.
أنت تبحث عن كرة ملكية موجودة على قبره
تحكي قصة جسد وردى رحم حمل روحاً في قلبه.

(Brown 2004: 374)

The TT makes the wrong decision! The key word towards the solution of the riddle is the correct interpretation of the signifier **Pope**. The search for a pope takes the characters (and the readers) down further lanes of suspense until the correct signified is brought back into unison with the signifier. The TT, however, uses the signifier بابا, which is the equivalent for "a pope". The interpretation for the TT reader thus remains handicapped.

Further, when the ST at last provides the correct signified that would help resolve the riddle, the TT continues in the use of wrong signifier.

(26)
TT.

مراسم دفن السير اسحق نيوتن، حضرها الملوك والنبلاء، وتراسها صديقه وزميله في العمل **الكسندر بابا**، الذى ألقى تأبيناً مؤثراً قبل أن يذرى التراب على قبره. نظر لانغدون إلى صوفي.
"لقد حصلنا على البابا الصحيح في بحثنا الثانى. ألكسندر.
A. Pope. صمت لحظة. "أ. بابا –

(Brown 2004: 430; *my emphasis*)

Not only is Alexander Pope a figure unknown to the TT reader, but the very mistaken construction of an alternative proper name of Alexander Baba would lead astray any curious TT reader who were to look up the name.

Semiotically speaking, it would seem as if the TT has managed to subvert the SL into a constituent component of the code of suspense. The ST seems to be aware of this potential in its code, stating at one point that "the verse is in English! *La lingua pura!*"

233

(27)
TT.

"إنه البحر الخماسى التفعيلات!" هتف تيبينغ والتفت نحو لانغدون. "والقصيدة مكتوبة باللغة الإنجليزية!
اللغة الصافية!
أومأ لانغدون. فقد كانت الأخوية، كالعديد من الجمعيات السرية فى أوروبة على خلاف مع الكنيسة، لذا
كانت تنظر إلى الإنجليزية على أنها اللغة الصافية الوحيدة على مدى قرون طويلة. حيث إن الإنجليزية
كانت منفصلة من الناحية اللغوية عن آلة الفاتيكان الإعلامية على عكس اللغة الفرنسية والإسبانية
والإيطالية التى كانت كلها ذات جذور لاتينية أى لغة الفاتيكان. ولهذا السبب، أصبحت الإنجليزية اللغة
السرية المقدسة لتلك الجمعيات السرية التى كانت على درجة من الثقافة لتتعلمها.
(Brown 2004: 338)

As a meta-linguistic / meta-narrative statement, this seems to celebrate the SL, hence the original text, which no doubt has a myriad of socio-cultural and political implications for the Arab reader. The most relevant one for this paper is the illocutionary impact: for the reader of the ST, the celebration of English is an act of enhancing self-esteem. For the reader of the TT, it is an act of challenging, if not threatening, the non-English speaker. This is further complicated by the fact that Arabic for the TT reader is perceived as the language of a holy text.

Similarly, when the ST provides a visual representation of what the characters perceive to be a Semitic language:

(28)
ST.

(Brown 2003: 323)

If the ST uses the script as an act of defamiliarization that is intended to make the reader construct suspense visually, but also perceive of "Semitic" scripts as a form of encryption, the TT obviously has a totally different impact on the reader. For the TT reader, Arabic **is** a Semitic language. English has already been largely established as the language of encryption, and the script for the TT reader does not seem in any way Semitic. On the other hand, the text is vibrantly rich with a myriad of (other) languages that range from the most accessible code (English for the American reader) to the most obscure. For the Arab reader, the most accessible seems to be the Arabic language, ranging from the most obscure codes represented in English and some unknown "Semitic language". The TT reader often ends up feeling more like Sophie when she wonders why "she had not spotted the linguistic ties immediately" (175). In fact, due to the constant destabilization of the signs in the TT, the target reader very often finds it difficult to recognize the linguistic ties between the signifiers they meet on the page and the mental-images / signified they are intended to reconstruct.

The ST seems to be aware of such discursive overtones, which takes us to the next and final section of the paper.

4. Discursive equivalence

The third level of analysis in this paper looks at the novel, its translation and their circulation in discursive terms. There is no doubt that the *Da Vinci Code*, though a world bestseller in record time, has also raised much controversy about its historicity. Over and over, Dan Brown has reiterated that much research has gone into the production of the novel, authenticating the truth-value of its portrayal of historical facts, figures, names and events. As Dennis Fisher, editor of RBC Research (2005: 8-9) points out, "When challenged on his fact, the author cannot rightfully say, 'It's only a novel.' Such positioning places the reader in a schizophrenic world of fact and fiction". This claim to historicity, posing the novel as a grand narrative, is indeed an attempt at writing an "alternative history" (Fisher 2005: 9).

Similarly, the novel is an attempt at destabilizing dominant discourses. One significant subversion is the deconstruction of discursive representations propagated by Hollywood. The reader is told by Langdon that "despite what you see in the movies, the pentacle's demonic interpretation is historically inaccurate. The original feminine meaning is correct, but the symbolism of the pentacle has been distorted over the millennia. In this case, through bloodshed" (Brown 2003: 41). For the TT reader this is a double-edged weapon. On the one hand, the creation of a counter-discourse resistant to biased Hollywood representations is always welcome. However, the alternative discourse of the sacred feminine and of the pentacle would seem to clash with dominant socio-cultural and religious discourses for the TT reader.

For feminists, the ST also introduces a powerful counter discourse to the dominant patriarchal discourses of both the Church and the state throughout the various ages of history.

(29)

ST.   "This is very common in times of turmoil," Langdon continued. "A newly emerging power will take over the existing symbols and degrade them over time in an attempt to erase their meaning. In the battle between the pagan symbols and Christian symbols, the pagans lost; Poseidon's trident became the devil's pitchfork, the wise crone's pointed hat became the symbol of a witch, and Venus's pentacle became a sign of the devil". Langdon paused. "Unfortunately, the United States military has also perverted the pentacle; it's now our foremost symbol of war. We paint it on all our fighter jets and hang it on the shoulders of all our generals". *So much for the goddess of love and beauty.* (Brown 2003: 41)

This extract is an excellent example to highlight the arbitrariness of the signifier-signified relationship, which in turn underpins the arbitrariness of ideological discursive formations. The symbols traced do not seem to have any semiotic resonance for the TT reader. However, words like "pagan" when translated into الوثنية instantly trigger religious discourses for the TT reader, which are adamantly dismissive of such concepts. The Arabic equivalent for pagan can only function as an immediate threat to paradigms of beliefs, religiosity etc. It is interesting, therefore, that it seems to be possible to textually forge the ST utterance into the TT, but the illocutionary impact thereof remains unachieved: the counter-discourse constructed in the ST is simply rejected in the TT. Religious discourse cannot be readily fictionalized in Arabic literary discourse. Its illocutionary impact seems to be restricted to religious contexts outside which it is taken only at the locutionary level[9].

5. Conclusion

In conclusion, it is obvious that due to limitations of time and space, this paper has only touched upon some of the most prominent strategies of the translation of suspense into Arabic. The very nature of Dan Brown's novel *The Da Vinci Code*, in terms of its own consciousness of the interplay of signs and languages, is a challenge both to the reader and the translator of the text –and to the researcher looking into the resonance of the ST in the TT. There are many points of research that still need to be addressed, in particular if translation itself is to be seen as a form of dialogue.

---

[1] For an in-depth and comprehensive discussion of the novel in Arabic, its history and development, see Roger Allen (1995)

[2] According to many translation scholars, such as Eugene Nida (1991: 25), "For effective impact and appeal, form cannot be separated from content, since form itself carries so much meaning". It is interesting to note how the intricate interconnectedness between form and meaning is further complicated in this text.

[3] For an interesting discussion of various definitions of the concepts of "equivalence" and "strategy",

as well as an examination of the intersection of the two terms in Translation Studies, see Erich Steiner & Colin Yallop (2001).

[4] For Nida (1991: 26), this is the socio-semiotic perspective of translation, the central focus of which "is the multiplicity of codes involved in any act of verbal communication ... In fact, the impact of the verbal message is largely dependent upon judgments based on these extralinguistic codes".

[5] Though an indispensible term in Translation Studies, "equivalence" remains a controversial concept. One way to explain equivalence can be in terms of the closeness/distance between the ST and the TT. The criteria adopted by various theorists, thus, vary. Arguing that "the transfer from ST to TT *inevitably* entails difference" (Dickins et al. 2002: 21), Dickins, Hervey and Higgins define equivalence in terms of an attempt to "avoid an absolutist ambition to *maximize sameness* between ST and TT, in favour of a relativist ambition to *minimize difference*" (2002: 20). Further, Gideon Toury (1980) is now quoted as the authoritative approach in which he states that "the question to be asked in the actual study of translations (especially in the comparative analysis of ST and TT) is not *whether* the two texts are equivalent (from a certain aspect), but *what type* and *degree* of translation equivalence they reveal" (1980: 47; cited in Baker and Saldanha (2011)

[6] Jamal Al-Qinai (2009) provides an interesting discussion of how punctuation and cohesive devices shift in the TT. As he points out, "Even with the absence of explicit cohesive devices, punctuation marks help native speakers of English to recognize the logical relationship between a group of phrases or sentences" (Al-Qinai 2009: 27). Thus, a translator should always be fully aware of the impact of carrying across the punctuation and/or cohesion conventions of the SL into the TT, and "the reproduction of rhetorical and cohesive devices should be closely scrutinized lest the target text be foreignized" (Al-Qinai 2009: 30). Though the issue here is not one of translation strategies such as foreignization, Al-Qinai's argument does hold in terms of the loss/gain of ideational content that may be lost in the TT.

[7] Roger Bell (1991: 211-212) argues that a text can be perceived of as a macro-speech act "with its own propositional content and illocutionary force and it is clear that 'retrieving the illocutionary force of the entire text, as well as the forces of the elements making up the text, are basic principles in explicating texture ... negotiating structure and ultimately reconstructing 'context' and that this ability is 'a precondition for efficient translation ...'".

[8] Paul St. Pierre (1993: 62) offers an interesting discussion of how Foucault's concepts of discourse can be reformulated in terms of translation. The main argument is that "Insofar ... as translation constitutes a transformation –a regulated transformation– of its object (an object which is also discursive in nature), it falls within the area explored by the work of Michel Foucault"

[9] In their discussion of the impact of power and status on translation as a discourse, Basil Hatim and Ian Mason (1990: 86) maintain that any "consideration of the translation of illocutionary force" must by necessity take into account "the social institutions within which linguistic communication takes place".

Laila C. Ahmad Helmi

Bibliography

Primary Sources

Brown, Dan. 2003. *The Da Vinci Code*. New York: Anchor Books.
———. 2004. *The Da Vinci Code*. Translated by Abd Rabu, S. M .Beirut: Arab Scientific Publishers.

Secondary Sources

Allen, Roger. 1995. *The Arabic Novel: An Historical and Critical Introduction*. Syracuse NY: Syracuse University Press.
Al-Qinai, Jamal. 2009. 'Style Shift in Translation' in *Journal of Pan-Pacific Association of Applied Linguistics* 13(2): 23-41. Online at ERIC, file EJ868850. (consulted 17.07.2012)
Baker, Mona and Gabriela Saldanha. 2011. *The Routledge Encyclopedia of Translation Studies*. (2nd Ed.) New York: Routledge.
Bell, Roger T. 1991. *Translation and Translating*. London and New York: Longman.
Boase-Beier, Jean. 2011. *Critical Introduction to Translation Studies*. London: Continuum International Publishing Group.
Dickins, James, Hervey, Sandor and Ian Higgins. 2002. *Thinking Arabic Translation. A Course in Translation Method: Arabic to English*. New York: Routledge.
Hatim, Basil and Ian Mason. 1990. *Discourse and the Translator*. London and New York: Longman
Munday, Jeremy. 2001. *Introducing Translation Studies: Theories and Applications*. New York: Routledge.
Nida, Eugene A. 1991. 'Theories of Translation' in *Traduction, Terminologie, Redaction* 4(1): 19-32. Online at: http://id.erudit.org/iderudit/037079ar (consulted 10.06.2012)
Searle, John R. and Daniel Vanderveken. 1985. *Foundations of Illocutionary Logic*. Cambridge: CUP.
Steiner, Erich and Colin Yallop (eds.). 2001. *Exploring Translation and Multilingual Text Production: Beyond Content*. Berlin: Mouton de Gruyter
St-Pierre, Paul. 1993. 'Translation as a Discourse of History' in *Traduction, terminologie, redaction* 6(1): 61-82. Online at: http://id.erudit.org/iderudit/037138ar (consulted 12. 08.2012)
Toury, Gideon. 1980. *In Search of a Theory of Translation*. Tel Aviv: The Porter Institute for Poetics and Semiotics. Tel Aviv University.
———. 1995. *Descriptive Translation Studies – and Beyond*. Amsterdam and Philadelphia; John Benjamins.
Wilson, Dan and Deirdre Sperber. 1993. 'Linguistic Form and Relevance' in *Lingua* 90: 1-25. Online at: http://dan.sperber.fr/wp-content/uploads/2009/09/Linguistic-form-and-relevance.pdf (consulted 11. 08.2012)

Corpus: Orig. Eng (parallel) — is the translator aware of differences?
Orig. Spanish
Eng. to Spanish) Comparable corpus
ways in which dialogue used as a narrative strategy in these 2 contexts.
- *Proportion of dialogue & dialogue tags in both subcorpora*
- *amount of informational load in them (plot, character, situations)*

Chapter 14: Analysis of the different features and functions of dialogue in a comparable corpus of crime novels[1]

Bárbara Martínez Vilinsky

Abbreviations

Rd. Nov. 18

Abstract
A comparable corpus of crime novels composed of a subcorpus of texts written originally in Spanish and a subcorpus of translations from American English into Spanish serves as a starting point and means for searching for differences and similarities between the ways in which dialogue is used as a narrative strategy in fiction in these two different communicative contexts. In order to do so, I will focus on aspects such as the proportion of dialogue and of dialogue tags present in both subcorpora and the degree of detail and informational load that is included in them, to find out whether they play a significant role in the development of the plot and the depiction of characters and situations. The corpus also includes a parallel subcorpus of original English novels which will help us establish whether the differences —or lack thereof— between the two components of the comparable Spanish corpus are due to the fact that the translator is aware or not of the influence of these variables, and alters them in any way in order to adjust to the Spanish communicative context.

concordance — words with their context

Keywords: Corpora, dialogue tags, verba dicendi, narrative strategies

diff. communicative contexts
orig. St & a novel translated into that lang.
em dash — before speech. Typographical sign

1. Introduction

The aim of this chapter is to compare the way fictional dialogue is represented in narrative literature that was originally written in Spanish, on the one hand, and that which has been translated into Spanish, on the other. The corpus compiled for this purpose is made up of contemporary crime novels, a genre that usually includes a fairly important amount of dialogue (de Haan 1996: 26) as a strategy to get the reader involved in the investigation and resolution of the cases. According to the US writer and scriptwriter Syd Field (1994: 184), dialogue is also used, among other things, to: help the story move along; reveal data and events; allow the reader to get to know the characters, their relationships and their emotional states better; comment on the action, and relate scenes to one another. Sometimes it just helps catch the reader's attention by adding a component that is both realistic and spontaneous.

purposes of dialogue

It is obvious that the crime novel traditions in the USA and in Spain differ in a number of aspects. If the focus is on linguistic and formal differences, the first thing that becomes immediately apparent is the difference in length, since the US novels tend to be substantially longer. For example, in the comparable

asked Katie — dialogue tags
asked
verba dicendi (verb introducing speech)

corpus, the mean number of words in the Spanish novels is barely 61,000 words, while the translations have around 97,500 (93,500 in the case of the originals). But what other kinds of differences are there between examples of this genre that were written in Spain and those that have been translated? Do the main features and functions of literary dialogue differ in some way? Are these differences merely a result of the influence of the characteristics of the English originals or might some of them be due to a conscious decision made by the translator? Is there a tendency among translators to adapt to the linguistic and stylistic norms of the target literary tradition? In this paper, I will focus on the following aspects of fictional dialogue which may provide us with important clues as to how to answer these questions.

First, I will determine the proportion of dialogue in each subcorpus. Then I will see whether dialogue tags² are normally used to qualify the situations illustrated by the dialogue or whether, on the contrary, the authors prefer to use the voices of their characters to convey most of the information. I will also establish the proportion in which interrogative and exclamatory sentences are employed in the Spanish dialogues with respect to the translated ones, since this is a trait that provides an indication of the emotional load that the dialogues are able to express in the story. Finally, I will analyse the range of *verba dicendi* used in the dialogue tags, together with the type of information that is included within them, in order to determine the extent to which the narrator intervenes in the dialogue in the different literary traditions.

2. Material and methods

To analyse these aspects of the construction of fictional dialogue, I will make use of the lexical analysis techniques and tools used in corpus-based translation studies. As Baker (1995: 235) and Laviosa (2003: 114) state in their works on the subject, compiling a comparable corpus of originals in a language, and translations into that same language, is a valid method for finding patterns of use that may be peculiar to translational language as opposed to non-translational language.

Given the size of the corpus (853,768 words), the aim of this work is not to focus on the specific functions of the dialogue in each novel or to go into details about the way in which particular cases have been translated. Instead, the intention is to offer an overview of the differences and similarities between novels that were written in Spanish and novels that have been translated into this language, in terms of some of the narrative and linguistic resources used by the authors to endow their texts with a certain degree of orality in the shape of literary dialogue. By observing large amounts of text I can draw certain preliminary conclusions about the way dialogue helps to construct the plot of a crime novel, to depict the characters and to situate the reader within the specific

240

communicative context of the Spanish detective novel. It also enables us to get some insight into whether (and if so, how and to what extent) these characteristic features of that context coincide with those of the translations into Spanish. The corpus also includes the parallel component of the subcorpus of translated novels, that is to say, their corresponding English originals. This will allow us to determine whether the differences or similarities are the result of the translator's being (or failure to be) aware of the influence of these variables, and thus alters them in some way to adapt them to the Spanish literary norms or, on the contrary, follows those of the source culture.

The corpus I base my study on contains six novels written by Spanish authors, which will be called ES subcorpus (366,263 words) and five novels by authors from the United States, translated by translators from Spain, called TRAD subcorpus (487,505 words). All of them were written, published and translated in the nineteen nineties. The list of works and their authors is included in the bibliography. The difference in the number of novels is due to the fact that, as I mentioned earlier, in this genre, the US novels tend to be considerably longer than the Spanish ones and I preferred to try to balance the number of words in order to increase the degree of comparability of the subcorpora.

To extract the data I used text analysis tools (Wordsmith Tools[3] for the comparable corpus and ParaConc[4] for the parallel corpus), which allow semi-automatic searches to be performed for particular linguistic elements and to see them in their context by extracting concordances.

Direct dialogue in the novels is easy to detect just by looking because, unless they are experimental texts in which the author plays with the form, the structure, the typography used in the language, or with the narrative techniques (Espunya 2012: 199), the dialogue is usually presented graphically with specific orthographic and typographical signs. In English, inverted commas are used to enclose the characters' words, while in Spanish each of their interventions usually has an em dash before it. If there are dialogue tags, in which the narrator qualifies those words and adds paralinguistic and extralinguistic information, then these are given between dashes.

The other typologies of the dialogue, however, are more difficult to detect using text analysis tools, since they are often intermingled with the narrator's discourse and making them stand out in a semi-automatic search for concordances is not so easy. For this reason, and partly owing to the method used to collect information, in this study I selected the type of direct dialogue which attempts to evoke oral discourse by the "exact reproduction" of the words of the characters.

The corpus was tagged with the software program TreeTagger,[5] although the search for concordances was conducted both in the original corpus without tagging, and in the tagged one, to ensure that the tagging had been performed correctly and that the lexical analysis programs collected all the appearances of the elements that I were looking for in both cases. Once the reliability of the tagged corpus had been verified, I began a joint search, using WordSmith, for the tags <FS> and <DOTS>, which represent punctuation marks that can indicate the end of a sentence, and very carefully screening the concordances that include ellipses. The figures can be seen in Table 1.

Table 1: Number of sentences in the two subcorpora

[handwritten annotation: Orig. Spanish authors]

[handwritten annotation: Orig. US authors / translated into spanish]

ES	No. sentences	TRAD	No. sentences
Giménez	7,751	Cornwell	8,907
Madrid	4,482	Ellroy	11,809
Martín	3,659	Grafton	8,598
Martínez	3,801	Highsmith	9,485
Núñez	5,073	Leonard	7,629
Vázquez	5,969		
Total	30,735	Total	46,428

The first of my aims was to calculate the proportion of dialogue present in each of the subcorpora. To do so, given the complications involved in delimiting interventions in dialogue form by searching for concordances, all the fragments of dialogue in each novel had to be extracted manually and then the sentences from those fragments were counted. Only paragraphs that included direct dialogue introduced by dashes were taken into account, along with their respective dialogue tags.

3. Results

3.1. Percentages of dialogue and dialogue tags

Dialogue, as a narrative technique, can be said to be widely used in this genre: the approximate percentage of dialogue found in the sample is above 50%. Two authors come close to 70% of dialogue, two are above 50% and two do not reach 40%. Table 2 shows the different percentages of dialogue sentences in the different texts in the subcorpus of Spanish originals.

Table 2: Percentage of dialogue in ES

Text	No. sentences	No. dialogue sentences	Percentage
Giménez	7,751	4,139	53.4
Madrid	4,482	3,012	67.2
Martín	3,659	1,671	45.7
Martínez	3,801	1,298	34.1
Núñez	5,073	1,942	38.3
Vázquez	5,969	4,437	74.3
Total	30,735	16,499	53.7

It is interesting to break down these figures into the percentage of dialogue tags, on the one hand, and the interventions uttered by the characters, on the other, in order to compare how this narrative technique is used in the two subcorpora.

I searched for all the concordances of dialogue dashes in the subcorpus and removed those that correspond to digressions within the narrative, as well as those that were duplicated because they divided a single sentence, spoken by one character, to allow an intervention by the narrator to be inserted. By so doing we were able to see from the concordances, which category the text that each dash precedes belongs to (see Table 3). *[handwritten: internal monologue pieces of dialogue with no]*

Table 3: Percentage of dialogue tags in ES

Text	No. Concordances	Direct dialogue (cases)	Direct dialogue (%)	Dialogue tags (cases)	Dialogue tags (%)
Giménez	2,862	2,668	93.2	194	6.8
Madrid	1,629	1,403	86.1	226	13.9
Martín	874	663	75.8	211	24.1
Martínez	701	602	85.9	99	14.1
Núñez	979	778	79.5	201	20.5
Vázquez	2,233	2,149	96.2	84	3.8
Total	9,278	8,263	89.1	1,015	10.9

The percentages of dialogue tags used by each author vary greatly from one to another, and a higher percentage of dialogue is not linked with a higher percentage of dialogue tags. For example, Vázquez, whose text includes the highest percentage of dialogue, has only 3.8% of dialogue tags. This is because this author resorts to lengthy interventions by the narrator in separate paragraphs to describe characters and situations (example 1):

(1)
TT.   Al vendedor se le había paralizado la sonrisa, la palabra, la gesticulación y por fin
       acertó a balbucir:
       —Pero hombre... (Vázquez 1996[6])

On the other hand, the three authors that use less dialogue, namely Martínez, Martín and Núñez, present the highest percentages of dialogue tags.

Table 4: Percentage of dialogue in TRAD

Text	No. sentences	No. dialogue sentences	Percentage
Cornwell	8,907	6,613	74.2
Ellroy	11,809	5,765	48.8
Grafton	8,598	5,089	59.2
Highsmith	9,485	5,826	61.4
Leonard	7,629	5,079	66.6
Total	46,428	28,372	61.1

As can be seen in Table 4, the proportion of dialogue in the subcorpus of translations into Spanish is approximately 7.4% higher than in that made up of texts originally written in Spanish. One author surpasses the 70% mark, two go beyond 60% and none of them are below 48%, which indicates that, generally speaking, there is a greater presence of dialogue in the translated novels in the corpus. *into Spanish*

It can also be seen this difference expressed in the number of words. The number of words that I found in the fragments of dialogue in ES (148,085) accounts for 40.4% of the total number of words in that subcorpus, whereas the words used in the dialogues (241,953) in TRAD account for 49.6% of the total number.

Moreover, I find a greater percentage of dialogue tags in the translated novels (as can be observed in Table 5, all of them have around 30% of dialogue tags, except Ellroy). These seem to include more descriptions of the surrounding action alongside the interventions of the characters, instead of in a separate paragraph (example 2):

(2)
—Deduzco que ha estado aquí, a menos que hayas empezado a fumar otra vez —Cerró la puerta del frigorífico y vino a la mesa. (Cornwell 1994/1993) [Spanish published translation]

Table 5: Percentage of dialogue tags in TRAD

Text	No. concordances	Direct dialogue (cases)	Direct dialogue (%)	Dialogue tags (cases)	Dialogue tags (%)
Cornwell	4,318	3,056	70.8	1,262	29.2
Ellroy	3,213	3,108	96.7	105	3.3
Grafton	2,533	1,845	72.8	688	27.2
Highsmith	3,426	2,052	59.9	1,374	40.1
Leonard	3,230	2,371	73.4	859	26.6
Total	16,720	12,432	74.3	4,288	25.6

As I have mentioned earlier, James Ellroy is rather an exception as he uses techniques that are quite unlike those employed by the other authors in their dialogues. Given that his narrator's comments are generally placed before the character's intervention, separated by a line break, they are not detected when searching for dashes. But a search conducted for a colon before the dialogue dash (by searching for the tags <COLON> and, in the context box, <DASH>) yields 539 results in ES and 648 in TRAD. These are sometimes isolated *verba dicendi*, sometimes descriptions of the context or characters and occasionally indications describing the gestures or actions performed by the character who is going to speak next (example 3).

(3)
TT.   (…) La joven esbelta, oscura y bastante guapa, contestó:
        –Sí, señora. (Leonard 1994) [Spanish published translation]

Sixty per cent of the cases in translations (388) are in the text by Ellroy, which evidences the author's preference for incorporating the additional information by means of this technique rather than using dialogue tags placed within or after the dialogue. The first practice seems to be more common in the original Spanish texts, taking into account the total number of sentences (Roland et al., 2007: 353): 17.5 (ES) versus 13.9 (TRAD) per thousand sentences (LL 15.20; p < 0.0001).[7] There are, on the other hand, more dialogue tags in the translations: 33 (ES) versus 92 (TRAD) per thousand sentences (LL 1047.05; p < 0.0001).

3.2. Presence of interrogative and exclamatory sentences

In this section I will offer a brief analysis of the proportion of exclamatory and interrogative sentences that can be found within the dialogues, since this is closely related to the choice of *verba dicendi*, which I will analyze in the following section. They can also provide us with clues about the main functions of the dialogue in the novels in the corpus. Exclamatory sentences denote greater emotionality on the part of the characters; they can express emotions such as joy, surprise, anger or irony, and they help characterise them and describe their reactions to the events. On the other hand, interrogative sentences are essential in crime and detective novels, since one of their main functions is to obtain information. The plot is often gradually built up as the characters discover things through the dialogues they have with other characters.

Table 6: Interrogative and exclamatory sentences in ES

Text	No. dialogue sentences	No. exclamatory sentences	%	No. interrogative sentences	%
Giménez	4,139	228	5.5	964	23.3
Madrid	3,012	131	4.3	799	25.5
Martín	1,671	146	8.7	361	21.6
Martínez	1,298	13	1	214	16.5
Núñez	1,942	29	1.5	306	15.7
Vázquez	4,437	121	2.7	844	19
Total	16,499	668	4	3,488	21.1

Table 7: Interrogative and exclamatory sentences in TRAD

Text	No. dialogue sentences	No. exclamatory sentences	%	No. interrogative sentences	%
Cornwell	6,613	43	0.6	1,093	16.5
Ellroy	5,765	304	5.3	1,060	18.4
Grafton	5,089	37	0.7	869	17.1
Highsmith	5,826	487	8.3	1,030	17.7

Leonard	5,079	16	0.3	1,144	22.5
Total	28,372	887	3.1	5,196	18.3

As can be seen in Tables 6 and 7, there is not much difference between the percentages, which would at first sight indicate a similarity in the two literary traditions in this narrative aspect of the construction of the crime genre. Yet, it can perhaps be catched a glimpse of the Latin character, which is more likely to allow itself be carried away by emotions, in the slight difference I found in favour of the Spanish texts (LL 25.10, p < 0.0001). Curiously enough, the translated text with the highest percentage of exclamatory sentences is set in France, and the French-speaking characters are the ones who most commonly express themselves by means of exclamations (example 4):

(4)
TT.   —Eh, Marie! Deux pastis! —Era la voz del gordo Georges (…) (Highsmith 1993)
[Spanish published translation]

Interrogative sentences, on the other hand, are better represented in the dialogue, accounting for around 20% of the total in the two subcorpora. Nevertheless, again it can be observed a small difference in favour of the subcorpus of originals (LL 42.57, p < 0.0001), which may mean that Spanish authors make more frequent use of the inclusion of questions and answers in the dialogues as a narrative technique in order to uncover aspects that are essential to the plot or to present characters.

3.3. Lexical diversity in the dialogue tags

I will now focus on the study of the degree of detail and informative load included in the dialogue tags, since they are the most important resource the narrator has at his or her disposal to express with what intent and in what way something is said (Axelsson 2011: 26). This will be undertaken, first, by analysing the variety of *verba dicendi* employed.

Verba dicendi designate linguistic communication acts or are used to express beliefs, deliberations or emotions (Villanueva 1989: 181-201). The first step will be to find out which *verba dicendi* are the most common in the two subcorpora by recording their frequency of occurrence in the concordances of dialogue (Tables 8 and 9).

Table 8: *Verba dicendi* by frequency of use in ES

Verbum dicendi		Frequency
1.	Decir	310
2.	Preguntar	109
3.	Contestar	53
4.	Gritar	24

5.	Exclamar	20
6.	Responder	18
7.	Añadir	17
8.	Insistir	15
9.	Comentar	12
10.	Dirigirse a	6
11.	Soltar	6
12.	Espetar	6
13.	Cantar / canturrear	5
14.	Confesar	5
15.	Saludar	5
16.	Murmurar	5
17.	Repetir	5
18.	Terciar	5

Another 67 verbs that appear fewer than 5 times were also found; thus, altogether there were 85 verbs, of which 19 do not appear in the subcorpus of translations.

Table 9: *Verba dicendi* by frequency of use in TRAD

Verbum dicendi		Frequency
19.	**Decir**	1233
20.	**Preguntar**	413
21.	**Responder**	200
22.	**Contestar**	141
23.	Explicar	110
24.	**Añadir**	64
25.	**Comentar**	60
26.	Proseguir	46
27.	**Exclamar**	41
28.	Replicar	40
29.	Observar	37
30.	Continuar	36
31.	**Insistir**	28
32.	**Repetir**	30
33.	Anunciar	23
34.	Asentir	23
35.	Concluir	23
36.	Apuntar	22

Adding up all the different verbs used in the dialogue tags in this subcorpus yields a total of 96, of which 30 do not appear in the dialogue tags in the subcorpus of originals.

The variety of *verba dicendi* in the two subcorpora, in terms of number (obviously I am referring to the number of types, not of tokens) is quite similar (the TRAD subcorpus has 11 more verbs). Perhaps a greater difference could have been expected given the divergence in the number of words in the two subcorpora. Yet, there are marked differences in terms of what verbs are to be found in each subcorpus: 31.2% of the verbs utilised in TRAD are not used even once in the dialogue tags of ES. With regard to this difference in the choice of *verba dicendi* in the two subcorpora I agree with Mauranen (2005: 80) when she claims that translators tend to utilise the resources of the target language by making relatively more use of what can be done than what is typically done in that language.

A tentative search in the parallel component of originals in English for a comma (or less frequently, other punctuation marks) followed by English close inverted commas (which is how the end of an intervention followed by dialogue tag is marked in the English originals) and followed by a space and open inverted commas (which is how an intervention preceded by a comment by the narrator is marked), reveales **88** different types of *verba dicendi*. There are more than in the Spanish originals, but fewer than in the translations. Moreover, it must be borne in mind that in these last two subcorpora I have only counted those that are included in post-positioned dialogue tags. In the case of the originals in English, however, I included the verbs that follow the interventions but also those that precede them, since many of them will become post-positioned dialogue tags on being translated, as it shall be seen later (if both possibilities are counted, the final number of verb types comes to 110 in ES and 105 in TRAD).

Hence, it is reasonable to think that this greater variety in the translations (albeit not very important, but nevertheless unexpected) may be due to the greater presence of dialogue tags in the originals and the translator's need to adapt to the stylistic preferences of Spanish, which recommend avoiding overuse of the two or three most frequent verbs, including *decir* ('say'), while this kind of repetition is far more acceptable in English. In order to check this hypothesis, I will perform a parallel search for some of the verbs that hardly appear in ES but which do appear several times in TRAD.

Let us take the verb *proponer* ('propose'), for example. If we search in the parallel corpus, it can be seen that all the cases in which the translator has used this verb (10) correspond to English sentences where the verb 'say' was used. The same thing happens with the verb *inquirir* ('inquire'), which always corresponds to 'ask', and is probably used to avoid an excessive repetition of its more usual equivalent preguntar. *Pedir* ('ask for'), on the other hand, is used on eight out of ten occasions to translate the verb 'say'. Of the 13 occurrences of the verb *conceder*, only five are translations of 'agree' or 'concede'. The others replace 'say' and, on one occasion, the *verbum dicendi* is added to a text with no dialogue tag in the original. *Advertir* (13) is used to translate 'say' on all occasions except one, where it translates its equivalent 'warn'. Finally, *puntualizar* ('point out') (14) is used as the translation of 'say' in all cases.

Of course, there are occasions where the opposite occurs. In English there are more lexical options with which to cover the semantic field of *murmurar*, *musitar* and *susurrar*. The translator alternates between these three options to translate a wider range of English verbs ('whisper', 'muse', 'mutter', 'mumble', 'murmur', 'hiss' and even 'say'). Yet, I believe there are enough examples of the opposite case to conclude that translators included in the corpus commonly extend the lexical diversity of the original *verba dicendi* in order to match the expectations of the target language.

The greater utilisation of the verb *decir* in TRAD (taking the total number of words of the dialogue fragments as the frame of reference) is very significant in statistical terms (LL 229.84; $p<0.0001$). The same thing occurs with the verb *preguntar* (LL 70.62; $p<0.0001$), a typical marker of the interrogative mode of enunciation, which may seem strange bearing in mind what I have said about the greater presence of interrogative sentences in ES. But to be able to draw conclusions, it would be necessary to take into account the frequencies of similar verbs like *inquirir* or *interrogar*. Also in relation to what was discussed in that respect, it can be seen that, apart from the fact that *clamar* ('cry out'), *explotar* ('explode') and *estallar* ('burst out') only appear in the originals in Spanish, the verbs *gritar* ('shout') and *exclamar* ('exclaim') (the latter used more often than *gritar* in translations) are ranked considerably higher in ES than in TRAD. This would account for the higher percentage of exclamatory sentences and would offer clues about one of the most significant purposes of dialogues in Spanish novels. The presence of both is significantly greater in the ES subcorpus (LL 7.93; $p<0.01$ and 5.70; $p<0.05$, respectively).

As it has been seen (and undoubtedly expected), the most frequent *verbum dicendi* in the dialogue tags in both subcorpora is *decir*, with 310 occurrences in ES and 1,233 in TRAD. Moreover, in ES we find 65 occurrences of this verb that are not included in dialogue (which they precede with a colon) and the same occurs on 114 occasions in TRAD. The difference in usage is not statistically significant but it must be taken into account that 389 of the 648 original concordances in TRAD (60%) belong to Ellroy, who surprisingly only has two examples of the verb *decir* placed before the character's intervention. This is because, on many occasions (237), the author removes the *verbum dicendi*, thus giving rise to examples like the following, which are almost stage directions (example 5):

(5)
TT.   Yo, con un bostezo:
    –¿Resultados? (Ellroy 1993) [Spanish published translation]

If added the omitted verb to many of these fragments, the difference in the frequency of use of the verb *decir* positioned before the character's intervention would increase considerably in favour of the corpus of translations.

From what can be read in interviews with the author, Ellroy's particular telegraphic style developed as a result of his publisher's telling him to reduce the length of his novels. Thus, he often chooses to introduce dialogue tags without *verba dicendi*, placed both before and after the character's intervention. In such cases, he limits himself to mentioning the character's name or, sometimes, to adding brief descriptions of actions or attitudes. By so doing, he gives the text a direct, fast, cutting style and makes his dialogues and characters both spontaneous and agile.

Thanks to the parallel corpus, it can be seen whether these strategies used in the translated text to represent dialogue directly reflect those used by the author or, in contrast, are somehow modified to adapt them to the stylistic conventions used in Spanish novels.

Searching for the word *said* in Ellroy's original text, in the cases in which it is used as *verbum dicendi* in dialogue (35), it can be found out that the most common order for dialogue tags in English (i.e. placed after the intervention) is used on only six occasions. In most of the concordances (29), the verb goes before the character's intervention, separated by a comma and open inverted commas (example 6):

(6)
ST.   Jack said, "Come see me." (Ellroy 2001)

However, the translation only conserves the verb before the intervention on five occasions and it is completely omitted on another five, which I assume will be for the sake of style (to avoid excessive repetitions). On two occasions direct speech is turned into indirect speech. In the others (17 cases), it is consistently altered and the dialogue tags are placed after the intervention, sometimes maintaining the verb *decir* or using others (example 7):

(7)
ST.   I said, "You will." (Ellroy 2001)
TT.   Tú sí –respondí. (Ellroy 1993) [Spanish published translation]

3.4. Degree of informative load in the dialogue tags

In the following I will focus on the amount of information the narrator adds in order to qualify the character's utterance by analysing whether the quantity and quality of this information differ in the two subcorpora. To do so, WordSmith was used to search for all the concordances of dash + different forms of the verb *decir* and they were classified in six categories, which were created ad hoc from observing the cases that occur in the corpus:

1) Only the verb (here are included the dative pronouns: *le digo*).
2) Verb and explicit reference to the subject.
3) Verb plus explicit subject and qualification, in a single clause, of specific aspects of the person who is speaking (by means of qualifying adjectives) or of the way they speak (by means of elements that indicate mood or intonation such as "sighing" or "sarcastically"), adverbial clauses of place or time or an indirect object.
4) Verb plus explicit subject and a more detailed description of characters, of their motivations and attitudes, of their gestures and body language or of complex actions that may require more than one clause or phrase.
5) The same as category 3 without making the subject explicit.
6) The same as category 4 without making the subject explicit.

Table 10: Information inside dialogue tags (ES)

Structure	No. of cases
1) V	52
2) V+explicit S	92
3) V+S+ simple qualification	23
4) V+S+ complex description	50
5) V+ simple qualification	40
6) V+ complex description	53
Total	310

Table 11: Information inside the dialogue tags (TRAD)

Structure	No. of cases
1) V	**232**
2) V+explicit S	**389**
3) V+S+ simple qualification	123
4) V+S+ complex description	**257**
5) V+ simple qualification	85
6) V+ complex description	**147**
Total	**1,233**

As can be observed in Tables 10 and 11, the commonest structure within dialogue tags that have *decir* as their main *verbum dicendi* is number 2, both in ES and in TRAD. The next three most frequent structures, in order of frequency, are 6, 1 and 4 in ES and 4, 1 and 6 in TRAD. According to these findings, the main function of the dialogue tags in the novels in this corpus is to make it clear to the reader who is speaking in the dialogues. This is achieved by making the subject who realises the utterance explicit, and also by the fairly frequent use of the verb on its own, which, given the inflective nature of the Spanish language, very often leaves it clear who the speaker is. These two structures (1 and 2) account for 46.4% in the original texts and 50.4% of the cases in the translations.

The most striking difference seen as regards the next two structures in order of occurrence (4 and 6, i.e. cases in which the dialogue tags include descriptions of gestures, characters, motivations and actions), which account for 33.2% of the total in ES and 32.8% in TRAD, is that there is a preference for making the subject explicit in the translations. In these, structure 4 appears more often than number 6, whereas in the Spanish originals the opposite occurs.

As for the least commonly used structures (20.3% in originals and 16.9% in translations), that is, categories 3 and 5, again it can be seen how the translations show a preference for the structure that includes the explicit subject (3), perhaps due to the influence of English, while it tends to be omitted more often in the originals (5).

These differences in distribution appear to be statistically significant, according to the chi-square test (X^2=21.49 (df=5), p<0.01) (Stefanowitsch 2004).

4. Conclusions

This chapter is based on a general analysis of five aspects that may point to differences in the narrative techniques used in the dialogues written by the authors (or translators) of crime novels in English and in Spanish. What I have found is that the use of direct dialogue seems to be more frequent in novels translated from English than in those written in Spanish, which contain a higher percentage of narrated fragments. The translations make more extensive use of dialogue tags to qualify the characters' words and actions, while the Spanish authors tend to leave these descriptions outside the fragments of dialogue. On the other hand, it can be found a higher degree of expressivity (in the form of exclamations) in the dialogues of Spanish novels. This may be a manifestation of a greater tendency to display emotion in this culture or is perhaps the result of a deliberate strategy implemented by the authors in order to represent their characters through the way they express themselves and how they deal with the situations that arise as the plot unfolds. It also can be found a higher proportion of interrogative sentences in the Spanish novels, which is an effective way of allowing the characters to discover elements that would otherwise have to be revealed by the narrator.

As regards the *verba dicendi*, the translated texts offer a degree of diversity that could be considered atypical, since it is not found to the same extent in the Spanish originals. It is probably a consequence of the need to translate the commonest verbs, like 'say', which appear with a frequency that is considerably higher than would be regarded stylistically acceptable in Spanish. The difference that was found between the originals in English and the translations, as regards the degree of intervention by the narrator, may have certain consequences on the way the translated text is received, due to the fact that the target reader has access to a higher degree of explicitation than the reader of the original text in terms of the way something was said (intonation, mood, etc.) and thus, of the communicative intention of the utterance. Finally, I have found that the most frequent function of the dialogue tags in both subcorpora is to make it clear which character is speaking. Furthermore, in the translations there is a preference for making the subject explicit in the dialogue tags, thus helping readers to identify who speaks or performs a particular action at any given time.

Here I have focused on the strategies used in both original Spanish and translated Spanish texts in a comparable corpus of crime novels and, thus, little has been done in terms of comparing those translations with their originals in English. Nevertheless, a couple of brief analyses of parallel concordances in the section on lexical diversity have allowed us to observe how translators sometimes modify the narrative strategies employed by the original author in order to match the stylistic, orthographic and typographical norms of fictional dialogue that prevail in the target culture. As a result, they can alter the stylistic effect sought by the original author. For example, if the systematic repetition of a particular verb such as 'say' is intentional or, if an author, as it has be seen with Ellroy, seeks to endow his novel with a telegraphic style in which most of the narrator's contributions are placed before the character's intervention rather than in dialogue tags, then altering these variables may be counterproductive. As Cadera (2012: 48) puts it, content is always important: "But maybe style or form has to be more important at the moment of translating from one language to another if the author's intention is to create a particular impression by form". Analyses such as this one can therefore be useful to researchers and translators when it comes to dealing effectively with certain factors that may have an effect on the way the dialogue in crime novels is translated into Spanish.

---

[1] This study was supported by a research grant from Universitat Jaume I, Spain (reference PREDOC/ 2008/03).

[2] Throughout this paper we use the term *dialogue tags* in the widest sense to refer to any of the digressions, explanations, descriptions, comments, etc. preceded by a dash (in Spanish) and given by the narrator to establish who is speaking and other information, such as how or where they are speaking.

[3] Version 3 (1999). Developed by Michael Scott and distributed by Oxford University Press.

[4] Version 1, build 269 (2004). Developed by Michael Barlow and distributed by Athelstan.

[5] Developed by Helmut Schmid in the TC project at the Institute for Computational Linguistics of the University of Stuttgart.

[6] Page numbers are not provided for the examples included throughout the text, since they are copied from the concordances extracted by Wordsmith and Paraconc, not from the actual novels that were

digitalized in order to create the corpus.

[7]According to the Log-likelihood test, which is very similar to the chi-square test but is more reliable, with low expected frequencies and big differences in the size of the corpora (Rayson and Garside 2000).

Bibliography

Primary Sources

Cornwell, Patricia. 1994. *Cruel and Unusual*. London: Warner Books [First edition published in 1993 by Little, Brown and Company].
———. 1994. *Cruel y extraño*. Translated by Jordi Mustieles. Barcelona: Ediciones B.
Ellroy, James. 2001. *White Jazz*. New York: Vintage Books [First edition published in 1992 by Random House].
———. 1993. *Jazz Blanco*. Translated by. Hernán Sabaté Vargas. Barcelona: Ediciones B.
Giménez Bartlett, Alicia. 1996. *Ritos de muerte*. Barcelona: Grijalbo.
Grafton, Susan. 1995. *L is for Lawless*. New York: Henry Holt and Company.
———. 1996. *L de ley (o fuera de ella)*. Translated by Antonio Prometeo-Moya. Barcelona: Tusquets.
Highsmith, Patricia. 2008. *Ripley Under Water*. New York: W. W. Norton & Company [First edition published in 1991 by Bloomsbury Publishing].
———. 1993. *Ripley en peligro*. Translated by Isabel Núñez. Barcelona: Anagrama [First edition published in 1992 by Cículo de Lectores].
Leonard, Elmore. 2004. *Rum Punch*. London: Orion Books [First edition published in 1992 by Viking].
———. 1994. *Rum Punch*. Translated by Enrique de Hériz Ramón. Barcelona: Ediciones B.
Madrid, Juan. 1995. *Cuentas pendientes*. Madrid: Alfaguara.
Martín, Andreu. 1992. *El hombre de la navaja*. Barcelona: Plaza y Janés Editores.
Martínez Reverte, Jorge. 1995. *Gálvez y el cambio del cambio*. Barcelona: Anagrama.
Núñez, Soledad. 1994. *La danza de los reptiles*. Gipuzkoa: Txertoa.
Vázquez Montalbán, Manuel. 1996. *El premio*. Barcelona: Planeta.

Secondary Sources

Axelsson, Karin. 2011. *Tag Questions in Fiction Dialogue*. Ph.D. thesis. University of Gothenburg, Göteborg. Online at: http://hdl.handle.net/2077/24047 (consulted 20.11.2012).
Baker, Mona. 1995. 'Corpora in Translation Studies: An Overview and Some Suggestions for Future Research'. *Target* 7(2): 223-243.
Cadera, Susanne M. 2012. 'Translating fictive dialogue in novels', in Brumme, Jenny and Anna Espunya (eds). *The Translation of Fictive Dialogue*. Amsterdam: Rodopi. 35-51.
De Haan, Pieter. 1996. 'More on the Language of fiction'. *ICAME Journal*, 20. 23-40.
Espunya, Anna. 2012. 'Sentence Connection in Fictive Dialogue', in Brumme, Jenny and Anna Espunya (eds). *The Translation of Fictive Dialogue*. Amsterdam: Rodopi. 199-215.
Field, Syd. 1994. *El libro del guión*. Madrid: Plot Ediciones.
Laviosa, Sara. 2003. 'Corpora and the Translator', in Somers, Harold (ed.). *Computer and Translation. A Translator's Guide*. Amsterdam: John Benjamins.
Mauranen, Anna. 2005. 'Contrasting languages and varieties with translational corpora'. *Languages in Contrast* 5(1): 73-92.
Rayson, Paul and Roger Garside. 2000. 'Comparing corpora using frequency profiling', in proceedings of the *workshop on Comparing Corpora, held in conjunction with the 38th annual meeting of the Association for Computational Linguistics (ACL 2000)* (Hong Kong, 1th-8th October 2000): 1-6. Online at: http://ucrel.lancs.ac.uk/llwizard.html (consulted 13.03.2013).
Roland, Douglas, Frederic Dick and Jeffrey L. Elman. 2007. 'Frequency of English Grammatical Structures: A Corpus Analysis'. *Journal of Memory and Language* 57(3): 348-379.
Stefanowitsch, Anatol. 2004. *Quantitative Thinking for Corpus Linguistics*. Online at http://www-user.uni-bremen.de/~anatol/qnt/qnt_dist.html (consulted 10.03.2013).
Villanueva, Darío. 1989. *Comentario de textos narrativos: la novela*. Gijón: Ediciones Júcar. 18-201.

<u>Glossary</u>.

(dead) Frozen metaphor - e.g.

he's a snake

Morphological e.g. tense
How a word is formed - roots,
prefixes, suffixes.
Semantically stronger adjs,
e.g. dreary for sad.
p. 267 Translation shift.
e.g. here in TT 1 character rather
than another in ST becs. unpleasant.
"mocking look" becs, 'malicious
expression'
p. 269 Microstructure level -
here lexical features expressing
emotion.

This is interesting - Read Nov. 18

[Handwritten notes at top of page:]

Expressions of emotion:-
P.260 paralanguage - tone, voice quality,
tempo, manner, onom at.
proxemics/kinesics - e.g. she strained closer
(corporal systems) Facial expressions.
Tone of voice + verba dicendi
Words of emotion (verb, adjs, nouns)

Chapter 15: Translating emotions expressed in nonverbal features of dialogues in the novel: *Schnee in Venedig*

Anita Pavić Pintarić and Sybille Schellheimer

Abstract
The aim of this paper is to investigate emotions expressed in nonverbal features of characters as well as their translation. The characters in novels express emotions using both verbal and nonverbal means. Thus, the reader can perceive the psychological features of the character, and the novelist can build suspense. This study is based on the German detective novel "Schnee in Venedig" written by Nicolas Remin and its Croatian and Spanish translations. Firstly, dialogues in which emotions are expressed in the original are identified. Further steps include determining which characters use emotions and in which situations, with expressions of emotions described according to their morphological and stylistic features. Finally, the translation of these expressions is analysed, and cultural similarities and differences are determined.

Keywords: Emotions, nonverbal behaviour, suspense, translation

1. Introduction[1]

Modern literary fiction shows the tendency of using dialogues as means of creating "feigned orality"[2] (Goetsch 1985), and is referred to as "stream of talk" (Lodge 1990: 81)[3] The usage of dialogues also contributes to creating suspense or making the text more dramatic[4] (Bal 2009: 64). Dialogues help build complex relationships between characters, and are set in certain contexts and situations. The contexts can be "verbal or nonverbal, consisting of utterances, questions, objections, comments, understanding, etc." (Nikulin 2006: 33). Nonverbal[5] contexts include gestures or facial expressions which help convey emotions and the state of mind of the characters. Nonverbal communication[6] "regulates relationships and may support or replace verbal communication" (Kleckova, Kral and Krutisova 2005) and attention is paid to it by those authors creating fictive orality, since we normally use these nonverbal activities / signs in everyday communication. These signs differ across cultures.

According to Fussell (2002: 1) "all languages provide speakers with an array of verbal strategies for conveying emotions". Vaňková (2010: 11) lists verbal, prosodic and nonverbal means for expressing emotions in a text, e.g. gestures, facial expressions, and posture. They all usually tell us more about the state of mind of the speaker than the verbal expressions. Enfield and Wierzbicka (2002) look at emotions as personal events which are expressed with words, in order to communicate, with the body playing an important role in the description of emotions.

We find that characters in novels express emotions using both verbal and nonverbal means. This way, on the one hand, the reader can perceive the psychological features of the character, and on the other, the novelist builds suspense. Suspense can be defined as "the doubt of the spectator as to the outcome of an intention of an actor in the story. Therefore, the first necessity in order to achieve suspense is the intention. A story without intentions cannot possibly cause suspense." (Vale 1987).[7] Yanal (1999: 126) sees suspense as "an emotion generated only in the presence of uncertainty of the outcome of a certain narrative situation". Readers' interest in the story is kept by raising questions in their minds about the "causality" and "temporality" (Lodge 1992).[8] This is especially important in detective stories, where an event usually influences the whole story, i.e. the possible outcomes,[9] the behaviour of the characters, and the expectations of the readers. Suspense "guides the reader's attention to an on-going episode, drives the reader to rivet his or her attention to the episode in question, and helps him or her to follow the story" (Iwata 2009: 256). In detective novels, it is often the nonverbal behaviour that can give clues to the reader about possible further development of the plot.

The aim of this paper is to investigate emotions[10] expressed in nonverbal features of characters and their translation. The study is based on the German detective novel "Schnee in Venedig" written by Nicolas Remin, and its Croatian and Spanish translations.[11] First of all, descriptions of nonverbal behaviour in which emotions are expressed in the original will be identified. Further steps include determining which characters use emotions, and in which situations. Expressions of emotions will be described according to their morphological and stylistic features. Finally, the translation of these expressions will be analysed and cultural similarities and differences will be determined.

[handwritten annotation: morphological – how words are formed items, roots, prefixes, suffixes]

2. Emotions

There are many definitions of what emotions are. They are set in the context of cognition,[12] evaluation, motivation, behaviour, etc. "Emotions are conceptually represented as cognitive models. [...] There are certain causes that lead to emotions, and the emotions we have make us produce certain responses" (Kövecses 2008: 134). Emotional reactions refer to physiological reactions (e.g. blood pressure, heartbeat), posture (e.g. body strain), expressive motoric reactions (e.g. gestures), expressive language reactions (syntactic and lexical) (cf. Jahr 2000: 7). The emotional system has different functions, among others, it "focuses attention, organizes memory, helps us to interpret social situations, and motivates relevant behaviour" (Salovey, Kokkonen, Lopes and Meyer 2004: 321).

Emotions are closely linked to feelings,[13] mood, and sensations, and cannot clearly be separated from them (Jahr 2000: 10) and, together with feelings they build "specific forms of experiencing"[14] (Fiehler 2002: 81). Emotions influence our behaviour and the course of conversations. Thus, language is seen as the product and the productive force of an emotional disposal (Jahr 2000: 56). Fiehler (1990: 30) sees three steps in the interaction between people which represent social relationships: self-presenting (Selbstpräsentation), evaluation[15] of the presentation of another person (Bewertung der Selbstpräsentation der anderen Person), and evaluation of the opinion the other person has to self-presentation (Bewertung der Stellungnahme der anderen Person zur eigenen Selbstpräsentation).

Speakers can express emotional state explicitly, e.g. with words that designate emotions (verbs like *love, hate*; nouns like *anger, sorrow*; or adjectives like *happy, sad*) (cf. Vaňková 2010: 12). These words form "the emotion vocabulary or lexicon of a language", which can also comprise "declarative formulas (*I felt myself, I had a feeling*), frozen metaphorical idioms, and metaphorical use of expressions (*Ich war völlig zu* – completely blocked)" (Fiehler 2002: 87-88). Kövecses (2000: 2) distinguishes between expressive and descriptive emotion words; "some emotion words can express emotions, e.g. *wow!* when impressed and enthusiastic; other emotion words can describe the emotions they signify (e.g. *angry, depressed*)". Some emotions can be more basic than others.[16] More basic ones in the English language include *anger, sadness, fear, joy* and *love*. Less basic ones include *annoyance, wrath, rage*, and *indignation* for anger, and *terror, fright* and *horror* for fear.

Emotion vocabulary can be found in novels. Vaňková (2010: 12-13) believes that texts have a certain emotional potential which can be expressed with lexical, grammatical and textual means in order to arouse emotions in recipients. That is also one of the fundamental tasks of literary works. Dialogues serve this purpose and are used in literary works to depict and develop characters. We can recognize what goes on in their minds, which emotions they feel or are feeling and how they evaluate the emotions of others. As Cupchik (1996 :196) states, "a complex, surprising, or disquieting text arrests the readers' attention, prompting an exhaustive search for meanings and emotions that can encompass and explain the event." One of the reactions that can be prompted in the reader by the use of emotion vocabulary is the anticipation of the novel's successive events, that is, suspense.

3. Nonverbal communication in novels

Writers of fictional texts use different techniques to depict the characters. Describing their nonverbal behaviour is one of them; e.g. their gestures, voice quality, or manner of speech can tell us something about their character (cf. Nord 1997: 107-108). Poyatos (2002: 5) differs between vocal-verbal (language), vocal-nonverbal (paralanguage), and nonvocal-nonverbal (kinesics, proxemics, and the other corporal systems) communication activity.[17] Speech is made up "basically of words, paralanguage[18] and kinesics, it must be specified that its basic instrument of transmission is the face, complemented by hand movements" (Poyatos 1997: 23), so that the whole body can contribute to communication.[19] Kinesic behaviour refers to chemical reactions (e.g. tears), dermal reactions (e.g. he muttered and blushed), audible kinesics (our body moves and makes sounds, e.g. while eating or drinking) (Poyatos 1997: 28). Hatim (1997: 56) names more paralinguistic and kinesic categories developed by Poyatos (1993): paralinguistic transcriptions (for momentary silence), paralinguistic descriptions ("exclaimed"), kinesic descriptions ("Catherine strained closer"), proxemic shift ("seeking to extricate himself"), chemical reactions ("the cold sweat ran from my forehead"), dermal reaction ("blanched with astonishment and rage").

According to Poyatos (1997: 37) novelists use four different ways of transmitting kinesic behaviour: a. describing the paralinguistic or kinesic behaviours and also explaining its meaning, b. by describing a behaviour but not its meaning, c. by identifying the meaning but not the behaviour, d. giving only the verbal expression which is always accompanied by a specific kinesic behaviour that completes the message, but which, not being described, may lead to the wrong image in the reader's mind.

Kinesics can refer to positive and negative feelings and reactions. These can differentiate across cultures, which can be seen in "certain folk, legal, protocolarian, religious or superstitious acts" (Poyatos 2002: 209).

Nonverbal systems "undergo profound changes through translations, and translators need to become extremely sensitive to all that happens or does not happen as they translate a text, for it is well known that translation is not only a interlinguistic exercise but an intercultural one" (Poyatos 1997: 18). In order to understand speech, one must also understand kinesics (gestures of face, eyes and hands, manners and postures) (Poyatos 1997: 22).

Nord (1997: 111) analyses the translation of "Alice in Wonderland" and gives the following aspects of utterance as part of paralanguage: tone (intonation, emphasis, indication of speech act), voice quality (loudness, pitch, emotional changes of voice), tempo (rhythm or speed of utterance, pauses, hesitations), manner of speech (indicating the speaker's emotions both explicitly and implicitly by referring to the speaker's attitude or behaviour towards the listener or the gestures and body movements accompanying the utterance), onomatopoeia (alternants, sound-reproducing verbs).

4. Emotions in *Schnee in Venedig*

Schnee in Venedig is a detective novel taking place in Venice in 1862. A royal army officer was murdered on a ship. At first, the investigation was conducted by Commissario Tron, but the case was soon taken over by the Austrian military police.

In the conversations and dialogues between the characters throughout the novel, nonverbal behaviour of the individuals is described by means of emotion vocabulary. These cases serve as the basis for the analysis carried out in the present paper. However, due to space limitations, we will not be able to show all instances, but will limit the study to the analysis of some exemplary cases, that best serve to illustrate the underlying thesis.

In most cases the emotions of male characters are described, which is not surprising, since mostly men are involved in the murder investigation. Commissario Tron's emotions are most often described (found in 17 cases), Pater Tomasseo (9), Sivry (8), Haslinger (5), Pater Abbondio (4), Alessandro (3), Oberst Pergen (2), Palffy (2), Zorzi (2), Spaur (2), Kovac (2), Ballani (2), Moosbrugger (1), Landrini (1), Sergente Bossi (1), Toggenburg (1), Grillparzer (1), Spadeni (1), Oberleutnant Bruck (1). The female character, Principessa, reveals her emotional state in 8 examples, Contessa (7), Elisabeth (4), Wastl (2), Könnigsegg (1).

The vocabulary refers mostly to anger, happiness / sadness, fear, anxiety and surprise, whereas the emotions of helplessness, pity, liking, pride, admiration and shame are less expressed. Table 1 gives the overview of the words[20] used to express these emotions.

Table 1. Words expressing emotions in the text

EMOTIONS	EXPRESSIONS
Anger	Empörung, gereizt, gekränkt, irritiert, fassungslos, grimmig, wütend, grollen, aufgeregt
happiness / sadness	traurig, Bestürzung, freudig, Vorfreude, verklärt
Fear	entsetzt, erschaudernd, erschrocken
Anxiety	nervös, Ungeduld, ungeduldig
Surprise	Erstaunen, Überraschung, überrascht
Helplessness	Resignation, gleichgültig, melancholisch
Pity	Mitleid, bedauernd
Liking	sympathisch, unsympathisch
Pride	Stolz
Admiration	Bewunderung
Shame	verlegen

Emotions are expressed with nonverbal behaviour, both with paralanguage and kinesics, and with emotion vocabulary. Paralanguage refers to the voice, the tone of voice and verba dicendi. The voice is present in 18 cases, the tone of voice in 5, smiling in 4, and the verb *sagen* (say) together with an adjective in 5 cases:

(1)
ST.   Pater Abbondios Stimme klang besorgt. (Remin 2004: 8)

(2)
ST.   „Und wann hast du Zeit für mich?", fragte die Contessa in gekränktem Ton, so als wäre dies alles die Intrige Trons, die einzig den Sinn hatte, sich um das Gespräch zu drücken.. (Remin 2004: 32)

(3)
ST.   „Das machen alle so, Tron", sagte Zorzi beleidigt. (Remin 2004: 72)

Kinesics is present in the gaze, facial expression, body parts, physiological reactions, and verbs of movement. Gaze is represented with eyes, eyebrows and the verbs of seeing. Gaze (*Blick*) is present in 3 cases, eyebrows (*Augenbrauen*) in 2, eyes (*Augen*) in 1 and verbs of seeing (*ansehen, anstarren, mustern*) in 6 cases.

(4)
ST.   Die Principessa hob die Augenbrauen. „Der Hofrat hatte ein Mädchen in seiner Kabine?" (Remin 2004: 56)

(5)
ST.   Der Polizeipräsident heftete einen nervösen Blick auf Tron. (Remin 2004: 86)

(6)
ST.   Die Principessa sah Tron überrascht an. „Dann sind sie einer von den Trons?" (Remin 2004: 94)

Facial expression refers to face (*Gesicht*) in 11 cases, and forehead (*Stirn*) in 4 cases:

(7)
ST.   Die Principessa runzelte die Stirn. „Jetzt kann ich ihnen nicht folgen, Commissario." (Remin 2004: 95)

(8)
ST.   Das schmale Gesicht der Contessa wirkte gereizt. (Remin 2004: 107)

The body parts are head (*Kopf* in 5 cases), shoulders (*Schultern* in 2 cases), knee (*Knie* in 2 cases), armpits (*Achseln* in 1 case) and hands (*Hände* in 1 case).

(9)
ST.   Tron hob bedauernd die Schultern. (Remin 2004: 111)

(10)
ST.   Sivry senkte traurig den Kopf. (Remin 2004: 120)

(11)
ST.   Grillparzer hob erschrocken die Hände. (Remin 2004: 199)

Physiological reactions refer to red cheeks (*Wangen*) in 1 case, and high pulse rate *(Puls)* in 1 case).

(12)
ST.   Tron spürte, wie seine Wangen heiß wurden. (Remin 2004: 332)

(13)
ST.   Tron spürte, wie sein Puls sich beschleunigte. (Remin 2004: 64)

Verbs of movement refer to jumping, nodding and bending (*aufspringen, nicken, beugen*), and are present in 6 cases.

(14)
ST.   Tron beugte sich überrascht vor. (Remin 2004: 30)

(15)
ST.   Pater Tommaseo nickte grimmig. „Diese Frau ist ein Mann." (Remin 2004: 136)

(16)
ST.   Sivry war erschrocken von seinem Schreibtisch aufgesprungen und starrte Tron mit weit aufgerissenen Augen an. (Remin 2004: 322)

The emotion vocabulary comprises adjectives (among them participles), e.g. *beleidigt, überrascht, melancholisch, gekränkt, nervös, spöttisch, entsetzt,* nouns like *Bestürzung, Empörung, Vorfreude,* verbs *grinsen, grollen,* and also (kinetic) phrasemes *die Stirn runzeln, die Augenbrauen heben, den Kopf schütteln, die Schultern heben, die Achseln zucken.*

The description of the characters' physical reactions in connection with the use of verbal expressions to display their emotional stance supports the creation of suspense. The clues expressed in the text help the readers to anticipate what is going to happen, and, therefore, prompt them to read on. If a character blushes or is described as being surprised, readers would like to know how these physical and emotional reactions will impact on the plot's continuation. Body posture and tone of voice can also enliven the story line and signal dangers or threats the protagonist is facing. This way, suspense is built around the characters' emotions. The description of nonverbal communication supports the actual verbal communication between the characters as expressed in the written dialogues, but can also add flair of uncertainty about the character's behaviour in a certain situation, and his or her actions during the plot's further developments. The novelist uses the description of the characters' emotions on the microstructure level to build up the narrative and also to evoke emotional reactions in the readers.

5. Translating Emotions in Nonverbal Communication

When looking into the translation of emotions we have to look at two levels: paralanguage / kinesics on the one hand, and emotion words (verbs, adjectives, nouns, phrasemes) on the other. These levels beckon a look at the following translation techniques, adapted according to Baker (1992): translation by the same / different body part; translation by the same / different paralanguage category; translation by the same / different word class; translation by the same / different word combination; translation by the same / different morphological category (e.g. tense).

5.1. Translation of Paralanguage in Croatian TT1

The translation at this level deals both with the structure of the verbal expression and the paralinguistic element included in it. According to the analysis, the expressions containing an adjective and the noun "Ton" are usually translated as an adjective and the noun "voice". This is also the case in example 17, where the structure of the verbal expression is the prepositional phrase containing an adjective and a noun in ST,[21] but which is translated without the preposition in TT1. The paralinguistic element in ST is the tone, translated in TT1 as voice. The conclusion to be drawn from these translation shifts is that paralanguage both in the ST and the TT1 guide the reader's attention in the same way.

(17)
ST. „Und wann hast du Zeit für mich?", fragte die Contessa in gekränktem Ton. (Remin 2004: 32)
TT1. „A kad ćeš imati vremena za mene?" upitala je kontesa uvrijeđenim glasom. (Remin 2005: 27)

The emotion is expressed with an adjective and the paralanguage with the tone in the voice in ST. The TT1 has the same structure of the emotion description, but the adjective is translated with a noun and a different verb is employed: "the tone of regret vibrates in the voice":

(18)
ST. Toggenburg hebt die Schultern. Er bringt es sogar fertig, einen bedauernden Tonfall in seine Stimme zu legen. "…"(Remin 2004: 103)
TT1. Toggenburg podigne ramena. Uspio je u nakani da mu u glasu zatitra ton žaljenja. "…" (Remin 2005: 97)

The third example contains the paralanguistic element of voice which is dripping with contempt. This description of emotion is also given in the TT1:

(19)
ST. „Sie meinen, dieser … Ballani?" Pater Tommaseos Stimme triefte vor Verachtung. (Remin 2004: 139)
TT1. „Mislite taj…Ballani?" Glas patera Tommasea cijedio se od prijezira. (Remin 2005: 131)

5.2. Translation of Kinesics in Croatian TT1

Kinesics must be described on two levels: the structure and the parts of the body used for expressing emotions. The analysis shows that different facial expressions, described with an adjective and the noun face in ST, are always translated as an adjective and the noun expression in TT1.

(20)
ST. Zorzi machte ein nachdenkliches Gesicht. Dann sagte er… (Remin 2004: 71)
TT1. Zorzijevo lice poprimilo je zamišljen izraz. Zatim je rekao… (Remin 2005: 66)

Zorzi made a pensive face in ST. In the Croatian translation, it is not the face which is pensive, but its expression. This changes the structure of the emotion expression. In ST it is Zorzi who does the action of making the pensive face, whereas in TT1, it is Zorzi's face that took on the pensive expression.

(21)
ST. Trons Kinn beschrieb eine unwillige Acht. Er warf Alessandro einen gereizten Blick zu. „Ich weiß, […].(Remin 2004: 24)
TT1. Tronova je brada nevoljko opisala oblik osmice. Dobacio je Alessandru razdražen pogled. „Znam […](Remin 2005: 20)

The kinesic movement of the chin which described an unwilling number eight in ST is translated as the chin which unwillingly described the shape of an eight in TT1. The translation, however, is not clear to the Croatian reader as one cannot understand what emotion is expressed with this movement.

(22)
ST. Ballanis Augenbrauen rückten irritiert nach oben. „Falls Ihr Besuch mit dem Mord […]" (Remin 2004: 143)
TT1. Ballanijeve obrve iznervirano su skočile uvis. „Ako vaš posjet ima veze […] (Remin 2005: 135)

The irritated lifting of the eyebrows in ST is translated as irritated jumping up in TT1. Using the unusual kinesic description of the jumping eyebrows in TT1 increases the interest of the reader to see how the character is going to react verbally.

5.3. Translation of Emotion Words in Croatian TT1

The words used for expressing emotions are sometimes translated with different word classes. This mostly happens with adjectives in ST. The adjective *bedauernd* (regretful) is translated with a preposition and a noun (with regret) in TT1:

> (23)
> ST.   Moosbrugger hob bedauernd die Schulter. „Das entzieht sich meiner Kenntnis, Commandante." (Remin 2004: 20)
> TT1.   Moosbrugger sa žaljenjem podigne ramena. „To, na žalost, ne znam, commandante." (Remin 2005: 16)

Sometimes semantically stronger adjectives are used in TT1, e.g. "dreary" for "sadly":

> (24)
> ST.   „Hat sich jemand für Tintoretto interessiert?" Sivry senkte traurig den Kopf. „Leider noch nicht." (Remin 2004: 120)
> TT1.   „Je li se netko zanimao za Tintoretta?" Sivry turobno sagne glavu. „Na žalost, nitko." (Remin 2005:113)

Surprise is often expressed in the ST, either with nouns or adjectives. The translation is sometimes stronger, e.g. the noun "surprise" in ST is "astonishment" in TT1:

> (25)
> ST.   „Am Hafen?" Tron gab sich keine Mühe, seine Überraschung zu verbergen. (Remin 2004: 36)
> TT1.   „U luci?" Tron se uopće nije trudio sakriti zaprepaštenost. (Remin 2005: 31)

The phrasemes in ST are translated as phrasemes in TT1. Sometimes a different verb is used, which changes the usual components of the phraseme, as in example 8.

> (26)
> ST.   „Meine Haushälterin, signora Bianchini, hat es mir gesagt." Tommaseo schüttelte fassungslos den Kopf. (Remin 2004: 137)
> TT1.   „Moja domaćica, signora Bianchini, rekla mi je to." Tommaseo je prenераženo tresao glavom. (Remin 2005: 130)

5.4. Translation of paralanguage in Spanish TT2

In contrast to the Croation translation, the noun "voice" in paralinguistic expressions is usually translated as "tono" in Spanish.

(27)
ST.   Himmel, Sivrys Stimme wurde richtig scharf. (Renim 2004: 120)
TT2.   ¡Dios mío! El tono de Sivry sonaba realmente implacable. (Remin 2007: 95)

Often, this translation shift is accompanied by a toning down of the associated emotion. In the following example, whereas in the German original, the character's voice is "dripping from contempt", in the Spanish translation, he is simply "asking with disdain".

(28)
ST.   „Sie meinen, dieser … Ballani?" Pater Tommaseos Stimme triefte vor Verachtung. (Renim 2004: 139)
TT2.   ¿Se refiere a tal… Ballani? —preguntó el sacerdote con desdén. (Remin 2007: 110)

Other paralinguistic features are modified in the translation and thereby change the emotion expressed. In this example, a "grin" which expresses malice becomes a "forced smile", a facial expression that would rather result from an embarrassing or uncomfortable situation. Also note the shift in the last part of the sentence: whereas in the original, Tron finds colonel Pergen disagreeable, in the Spanish translation, it is the other way round. This kind of translation shifts – may they be voluntary or originate from the translator's carelessness or lack of language skill – alters the characters' nonverbal behaviour and emotional stance as described by the author in the ST and therefore affect the creation of suspense in the TT2.

(29)
ST.   Pergen grinste, und Tron stellte fest, dass ihm der Oberst schlagartig unsympathisch wurde. (Renim 2004: 52)
TT2.   Pergen esbozó una sonrisa forzada que daba a entender que Tron empezaba a resultarle algo antipático. (Renim 2007: 39)

5.5. Translation of Kinesics in Spanish TT2

As for the kinesic features in the Spanish TT2, the translator opts for a literal translation of most gestures, including those gestures that are probably not as frequent in original literature in Spanish language as in German, such as "frowning" and "shrugging". Some of the gestures, however, receive a different interpretation in the target text. In this example, a "mocking look" becomes a "malicious expression":

(30)
ST.   Landrini sah Moosbrugger spöttisch an. (Renim 2004: 21)
TT.   Landrini le miró con un gesto malicioso. (Renim 2007: 14)

Very frequently, the emotions are toned down in the TT2 by the use of the adverb "algo" ("a bit"). A "sullen look" is translated by a "somewhat sullen expression" in Spanish:

(31)
ST.   Die Contessa warf Tron einen verdrossenen Blick zu. (Renim 2004: 182)
TT2.   La condesa observó a Tron con un gesto algo malhumorado. (Renim 2007: 146)

Some not very common gestures are interpreted differently in the TT2. The gesture described in this example expresses irritation, whereas the Spanish translation expresses contempt and indifference:

(32)
ST.   Trons Kinn beschrieb eine unwillige Acht. Er warf Alessandro einen gereizten Blick zu. (Renim 2004: 24)
TT2.   El gesto de Tron, con la barbilla fruncida, daba a entender un claro desinterés mientras sus ojos arrojaban a Alessandro una mirada llena de inquina. (Renim 2007: 18)

5.6. Translation of Emotion Words in Spanish TT2

In respect of the translation of emotion words, many adjectives of the ST are translated with nouns in the TT2. Also, once again the translator frequently introduced toning down by adding the adjective "cierto", or "certain". In this example, the character is "irritated" in the ST, whereas in the TT2 he "reacts with certain irritation".

(33)
ST.   Einen Moment war Tron irritiert. (Renim 2004: 68)
TT2.   Tron reaccionó con cierta irritación. (Renim 2007: 54)

Some descriptive adjectives that help to interpret the gesture are omitted in the TT2, like in this case of the "sympathetic shrug". In the Spanish translation, the reader has no clue as to why the character shrugs: it could be out of ignorance, or indifference, etc.

(34)
ST.   Moosbrugger hob bedauernd die Schulter. (Renim 2004: 13)
TT2.   Moosbrugger se encogió de hombros. (Renim 2007: 20)

And finally, some emotion words are mistranslated. In this example, the translator confused the adjective "verlegen" (i.e. "embarrassed") with the verb "etwas verlegen", "to mislay something".

(35)
ST.   Die Wastl dreht sich um und deutet einen Knicks an, ein Zeichen dafür, dass sie
        verlegen ist. (Renim 2004: 75)
TT2.   La doncella se gira y hace una reverencia que indica que ha cambiado de posición.
        (Renim 2007: 60)

6. Conclusion

The novelist described nonverbal behaviour of his characters mostly combining paralinguistic and kinesic elements with emotion words, which served as support to the verbal behaviour expressed in the dialogues. In our opinion, this technique has helped create suspense. The description of the behaviour prolonged the dialogues, which in turn gave more information about the characters' emotions and implied further developments in the story. Suspense is the element that authors use to make the reader anticipate the novel's successive events. This anticipation can be created by giving clues about the characters' emotions at a microstructure level. The sum of many of these clues in connection with the individuals' actual deeds build up their personality, shed light on their motives and help the reader to interpret their behaviour, as well as anticipate future actions.

The main characters are more often depicted with nonverbal behaviour, their characterisation is thus more vivid. Emotion words are used to emphasize paralanguage and kinesics. Mostly negative emotions are expressed, which is not unusual taking into account that the plot is developed around the unsolved murder case.

The translation of nonverbal behaviour in both languages does not show a specific pattern or strategy pursued by the translator. There are some slight differences in the cultural norms of the presentation of nonverbal behaviour. In the Croatian translation the tone of voice is translated with voice, face is translated as facial expression. In the Spanish translation, however, voice is translated as tone. Some gestures are translated literally as gestures that are unusual both in the Croatian and in the Spanish languages. Also, there is a relatively high frequency of translating adjectives with prepositional phrases in both languages.

There seems to be a certain tendency to tone down the emotions expressed in the Spanish text. This is achieved mainly through the use of modifiers such as "cierto" and "algo", and through the change or omission of adjectives denoting emotions or through the reinterpretation of gestures. The emotions in the

Croatian text, on the other hand, tend to be expressed more intensively than in the source text, with the choice of stronger adjectives and nouns.

All in all, the result is a somewhat careless translation of emotions in nonverbal features. By omission or modification of nonverbal features the reader receives different information about the text and cannot interpret correctly the nonverbal behaviour of the character. This can lead to a loss of interest, and may influence the creation of suspense achieved in the original.

---

[1] This paper was written as part of the research project The Translation of Fictional Dialogue. Literary Texts and Multimodal Texts (TRADIF), reference number FFI2010-16783, financed by the Spanish Ministry of Science and Innovation. Head researcher: Jenny Brumme.

[2] According to Goetsch, orality in literature is author's creation and is therefore feigned.

[3] Cited from Cadera (2012: 36).

[4] "The more dialogue a narrative text contains, the more dramatic that text is." (Bal 2009: 64). Researchers have observed "that narration is more vivid when speech is presented as first-person dialogue (…) rather than third-person report" (Tannen 1986: 311).

[5] Poyatos (2002: 5) believes that "communication activity can be vocal-verbal (language), vocal-nonverbal (paralanguage), and nonvocal-nonverbal (kinesics, proxemics, and the other corporal systems)". When we talk about nonverbal activities in this paper, we refer to nonvocal-nonverbal activities.

[6] Planalp and Knie (2002: 55) believe that "verbal and nonverbal cues fit together into integrated messages like interlocking pieces of a puzzle, but nobody really knows how. [...] We know that emotion is expressed or communicated with words, faces, voices and bodies, usually in rich combinations, but we know very little how these cues work in concert or in conflict."

[7] Cited from Wulff (1996: 13).

[8] Cited from Iwata (2009: 19). Causality refers to the question "whodunnit?" and temporality "what will happen next?"

[9] Iwata (2009: 83) believes that "suspense arises when an event/situation which the reader does not want to occur seems more likely to occur than the one the reader wants to transpire".

[10] Emotions are determined according to semantic fields by University of Texas. On line at: http://www.utexas.edu/cola/centers/lrc/iedocctr/ie-ling/ie-sem/pie-emotion.html(consulted 21.7.2012)

[11] The novel was translated into Croatian by Sandra Markota Sever in 2005 and into Spanish by Ana María Andreu Baquero in 2007.

[12] Emotions are mental systems of cognition and evaluation (Schwarz-Friesel 2008: 284).

[13] More to the differences in terms *emotions* and *feelings* in Fries (2007) and Wierzbicka (1999).

[14] Fiehler (2002: 81) explains this in the following way: "People experience a multiplicity of internal-psychological processes and states in everyday life, not all of which they would define as emotions. [...] Experience and action are the two central strands of the personal-environmental reference. [...] Experiencing results from actions, accompanies actions, and leads to actions. [...] One can experience annoyance disgust, and joy, which represent prototypical emotions. But one can also experience irritation, uncertainty, curiosity, tiredness, and hunger, which are not emotions, or at least not 'pure' emotions."

[15] According to Fiehler (1990: 36), communication is the exchange of information and evaluation. Communicating emotions is part of evaluation.

[16] Kövecses (2000: 5) names 5 general and possibly universal basic emotions in 11 languages, based on previous studies: happiness, sadness, fear, anger, love.

[17] In Poyatos (2002: 5) opinion, "if culture is communication and a product of interaction, it is also a dynamic continuum of activities, and that interaction among members of a culture is an uninterrupted

activity along many different channels, thanks to which the [...] systems of that culture remain active and are transmitted from one day to the next, [...]"

[18] Poyatos (1997: 42) defines paralanguage as "the nonverbal voice qualities, modifiers, and independent sound constructs we use consciously and unconsciously supporting, contradicting or accompanying the linguistic, kinesic or proximic messages mainly, either simultaneously to or alternating with them". Kinetics "comprise gestures (e.g. smiles, eye movements, beckoning), manners (the manner in which we perform a gesture), postures, (...)" (Poyatos 1997: 43).

[19] We qualify our movements with communicative qualities, e.g. when someone comes into the room, conveys his mood without saying anything (He slammed the door angrily) (Poyatos 1997: 32).

[20] These words occur in the text more than once.

[21] The example from the original is denoted as ST and is always given first. The Croatian translation is indicated as TT1 and the Spanish as TT2.

Bibliography

Primary Sources

Nicolas Remin. 2004. *Schnee in Venedig*. Reinbek: Kindler.
———. 2005. *Snijeg u Veneciji*. Translated by Sandra Markota Sever. Zaprešić: Fraktura.
———. 2007. *Nieve en Venecia*. Translated by Ana María Andreu Baquero. Barcelona: Starbooks.

Secondary Sources

Baker, Mona. 1992. *In Other Words: A coursebook on translation*. London: Routledge.
Bal, Mieke. 2009. *Narratology. Introduction to the Theory of Narrative*. Toronto: University of Toronto Press.
Cadera, Susanne M. 2012. 'Translating fictive dialogue in novels' in Brumme, Jenny and Anna Espunya (eds.) *The Translation of Fictive Dialogue*. Amsterdam and New York: Rodopi. 35-48.
Cupchik, Gerald. 1996. 'Suspense and Disorientation: Two Poles of Emotionally Charged Literary Uncertainty' in Vorderer, Peter, Hans J. Wulff and Mike Friedrichsen (eds.) *Suspense: Conceptualizations, Theoretical Analyses, and Empirical Explorations*. Hillsdale, NJ: Erlbaum. 189-198.
Enfield, N.J. and Anna Wierzbicka. 2002. 'The body in description of emotion' in *Pragmatics & Cognition* 10, 1/2: 1-25.
Fiehler, Reinhard. 1990. *Kommunikation und Emotion: theoretische und empirische Untersuchungen zur Rolle von Emotionen in der verbalen Interaktion*. Berlin and New York: de Gruyter.
———. 2002. 'How to Do Emotions With Words: Emotionality in Conversations' in Fussell, Susan R. (ed.) *The Verbal Communication of Emotions: Interdisciplinary Perspectives*. Lawrence Erlbaum Associates. 79-108.
Fries, Norbert. 2007. 'Die Kodierung von Emotionen in Texten. Teil 1: Grundlagen' in *JLT* 1/2: 293-337.
Goetsch, Paul. 1985. 'Fingierte Mündlichkeit in der Erzählkunst entwickelter Schriftkulturen' in *Poetica* 17: 202-218.
Hatim, Basil. 1997. 'Discourse features in non-verbal communication. Implications for the translator' in Poyatos, Fernando (ed.) *Nonverbal Communication and Translation: New Perspectives and Challenges in Literature, Interpretation, and the Media*. Amsterdam and Philadelphia: John Benjamins. 49-67.
Iwata, Yumiko. 2009. *Creating suspense and surprise in short literary fiction: A stylistic and narratological approach*. PhD thesis. University of Birmingham.
Jahr, Silke. 2000. *Emotionen und Emotionsstrukturen in Sachtexten*. Berlin and New York: Walter de Gruyter.
Kleckova, Jana, Pavel Kral and Jana Krutisova. 2005. 'Use of Nonverbal Communication in Dialog System' in *Proceedings of the 4th WSEAS / IASME. Int. Conf. on System Science and Simulation in Engineering*. Tenerife / Spain. December 16-18: 1-4. (available online: http://www.wseas.us/e-library/conferences/2005tenerife/papers/502-634.pdf)
Kövecses, Zoltán. 2000. *Metaphor and Emotion: Language, Culture, and Body in Human Feeling*. Cambridge, New York and Melbourne et al: Maison des Sciences de l'Homme and Cambridge University Press.
———. 2008. 'The Conceptual Structure of Happiness' in Tissari, Heli, Anne Brigitta Pessi and
Nikulin, Dmitri V. 2006. *On Dialogue*. Lanham: Lexington Books.
Nord, Christiane. 1997. 'Alice abroad. Dealing with descriptions and transcriptions of paralanguage in literary translation' in Poyatos, Fernando (ed.) *Nonverbal Communication and Translation: New Perspectives and Challenges in Literature, Interpretation, and the Media*. Amsterdam and Philadelphia: John Benjamins. 107-130.

Planalp, Sally and Karen Knie. 2002. 'Integrating Verbal and Nobverbal Emotion(al) Messages' in Fussell, Susan R. (ed.) *The Verbal Communication of Emotions: Interdisciplinary Perspectives.* Mahwah, NJ: Lawrence Erlbaum Associates. 55-77.

Poyatos, Fernando. 1997. 'Aspects, problems and challenges of nonverbal communication in literary translation' in Poyatos, Fernando (ed.) *Nonverbal Communication and Translation: New Perspectives and Challenges in Literature, Interpretation, and the Media.* Amsterdam and Philadelphia: John Benjamins. 17-47.

————. 2002. *Nonverbal communication across disciplines.* Volume 1: *Culture, Sensory Interaction, Speech, Conversation.* Amsterdam and Philadelphia: John Benjamins.

Salovey, Peter, Marja Kokkonen et al. 2004. 'Emotional Intelligence. What Do We Know?' in Manstead, Antony S.R., Nico Frijda, Agneta Fischer (eds.) *Feelings and Emotions. The Amsterdam Symposium.* Cambridge: Cambridge University Press. 321-340.

Schwarz-Friesel, Monika. 2008. 'Sprache, Kognition und Emotion: Neue Wege in der Kognitionswissenschaft' in Kämper, Heidrun and Ludwig M. Eichinger (eds.) *Sprache-Kultur-Kognition. Sprache zwischen mentaler Struktur und kultureller Prägung.* Berlin and New York: Walter de Gruyter. 277-301.

Tannen, Deborah. 1986. 'Introducing constucted dialogue in Greek and American conversational and literary narrative' in Coulmas, Florian (ed.) *Direct and Indirect Speech.* Berlin / New York and Amsterdam: Mouton de Gruyter. 311-322.

Tissari, Heli, Anne Birgitta Pessi and Mikko Salmela (eds.) *Happiness: Cognition, Experience, Language.* Helsinki: Helsinki Collegium for Advanced Studies.

Vaňková, Lenka. 2010. 'Zur Kategorie der Emotionalität. Am Beispiel der Figurenrede im Roman Spieltrieb von Juli Zeh' in *Studia Germanistica* 6: 9-18.

Wierzbicka, Anna. 1999. *Emotions Across Languages and Cultures: Diversity and Universals.* Cambridge: Cambridge University Press.

Wulff, Hans J. 1996. 'Suspense and the Influence of Cataphora on Viewers Expectations' in Vorderer, Peter, Hans J.Wulff, Mike Friedrichsen (eds.) *Suspense. Conceptualizations, Theoretical Analysis, and Empirical Explorations.* Mahwah, New Jersey: Lawrence Erlbaum Associates. 1-17.

Yanal, Robert J. 1999. *Paradoxes of Emotion and Fiction.* University Park: The Pennsylvania State University.

Chapter 16: English-Spanish subtitling and dubbing (1960s and 1970s): Voices of suspense in Polanski's *Repulsion*[1]

Camino Gutiérrez Lanza

Abstract
This paper aims to explore the way in which suspense has been created in one of the classic psychological thrillers of the 1960s, Roman Polanski's first film in English *Repulsion*, and the way it has been recreated for the Spanish audience in dialogue translation. Drawing on the theoretical and methodological framework of Descriptive Translation Studies (particularly on the relevance of translations as cultural facts of the target culture and on the close relationships that can be established between texts and contexts). *Repulsion* constitutes a highly interesting object of study, especially from the point of view of the target context. The film reached the Spanish cinemas both in its subtitled and dubbed versions for both specialized and commercial circuits at two particularly interesting periods of time within Franco's dictatorship: the period of socio-political aperture (1962-1969) and the final years of the regime (1970-1975). The fascinating socio-political and economic role played by both audiovisual translation types (subtitling and dubbing) in Spain during the sixties and seventies will also be examined in detail.

Keywords: *Repulsion*, subtitling, dubbing, suspense, censorship

1. Introduction: Thrilling suspense and suspense thrillers

There seems to be general agreement that in order to make most films attractive "the narrative has to convince the audience that it is worth their while to sit down through the movie (and enjoy it) until the end" (Cattrysse and Gambier 2008: 46). So, assuming that nearly all films intend to raise a certain feeling of expectation and anticipation to keep the audience attention, most films are likely to contain a certain degree of suspense. Suspense can thus be understood as both a structural device which allows "the spectator to anticipate plot developments (especially of the threatening variety) before the protagonists themselves" (Derry 1988: 7) and a psychological device "which directly engages the spectator by causing anxiety and setting off complex subconscious mechanisms" (Derry 1988: 19).

Suspense as "an emotional response to narrative fictions" (Carroll 1996: 74) is usually associated with thrillers. "Virtually all narrative films could be considered thrilling to some degree, because they contain suspense and action and a sense of departure from the routine world into a realm that is more marvelous and exciting" (Rubin 1999: 5). When the creation of intense excitement becomes the focus of the film, it is fully achieved not only by producing some kind of expectation and anticipation in the audience, but also by generating noticeable feelings of tension, anxiety, nervousness, apprehension, or even pleasure. The thrilling elements usually appear in combination and excess, becoming, then, "an end in themselves" (Rubin 1999: 6). Audiences, in turn, feel so attracted by these emotions that, ever since the birth of cinema, suspense-thriller films have been in constant evolution and have enjoyed world-wide success.

2. Texts and their contexts

One of the suspense-thriller films whose world-wide recognition has survived over decades is *Repulsion*, which constitutes a highly interesting object of study from the point of view of the Spanish 1960s and 1970s. Drawing on the theoretical and methodological framework of Descriptive Translation Studies – particularly on the relevance of translations as cultural facts of the target culture (Toury 1995/2012: 23-39) and on the close relationships that can be established between texts and contexts (Tymoczko 2002: 11)–, we will analyse in the following pages the way suspense has been recreated for the Spanish audience both in the subtitled and in the dubbed versions of the film.

2.1. *Repulsion* (1965), art suspense thrillers, the new European cinema

After *Noz w wodzie / Knife in the Water* (1962), *Repulsion* is the second film directed by Polish director Roman Polanski. The screenplay was co-written by Polanski and Brach in 1964, while David Stone was in charge of the adaptation and additional dialogue.[2] As Polanski declared in *A British Horror Film* (Gregory 2003), being in precarious circumstances when they first arrived in London in 1964, "we needed to come up with something that had chances of being accepted. Therefore, we thought of a kind of horror film. I had Deneuve in mind all the time as we were working on it". The point of departure was the story of a friend who was dating a seemingly fragile, sweet, innocent girl, only to discover that there was an entirely different side to her. The film was released in 1965 in France (Cannes Film Festival), the UK, West Germany, Denmark, Japan, Sweden, the USA, Norway and Finland, and met all expectations when, in the same year, it won the Silver Bear in the Berlin International Film Festival.

Although *Repulsion* was made by a young team headed by a relatively novel director, over the years it has become one of the classic art suspense thrillers of all times, together with classics such as *Psycho*. As pointed out in the periodical, *Movie*, when it was first released,

> *Repulsion* has a Norman-Bates-like heroine, Carol, driven by early experiences – implied ones – into a violent revulsion from sex. There are two savage murders, placed at intervals similar to

those in *Psycho*, the first one coming after 50 minutes. The picture ends with Carol, like Norman, totally cut off from her environment. There is no doubt that the influence is conscious. (Barr 1965: 26)

Highly influenced by surrealism, "in its presentation of a sexual obsessive and in its recurrent imagery, is [sic] the most Buñuelian of films. Indeed, it is explicitly a *hommage*" (McArthur 1968/69: 15). Especially remarkable is the way the opening titles appear on the screen on top of a close-up of Carol's eye. Only a moment later, just before the start of the film, the audience gets the first thrill: when "the credit 'directed by Roman Polanski' comes up, it moves precisely from right to left across the centre of the eyeball, recalling the notorious opening sequence of *Un Chien Andalou* in which an eyeball is sliced by a razor" (McArthur 1968/69: 15).

"The use of a protagonist, a dramatic goal and a convincing 'or else'-factor are devices that can be used in a million different ways, according to the genre or type of story being told" (Cattrysse and Gambier 2008: 46). *Repulsion* uses all the typical devices of art cinema (Bordwell 1985: 205-227), suspense thrillers (Derry 1988: 21-54), and the so-called new European cinema narration (Monterde, Rimbau and Torreiro 1987: 181-262): an interest in character and not in plot, which is usually confined to a critical situation, the protagonist is very often a passive, solitary and vulnerable hero, psychological problems such as alienation or lack of communication, emotional insecurity, verisimilitude of behaviour and space, calculated gaps in the story, lack of an ongoing causal chain of events (e.g. prototypical characters without clear-cut goals), subjectivity combined with various temporal manipulations (e.g. dreams, memories, hallucinations), an open end, a focus on form (spaces and objects which relate to the characters' imagination, strange camera angles and movements, etc.), and the occasional presence of jazz in the soundtracks (e.g. Chico Hamilton's soundtrack in *Repulsion*). Furthermore, dialogue serves the main functions identified by numerous authors (e.g. García Jiménez 1994/2003: 215-223; Li 1998: 153; Brumme and Espunya 2012: 16-24), two of which are plot development and character portrayal. As a result, "a highly self-conscious narration weaves through the film" (Bordwell 1985: 211) and the spectators comprehend the film by abandoning traditional expectations and by adapting to the particular authorial address.

2.2. Subtitled *Repulsión* (1967), *Salas Especiales, apertura*

Repulsion's first release in Spain took place during the so-called *apertura*, a controversial period of relative socio-political opening which started in 1962 with the reorganisation of the *Junta de Clasificación y Censura de Películas Cinematográficas* and lasted up to 1969, with Manuel Fraga Iribarne as the Minister of Information and Tourism (Gutiérrez Lanza 2011a: 308-315). One of the key factors of this period was the regulation of the *Salas Especiales* by Ministerial *Orden* published in the *Boletín Oficial del Estado* (MIT 1967: 895). They were special cinemas of no more than 500 seats placed either in provincial capitals, in cities of more than 50,000 inhabitants, or in places of tourist interest, which allowed the exploitation in Spain of both foreign subtitled films and Spanish films of special interest. Subtitled films, only exhibited in these *Salas Especiales*, were specially directed to the tourist population, who supposedly lacked the skills needed to watch films dubbed in Spanish, thus satisfying the demand for a more experimental type of cinema which could not be seen in the Spanish commercial circuits. Thus, although none of them escaped the effects of censorship, Hollywood-type films, specially directed to the Spanish population, were suitable to be shown in their dubbed versions in commercial circuits, where they enjoyed popular success (Gutiérrez Lanza 2003: 281-282; 285-286), and, from October 1967 onwards, subtitled experimental films, specially directed to the tourist population, started to be exhibited in *Salas Especiales* (Gutiérrez Lanza 2008: 228; Gutiérrez Lanza 2011a: 313). This way, both audiovisual translation types (subtitling and dubbing) were used according to very clear socio-political and economic interests in the target context.

Repulsión was the second film to be released in Madrid's *Salas Especiales*, after Pasolini's *Mamma Roma* (Anon 1967: 2; Gutiérrez Lanza 2008: 228; Gutiérrez Lanza 2011b: ID 2070). According to the documents kept in Censorship File 40.168, the subtitled version of *Repulsion* was first banned by the *Junta de Censura y Apreciación de Películas* in July 1966 and later on, in April 1967, it was authorised for people over 18 years of age with certain changes suggested by censors in the Spanish subtitles[3]. The final version of the subtitles was authorised in July 1967 and the fact that the film received a "4, highly dangerous" verdict from church censorship (Anon 1967: 2) did not prevent it from being shown in Barcelona on 3rd July 1967 and in Madrid, in *Sala de Arte y Ensayo* Palace, on 2nd October 1967.

2.3. Dubbed *Repulsión* (1974), commercial circuits, the late Franco years

In the late Franco years the controversial nature of the film no longer seemed to be a problem and it was even considered by some of the censors of the new *Junta de Ordenación y Apreciación de Películas* as one of the best films about mental disorders ever made. Following this radical change of opinion, according to the documents kept in Censorship File 40.168, on 30th January 1974 the dubbed version of *Repulsión* was authorised to be shown in commercial circuits for people over eighteen with only one cut: "la duración del jadeo amoroso que la protagonista está oyendo desde su cama" (the duration of the moans of pleasure the protagonist is listening to from her bed) [*my translation*]. On 21st August 1974 the dubbed film was authorised and it was distributed by Columbus Films.[4]

3. Original, subtitled and dubbed voices of suspense in *Repulsion*

For the purpose of the present analysis, the following texts will be used: the original version filmed in English and released in 1965 (ST), the unpublished translation of the dialogue done in 1967 for the subtitled version and kept in Censorship File 40.168 (TT1),[5] and the dubbed version in Spanish released in 1972 (TT2). A selection of fragments of dialogue will be compared and further reflections will be made on the nature of both types of translation: subtitling and dubbing.

Subtitling presents "a written text [...] that endeavours to recount the original dialogue of the speakers, as well as the discursive elements that appear in the image [...], and the information that is contained on the soundtrack [...]" (Díaz Cintas and Remael 2007: 8). Consequently, this translation practice "does not replace the original language, but leaves it intact and adds a form of translation" (Smith 1998: 142), which means that "the foreign language dialogue is received by the viewers of a subtitled film as the original dialogue. The subtitles are read as a translation" (O'Sullivan 2011: 118). On the other hand, interlinguistic dubbing technically "consists of replacing the original track of a film's (or any audiovisual text) source language dialogues with another track on which translated dialogues have been recorded in the target language" (Chaume 2012: 1). Therefore, the voices of the actors in the original version of *Repulsion* are complemented by the Spanish subtitles in TT1 and substituted by the voices of the Spanish dubbing actors in TT2.[6]

In *Repulsion*, images are strong indicators of suspense and greatly contribute to the creation of an atmosphere of terror. Objects and surreal images become symbolic references of Carol'alienation and mental illness: the rotten rabbit, the cracks on the wall, the darkness of the flat, strange camera movements and angles, peculiar close-ups etc. Dialogue seems to play a secondary role, but draws viewers' attention in many ways: e.g. Carol's French accent, the low volume of her cold and distant voice, her deficient oral skills, and her limited use of language are strongly emphasised and highly noticeable. Her problems to communicate at the beauty salon are the first unmistakeable signs of her fragile mental state. However, the main topic of the film is her repulsion for men. Subtle proofs of it are scattered through more than half of the film, while the topic is slowly being introduced. For example, when Carol is walking the streets of London, she receives the first visual and verbal threat from a bare-chested road labourer and, annoyed, lowers her head:

(1)
ST.   WORKMAN: Hello darling. How about a date?
TT1.   OBRERO: Hola, guapa. / ¿A ver una sonrisita?
TT2.   TRABAJADOR: Hola, guapa. Quédate a hacernos compañía.

Soon after, when, in a brief break from work, Carol sits at a restaurant in front of a plate of fish and chips, Colin, who is in love with her, enters and sits opposite showing he is very glad to see her. However, Carol's elusive answers turn what is supposed to be a nice situation into a moment of despair. Later on, back at the flat, she is annoyed at some objects left by Michael, Helen's married boyfriend, in the bathroom:

(2)
ST.   CAROL: Does he have to leave his things in the bathroom? […]
          CAROL: Why does he put his toothbrush in my glass?
TT1.   CAROL: ¿Es necesario que deje sus cosas en el cuarto de baño? […]
          CAROL: ¿Por qué pone su cepillo de dientes en mi vaso?
TT2.   CAROL: ¿Es imprescindible que deje sus cosas en el lavabo? […]
          CAROL: ¿Por qué tiene que dejar su cepillo de dientes en mi vaso?

Michael, in turn, overtly refers to Carol's worrying mental state when he is alone with her sister:

(3)
ST.   MICHAEL: She's a bit stung up, isn't she?
          HELEN: She's just sensitive.
          MICHAEL: You can say that again…She should see a doctor.
TT1.   MICHAEL: Es un poco rara, no?
          HELEN: Es muy sensible, nada más.
          MICHAEL: Ya lo creo que lo es. Debería ver a un médico.
TT2.   MICHAEL: Está un poco nerviosa, ¿no?
          HELEN: Es que… es muy sensible.
          MICHAEL: Eso desde luego. Debería ver a un médico.

After listening to Helen and Michael making love, Carol mentions her disgust at Michael staying overnight:

(4)
ST.   CAROL: Is he going to stay here every night? […]
          CAROL: He's married though.
TT1.   CAROL: ¿Se va a quedar aquí todas las noches? […]
          CAROL: Pero está caso. [sic].
TT2.   CAROL: ¿Se va a quedar aquí todas las noches? […]
          CAROL: Pero está casado.

Back at the beauty salon, Bridget has a private conversation with Carol, and she overtly reveals her dislike of men's disgusting behaviour:

(5)
ST.   BRIDGET: Oh, he was a pig… forget it… oh, my eyes. […] I'll tell you the sordid
          details later… ugh, why are they all so filthy?
TT1.   BRIDGET: Era un cerdo. Déjalo. Ah! Fíjate qué ojos!… […] Luego te contaré los
          detalles. ¿Por qué serán tan sucios?

TT2.   BRIDGET: No hablemos de él. Es un imbécil. ¡Qué ojos me he puesto! [...] Luego te
         contaré todo con detalle. ¿Por qué serán tan odiosos?

During the following scene, which seems to be part of a clever narrative strategy
designed to get the audience to instantly identify with the protagonist, just to
confirm how disgusting men can be, John and Reggie, two young, fairly
snobbish Chelsea men who are having a drink in a pub, approach Colin, who,
according to his lack of response, is not very interested in their conversation:

(6)
ST.   JOHN: [...] One of them, big girl with bloody great tits, tried to claw the other's face to
         bits. Got her hand right down her throat. [...]
         REGGIE: Lesbians? [...]
TT1.   JOHN: [...] Una era muy grande, con montañas de pelo, y trataba de arañar la cara a la
         otra. Le metió el puño por la boca. [...]
         REGGIE: ¿Estaban locas? [...]
TT2.   JOHN: La más grandota, que tenía unos músculos impresionantes, intentó clavarle las
         uñas a la otra. ¡Estaba como loca, como loca! Casi le mete el puño en la garganta. [...]
         REGGIE: ¿Lesbianas? [...]

After this, Carol shows numerous signs of her poor mental health and worrying
frailty. She lets herself be kissed by Colin in his car with no reaction whatsoever;
she does not want to be left alone by Helen, who is about to go to Paris with
Michael, she behaves strangely again at the beauty salon, and suffers terrifying
hallucinations when she is finally left home alone. Back at the pub, she is the
subject of John and Reggie's offensive conversation with Colin:

(7)
ST.   JOHN: Still keeping her legs crossed? [...]
         REGGIE: Just tell her, either, or... she'll soon strip off. [...]
TT1.   JOHN: ¿Sigue dándote calabazas?... [...]
         REGGIE: No te impacientes... ya caerá.
TT2.   JOHN: ¿Sigue haciéndose la interesante? [...]
         REGGIE: Cántale las cuarenta, verás cómo cambia. [...]

This series of clues help the audience anticipate that something terrible is about
to happen to Colin when he is alone with Carol in her flat. The scene is a perfect
example of a narrative device known as "*counter-dialogue*, in which characters
talk while performing certain actions. Here, the dialogue remains in the
background, the focus going to the dramatic action" (Cattrysse and Gambier
2008: 51). Finally, our worst fears come true when Colin breaks into the flat and,
after his disturbing monologue, she kills him with a candlestick:

(8)
ST.   COLIN: Carol... I'm sorry, oh Christ, I'm sorry for that... it's so sordid... but I just had
         to see you.... Honestly, it's so miserable without you... you don't know what it's been
         like... I've telephoned you till I thought I'd go mad listening to that ringing tone... I

mean, is it something I've done, Carol, please tell me... I'm not really like this. Oh Christ, I wish I could put it properly but things just go round and round in my mind... I just ...I just want to be with you ... all the time... all the time...

TT1.   COLIN: Lo siento. Perdona. Todo esto es... ¿Qué te pasa? Perdóname... Necesitaba verte, eso es todo. De verdad, no podía seguir sin verte. Te llamé muchas veces. El sonido del teléfono me ha vuelto loco... ¿Es...? ¿Es que te he hecho algo? Carol... Por favor... dímelo... En realidad... yo no soy así... Ojalá encontrara las palabras... No hacen más que darme vueltas en la cabeza. Sólo quiero... Sólo quisiera... estar contigo... siempre...

TT2.   COLIN: ¡Lo siento!... ¡Perdona!... No entiendo nada... ¿Qué... qué te pasa? Lo siento... Es que... tenía que verte, sencillamente... No sabes lo preocupado que estaba... Te he llamado una y otra vez... Y al no contestarme creí volverme loco... Dime, ¿te he hecho algo malo? Carol, por favor... dímelo... Está bien... Me gustaría encontrar las palabras adecuadas... Quisiera expresarte... pero se me amontonan las ideas, tengo la cabeza hecha un lío. Sólo quiero verte, estar contigo... hablarte...

Once the first murder has been committed, the second one, an immediate consequence of the landlord's verbal and physical attack, is more than expected:

(9)

ST.   LANDLORD: I can be a good friend to you ... you look after me, and you can forget the rent... eh?... come on, a little kiss between friends...

TT1.   CASERO: Yo podría ser un buen amigo suyo, sabe? Sea amable... y olvidaremos el alquiler. Un besito entre amigos, ¿quiere? Vamos...

TT2.   CASERO: Yo podría ser un buen amigo tuyo, ¿sabes? Tú te ocuparías de mí y no tendrías que pagar el alquiler. Vamos, vamos, dame un besito de amiga, ¿eh? Anda... Vamos...

At the end of the film Helen and Michael come back from France only to find great disorder and both dead bodies in the flat. Michael enters, followed by some neighbours, and takes Carol in his arms. She is in a state of total madness. The camera moves towards the family photo "isolating CAROL, then framing her face, then still closer to her beautiful and proud implacably vague child's eyes where madness had already gained the day" (Polanski, Brach and Stone 1964: 79). This final close-up shows a very young Carol looking sideways at a man, a subtle clue to the reason for her repulsion.

Although the narrative devices used to help the audience anticipate the terrifying sequence of events have not been significantly altered, there are some noticeable differences concerning the use of language and suspense building in both translations. In this respect, we shall briefly comment the following: the features of Carol's speech, the use of (in)formal language, and the effects of censorship.

3.1. The features of Carol's speech

As has been said before, although at first dialogue seems to play a secondary role in *Repulsion*, Carol's French accent, her deficient oral skills, and some suprasegmental features of her speech are highly noticeable and greatly contribute to character portrayal in the original version. Indeed, her foreign accent, together with the low volume of her cold, distant, mellow voice make her appear more displaced, fragile and delicate than every other female character in the film and help suspense building by highlighting her weakness.

Since the original dialogue can be heard in the subtitled version of the film (TT1), the extra information it provides helps viewers spot her as the victim of a terrible set of circumstances. However, when the original dialogue disappears from the dubbed version (TT2) and original voices are substituted by those of the dubbing actors, different effects are often caused in the target audience. In the case of Carol, her original voice is substituted by the nice, low-toned voice of María Luisa Rubio, who successfully tries to preserve a hint of uneasiness in Carol's speech, but her original French accent vanishes turning into standard peninsular Spanish, "thus losing the connotations of the foreign accent in the original film" (Chaume 2012: 138).

3.2. The use of (in)formal language

Carol's encounter with the landlord is one of the most terrifying moments of the film. While she remains silent, in his monologue there is a noticeably different use of *tú* and *usted* in both translations. Example 9 above shows that in the subtitled version (TT1) the landlord uses the formal second person singular form of address *usted*, both in the possessive adjective *suyo*, and in the verb forms *sabe, sea,* and *quiere*. In the same fragment of the scene, in the dubbed version (TT2), he uses the informal second person singular form of address *tú*, both in the possessive adjective *tuyo*, and in the verb forms *sabes, te ocuparías, tendrías,* and *dame*.

The formal term of address *usted* used in the Spanish subtitles (TT1) would typically be expected from both characters in order to keep an equal, horizontal relationship of formal solidarity (Fontanella de Weinberg 1999/2000: 1414-1415) between two people who meet for the first time (Matte Bon 1992/2002: 244). However, the fact that Carol is addressed informally all throughout the scene in the dubbed dialogue (TT2) may reveal a less respectful attitude on the part of the landlord, who consequently places himself in a position of power. These facts may increase in TT2 the audience's feeling of anticipation of the risk she is running.

3.3. The effects of censorship

One of the key issues that need to be taken into account when analysing the translation of original dialogues during the sixties and seventies in Spain is the existence of both religious and state censorship on the part of both religious and political authorities respectively. Since 17 February 1950 until the early 1980s, the *Instrucciones y normas para la censura moral de espectáculos* (Instructions and Standards Regarding Moral Censorship of Public Performances) [*my translation*] were used by Spanish ecclesiastical authorities as "a written code of censorship norms which coexisted with the official, political censorship system and provided a unified moral guide for public performances aimed at critics, priests and audiences" (Gutiérrez Lanza 2011a: 08). Following this code, the moral classification of films ranged from the less to the most offensive ones in a scale from 1 to 4, the last of which indicated that, in the opinion of the church, the films should be banned. However, only the *Juntas*, that is to say, the official boards of censorship, had the power to issue the final verdict.

As has already been stated, *Repulsion* was awarded first place, "4, highly dangerous" (Anon 1967: 2), in the moral scale of offensiveness. In fact, the subtitled version was authorized for people over 18 years of age by the *Junta de Censura y Apreciación de Películas* on 14 April 1967 on one condition, namely that, according to Censorship File 40.168, seven changes suggested by censors had to be made in the subtitles in order to tone down the most offensive terms. Four of these changes appear in the examples quoted above: the elision of *lúridos* ("sordid" in example 5) both in TT1 and TT2, the modification of *tetas* ("tits" in example 6), translated as *pelo* (hair) in TT1, and *músculos* (muscles) in TT2, *tortilleras* ("lesbians" in example 6), translated as *¿estaban locas?* (were they mad?) in TT1, but as *lesbianas* (lesbians) in TT2, and *¿Todavía se mantiene con las piernas cruzadas?* ("Still keeping her legs crossed?" in example 7), translated as *¿Sigue dándote calabazas?* (Is she still rejecting you?) in TT1, and *¿Sigue haciéndose la interesante?* (Is she still trying to catch you attention?) in TT2 [*my translations*]. With the exception of *lesbianas*, seven years later TT2 seems to follow the same censors' directions as TT1 (although they were never made explicit in the 1974 censorship report) and adds a new change upon request by the *Junta de Ordenación y Apreciación de Películas*: the shorter duration of the moans of pleasure heard by Carol from her bed.

These examples highlight the essential role played by the use of explicit sexual language mainly in the speech of certain male characters in the original version of the film. At the same time, they demonstrate that the restrained use of this type of language in both translations, promoted by the Spanish censors, may alter character portrayal, may diminish the impact it was originally meant to have and, as a consequence, may have a less chilling overall effect on the target audience.

4. Conclusions

Since iconic elements are so relevant in *Repulsion*, dialogue, quite scarce when compared to other films, seems to play a secondary, not so significant narrative role in the development of the story. However, this paper emphasizes the main role played by dialogue in the (re)creation of thrilling supense both in the original version of the film and in its first two translated (subtitled and dubbed) versions into Spanish. In this sense, it can be stated that

> [...] the characters exchange may be fictional in many ways, including the less than real features of their oral communication, but what is real, to a greater or lesser extent, is what the director wishes to communicate to the audience. (Zabalbeascoa 2012: 65)

Our analysis confirms that there are certain differences in the way the use of language contributes to suspense building not only in the original and translated versions but also in the two translations. It also proves that the two different types of audiovisual translation (subtitling and dubbing) used in the release of *Repulsion* in Spain satisfied two different socio-political and economic needs of the target context in two different periods of time: the sixties and the seventies. During the sixties, while dubbed versions of Hollywood-type films were mainly directed to the Spanish audience and, therefore, exhibited in commercial cinemas, due to their controversial nature, subtitled art films were mainly directed to tourists and exhibited in *Salas Especiales*. This way, Spain could no longer be accused of keeping experimental, art cinema outwith its borders; however, it was made accessible only after being censored, and only for a very limited and mainly foreign type of audience. It was not until the first half of the seventies that the dubbed versions of art films started to be exhibited in mainstream commercial circuits for Spanish adults.

---

[1] Research for this paper has been undertaken as part of the TRACE project (*Traducciones censuradas* / Censored translations), funded by the Spanish Ministry of Economy and Competitiveness (FFI2012-39012-C04-03). More information on line at: http://trace.unileon.es; http://www.ehu.es/trace/

[2] More information about full cast and crew and further data about *Repulsion* in 'IMDb'. On line at: http://www.imdb.com/title/tt0059646/faq#.2.1.3 (consulted 05.12.2012).

[3] They will be analysed in more detail in section 3.3 of this paper.

[4] It has later been shown on television, and its subtitled version has recently been re-released in 2011 in a summer cinema festival celebrated at cinemas Verdi both in Barcelona and Madrid ('IMDb') (consulted 05.12.2012). It has also been released both in VHS and DVD (MECD. 'Base de datos de películas calificadas') (consulted 05.12.2012). For the purposes of this paper, only the first subtitled and dubbed versions will be analysed.

[5] The currently available subtitled versions of the film (shown on Spanish TV or recorded on VHS and DVD) have not been used because the dialogue has been retranslated.

[6] The main original and dubbing actors are: Carol Ledoux: Catherine Deneuve / María Luisa Rubio, Michael: Ian Hendry / Luis Carrillo, Colin: John Fraser / Víctor Agramunt, Helen Ledoux: Yvonne Furneaux / Pilar Gentil, Landlord: Patrick Wymark / Vicente Bañó, Madame Denise: Valerie Taylor / Ana Díaz Plana, John: James Villiers / Rafael de Penagos, Bridget: Helen Fraser / María Dolores Díaz, Workman: Mike Pratt / Joaquín Escola ('IMDb' and 'Eldoblaje.com') (consulted 05.12.2012).

Bibliography

Primary Sources

Polanski, Roman, Gérard Brach and David Stone. 1964. *Repulsion*. Unpublished script. BFI Script Collection. S9987.
Polanski, Roman. 1965. *Repulsion*. UK.
Polanski, Roman, Gérard Brach and David Stone. 1967. *Repulsión. Diálogos en español* (Translated by Anon) (Unpublished translated dialogue). Cinematográfica Comercial S.A. Ministerio de Información y Turismo. Expediente n° 40168.
Polanski, Roman. 1967. *Repulsión*. UK. (Original version with Spanish subtitles) (Broadcast on Spanish TVE-2 24.11.1998).
Polanski, Roman, Gérard Brach and David Stone. 1974. *Repulsión. Diálogos en español*. Translated by. Anon. (Unpublished translated dialogue). Columbus Films. Ministerio de Información y Turismo. Expediente n° 40168.
Polanski, Roman. 1974. *Repulsion*. UK. (Dubbed into Spanish. VHS. Oro Films. Expediente n° 39.496) (Videoteca Municipal Conde Duque. Madrid).

Secondary Sources

Anon. 1967. 'Repulsion' in *Cine asesor. Hojas archivables de información – exclusivas para empresas. Películas estrenadas en Salas de Arte y Ensayo y Salas Especiales*: 2.
Barr, C. 1965. 'Repulsion' in *Movie* 14: 26-27.
Bordwell, David. 1985. *Narration in the Fiction Film*. London: Methuen.
Brumme, Jenny and Anna Espunya. 2012. 'Background and justification: research into fictional orality and its translation' in Brumme, Jenny and Anna Espunya (eds). *The Translation of Fictive Dialogue*. Amsterdam and New York: Rodopi. 7-31.
Carroll, Noël. 1996. 'The Paradox of Suspense' in Vorderer, Peter, Hans J. Wulff and Mike Friedrichsen (eds). *Suspense: Conceptualizations, Theoretical Analyses, and Empirical Explorations*. London: Routledge. 71-91.
Cattrysse, Patrick and Yves Gambier. 2008. 'Screenwriting and translating screenplays' in Diaz Cintas, Jorge. (ed.). 2008. *The Didactics of Audiovisual Translation*. Amsterdam and Philadelphia: John Benjamins. 39-56.
Chaume, Frederic. 2012. *Audiovisual Translation: Dubbing*. Manchester, UK and Kinderhook (NY), USA: St. Jerome Publishing.
Derry, Charles. 1988. *The Suspense Thriller. Films in the Shadow of Alfred Hitchcock*. Jefferson, North Carolina: McFarland & Company, Inc.
Diaz Cintas, Jorge and Aline Remael. 2007. *Audiovisual Translation: Subtitling*. Manchester, UK and Kinderhook (NY), USA: St. Jerome Publishing.
'Eldoblaje.com'. On line at: http://eldoblaje.com/ (consulted 05.12.2012).
Fontanella de Weinberg, María Beatriz. 1999/2000. 'Sistemas pronominales de tratamiento usados en el mundo hispánico' in Bosque, Ignacio and Violeta Demonte (eds). *Gramática descriptiva de la lengua española 1. Sintaxis básica de las clases de palabras*. Madrid: Espasa Calpe. 1399-1425.
García Jiménez, Jesús. 1994/2003. *Narrativa audiovisual*. Madrid: Cátedra.
Gregory, David. 2003. *A British Horror Film*. UK. Documentary film.
Gutiérrez Lanza, Camino. 2003. 'Cine nacional y cine importado en España: alcance social, político y económico de la colonización' in Muñoz Martín, Ricardo (ed.) *I AIETI. Actas del I Congreso Internacional de la Asociación Ibérica de Estudios de Traducción e Interpretación. Granada, del 12 al 14 de febrero de 2003*. Granada: AIETI. 277-289.
———. 2008. 'Traducción inglés-español y censura de textos cinematográficos: definición, construcción y análisis del Corpus 0 / Catálogo TRACEci (1951-1981)' in Merino, Raquel (ed.)

Traducción y censura en España (1939-1985). Estudios sobre corpus TRACE: cine, narrativa y teatro. Bilbao: UPV / EHU and ULE. 197-240.

———. 2011a. 'Censors and Censorship Boards in Franco's Spain (1950's-1960s): An Overview Based on the TRACE Cinema Catalogue' in Asimakoulas, Dimitris and Margaret Rogers (eds). *Translation and Opposition.* Clevedon: Multilingual Matters. 305-320.

———. 2011b. 'Repulsion' in *TRACEci (1951-1975) Catalogue of English-Spanish Translated and Censored Cinema:* ID 2070. On line demo version at: http://trace.unileon.es (consulted 05.12.2012).

'IMDb'. On line at: http://www.imdb.com and http://www.imdb.es (consulted 05.12.2012).

Li, Jian. 1998. 'Intonation Unit as Unit of Translation of Film Dialogue: *FIT* to Keep' in Gambier, Yves (ed.) *Translating for the Media.* Turku: University of Turku. Centre for Translation and Interpretation. 151-184.

Matte Bon, Francisco. 1992/2002. *Gramática comunicativa del español. De la lengua a la idea. Tomo I.* Madrid: Edelsa.

McArthur, C. 1968/69. 'Polanski' in *Sight and Sound* 38 (1): 14-17.

MEC (Ministerio de Cultura). 1966. '*Repulsión'.* Archivo General de la Administración: File 40.168. SIGNAGA 36/04324.

MECD (Ministerio de Educación, Cultura y Deporte). 'Base de datos de películas calificadas'. On line at: http://www.mcu.es/cine/CE/BBDDPeliculas/BBDDPeliculas_Index.html (consulted 05.12.2012).

MIT (Ministerio de Información y Turismo). 1967. 'Orden de 12 de enero de 1967 sobre programación de salas cinematográficas especiales' in *Boletín Oficial del Estado* 17 (20 enero 1967): 895.

Monterde, José Enrique, Esteve Rimbau and Casimiro Torreiro. 1987. *Los "nuevos cines" europeos. 1955-1970.* Barcelona: Lerna.

O'Sullivan, Carol. 2011. *Translating Popular Film.* Basingstoke: Palgrave Macmillan.

Rubin, Martin. 1999. *Thrillers.* Cambridge: Cambridge University Press.

Smith, Stephen. 1998. 'The Language of Subtitling' in Gambier, Yves (ed.) *Translating for the Media.* Turku: University of Turku. Centre for Translation and Interpretation. 139-149.

Toury, Gideon. [1995] 2012. *Descriptive Translation Studies – and beyond. Revised Edition.* Amsterdam and Philadelphia: John Benjamins.

Tymoczko, Maria. 2002. 'Connecting the Two Infinite Orders. Research Methods in Translation Studies' in Hermans, Theo. (ed.) *Crosscultural Transgressions. Research Models in Translation Studies II. Historical and Ideological Issues.* Manchester, UK and Northampton MA: St. Jerome Publishing. 9-25.

Zabalbeascoa, Patrick. 2012. 'Translating dialogues in audiovisual fiction' in Brumme, Jenny and Anna Espunya (eds). *The Translation of Fictive Dialogue.* Amsterdam and New York: Rodopi. 63-78.

Name index

Subject index

P.198

deictic ('now') - word whose meaning
~~dependent on context~~ Here, you, next Tues.
Reflector - character thinking.

aggregative clause - Beginning a query
Here - building up, but suggesting
a query.

Free indirect thought e.g. "yes, she
was afraid"

Parataxis - no linking conjunction.
It was cold; the snows came
Hypotaxis - using conjunctions.
dialogic - communication presented
as dialogue (!)
Modifier, "in a confused fashion"
locative verb - verb indicating
location.
stair figure a new sequence anchored
in the previous one. "~~Perfectly~~ nice"

colloquial formulaic construction.
Colloquial — one goes & has silly ideas.
formulaic
Construction
Prosodic focus action - intonation, tone,
stress, rhythm.

P. 200

Dialogue as source of delay &
heightening of tension.

Precision of description in dedective
fiction.

Role of the copy editor.

hypotaxis -

unequal constructs in a sentence

- Some more important than
others e.g. clause inside a
sentence.

Free direct thought

deictic - meaning of a word
dependent on context.
Chere, there, next Tuesday

Anaphora P. 203

P. 176 - Toury Descriptive
Translation Studies.
target culture